STEREOTYPE DYNAMICS

Language-Based Approaches to the Formation,
Maintenance, and Transformation
of Stereotypes

STEREOTYPE DYNAMICS
Language-Based Approaches to the Formation, Maintenance, and Transformation of Stereotypes

Editors

Yoshihisa Kashima
Klaus Fiedler
Peter Freytag

Psychology Press
Taylor & Francis Group

New York   London

Cover Design: Tomai Maridou

First published 2008 by Lawrence Erlbaum Associates

This edition published 2013 by

Psychology Press
Taylor & Francis Group
711 Third Avenue
New York, NY 10017

Psychology Press
Taylor & Francis Group
27 Church Road, Hove
East Sussex, BN32FA
Oxon OX14 4RN

© 2008 by Taylor & Francis Group, LLC
Psychology Press is an imprint of Taylor & Francis Group, an Informa business

International Standard Book Number-13: 978-0-8058-5677-4 (case) 978-0-8058-5678-1 (paper)

Visit the Taylor & Francis Web site at
http://www.taylorandfrancis.com

Contents

Preface

History brings a new horizon—and a new challenge. In today's globalizing world, the age old problem of stereotypes has taken on a new dimension, and presents a new challenge to social psychology. At the beginning of the 21st century, globalization has provided the unprecedented opportunities for us to communicate with each other, and to obtain information from far flung parts of the world. In an instant, we send and receive a message, communicating with someone on the other side of the planet; a telecommunication device presents an image of a distant land and voices of people whom we have never seen or even heard of. At the same time, globalization has ushered in the era in which we are making decisions and judgments that affect groups of people who live in a distant corner of the world, and with whom we have little direct contact. Should we support our government's policy to send troops to a foreign country; should we express support or opposition, moral outrage or sympathy, to one side or the other of an international conflict; or should we support an effort to provide a humanitarian aid to the victims of a natural disaster thousands of miles away? Such decisions and judgments are, more often than not, colored by stereotypes. If so, how do we form and maintain those stereotypes of the people about whom we have little firsthand information? Secondhand information we obtain from other people through communication must play a significant role in the contemporary world.

Certainly, social cognitive approaches to stereotypes have provided us with a wealth of knowledge about how the individual mind handles information about social groups and what effects stereotypes may have—how information is encoded, stored, and retrieved to affect judgments, decisions, and a variety of behaviors in social context. However, when we consider stereotyping in the contemporary world, interpersonal communication emerges as one of the neglected topics in social psychological inquiries about the dynamic formation, maintenance, and transformation of culturally shared stereotypes. Namely, stereotypes based on secondhand information may affect our judgments and decisions with equally important, or even greater, social consequences. This volume addresses the role of communication—especially language-based communication—in stereotype dynamics, which complements the social cognitive insights with language-based approaches to stereotypes that take communication seriously. By examining the dynamic interplay of stereotype and language-based communication, the book places the phenomenon of social stereotypes squarely in socio-cultural context where it rightly belongs.

First, in part 1, *Stereotype Dynamics*, meta-theoretical perspectives are presented, which are nonetheless strongly informed by theories and empirical research. Although they represent diverse perspectives, the central claim of these chapters is unanimous: the dynamic processes of stereotype formation, maintenance, and transformation can be explained more comprehensively by analyzing interpersonal facets of communication rather than by examining intrapersonal factors alone. Here, stereotyping is conceptualized as a phenomenon involving not only intra-personal cognitive, affective, and motivational processes, but also inter-personal communication processes mediated by language—undoubtedly, the most significant aspect of human communication.

Taking the view that language is a *semiotic system*, which provides *signs* (e.g., words, phrases, sentences) that carry meaning in communication, subsequent parts address the following research questions in the perspectives of language-based communication.

1. What do the signs in a language *mean*, and how do the meanings of the signs shape stereotypes?
2. How do people *use* those signs intentionally or unintentionally? Is language use biased in some way?
3. How do language users' identities affect the *meaning of a particular language use* in social context?
4. What are the social consequences of language-based communication? Does language-based communication provide a basis for the formation, maintenance, and transformation of social stereotypes?

In particular, part 2, *Symbolic Mediation and Stereotyping*, examines question (1), namely, how the meaning of linguistic signs could shape stereotypes. For instance, words like "gay" or "fag" convey different meanings about the same referent group. Do such manipulations of words and phrases have any implications for everyday stereotyping? The chapters in this part are unanimous in their affirmation though each presents a unique and innovative approach. Part 3, *Stereotype and Language Use*, addresses question (2), unintentional and strategic uses of language in stereotype dynamics. Using word categories such as adjectives and verbs as a main vehicle of investigation, chapters in this part examine the psychological processes involved in language use in social context. Part 4, *Stereotype Sharedness and Distinctiveness*, addresses question (4), social consequences of language-based communication. Here, the forces at work in communication chains and small group discussions, which can give rise to the shared stereotypes as distinctive beliefs about social groups. Finally, in part 5, *Identity, Self-Regulation, and Stereotyping*, provides some striking examples that drive home the importance of question (3), how language users' identities can influence the meaning of language used in social context.

In total, the present volume presents contemporary answers to the four central questions in the semiotic mediation of stereotypes, provided by the researchers most active in the field of language-based communication in social psychology. The book is intended for advanced students, scholars, and researchers in social psychology (especially in the areas of social cognition, group processes, and interpersonal communication) and related social scientific disciplines such as human communications and socio linguistics. It may also be used as a supplement in upper level courses on prejudice and stereotyping. We thank Professors Chuck Stangor, University of Maryland, and David Roskos-Ewoldsen, University of Alabama, for their helpful reviews of our proposal on this volume. A grant to Klaus Fiedler from Deutsche Forschungsgemeinschaft made possible a small group meeting of the researchers in Heidelberg, Germany, which formed a basis of this volume. We also acknowledge this contribution and express our gratitude.

Contributors

Herbert Bless
University of Mannheim, Germany

Matthias Blümke
University of Heidelberg, Germany

Janine Bosak
University of Berne, Switzerland

Markus Brauer
Université Blaise Pascal, France

Andrea Carnaghi
Università di Padova, Italy

Anna Clark
Free University of Amsterdam,
   The Netherlands

Amanda B. Diekman
Miami University, USA

Karen M. Douglas
The University of Kent at Canterbury,
   United Kingdom

Tracey J. Elder
University of Kent at Canterbury,
   United Kingdom

Klaus Fiedler
University of Heidelberg, Germany

Peter Freytag
University of Heidelberg, Germany

Peter J. Hegarty
University of Surrey, United Kingdom

Matthew Hornsey
University of Queensland, Australia

Yoshihisa Kashima
The University of Melbourne,
   Australia

Minoru Karasawa
Kobe University, Japan

Johannes Keller
University of Mannheim, Germany

Olivier Klein
Université Libre de Bruxelles, Belgium

Sabine Koch
University of Heidelberg, Germany

Josephine D. Korchmaros
Southern Illinois University–
   Carbondale, USA

Tim Kurz
University of Newcastle upon Tyne,
   United Kingdom

Anthony Lyons
University of Newcastle upon Tyne,
   United Kingdom

Anne Maass
Università di Padova, Italy

Craig McGarty
The Australian National University,
   Australia

Felicia Pratto
University of Connecticut, USA

Sabine Sczensny
University of Berne, Switzerland

Gün Semin
*Free University of Amsterdam,
   The Netherlands*

Sayaka Suga
Kobe University, Japan

Robbie M. Sutton
*The University of Kent at Canterbury,
   United Kingdom*

Mark Tarrant
Keele University, United Kingdom

Scott Tindale
Loyola University of Chicago, USA

Jean Twenge
San Diego State University, USA

Christian Unkelbach
University of Heidelberg, Germany

Clemens Wenneker
University of Amsterdam, The Netherlands

Daniël Wigboldus
*Radboud University Nijmegen,
   The Netherlands*

Vincent Yzerbyt
*Université Catholique de Louvain,
   Belgium*

STEREOTYPE DYNAMICS
Language-Based Approaches to the Formation,
Maintenance, and Transformation
of Stereotypes

Chapter 1

Stereotype Dynamics: An Introduction and Overview

Yoshihisa Kashima
University of Melbourne, Australia

Klaus Fiedler and Peter Freytag
University of Heidelberg, Germany

Given the current human historical context, it is perhaps not at all surprising that stereotyping is a pressing concern in social psychology. In today's globalizing world, we are faced with the circumstances in which we not only interact with individuals who belong to a variety of different social groups, but also have to make significant, even history-defining, decisions about social groups without first-hand experience about them. How do we decide whether to support a policy that can affect refugees and asylum seekers; how do we decide whether to support our government's proposal to send troops to a foreign country; and how do we decide whether to support an international organization such as the United Nations, the European Union, and the like? Events around the world can change international alliances and transform the global scene in a matter of weeks or months. Citizens in this fast-changing world are faced with momentous decisions that could affect tens of thousands of people, with whom they have little direct contact. One wonders whether such judgments and decisions are well informed by all the known facts, or shaped in some way by stereotypes.

Dominated by social cognitive approaches, there is a great wealth of knowledge concerning how the individual mind handles information about social groups and what effects stereotypes may have—how information is encoded, stored, and retrieved to affect judgments, decisions, and a variety of behaviors in social context (e.g., Hamilton & Sherman, 1996; Hilton & von Hippel,

1996; Kashima, Woolcock, & Kashima, 2000; Major & O'Brien, 2005; Schneider, 2004). What type of information is available to the individual mind and what information is likely to be sampled in the environment is then a critical question (Fiedler, 2000). In much of the social cognition literature (with some exceptions; e.g., Linville & Fischer, 1993), there has been an implicit assumption that the information derives from direct observation and experience with members of the social group. *Firsthand* information we gain from direct interaction with group members would surely affect our views about the group. However, when we are dealing with social groups with which we have little direct contact, *secondhand* information, or hearsay, which we obtain from other people, must play a significant role.

SOCIAL MINDS EXIST IN COMMUNICATION WITH OTHER MINDS

Thus, when we begin to consider stereotyping in the contemporary world, the dynamic formation, maintenance, and transformation of stereotypes in interpersonal communication emerge as neglected issues in social psychology. Furthermore, the uniqueness of *human* communication lies in our capacity to use language. Although nonverbal behaviors and other symbolic mediums too can act as signs, language-mediated communications would be the major source of secondhand information for humans, especially when the information is complex. These realizations have led a number of researchers to begin to complement social cognitive insights with language-based approaches that take communication seriously. A small group meeting of like-minded researchers was organized in Heidelberg, Germany, by Peter Freytag, Klaus Fiedler, and Yoshihisa Kashima. Further inviting other researchers who share similar concerns to contribute their chapters, this volume collects papers that address the role of communication—especially language-based communication—in stereotype dynamics, an emerging issue in social psychology.

Part 1 of this volume, Stereotype Dynamics, collects papers that illustrate the central problem of the book, namely, how ongoing dynamic interpersonal communication shapes constantly evolving stereotypes. Semin sets the scene by calling for researchers to examine "stereotypes in the wild," pointing out the constantly changing dynamic nature of interpersonal communication surrounding stereotypes, while squarely placing the social phenomenon of stereotyping within the context of communication and framing it as an aspect of the even broader context of communicative regulation of intergroup relationships. Similarly, Yzerbyt and Carnaghi provide a socially situated view of stereotype change, pointing out that stereotype communication does not take place in a social vacuum. Social-contextual influences that shape and moderate the change and maintenance of stereotypes include audience effects, attitudes of reference groups, and group membership. Finally, Lyons, Clark, Kashima, and Kurz consider cultural implications of stereotype dynamics, examining in particular how the composition and configuration of social networks affect the diffusion of stereotype information. As a whole, these papers collectively point to the dynamic nature of stereotyping and the role of interpersonal communication in it.

The other four parts of the book examine different aspects of language-based stereotype communication. To orient the sections and to describe their interrelationships, let us first consider the following simple statement:

"Australians are racists."

Perhaps someone's utterance like this can be regarded as a clear instance of a stereotyped communication. However, a moment's reflection reveals the complexity of the issue. As Fiedler (in press) noted, social communication consists of relationships among at least four elements, communicator (C), recipient (R), signs that are used for communication (S), and the target that the signs refer to (T). Suppose that it was Donald who made the utterance, "Australians are racists," to James. The communicator is Donald, the recipient is James, and the utterance contains, among other things, the linguistic signs, *Australians* and *racists*, which refer to certain targets in the world; Donald the communicator presumably encodes his thought into the utterance and James the receiver decodes the utterance and understands it. As far as the *referential relationship* between the signs and the targets is concerned, the example may be regarded as a stereotyped statement that universally imputes the attribute of "racism" to a group of people, "Australians," thus making a generalizing statement about the group.

However, what if there is no such linguistic sign as *racists?* Suppose that there is a hypothetical language, English₂, which lacks the word *racists*. Instead, in English₂, there may be a phrase like *outgroup haters*. If the referent (T) of the "racists" is roughly understood as individuals who hold unjustified negative beliefs about individuals who belong to racial groups other than their own, then to refer to these individuals, one may say, "racial outgroup haters." Then, using English₂, where the word *racist* does not exist, a communicator does not have a choice but to say, "Australians are racial outgroup haters." Note, however, *racists* and *racial outgroup haters* may not refer to the exact same set of people; some racists may hate people of other races, but other racists may fear people of other races. The phrase *racial outgroup haters* then excludes those who are fearful of people of other races, whereas the word *racists* does not. Then, as far as their reference is concerned, those linguistic signs are not perfectly synonymous. In fact, this is at the heart of the process of translation. If there are two languages understood as linguistic sign systems (a Swiss linguist, Saussure, called it *langue*), a word or phrase in one system may not have the exact same referent as a word or phrase in the other system.

Part 2 of the present volume, Symbolic Mediation and Stereotyping, addresses the question of referential relationship in stereotyping. Fiedler et al.

clarify this critical issue in symbolically mediated communication, devise an experimental paradigm to examine this question, and the report results of their investigation for the first time in the literature. The result is a surprising effect of a sign system—conceived as transmitters of information, as distinguished from the intrapersonal processes within senders and receivers—that can generate stereotypes without the communicators' intent. Carnaghi and Maass point out that the meaning of a symbolic message is not exhausted by its referent; recalling the classical distinction between reference (what a sign refers to) and sense (what a sign implies other than its referent), they report the results of their ongoing investigation that show the importance of linguistic signs in stereotype dynamics. Sczesny, Bosak, Diekman, and Twenge focus on the contemporary dynamism of gender stereotypes, highlighting the changing nature of the referential relationship of gender-related signs (e.g., men and women) with the social roles such as breadwinners and caretakers. Once upon a time, being a man was to work outside the family and being a woman was to raise family. However, as the association between gender and role occupancy became less tight, the gender stereotypes themselves changed—hence the remarkable transformation of gender stereotypes over time.

Returning to the first statement about Australians, in using real English, people rarely make so straightforward a statement as "Australians are racists." As noted by a number of researchers, investigating interpersonal discourse about race and stigmatized groups (e.g., van Dijk, 1984, 1986, 1993; Wetherell & Potter, 1992), communicators use a number of communicative devices (e.g., "My best friend is so and so, but . . ."). When making a statement that may bear negatively on a social group, communicators may make subtle adjustments to the manner in which the propositional content is rendered. One such device is the type of words that are used. Semin and Fiedler (1988) postulated that different linguistic categories convey different senses in which a certain proposition is applicable to the subject it describes. So, adjectives and nouns such as "bigoted" and "racists" would convey a strong sense of dispositionality, stability, and generalizability, among other things, whereas state verbs such as "hate people of other race" would imply this sense a little less, interpretive action verbs like "abused people of other race" still less, and descriptive action verbs like "spoke loudly to people of another race" even less.

Section 3, Stereotype and Language Use, examines the question of how people use the existing language (Saussure's *parole*), mostly focusing on the unintentional and intentional use of lexical terms. Wigboldus and Wenneker review the literature on linguistic expectancy bias (LEB) and linguistic intergroup bias (LIB), in which people appear to use unwittingly more abstract linguistic categories, such as adjectives, for describing an observation that conforms to their expectation (LEB), for instance, outgroup members' negative behavior and ingroup members' positive behavior (LIB). They then propose a process model of intentional and unintentional biased language use, while pri-

NOTE: may be out of date

marily focusing their discussion on its unintended and relatively automatic aspect. On the other hand, Douglas, Sutton, and McGarty explore the extent to which communicators can strategically deploy different linguistic categories to convey different impressions. Following these chapters, Freytag provides a critical analysis of the existing LIB/LEB literature, calls for a greater emphasis on the communicative context including the communicator (C) and receiver (R) identities, and proposes an integrative framework in which to conceptualize the current findings and to suggest future directions of research.

Let us return again to the statement *Australians are racists*. Supposing that someone has made this utterance, can we conclude that the speaker is communicating a stereotype about Australians? After all, it makes a generalizing statement about a group of people; if this is not stereotyped communication, what is? Again, the issue is not so simple. This utterance is in fact very similar to the kind of statements made by Australians shortly after December 11, 2005, when a crowd of Australians mobbed those who they thought were Australians of Lebanese descent in a seaside suburb near Sydney. The next day, the news headline in an Australian newspaper, *The Age*, read, "Racist furore as 'Aussie' mob riots on beach." In this context, when statements like "Australians are racists" are made by non-Australians, it would be regarded as stereotyping; when they are made by Australians themselves, however, it would sound more like a self-criticism. Although the words may be exactly the same, and therefore the signs and targets (S and T) may be identical, the meaning of the utterance may depend on who said this to whom. This example points out that the *social relationship* between the communicator and the receiver is a significant determinant of the meaning of generalizing statements about social groups such as "Australians are racists."

This and other issues related to the identity of the communicators and recipients (C and R), and their psychological and embodied underpinnings are addressed in Section 5, Identity, Self-Regulation, and Stereotyping. The chapters by Hornsey and Sutton et al. are strong reminders that the social context matters in stereotype dynamics. Hornsey's research shows that a negative statement about a social group may be interpreted to be stereotyping if it is made by an outgroup member. He summarizes his research program on intergroup sensitivity effect: people regard an outgroup member's negative statement more negatively than the same statement made by an ingroup member. Sutton et al. argues that this phenomenon can be interpreted within the broader normative context, which shuns people's negative statement made about their outgroup. Keller and Bless further examine the consequence of stereotyped communication especially when its recipient is also the target of the stereotype. Their research acts as a strong reminder of the central importance of the motivated being in interpersonal communication. In all, the papers in this section illustrate the role of social relationships in stereotype dynamics.

automatic vs motivated

homophily
social influence

Thus, using language in social context, people affect each other in constant and ongoing interaction with each other. The decades of research in social psychology inform us of the consequence of such interaction: people who interact with each other often share their beliefs, attitudes, and values as a result of ongoing social influence processes. Section 4, Stereotype Sharedness and Distinctiveness, explores the dynamics involving shared and distinctive information in interpersonal communication. Klein, Tindale, and Brauer examine the process by which people form consensual stereotypes in language-mediated interaction within small groups. Depending on what type of information is originally shared or unshared by people, they may bring out different types of information. If shared information dominates communication, consensual stereotypes are formed; if unshared information is presented, consensus may be less likely to form. Although shared information typically plays a dominant role in group interaction, they further suggest that under some circumstance, it may be possible to facilitate the communication of unshared information, implying that there may be a possibility of stereotype change and transformation through communication.

However, once consensus is formed and known to be formed, does it affect people's communication of stereotype relevant information? Karasawa and Suga tackle this question by examining the type of information that is likely to be communicated, and the way in which it is communicated, through a communication chain, suggesting that stereotype-consistent information may be communicated in a more abstract way. However, does this mean that information that is shared in society is communicated more often generally? Under what circumstances do people communicate what is distinctive? Pratto, Hegarty, and Korchmaros suggest that people communicate what is assumed to be shared and therefore normative, while subtly distinguishing what is not normative. This process, however, can potentially serve to strengthen what is regarded as normative. Beukeboom's work fits here & LEB

An obvious omission is the research on the effect of mass media on stereotypes. There is voluminous research on the mass media content as it related to stereotypes (e.g., Bullock, Wyche, & Williams, 2001; Durkin, 1985a,b,c; van Dijk, 1984, 1986; see Ruscher, 2001). It is arguably the case that the study of mass media should not be excluded from a volume such as this. However, at this stage, we decided to concentrate on the primary questions of language as a system and language use in social context. As a discipline, social psychology is mostly concerned with human social behavior in concrete social situations; as a result, it typically focuses on the implications of language as a system and language use in *interpersonal* communication. Furthermore, mass media effects are complex processes, which are often moderated by a number of factors. Indeed, interpersonal communication is consistently regarded as one of the factors that are postulated to strengthen the effect of mass media communication (e.g., Katz & Lazarsfeld, 1955; Lazarsfeld, Berelson, & Gaudet, 1948; see

Perse, 2001). Clearly, the interaction between mass media content and interpersonal communication processes is one of the pressing questions that will need to be further addressed in future research.

All in all, this volume collectively provides perspectives that are relevant to the emerging research tradition of language-mediated interpersonal stereotype dynamics. This paradigm takes seriously the intrapersonal social cognitive processes; however, it places the social cognitive mind within its natural milieu, social communication: communicators (C) transmission of semiotic messages (S) about targets (T) to recipients (R). We hope the book serves as a good illustration of how these social communicative components shape the meaning of social groupings.

formula ?

ACKNOWLEDGMENTS

The small group meeting, which formed the basis of this volume, was funded by a grant to Klaus Fiedler from Deutsche Forschungsgemeinschaft.

REFERENCES

Bullock, H. E., Wyche, K. F., & Williams, W. R. (2001). Media images of the poor. *Journal of Social Issues, 57*, 229–246.

Durkin, K. (1985a). Television and sex-role acquisition. 1: Content. *British Journal of Social Psychology, 24*, 101–113.

Durkin, K. (1985b). Television and sex-role acquisition. II: Effects. *British Journal of Social Psychology, 24*, 191–210.

Durkin, K. (1985c). Television and sex-role acquisition. III: Counter-stereotyping. *British Journal of Social Psychology, 24*, 211–222.

Fiedler, K. (2000). Beware of samples! A cognitive-ecological sampling approach to judgment biases. *Psychological Review, 107*, 659–676.

Fiedler, K. (in press). Introduction to social communication. In K. Fiedler (Ed.), *Social communication.* Psychology Press.

Hamilton, D. L., & Sherman, J. W. (1996). Stereotypes. In R. S. Wyer, Jr., & T. K. Srull (Eds.), *Handbook of social cognition* (2nd ed., Vol. 2, pp. 1–68). Mahwah, NJ: Lawrence Erlbaum Associates.

Hilton, J. L., & von Hippel, W. (1996). Stereotypes. *Annual Review of Psychology, 47*, 237–271.

Kashima, Y., Woolcock, J., & Kashima, E. S. (2000). Group impressions as dynamic configurations: The tensor product model of group impression formation and change. *Psychological Review, 107*, 914–942.

Linville, P. W., & Fischer, G. W. (1993). Exemplar and abstraction models of perceived group variability and stereotypicality. *Social Cognition, 11*, 91–125.

Major, B., & O'Brien, L. T. (2005). The social psychology of stigma. *Annual Review of Psychology, 56*, 393–421.

Perse, E. M. (2001). *Media effects and society.* Mahwah, NJ: Lawrence Erlbaum Associates.

Ruscher, J. B. (2001). *Prejudiced communication: A social psychological perspective.* New York: Guilford Press.

Schneider, D. J. (2004). *The psychology of stereotyping.* New York: Guilford Press.
Semin, G. R., & Fiedler, K. (1988). The cognitive functions of linguistic categories in describing persons: Social cognition and language. *Journal of Personality and Social Psychology, 54,* 558–568.
van Dijk, T. A. (1984). Prejudice in discourse. Amsterdam: Benjamins.
van Dijk, T. A. (1986). *Communicating racism: Ethnic prejudice in thought and talk.* Beverly Hills, CA: Sage.
van Dijk, T. A. (1993). *Elite discourse and racism.* Newbury Park, CA: Sage.
Wetherell, M., & Potter, J. (1992). *Mapping the language of racism.* London: Harvester Weatsheaf.

Part 1

STEREOTYPE DYNAMICS

Chapter 2

Stereotypes in the Wild

Gün R. Semin
Free University Amsterdam, the Netherlands

The subject of stereotypes constitutes a substantial chapter in the annals of social psychology. Historically, its roots are often traced back to Lippman's (1922) famous "pictures in the head" metaphor. This metaphor drew attention to the perilous discrepancy between mental pictures and the reality to which they were supposed to refer. It is therefore not surprising that this dangerous residue of our "mental life" presents a fascinating subject. The chief idea is that such pictures shape people's views of the social world. Obviously, an improved understanding of the psychological mechanisms that drive stereotypes is important on its own right. However, the significance of this focus becomes more self-evident, since understanding this phenomenon can also furnish possible routes to responsibly taming these "irrational" forces and paving the way for society to become a "better" place. It is therefore not surprising that there are diverse research traditions focusing on stereotypes. For instance, there is a substantial literature on cognitive processes underlying stereotypes (for reviews, see Brown, 1995; Fiske, 1998; Macrae & Bodenhausen, 2000). Another research emphasis that was popular in the 1930s (e.g., Katz & Braly, 1933) is gaining renewed prominence, namely the content of stereotypes (e.g., Fiske, Cuddy, Glick, & Xu, 2002). A further research focus is to be found in the treatment of stereotypes as social representations (cf. Stangor & Lange, 1994) that are driven by norms and constitute "collective" or "cultural" guidelines (see Stangor & Shaller, 1996).

It is possible to justly ascribe this diversity to the serious complexity of the subject and argue that a multipronged approach is the best way to tackle it. Yet, one may also question if this diversity may be due to reasons other than the complexity of the phenomenon. In this chapter, I take an explicitly oppositional stance. Diversity in approaches can also come about by the absence of functionally grounding the phenomenon under investigation. Thus, if stereotypes are specific social phenomena that are manifested in communicative contexts and have the characteristic of inducing social distance between a speaker and a receiver, then we have defined a specific functional context. Such a context provides the parameters of what is manifested, and when and where. However, if one takes a mentalist metaphor that is detached from the context and content of what is manifested, then it is possible to engage in and introduce conceptual diversity, since the phenomenon is underdetermined conceptually in the first place.

I therefore suggest that these approaches share a mentalist metaphor, fostered by a cognitive representational focus that social psychology has inherited largely from cognitive psychology. I take this position in the hope that this may sharpen the argument and to suggest that the mentalist view has blinded us to the fact that stereotypes are manifested in social contexts in the form of social action (often verbal). The mentalist stance has diverted attention from this important feature of stereotypes (or rather *stereotyping*) by reducing the phenomenon to separate components (computational, representational models—e.g., of semantic contents and their properties, etc.) and thus obfuscated the context within which stereotypes are "active."

The approach adopted in this chapter is that stereotypes are the result of socially situated interactions between individuals, rather than a product that resides within the head of an individual. I shall outline a conceptual framework that attempts to extract the idea of stereotypes from the confines of representations locked as pictures in the head and reintroduce it where it takes place and is manifested, namely the public domain—communication. I therefore use the metaphor of "stereotypes in the wild," adapting the title of E. Hutchins' (1996) work, which treats cognition as a phenomenon emerging in interpersonal communication. In doing so, the current framework focuses on the public domain as the location where stereotypes are manifested in the dynamic communicative interplay between two or more interlocutors.

In the following, I begin by providing the set of assumptions behind the approach adopted here and draw attention to the differences between the current approach and process-driven approaches to stereotypes. These differences are largely the result of adopting a framework where the emphasis is on the function of language in implementing cognition.

The next section makes up the empirical focus of the chapter. Here I address features of language that are implicitly used in communication and mediate feelings of social distance and proximity between a speaker and a listener. The core of this section relies on seeing stereotyping as an emergent process that is driven by systematic biases in language use during communication. These biases are regarded as responsible for perceived and experienced feelings of social proximity or distance. In the concluding section, I outline a model (Semin, 2000a) that furnishes a framework within which the current approach and research can be best summarized.

CONTEXT dependent

SOCIALLY SITUATED COGNITION AND STEREOTYPING

The way we define specific social phenomena and subject them to scientific inquiry contains a host of hidden assumptions embedded in the methodological commitments and the amenability of phenomena for empirical analysis. These have a number of unintended consequences, which *can* have adverse effects on what we examine in social psychology. As McGuire and McGuire (1988) noted, "Psychological research often has a reverse-Midas touch in that it turns to dross such topics of golden promise as self, love, anxiety, etc., by cutting the topic to fit a Procrustean bed of conventional methods, even at the price of extirpating the bases of the topic's interest, so that it is dead on arrival at the laboratory" (p. 97). *dangers of experimental method*

The point that I would like to make is not to declare that the voluminous research on stereotypes is dead, but that it is in dire need of resuscitation. Resuscitation requires the introduction of a different perspective that brings the phenomenon to life again. The prevailing information-processing perspective on stereotypes focuses on cognition for its own sake. This is done at the expense of the links between cognition and action, as well as the dynamic and adaptive function cognition serves. The prominent implicit model is of cognition as reception, where the person is treated as a passive observer of ongoing stimuli. (This is certainly the mode in which participants are placed in most social cognition studies within social psychology.) Cognition becomes the construction and manipulation of inner representations, rather than real interaction with the world, conversation, etc.

The solution, as is argued in this paper, is to put stereotypes back where they breathe, namely out of the head and where they happen—the *wild*, as Edwin Hutchins (1996) aptly put it. The place proper is the context of social interaction and communication and not in the head, as mainstream social cognition has allocated it. *where stereotypes live*

Why should one take stereotyping out of the head and put it in the public domain? From a situated perspective, an examination of stereotyping only in terms of cognitive processes neglects the adaptive function of cognition. Cognition, in the socially situated perspective (Smith & Semin, 2004), is not identified with detached thought but with adaptively successful social interaction.[1] It is for the adaptive regulation of action and *emerges* in social interaction. A number of converging traditions—outside of mainstream social cognition—have for a considerable period emphasized the adaptive function of cognition, as in the case of symbolic interactionism and the sociocultural school of

Mead Cooley

... Goffman

---

[1] I refer to social interaction in the context of this chapter, but of course cognition is about adaptive interaction with persons as well as the world in general.

How we think & feel impacted by our interxns [handwritten annotation]

SEMIN

thought (e.g., Mead, 1934; Vygotsky, 1962/1986). Converging perspectives can be found in recent work in artificial intelligence and psychology (e.g., Barsalou, 1999; A. Clark, 1997, 1999; Clancey, 1997). Thus, as Smith and Semin recently (2004) summarized, cognition has an adaptive function, namely the regulation of social interaction. Moreover, cognition and action are the *emergent* outcome of dynamic processes of interaction between people. Finally, the socially situated approach takes cognition out of the head and suggests approaching it as being distributed between social agents.

LANGUAGE AS A DEVICE TO IMPLEMENT COGNITION

Doesn't occur in isolation [handwritten annotation]

If cognition is for action, then how is cognition implemented in social interaction? One of the chief tools by which cognition is extended in social interaction and implemented is by language (Semin, 2000). For cognition to happen it has to be coupled with an external entity in a two-way interaction. In the case of human communication, one can refer to this process as social coupling. Language in this context is the chief means by which action is brought about and is a tool for effecting change. "Without language we might be much more akin to discrete Cartesian 'inner minds', in which high-level cognition, at least, relies largely on internal resources. . . . Language thus construed, is not a mirror of our inner states but a complement to them. It serves as a tool whose role is to extend cognition in ways that on-board devices cannot" (Clark & Chalmers, 1997, p. 14) (Language is the means by which action is brought about and is the medium for practical activity (Chiu, Krauss, & Lau, 1998; Higgins, 1981; Krauss & Fussell, 1996) and thus a tool for implementing cognition in communication and thereby transforming reality by conveying meaning.) The implementation of cognition takes place by use of language as a strategic resource in order to structure how reality is represented, thereby shaping and influencing the cognitive processes of the *recipient* of a message. The way the speaker structures his or her speech act also shapes the structure of the listener's response (Semin, 2000b). This perspective treats cognition as intended action and language as the tool that facilitates the implementation of intended action (Semin, 2000a,b). Strategic use of language comes about because any single intention or event can be represented in a number of different ways by language, since language is creatively indeterminate (Semin, 2006). Thus, any single event, such as *John's fist travels with high speed in space only to make violent contact with David's chin and thus knock him out flat,* can be represented in a number of different ways, all of which can be considered appropriate descriptions of this event (e.g., *John punched David, John hates David, John is aggressive*). The choice of a linguistic utterance is intended to structure not only an addressee's representation of an event in a particular way, but also the flow of the verbal interaction. Language therefore constitutes a structuring resource.

To understand how a message is shaped we have to know first of all what the properties of the different linguistic devices are. It becomes possible to understand and examine why a speaker makes a particular strategic choice rather than another one and how such choices may influence a listener once we know the systematic differences of the properties of different linguistic tools. Thus, choices such as those illustrated above can become indicative of the psychological process driving the strategic language choices and the psychological impact such strategic choices may have upon their recipients. But before we go to this detail, which is covered in the next section, we need a brief overview of the properties of interpersonal language that a speaker can use in order to structure a listener's representation.

Interpersonal language has two correlated properties (Semin, 2000b). These are the (1) *propositional* properties and (2) *structural* properties of a message. These two correlated features can be illustrated with the above "flying fist" example. A witness can represent this event in a number of different ways: *John punched David, John hit David, John hurt David, John damaged David, John dislikes David, John hates David, John is aggressive.*

All of these options express a surface meaning or semantic meaning in the traditional linguistic sense. In that vein, all of these sentences express a proposition that preserves a truth reference to the "flying fist" event. No witness is likely to question the veracity of these statements. This is what I refer to as "propositional properties." It is noteworthy that the truth-value of such statements can be checked. Obviously, the type of event determines the type of lexical selections that will be made to represent that event. This will vary from event to event.

There is, however, a second feature of such selections that is hidden and orthogonal to the specific propositional properties. Let me elaborate briefly. Some of the sentences preserve perceptual features of the event (e.g., *John punched David*—"punching" always involves the fist). Other types of predicates also refer to the same event but lose the tight perceptual link and do not preserve the perceptual features of the action (*John hit David*—one can hit in a number of different ways, from a fist to a baseball bat). Others are removed from the precise act (*John hates David*—John is aggressive). The absence of preserving a perceptual link does not make this type of representation less valid. An event, any event, can therefore be represented with predicates that vary in terms of their linguistic proximity to or distance from the action and event, in other words in terms of their degree of abstraction. The *linguistic category model* (LCM) (Semin & Fiedler, 1988, 1991) captures this meta-semantic or structural property of language. The LCM is designed to identify the general cognitive functions of various linguistic devices (predicates), namely interpersonal verbs and adjectives. It furnishes the means of investigating the properties of message structure and thereby interfacing psychological processes underlying message production, message structure, and message comprehension (Semin, 2000a,b). The LCM makes a distinction between four different levels of abstraction:

> *Descriptive-action verbs* are the most concrete terms. These are used to convey a noninterpretive description of a single, observable event and preserve perceptual features of the event (e.g., *A punches B*).
>
> *Interpretive-action verbs* also describe a specific event but are more abstract in that they refer to a general class of behaviors and do not preserve the perceptual features of an action (e.g., *A hurts B*).
>
> *State verbs* constitute the next category in degree of abstraction and describe an emotional state and not a specific event (e.g., *A hates B*).
>
> The most abstract predicates are *adjectives* (e.g., *A is aggressive*). Adjectives generalize across specific events and objects and describe only the subject. They show a low contextual dependence and a high conceptual interdependence in their use. In other words, the use of adjectives is governed by abstract, semantic relations rather than by the contingencies of contextual factors, with the opposite being true for action verbs (e.g., Semin & Fiedler, 1988; Semin & Greenslade, 1985).

The most concrete terms retain a reference to the contextual and situated features of an event. Thus, the second distinctive property is the concreteness versus the abstractness of the predicates that people choose to represent any interpersonal event.

It is important to note that the properties of abstractness-concreteness and causal (thematic) inference are *generic to the entire predicate classes* represented in the LCM. The properties are generic in that they are independent from *specific surface* meanings or implications. Thus, the semantic domain of *helping-assisting* comprises a set of terms circumscribed by the words that are all associated by one rule or another with helping-assisting. This is the subject of the more conventional study of meaning, namely semantics. The more conventional approaches in linguistics are the study of meaning in terms of *semantic fields, semantic relations,* or the analysis of lexical items in terms of *semantic features* to investigate the semantic component of a grammar's organization. Whereas semantic fields are concerned with how vocabulary is organized into domains or areas within which lexical items interrelate (domain of economic exchange—*to sell, to buy, to pay; to get, to obtain, to purchase,* and so on), semantic or sense relations address relationships such as synonymity (e.g., *affable, amiable, friendly*) and antonymity (e.g., *friendly* vs. *unfriendly, good* vs. *bad*). The *inferential properties* identified by the LCM are not domain specific, nor are they expressed in terms of interrelationships between the surface properties of terms. One may refer to the meaning domain identified by the LCM as *metasemantic,* since the inferential properties apply across semantic fields.

How do people use different predicates strategically and, in particular, how do they do so in the context of stereotyping? This is the question I address in the next section, where I report on the research that has examined why and how people shape specific linguistic features of their communicative acts in the context of communicating stereotypes. But it is not only the communication of stereotypes and systematic lexical decisions that are relevant if one wants to investigate stereotyping as a socially situated phenomenon. One also has to address how such messages get coupled with a recipient who is the target of such messages and what consequences the reception of such biased messages have for the recipient.

effects of bias

STEREOTYPES AS PUBLIC PHENOMENA

We now turn to how stereotypes are realized in their proper context, namely in social interaction and communication. As public phenomena we do not encounter stereotypes but essentially remarks, observations, and comments in routine daily exchanges. Thus, we come across stereotypes as public phenomena in specific social situations. This can be experienced in direct verbal expressions of prejudice and discrimination toward members of outgroups in a variety of contexts. However, it largely has become politically incorrect to engage in such direct expressions, because of the prevalence of egalitarian social norms (Dovidio & Gaertner, 1986), which often attract negative sanctions. Nevertheless, prejudice and discrimination are still the order of the day. Their expression has only taken more sophisticated forms of expression, is subtler and less easily detected from manifest comments (Schnake & Ruscher, 1998). Whichever form the expression of stereotypes takes, as public phenomena they are manifested only in terms of verbal exchanges or statements from which we infer what Lippman termed a "stereotype," irrespective of whether such images actually exist. Thus, the proper place for examining stereotypes is situated communication contexts. The parties to such contexts can be varied, in terms of different types of group membership (supporters of two football clubs, gender membership, proponents of different political parties, members of different social, racial classes, and so on). The point is that discrimination and prejudice are conveyed by communication, and on occasion this can rely on extremely subtle linguistic cues, such that one may not be able to put one's finger on why one is feeling somewhat isolated or offended. It has taken more sophisticated forms of expression and occurs in subtler and less detectable ways (Schnake & Ruscher, 1998). Such subtle expressions lead to the experience of feelings of proximity or distance, without knowing precisely why we feel as we do. The expression of such prejudice can take a number of different forms (Swim, Aikin, Hall, & Hunter, 1995; Swim, Ferguson, & Hyers, 1999).

An examination of stereotypes in the wild in effect means studying everyday social situations where prejudice is expressed, subtly or otherwise, and systematically investigating its emergence and consequences. This type of research strategy, while maintaining the wealth of the natural expression of stereotypes in the wild, makes it somewhat difficult to investigate systematically the psy-

aversive racism

microaggressions

chological factors driving such expressions and the psychological consequences for the receiver of such messages. A possible experimentally appropriate approximation to such situations is to dissect such social situations to (a) precursors to the expressions of stereotypes in the public domain and (b) consequences of such expressions for the receiver of such messages. Such a dissection means that one can investigate the cognitive and motivational processes responsible for the production of systematically biased messages that convey stereotypes and transmit them. Moreover, having discovered the systematic properties of language use in such expressions, one can then construct experimental situations in which properties of messages can be experimentally controlled in terms of the language properties of messages. Such a two-step process, albeit an approximation, is a possible systematic avenue to the investigation of how stereotypes are manifested in the public domain—namely in the composition of messages people pass on to each other in conversations, and their impact (e.g., psychological consequences) upon receivers.

Consequently, the research that addresses these points comes in two parts. One part is concerned with how people use language strategically when they are communicating about stereotypes. This is concerned with the linguistic composition of the message. The other part addresses the question of how messages affect the inferences people make when they read them. This research was first of all conducted with participants who were in no particular relationship to the transmitter or the behaviors that were represented in the message—thus, participants were independent. An extension of this second part is research that utilized participants who were the targets of the message and the recipients of the message. It is in this particular situation that it is possible to investigate the influence of a message that is serving stereotype transmission in a fully interdependent context. In the following I review the research on message composition, message impact, and finally the interface between message transmission and its impact.

The first steps toward answering this question were introduced by Anne Maass's seminal work on the transmission and maintenance of stereotypes. The objective of this research was to examine how motivational (and later cognitive) processes influence strategic language use in the description of positive and negative behaviors performed by ingroup and outgroup members (Maass, Salvi, Arcuri, & Semin, 1989). The chief contribution of this research is the finding that people use language strategically to protect and enhance the identity of their ingroup and derogate the outgroup identity (see Maass, 1999, for an overview). This is achieved by describing positive behaviors of ingroup members with abstract language. This indicates that the behavior in question is not due to some situational fluctuations or factors outside of the person's control, but rather to his or her enduring positive qualities. This puts the ingroup member in a positive light in communication contexts. Similarly, negative outgroup behaviors are described with abstract language, thereby implying that such negative behaviors are due to some inherent and enduring qualities of these per-

good explanation of LIB ✓

sons. In contrast, negative ingroup behaviors as well as positive outgroup behaviors are represented with a more frequent use of concrete terms. In these cases, the implied suggestion is that these behaviors are incidental and due to situational circumstances that play a more important role in shaping the behavior in question, rather than some dispositional tendency (see Maass, 1999, for a review). Another interpretation of these patterns of language use is to use a cognitive account which states that expected behaviors are described with abstract language and unexpected behaviors by the use of concrete predicates (e.g., Rubini & Semin, 1994). Both processes appear to be operative, depending on the motivational circumstances under which the strategic language is produced (Maass, 1999; Maass, Milesi, Zabbini, & Stahlberg, 1995). Whatever the processes responsible for the production of the biased message, the inferences that uninvolved persons and recipients of such communications draw are precisely what was implied in the message (Werkman, Wigboldus, & Semin, 1999; Wigboldus, Semin, & Spears, 2000). Extending this line of thinking and building on their earlier work (2003), Douglas and Sutton have shown that linguistic choices implicitly convey to listeners of messages the type of attitudes one holds toward people and groups (Douglas & Sutton, 2006).

The hallmark of the LIB is that a concrete or abstract behavioral description of a social event is, as I mentioned earlier on, commensurable in a number of important ways—except for the relative use of predicate categories. In short, they are "truthful" renderings of the behaviors in question. Thus, the messages are representationally commensurable irrespective of whether a description is abstract and the others are concrete. Moreover, the descriptions should not be disputable when it comes to the accuracy with which they reflect the event and behaviors in question. This is precisely why the LIB has a specific fascination. The communications are "politically correct" and yet biased in an *implicit* way. Research has shown that while strategic predicate use in LIB messages is related to implicit, unobtrusive measures of discrimination and stereotyping, it is not related to explicit measures (Franco & Maass, 1996, 1999; Douglas & Sutton, 2006; von Hippel, Sekaquaptewa, & Vargas, 1997; see also Semin & De Poot, 1997a,b).

The research I have briefly covered above is about how people communicate about positive and negative members of ingroups and outgroups, and the inferences that neutral recipients draw when they read or hear messages with such bias in language use. Although this is informative about stereotype communication, it tells us little to nothing about stereotyping in an interpersonal situation. This is a situation in which the *recipient* of such messages is someone who is the person that has just behaved positively or negatively and hears another person describe his or her behavior. This is the central issue in this chapter. Depending on the condition, the recipient hears that her positive behavior is described either with abstract predicates or (in another condition) with concrete predicates. In the two other conditions, recipients hear their negative behavior described in either abstract or concrete terms.

recipient is the target of L113 NOT group as a whole.

Earlier work has revealed that with samples of *independent* recipient participants these participants draw dispositional inferences from abstract narratives and situational ones from concrete narratives (Werkman et al., 1999; Wigboldus et al., 2000). The question that is relevant in this context is how would such messages affect *interdependent* recipients? By "interdependent" I mean here a person who hears another reporting or talking about his or her own positive or negative behavior. How would the involved recipient of such messages feel toward the transmitter and in particular the social distance or proximity the recipient feels toward the recipient? Note that the type of situation does not involve any overt derogation, slur, or insult, but a description of the event that can be regarded as truthful.

This is precisely what we investigated in an unpublished vignette study (Semin, 2006).[2] Participants were given cartoons depicting an event sequence that could end with either a positive or negative behavior being displayed. Thus, the central person (genderless in the cartoon), with whom the participant was asked to identify, is, for example, in a lift and sees someone running to catch the lift. In one condition (positive), he stops the lift and waits for the running person to enter. In the other condition (negative), the central person lets the doors close and frustrates the running character. Participants were asked to imagine that they accidentally overheard somebody describing what they had done in this hypothetical situation. The findings provided support for the specific predictions that were advanced. The prediction was that concrete descriptions of positive and abstract descriptions of negative behavior would lead to perceived distance, whereas abstract descriptions of positive behavior and concrete descriptions of negative behavior were expected to lead to perceived proximity to the narrator. Consistently, an abstract description of positive and a concrete description of the negative events yielded high ratings on social proximity.[3] Participants noted that the witness knew them better personally; was closer to them; and they judged the likelihood of developing a friendly relationship higher relative to the other two conditions. The reverse pattern was obtained in the conditions where the witness depicted a positive event concretely and a negative one abstractly. This is precisely the type of everyday situation where we hear something mentioned about us or are told so directly. Notably, the receiver of such a message does not have access to alternative wordings. This is a situation where it is very difficult to put our finger on what it is that makes us *feel* that the person who is passing on the message is — *abstraction*

[2]I would like to express my thanks to Ismintha Waldring and Sophie Lingier, who conducted these two studies.

[3]The three relevant proximity and distance variables were: "How likely is it that you will develop a friendly relationship with the witness? How close do you think the witness is to you personally? How well does the witness know you?" On all of these dependent variables we noted significant interactions (all F's$(1,27) > 9.00$; p's $< .005$).

close to us or why we want to put as much distance as we can between ourselves and this person.

Thus, what we find is that what is generally known as the linguistic intergroup bias is, in its situated use, a way of conveying information about the nature of an interpersonal relationship and in fact affecting the perceived social distance between two interlocutors. This type of experimental paradigm puts the LIB into a socially situated context (Smith & Semin, 2004) and one that is a *functional* context about the situated regulation of interpersonal relationships and situations where stereotyping occurs. Admittedly, the study I reported above was a simulation or vignette study, and often there may be justified concern about the validity of such studies, particularly with respect to whether it is possible to generalize from such studies to what the effects are of in situ communication with the same independent variables.

This is precisely what we did in a recent study (Reistma-van Rooijen, Semin, & van Leeuwen, 2006). Participants (transmitters) were asked to describe an event when they had acted in either a socially responsible (positive) or socially irresponsible (negative) way. These descriptions were then passed on allegedly to another participant, who wrote his or her thoughts about this event, and this handwritten feedback was given to the transmitter. The feedback was either abstract or positive and was controlled for valence. We then measured social distance with the Inclusion of Other in Self scale (Aron, Aron, & Smollan, 1992) as a function of behavior valence (positive vs. negative) and message abstraction (abstract vs. concrete). As expected, the interaction was significant, showing that the participants in the abstract positive feedback and the concrete negative feedback condition were more likely to include the transmitter in their "self" relative to the concrete positive and abstract negative feedback conditions. Again, we find the same pattern with different manipulations and in situ experimentation.

Depending on the language used, a particular state of relationship emerges that influences the social distance we feel toward the other. Obviously, the particular linguistic bias in the message will depend on what the other person thinks of us. Are we a member of the ingroup or not; are we a friend or a foe? *That shapes the strategic language that is deployed in constructing the message. On the face of it, such messages may appear to be tactically sterile, but strategically and implicitly they convey social proximity or distance.* This is precisely the type of situation in which a stereotype is put into subtle operation without the recipient knowing what the cause of his or her feelings toward the transmitter is. Similarly, the transmitter is also unlikely to know that he or she has just engaged in stereotyping their interlocutor, as the extant research evidence suggests that people do not have access to the biases in their language use in such situations (Franco & Maass, 1996, 1999; Douglas & Sutton, 2006; von Hippel, Sekaquaptewa, & Vargas, 1997; see also Semin & De Poot, 1997a,b).

These preliminary studies suggest that interpersonal relationships regulated by the way we describe what we have done and the induced "feeling" of distance and proximity are something that we cannot put our finger on. The communication is accurate, it does not bias the event, and it does not use explicit remarks or indicators of prejudice or stigmatizing language. Nevertheless, what we communicate is intimacy, proximity, better knowledge, and some sense of unity, or precisely the reverse. This type of language use is an implicit means by which a transmitter is able to convey his or her feelings toward another, since the inference is implicit and consequently not open to debate or discussion. Moreover, we cannot put our finger on what the precise source of the feeling is. What is done is "politically correct"—certainly on the surface but a clear instance of stereotyping—positively or negatively.

CONCLUSION

The voluminous research on the LIB has revealed the psychological processes that are responsible in the production of biased language. This has been extremely invaluable. The current perspective suggests that we can add a social level to this intrapersonal level of analysis. By doing so, we complete the circle from message production, to message characteristics and message reception and its implications. The research also allows us to specify the situated features of such communication by identifying the conditions under which a message will be produced, when they will have a function and when not. Thus, the contribution of this research is to be able to experimentally delineate the situated features of a phenomenon by determining the conditions under which a phenomenon will occur and those that will prevent it from being manifested. In this view, the LIB is not an automatic phenomenon that is triggered by any ingroup or outgroup behavior. On the contrary, the message has to have a communicative function, and if it does not then the bias is not manifested. Semin, de Montes, and Valencia (2003; de Montes, Semin, & Valencia, 2003) have demonstrated that strategic language use occurs only when the message has a communicative function. However, no systematic bias in language is observed in the same situation if the message does not fulfill any communicative function. Similarly, Douglas and Sutton (2003) have shown across a series of elegant studies that in hypothetical situations participants are able to monitor strategic language use as a function of the type of experimentally induced goals. Thus, taken together, the research by Semin et al. (2003) and Sutton and Douglas (2003) provides evidence for the flexibility and situated and dynamic nature of the LIB. Notably, despite the fact that communication goals exert an influence upon the manifestation of the bias, the precise nature of strategic language production escapes the conscious access of both producer and perceiver, which makes this type of stereotyping possible. So, where does this all lead us, in terms of how stereotypes are realized in socially situated contexts? A concluding model is provided by the *message modulation model* (Semin,

2000a), which provides a systematic framework for the research reviewed in the previous section.

The gist of what the model attempts to capture is best illustrated by an example. The illustration I used was a simple exchange that two different visitors engage in with local information in order to find their ways to the main train station in Amsterdam.

One of the visitors is a tidily dressed woman and the other visitor is an archetypal soccer hooligan from a European country that has a reputation:

> In the first case, the local's response is something like "Take the first road to the left. When you see the McDonald's, turn right. Then you arrive at a T-junction and then . . . etc., etc.". The answer in the second case is much more likely to be "Just go straight ahead and you will get there. Good luck." In the first instance, we have a helpful, detailed and accurate instruction. In the second case, the instruction is as misleading as it can be. The messages (verbal instructions) constitute situated knowledge structures by which *social coupling* is achieved. Their production is regulated by the cognitive and motivational implications of the speaker-audience relationship. The message is a product of motivational (like or dislike for the target), cognitive (preparation of instructions) and behavioral (speech acts conveying a cognitive map) processes. The message is designed to impact the audience cognitively, behaviorally and motivationally. The impact of the message can be seen as (1) providing a cognitive map, that guides the 2) "stranger's" behaviors to reach a destination, and as having (3) clear motivational consequences (a very satisfied or highly angered inquirer). In this context, both speaker and audience present external memory tools (Semin 2000; Smith & Semin, 2004) for the event to occur. The speaker is identified as a local and thus approached; the addressee is identified as a tidily dressed woman or a soccer hooligan. *The knowledge structure as presented in the message is a situated one and is the emergent outcome of the relationship between speaker and audience, and its psychological function and status cannot be understood independently of this relationship.* (Semin, 2000, p. 610)

I capture the dynamics of this situated exchange in what I refer to as the message modulation model, which is expressed in three general propositions:

I.   Messages are *publicly accessible situated knowledge structures* that are mediated by the propositional and structural properties of language (Semin, 2000, p. 603).

Thus, a message (a speech act; Searle, 1969) is a publicly accessible linguistic behavior, which in the above example consists of the instructions for how to reach the train station. In the case of the type of research revealing LIB, the linguistic behavior is systematically biased. The message has manifest surface or propositional properties. It is about how to get to the train station or, in the case of LIB messages, it's a linguistic representation of an event or behavior. However, the message also contains structural properties as indicated by the LCM, namely their degree of abstraction or concreteness. These two features of the message are both publicly accessible and are both emergent properties (see proposition III below).

Notably, the knowledge structure that is manifested in verbal behavior is not something that is internal to the speaker. It is something that is in the public domain. It is in this context that it has specific functions.

II.   The function of messages is the regulation (e.g., coordination and synchronization) of the cognitive, behavioral, and motivational processes between speaker and audience (Semin, 2000a, p. 604).

Obviously, in the absence of an audience a message does not have any function (Semin et al., 2003). The function of a message is the coordination of the interaction between a producer and a receiver. In the example of the visitor seeking the train station the message is designed to get the visitor to her desired destination. But messages are generally designed for the particular purpose at hand and—all other things being equal—are truthful, informative, relevant, clear, brief, and orderly (Grice, 1975). However, producer–receiver relationships are not only neutral. On many occasions they are motivated as in example I provided above or in LIB research. Thus, the motivational and cognitive features of the producer–perceiver relationship will affect the shape that the linguistic behavior will take. This in turn will leave its stamp upon the nature of the relationship between producer and perceiver. Thus, as the research reviewed earlier suggests, one may have a feeling of being either close to or distant from the producer, depending on the behavior in question and how it is represented linguistically.

Interestingly, one can detect the nature of the producer–perceiver relationship from the type of language that the producer has used. Thus, the concreteness or abstractness of the message will give an indication of what the producer's attitude toward the receiver is, as some recent research by Douglas and Sutton (2005) reveals. Messages therefore contain information not only about the psychological processes (cognitive, motivational) driving the distinctive pattern of language use, but also those processes (cognitive, motivational) that constitute the intended impact of a message on its audience.

III.   The type of situated knowledge structure that a message constitutes is an emergent property resulting from the speaker–audience relationship (Semin, 2000, p. 604).

The shape that a message takes reflects the emergent quality of the speaker–audience relationship. The particular message cannot be reduced to the transmitter, the receiver, the head of the transmitter, etc. The message cannot be simply reduced to individual components. It is a unique product of the specific constellation that comes about by the composition of the specific interlocutors, the nature of their relationship or absence thereof, by the social context they provide and the type of behavior in question. Therefore, it is impossible to understand the function, type, and shape of a message independently from the type of relationship between the speaker and receiver. The speaker–audience relationship is an *emergent and regulatory property that characterizes the intersection between speaker and audience*. It does not reside in some internal qualities of either party. The nature of the speaker–listener relationship grounds the regulatory motivational and affective processes that shape the message. Conversely, the shape of the message conveys information about the relationship between speaker and audience.

The message modulation modal conceptualizes cognition (stereotypes) as an emergent and situated process that is manifested in the public domain and is regulated by motivational and cognitive processes inherent to the relationship between the speaker and receiver. Language in this context is seen as the tool that extends cognition, thereby not only giving expression to a person's goal, but constituting a crucial but not the only means (Semin, 2007) of achieving social coupling.

In the specific context of situated communication, biased language is the means by which people convey social proximity to and distance from each other. Since this point may require emphasis, it is useful to repeat its dynamics. As we know, people utilize predominantly abstract terms to describe positive behaviors of an ingroup member and negative behaviors of an outgroup member. The descriptions people use for the negative behaviors of an ingroup member and positive behaviors of an outgroup member use more concrete predicates. As we know from work reviewed here, concrete terms imply that the behavior in question is incidental and cannot be ascribed to some enduring property of the person who performed it. In contrast, abstract terms invite the inference that the behavior in question is due to enduring characteristics, a trait-like propensity, and is therefore unlikely to change and typifies the person who has performed the action. Moreover, we also know from the research we reviewed earlier that these biases escape conscious access and are implicit. This goes not only for the procedure of the message, but also for the recipient. The recipient of biased messages therefore is unable to detect the bias, since it is subtle and is not a direct derogation or discriminative remark. This, as we have reviewed, has been revealed to give rise to the feeling of social distance or proximity in targets to such messages. Thus, people whose positive behavior was described in abstract terms and negative behavior in concrete terms felt closer to the transmitter than recipients of concrete messages upon a positive behavior and abstract messages upon a negative behaviors. The latter recipients expressed social distance from the transmitter. But this is precisely what stereotypes are about when they are expressed in "politically correct" ways, namely without blatantly distorting reality. They convey this awkward feeling that one is not wanted, without being able to put one's finger on it. Or, alternatively, one has this warm feeling while being not quite aware of how it has come about. Thus, although we are not aware of their powerful machinations, generic structural properties of words can play with our feelings and convey a feeling of being wanted or rejected. This is the emergent property of such situated exchanges that we refer to as stereotypes.

ACKNOWLEDGMENTS

The Royal Netherlands Academy of Arts and Sciences PAH program facilitated the writing of this chapter.

REFERENCES

Aron, A., Aron, E. N., & Smollan, D. (1992). Inclusion of other in the self scale and the structure of interpersonal closeness. *Journal of Personality and Social-Psychology, 63*, 596–612.

Barsalou, L. W. (1999). Perceptual symbol systems. *Behavioral and Brain Sciences, 22*, 577–660.

Brown, R. (1995). *Prejudice: Its social psychology.* Oxford, England: Blackwell.

Chiu, C., Krauss, R. M., & Lau, I., Y. M. (1998). Some cognitive consequences of communication. In S. R. Fussell & R. J. Kreuz (Eds), *Social and cognitive approaches to interpersonal communication* (pp. 259–279). Mahwah, NJ: Lawrence Erlbaum Associates.

Clancey, W. J. (1997a). *Situated cognition: On human knowledge and computer representations.* New York: Cambridge University Press.

Clark, A. (1997). *Being there.* Cambridge, MA: MIT Press.

Clark, A. (1999). Where brain, body, and world collide. *Cognitive Systems Research, 1*, 5–17.

Clark, A., & Chalmers, R. (1997). The extended mind. *Analysis, 58*, 7–19.

Douglas, K. M., & Sutton, R. M. (2003). Effects of communication goals and expectancies on language abstraction. *Journal of Personality and Social Psychology, 84*, 692–696.

Douglas, K. M., & Sutton, R. M. (2006). When what you say about others says something about you: Language abstraction and inferences about describers' attitudes and goals. *Journal of Experimental Social Psychology, 42*, 500–508.

Douglas, K. M., & Sutton, R. M. (2006, unpublished manuscript). Could you mind your language? On the (in)ability to inhibit linguistic bias

Fiedler, K., Semin, G. R., & Finkenauer, C. (1993). The battle of words between gender groups: A language-based approach to intergroup processes. *Human Communication Research, 19*, 409–441.

Fiske, S. T. (1998). Stereotyping, prejudice, and discrimination. In D. T. Gilbert, S. T. Fiske, & G. Lindzey (Eds.), *Handbook of social psychology* (4th ed., Vol. 2, pp. 357–411). Boston: McGraw-Hill.

Fiske, S. T., Cuddy, A. J. C., Glick, P. S., & Xu, J. (2002). A model of (often mixed) stereotype content: Competence and warmth respectively follow from perceived status and competition. *Journal of Personality and Social Psychology, 82*, 878–902.

Franco, F. M., & Maass, A. (1996). Implicit versus explicit strategies of out-group discrimination: The role of intentional control in biased language use and reward allocation. *Journal of Language and Social Psychology, 15*, 335–359

Franco, F. M., & Maass, A. (1999). Intentional control over prejudice: When the choice of the measure matters. *European Journal of Social Psychology, 29*, 469–477

Hutchins, E. (1995). *Cognition in the wild.* Cambridge, MA: MIT Press.

Katz, D., & Braly, K. (1933). Racial stereotypes of one hundred college students. *Journal of Abnormal and Social Psychology, 28,* 280–290.

Krauss, R. M., & Fussell, S. R. (1996). Social psychological models of interpersonal communication. In E. T. Higgins & A. W. Kruglanski (Eds.), *Social psychology: Handbook of basic principles* (pp. 655–701). New York: Guilford.

Maass, A. (1999). Linguistic intergroup bias: Stereotype perpetuation through language. In M. P. Zanna (Ed.), *Advances in experimental social psychology* (Vol. 31, pp. 79–121). San Diego: Academic Press.

Maass, A., Milesi, A., Zabbini, S., & Stahlberg, D. (1995). Linguistic intergroup bias: Differential expectancies or in-group protection. *Journal of Personality & Social Psychology, 68,* 116–126.

Maass, A., Salvi, D., Arcuri, L., & Semin, G. (1989). Language use in intergroup contexts: The linguistic intergroup bias. *Journal of Personality and Social Psychology, 57,* 981–993.

Macrae, C. N., & Bodenhausen, G. V. (2000). Stereotypes.. In S. T. Fiske, D. L. Schacter, & C. Zahn-Waxler (Eds.), *Annual review of psychology* (Vol. 51, pp. 93–120). Palo Alto, CA: Annual Reviews.

Mead, G. H. (1934). *Mind, self, and society.* Chicago: University of Chicago Press.

de Montes, G. L., Semin, G. R., & Valencia, J. F. (2003). Communication patterns in interdependent relationships. *Journal of Language and Social Psychology, 22,* 1–22.

Rubini, M., & Semin, G. R. (1994). Language use in the context of congruent and incongruent ingroup behaviours. *British Journal of Social Psychology, 33,* 355–362.

Ryle, G. (1949). *The concept of mind.* Chicago: University of Chicago Press.

Searle, J. R. (1969). *Speech acts.* Cambridge: Cambridge University Press

Semin, G. R. (2000a). Agenda 2000: Communication: Language as an implementational device for cognition. *European Journal of Social Psychology, 30,* 595–612.

Semin, G. R. (2000b). Language as a cognitive and behavioral structuring resource: Question-answer exchanges. In W. Stroebe & M. Hewstone (Eds.), *European review of social psychology* (pp. 75–104). Chichester: Wiley.

Semin, G. R. (2006). Modeling the architecture of linguistic behavior: Linguistic compositionality, automaticity, and control. *Psychological Inquiry, 17,* 246–255.

Semin, G. R. (2007). Grounding communication: Synchrony. In E. T. Higgins & A. Kruglanski (Eds.), *Social psychology: Handbook of basic principles* (2nd ed.), (pp. 630–649) New York: Guildord Publications.

Semin, G. R., & Fiedler, K. (1988). The cognitive functions of linguistic categories in describing persons: Social cognition and language. *Journal of Personality and Social Psychology, 54,* 558–568.

Semin, G. R., & Fiedler, K. (1989). Relocating attributional phenomena within the language-cognition interface: The case of actor-observer perspectives. *European Journal of Social Psychology, 19,* 491–508

Semin, G. R., & Fiedler, K. (1991). The linguistic category model, its bases, applications and range. In W. Stroebe & M. Hewstone (Eds.), *European review of social psychology* (Vol. 2, pp. 1–30). Chichester: Wiley.

Semin, G. R., de Montes, G. L., & Valencia, J. F. (2003). Communication constraints on the linguistic intergroup bias. *Journal of Experimental Social Psychology, 39,* 142–148.

Semin, G. R., & De Poot, C. J. (1997b). The question-answer paradigm: You might regret not noticing how a question is worded. *Journal of Personality and Social Psychology, 73,* 472–480.

Stangor, C., & Lange, J. E. (1994). Mental representations of social groups: Advances in understanding stereotypes and stereotyping. *Advances in Experimental Social Psychology, 26,* 357–416.

Vygotsky, L. (1962/1986). *Language and thought.* Cambridge, MA: MIT Press (original publication 1962).

Werkman, W. M., Wigboldus, D. H., & Semin, G. R. (1999). Children's communica-
      tion of the linguistic intergroup bias and its impact upon cognitive inferences.
      European Journal of Social Psychology, 29, 95–104.
Wigboldus, D., Semin, G. R., & Spears, R. (2000). How do we communicate stereotypes?
      Linguistic bases and inferential consequences. *Journal of Personality and Social Psy-
      chology, 78,* 5–18.

Chapter 3

Stereotype Change in the Social Context

Vincent Yzerbyt
Catholic University of Louvain at Louvain-la-Neuve, Belgium

Andrea Carnaghi
Università di Padova, Italy

> That attitudes have [such] social roots and implications has consequences for their cognitive and emotional functioning. . . . Their content and their persistence and change must be seen as an expression of the need to maintain viable group relations. Only in this way can we fully understand the pull of social conditions in the formation and modification of attitudes and the fact that they vary lawfully with group membership. . . . For a Southerner to deny the prevailing views about Negroes requires a drastic intellectual reorientation and a serious snapping of social bonds. It would be tantamount to questioning the perceptions and cherished values of those nearest to him and to casting himself out of the group. (Asch, 1952, pp. 577–578)

What do Brits think are the distinctive features of Muslims? How does a male employee expect his new female colleague to be? More crucially, why do the positive pieces of information about this asylum seeker fail to alter my views about immigrants? We know that social perceivers associate human groups with a series of characteristics regarding what they think (their beliefs), what they do (their behaviors), and how they feel about their environments (their emotions). In fact, people entertain various assumptions about the features that are emblematic of a variety of other groups and have a definite idea of which personality characteristics to expect when they are confronted with their specific members. Within social psychology, an impressive body of literature is devoted to the measurement of these so-called stereotypes (Judd & Park, 1993; Park & Judd, 1990; Leyens, Yzerbyt, & Schadron, 1994). A substantial

level of effort has also been directed toward understanding the consequences
that such stereotypical beliefs may have on social relations (Fiske, 1998, 2000;
Schneider, 2004; Yzerbyt & Corneille, 2005). Perhaps even more central to social psychologists' research agendas is the work concerned with the variables
that shape and possibly alter stereotypes. What are the different factors that
may help change what people think about other groups?

Such a focus on stereotype change is hardly surprising given the general
agreement regarding the costs of stereotypical beliefs. Indeed, although the
vast majority of stereotypes may well be useful cognitive tools, many observers
also see them as offensive and inaccurate (Dovidio, Glick, & Rudman, 2005).
When using stereotypes, people make the blanket assumption that a specific
member of a group is like any other member of the group. Stereotypes are also
thought to perpetuate defiance between members of different groups and to
generate misunderstanding among individuals with dissimilar backgrounds.
The least one could do, it would seem, is to fight derogatory beliefs and
replace unfavorable and potentially wrong views about the social world with
more encouraging ones.

This chapter is about stereotype change and how communication may affect the extent to which stereotypes are modified or maintained. Our ambition
is to propose a perspective on the modification of stereotypical beliefs which
takes into account the social nature of the process. We argue that in order to
change people's stereotypes, one has to give serious consideration to the social
significance of stereotypes. Stereotyping takes place in the context of relations with other people and any attempt at orienting social perceivers' beliefs
into one direction or another without giving the social environment proper
weight is likely to be short-lived at best and counterproductive at worst. By
evidencing the role of communication in matters of stereotype change, we
intend to stress the complementarities of a cognitive approach and of a social
perspective on these important issues.

This chapter is divided in three sections. The first section details three main
research traditions that we see as directly relevant to our socially situated view
of stereotype change and clarifies how they stimulated our research program.
We begin by reviewing the work inspired by the social influence tradition and its
extensions on the issue of stereotypical beliefs. We then spell out the most significant lessons emerging from the work on stereotype change conducted in the
social cognition tradition. We conclude with an overview of the research that has
examined the impact of communication settings on information processing.

The next section is devoted to a presentation of our empirical work. We review a series of studies conducted in recent years. These studies allow us to
build a case for what we call socially situated stereotype change. Although the
paradigm we rely upon remains largely identical across the different studies,
our dependent measures range from the traditional explicit measures, such
as the evaluative judgments and ratings of typicality, to a more spontaneous
and implicit measure of accessibility, such as the lexical decision task.

We conclude this chapter with a more general consideration of the role of social factors in information processing. In particular, we will see how other phenomena that have generally been studied at the individual level are profitably examined in a more social context.

THEORETICAL BACKGROUND

Consensus and the Change of Stereotypical Beliefs

similar of ingrou

A long tradition of work in social psychology shows that people expect to agree with relevant others on particular statements or beliefs (Asch, 1951; Deutsch & Gerard, 1955; Moscovici, 1976). In line with this idea, social identity and self-categorization theorists proposed that the expectation of consensus essentially involves members of one's in-group (Turner, 1991). When the context activates a specific social identity, people are induced to actively reach a consensus on relevant issues with the other members of their salient in-group. This search for consensus cannot be separated from its outcome, such as the validation of people's statements and beliefs (Haslam et al., 1999; Turner, 1991). In other words, only the consensus within one's in-group would transform an idiosyncratic perception about the social environmental into a shared and subjectively valid point of view on social reality. In line with this reasoning, a large body of research in the social influence domain showed that the validity of a persuasive message is largely determined by source membership and that people are more influenced by in-group than by out-group sources (Abrams & Hogg, 1988; Abrams, Wetherell, Cochrane, Hogg, & Turner, 1990; Cialdini, 1988; Clark & Maass, 1988; David & Turner, 1996; Hogg & Turner, 1987; Mackie, 1986).

Compared to the wealth of studies examining attitude change and persuasion, only a few researchers adopted this framework to examine people's stereotypical beliefs. As it happens, a study by Asch (1940) offered an early, but truly impressive, illustration of the role of social factors in shaping people's conceptions. Participants, all university students, were asked to rank order a series of 10 professions, among which was politician. Before doing this, some participants learned that other students had ranked politician number one. Another group was informed that other students had placed politician in the last position. A third and final group received no information about how other students viewed politician.

Results showed that participants expressed very different opinions as a function of the preliminary information given to them. Specifically, the rank given to politician was largely isomorphic to what participants thought had been indicated by other students, the control condition falling in between the two extreme conditions. An interesting feature of this admittedly simple study concerns the fact that Asch (1940) did not only record the ranking of his participants in the three conditions. He also asked them to provide a description of what they had in mind when they were evaluating the various professions. Interestingly, the kind of politician evoked by the participants in the three conditions was very different. More respected political figures were mentioned and more likable qualities referred to when participants believed others like them had singled out politician as the most prestigious profession than when politician had allegedly been relegated to the last position.

More recently, the role of the reference group as a source of consensus information was illustrated in several studies specifically devoted to the maintenance and change of stereotypical beliefs (Haslam, Oakes, McGarty, Turner, Reynolds, & Eggins, 1996; Sechrist & Stangor, 2001; Stangor, Sechrist, & Jost, 2001; Wittenbrink & Henly, 1996). For instance, Haslam et al. (1996) found that participants shifted their a priori beliefs about national groups toward the beliefs publicly held by members of a positively evaluated in-group. In contrast, participants shifted their stereotype away from the stereotype expressed by an undesirable out-group. In one illustrative study, Stangor et al. (2001) told participants about the beliefs held by other individuals (e.g., in-group members) regarding African Americans. This information was either systematically more favorable or more unfavorable than the stereotype participants thought was shared within their in-group. Participants reported a more positive (negative) stereotype when they first learned that relevant others held a more favorable (unfavorable) stereotype.

In another study, Sechrist and Stangor (2001) had participants come to the laboratory and fill in a prejudice scale. Depending on conditions, participants were then informed that 19% or 81% of the other respondents shared the same viewpoint as themselves. They then had to leave the laboratory and wait in the hall where they were confronted with several seats, as well as an African American participant, actually a confederate of the experimenters, sitting on one of the seats. After a couple of minutes, participants were brought back to the laboratory and asked to convey their stereotype about the target group on several positive and negative stereotypical traits. Results showed that high-prejudice participants sat farther away from the confederate when they were provided with high rather than low consensus feedback. Conversely, low-prejudice participants sat closer to the confederate after being given high rather than low consensus feedback. Moreover, participants' stereotypical judgments also revealed that high-prejudice participants, compared to low-prejudice participants, assigned a higher percentage of negative traits and a lower percentage of positive traits after having received a high-consensus feedback. Correlational analyses also confirmed that providing people with a high compared to a low-consensus feedback bolstered the link between the initial attitude and both their stereotypes and their overt behavior.

Together, these studies stress the importance of the in-group as a source of influence playing a role in stereotype maintenance or change. Results such as those, presented by Haslam et al. (1996), Sechrist and Stangor (2001), and

Stangor et al. (2001), all pointed to the fact that information about the consensus within the in-group has group members align their view about the target category to the in-group norm. The fact that the pattern emerging from self-reported measures were paralleled by data obtained on behavioral and cognitive measures is encouraging evidence that people's adoption of the consensual viewpoint is not merely a matter of superficial compliance but derives from some genuine belief change.

In sum, the idea here is essentially that social perceivers are sensitive to the referential beliefs attributed to in-group members. Informative as this line of work may be, it should be noted that the above efforts are not directly concerned with aspects of communication but shows that members start reacting differently when they are made aware of the viewpoint of in-group members.

Subtyping and Cognitive Resources

Some 50 years ago, Allport (1954) laid the foundation of a cognitive approach of stereotype change (for a review, see Dovidio, Glick, & Rudman, 2005). In this seminal contribution, Allport (1954) proposed that the promotion of intergroup contact constituted a prime strategy for changing stereotypes. To be sure, a cursory look at the literature on the contact hypothesis shows that even its strongest supporters knew quite well that the mere promotion of intergroup contact would fail to alter people's stereotypes (Allport, 1954; Sherif, 1966). Given this state of affairs, many researchers started to investigate the cognitive strategies, allowing people to maintain their stereotypes largely intact even in face of contrary evidence. The subtyping strategy is undoubtedly one of the best-studied strategies of stereotype maintenance (Johnston & Hewstone, 1992; Kunda & Oleson, 1995, 1997; Maurer, Park, & Rothbart, 1995; Park, Wolsko, & Judd, 2001; Rothbart & John, 1985; Weber & Crocker, 1983; Yzerbyt, Coull, & Rocher, 1999).

Social psychologists define subtyping as a process that allows people to exclude the deviant member from their representation of the group. Because the deviant is recategorized as an exception to the rule, the group can still be perceived as equally, if not more, stereotyped than before the encounter with the deviant. Somehow, meeting a counterstereotypical out-group member has people consider that the group comprises true members, those who confirm people's stereotype, on the one hand, and untrue members, those who fail to be incorporated in the boundaries of the group, on the other.

Early approaches of the subtyping strategy emphasized the importance of data-driven processes in stereotype change. Several studies stressed the role of the presentation format of the disconfirming evidence (Weber & Crocker, 1983; Johnston & Hewstone, 1992) or the general representativeness of the contrary evidence as a crucial determinant in stereotype revision (Weber & Crocker, 1983;

Wilder, 1986; see also, Hewstone, Hassebrauck, Wirth, & Waenke, 2000). These studies showed that the actual degree of deviance of the exemplar could account for its impact on the category as a whole. The typicality of the deviant exemplar on other characteristics than the critical one was seen to be a necessary condition for the emergence of stereotype revision (Rothbart & John, 1985; Rothbart & Lewis, 1988). Presumably, the limited change resulting from the confrontation with a deviant results from the fact that the deviant did not activate the target category in the first place (see also Bless et al., 2001).

A somewhat different approach to subtyping builds upon the idea that some construal of information takes place upon encountering a deviant group member (Kunda & Oleson, 1995; Yzerbyt et al., 1999). According to this view, subtyping results from a constructive attempt to try and discard an individual who violates the stereotype. Indeed, several studies suggest that perceivers who come across a deviant member are especially likely to engage in a causal reasoning aimed at refencing the contrary evidence and transforming the deviant into an exception to the rule. Perceivers try to find a good reason to consider the deviant as a special case who is hardly providing any information about the group as a whole. The underlying assumption of this perspective is that perceivers have a vested interest in the maintenance of their stereotypical views and are ready to pay the cognitive cost of preserving them even in the face of contrary evidence (Yzerbyt et al., 1999; Sherman, Stroessner, Conrey, & Azam, 2005).

A variety of reasons may explain why social perceivers are not ready to easily give up their convictions regarding surrounding social categories. In addition to the intrinsic value of possessing an orderly representation of the social word, the inertia characterizing people's beliefs and attitudes about their own group as well as other groups may also find its origin in personal and social motives (Yzerbyt et al., 1999). As it turns out, only a handful of studies focused their attention on the individual factors that prompt observers to dismiss or include a deviant member within the boundaries of the group. One study (Coull, Yzerbyt, Castano, Paladino, & Leemans, 2001) investigated the role of in-group protective motivation as an antecedent in the refencing of a deviant member. Using a dual task paradigm, we presented a deviant in-group member to participants who varied in terms of their level of identification with their in-group. Compared to low identifiers, high identifiers allocated more of their limited cognitive resources to process and discount the information about the deviant in-group member.

Results such as these indicate that individual factors, such as the identification with the in-group, contribute to the perpetuation of the images people form about others. Still, it would appear that more social factors are also likely to play a role in the maintenance of stereotypes. Before we turn to more recent research on these issues, we devote some space to a last source of inspiration for our work—namely the work focusing on the impact of the communication situation on cognitive factors.

Audience and Communication

Communication offers an ideal means for investigating how and why social aspects of the situation tailor the message that gets communicated as well as the cognitive processes that constitute the underpinnings of the construal of the message (Zajonc, 1960; Rusher, Fiske, & Schanke, 2000; Ruscher & Hammer, 1996). Zajonc (1960) was among the first to report a modification in people's cognitive processes as a function of their role in a communication setting. Specifically, he showed that compared to participants assigned the role of receivers those who expected to be communicators tended to exclude or minimize contradictory information and exhibited more polarized impressions on a given target. When it comes to examining communication, a widespread experimental paradigm is the anticipated public context. Concretely, people are asked to communicate or justify their view about a specific issue to someone else. This audience, such as the recipient of the communication, may be present or only symbolically evoked. — very powerful

Within social psychology, several lines of research have implemented this paradigm, of which the Communication Game model and the Accountability model. Taken together, these models have repeatedly shown that either the identity of the audience or its viewpoint on a given issue affects perceivers' impressions of a target (Higgins et al., 1982, Higgins & McCann, 1984) or perceivers' attitudes (Tetlok, Skitka, & Boettger, 1989) and perceivers' endorsement of the group norm (Barreto & Ellemers, 2000). Using their communication game, Higgins and colleagues (Higgins et al., 1982) found that communicators do not only convey an attitude regarding the target of impression that mirrors the view of the audience toward that same target but that participants also tailor their message in order to espouse the position of the audience. For instance, Higgins et al. (1982) showed that participants tended to describe the target of impression by using traits with evaluative implications that were consistent with the attitude of their recipients (for similar results in dyads, see Ruscher & Hammer, 1996; Ruscher, Hammer, & Hammer, 1996).

In the context of the accountability model, researchers not only focused on the content of the message but also on the cognitive processes that contribute to the formation of the message. Regardless of the message being communicated, it would seem that awareness of the position of the audience leads communicators to engage in a less complex and scrupulous thinking process (Tetlock & Lerner, 1999; Tetlock, Armor, & Peterson, 1994). Also, when participants know the attitude of the audience, they usually shift their positions toward the attitude advocated by the audience (Tetlock et al., 1989). Although a possible explanation for this finding is that people adopt the position advocated by the audience as a means to forgo the stress of arguing with opponents, to avoid public rejection, and to achieve self-presentational goals, research would suggest that the attitudinal shift is far from being a superficial change (Cialdini, Levy, Herman, & Evenbeck, 1973; Quinn & Schlenker, 2002). People may well take into account the perspective of the audience with respect to the attitudinal object in such a way that, once the target of judgment has been re-framed under the influence of the prospective audience, the position of the audience still exerts its impact on people's judgment even in a private con-text (Pennington & Schlenker, 1999).

Quite a different story emerges when the position of the audience remains unknown. In this case, participants tend to work on the available target infor-mation in a more conscientious manner as to avoid objections coming from potential opponents (for similar results in the stereotype area, see Moreno & Bodenhausen, 1999). In particular, thought-listing data revealed that, com-pared to participants who are made aware of the position of the audience, peo-ple who do not know the audience's viewpoint engage in a more complex and effortful thinking process (Lerner & Tetlock, 1999; Tetlock et al., 1994).

Interestingly, Kashima (2000; Lyons & Kashima, 2003) recently proposed that cognitive tuning could also play a key role with respect to stereotype main-tenance. Kashima (2000) showed that participants in earlier positions of a communication chain reproduced more inconsistent information than con-sistent information and that participants toward the end of the chain repre-sented consistent information better than inconsistent information.

Although these various efforts make strong predictions regarding people's endorsement of the audience's position in actual or anticipated public con-texts, they fail to spell out specific hypotheses regarding the way people process information when they are embedded in a meaningful social setting such as the anticipated public context. Is it the case that perceivers take into ac-count the audience's position when they appraise information that is consis-tent or inconsistent with the audience's view? Questions such as these deserve closer scrutiny.

Summary

Perhaps the most striking lessons emerging from the above three traditions of work is that they all seem to point to a facet that potentially plays an impor-tant role in stereotype change while largely remaining silent with respect to the other aspects. Work conducted in the social influence and self-categorization tradition strongly points to the social embedment of social believers. What is being stressed is the importance for people to embrace views about other groups and group members that would echo those championed by their fellow in-group members. Social cognition research chooses to draw attention to the cognitive strategies that people rely on in order to handle the emergence of stereotype-inconsistent information. In this approach, the strategy know as subtyping, as well as the cognitive work people engage in, are paramount to people's abilities to maintain their stereotypical beliefs. Finally, efforts under-taken in the context of the communication game and the accountability model emphasize the importance of examining cognitive processes in light of the communication goals of the perceivers. *motivation in interpersonal context*

It is our belief that these three perspectives need to be brought together. Stereotype change offers an ideal illustration of the fact that people do not handle information in a social vacuum. Perhaps more than any other type of information, social perceivers' beliefs about what characteristics describe their own as well as others' groups is likely to be sensitive to considerations that are social in nature. These social goals ought to shape the extent to which people's cognitive processes unfold. Over the past few years, we conducted a series of studies aimed at checking several hypotheses based on our view that cognitive processes and social concerns are likely to combine when it comes to creating and altering beliefs about other groups. We now turn to a rather systematic presentation of the various empirical steps that we took to evaluate the validity of our socially situated view of cognitive processes in general and stereotype change in particular.

EMPIRICAL EVIDENCE

The Initial Evidence

What happens when people encounter information about a target person that contradicts prevailing stereotypes? A first, admittedly very simple, issue that we wanted to investigate concerned the impact of the mere presence of an audience. We expected the presence of an audience to induce a more scrupulous examination of the information. Moreover, we conjectured that the identity of the audience, whether it is a known audience or an unknown audience, would likely influence the way perceivers process the information and the resulting judgment. We designed a study in which we asked our participants to form an impression about a target person (Carnaghi, Yzerbyt, Cadinu, & Mahaux, 2005). We carefully selected the information given to our participants so that the target person would be seen as an ambiguous member of a stereotyped category. Specifically, we first selected a series of four positive and four negative traits that were either stereotypical (e.g., elegant, sensitive) or counterstereotypical (e.g., strong, rude) of the category of homosexuals. We then asked a group of students to provide us with behaviors that they saw exemplified these traits. Still another group of students evaluated the ability to diagnose various behaviors for the different traits, allowing us to retain eight behaviors (e.g., he dresses in a smart way; he used to say slurs) that had a comparable level of diagnosis for inclusion in the experimental materials.

Before experimental participants received the behavioral information about the target person on their computer screen, some learned that they would have to communicate their impression to other people whereas others received no such instruction. Moreover, whereas half of the audience participants were informed about the identity of the audience, a group of other students like them, the remaining half received no further information about the audience. All participants could then read the various behaviors at their own pace and rate the target person on a series of traits corresponding to the behaviors that had been presented.

Our hypotheses concerned both the process and the content aspects of participants' reactions to the information concerning the target person. As far as information processing indicators were concerned, we expected participants to be more meticulous when made accountable than when confronted with the target information in a more private mode. Moreover, we hoped to see the prevailing views of the audience to alleviate the need to examine stereotypical information in a careful way. Turning to the judgment, we expected that more time spent examining the information would result in more moderate judgments.

Our predictions were borne out. In general, participants took less time to examine the information that was stereotypical than the information that ran counter to prevailing expectations about homosexuals. As confirmed by a significant interaction with audience, this pattern emerged only when the audience was known to the participants. In the presence of an unknown audience, participants took more time to read all the information that was given to them, be it stereotypical or counterstereotypical. In sharp contrast, the absence of any audience had participants read all the information much more quickly. Our hypothesis regarding judgments was also supported. Participants expressed more stereotyped judgments in the absence of an audience versus the presence of a known audience, with the unknown audience participants falling in between.

These findings can be seen as initial evidence for the influence of social concerns on information processing. To the extent that participants intended to preserve consensus with the audience, they seemed ready to mobilize their cognitive resources in order to debunk whatever information clashed with the stereotype held by the audience. Promising as this demonstration may be, one obvious limitation concerns the fact that we exert no control over the stereotypes believed to be held in the group of students. This potential confound between the nature of the behaviors and the degree to which they may be stereotyped may seem difficult to avoid, but we decided to conduct a study in which we would be able to show that perceivers do indeed pay relatively more attention to counterstereotypical than to stereotypical information in a context in which we manage to alter the assumed stereotype of the audience.

The study (Carnaghi & Yzerbyt, 2006) relied heavily on the procedure used in the first study. This time, however, we dropped the no-audience condition. Also, we used two known audience conditions (again using the in-group of students) in addition to an unknown audience condition. We thought it would be somewhat unrealistic to provide participants with bogus information that would blatantly clash with their assumptions regarding the ambient stereo-

types. Therefore, we selected two positive (e.g., athletic, careful) and two negative traits (e.g., easygoing, spiritual) that were seen as rather irrelevant of homosexuals in general. As in our first study, we then secured behaviors that were
diagnostic of these traits (e.g., he used to play basketball). For each one of
these traits, we also chose an equally irrelevant antonym (e.g., sedentary, care-
less, irritable, materialistic). These eight traits allowed us to present one audience as holding a positive stereotype about homosexuals and the other audience as holding a negative stereotype about homosexuals.

Upon their arrival at the laboratory, participants were seated in front of a
computer and were told that the study concerned the way people form an impression about a target and communicate it to others in a face to face interaction. Participants in the positive or negative stereotype audience conditions
were informed that the experiment comprised three phases. In the first phase,
participants had to learn the stereotype held by the audience about a given
group. Whereas the positive audience was said to hold beliefs embodied in
the four positive traits, the four negative traits were used to describe the beliefs
of the negative audience. In the second phase, participants had to form an
impression about a member of that group. In addition to the four behaviors
corresponding to the irrelevant traits, participants were also shown four moderately typical behaviors so as to ensure the credibility of the target person as
a homosexual. In an ostensibly final phase, participants were expected to
communicate their personal impression of the target to the audience. Participants in the unknown audience condition were simply told about the two last
phases. The third phase never took place. Importantly, as far as the known
audience conditions are concerned and because our careful selection of the
two sets of eight traits, the target always partly confirmed and partly disconfirmed the alleged beliefs of the audience about homosexuals. Participants
paced themselves through the behavioral information, pressing the space bar
when they felt ready to examine the next behavior. As before, we took reading time of behavioral items to be a valid online measure of attention allocation and stimuli interpretation (e.g., Fiske, 1980).

Leaving a rather trivial valence effect aside—not surprisingly, participants
took more time to read the negative than the positive behaviors—results revealed that the hypotheses were strongly supported. As expected, people took
longer to examine the four behaviors when they found themselves in the unknown condition than when they had been informed about the stereotype of
the audience. More interestingly, there was an interaction in the time people
took to examine the information in the known audience conditions. Confirming the importance of the social context on information processing, participants took relatively more time to examine the behaviors that proved to
be inconsistent with the views of their prospective audience than to read those
behaviors that were in line with the assumed stereotype of their audience. It
is noteworthy that this effect emerged despite the fact that the alleged audience was in fact the same in both known audience conditions. The only dif-

ference between the two conditions was the alleged set of beliefs that had been attached to the audience.

Clearly, this pattern of findings strongly suggests that our participants were sensitive to the social repercussions of their impressions and realized that they needed to make sure they had devoted enough attention to information that could prove problematic in light of the a priori position of the audience. The data also emphasized the fact that perceivers are not approaching new information from their idiosyncratic perspective but take into account the potential divergence with the surrounding social world.

Subtyping the Target

In light of the encouraging message coming from the two initial studies (Carnaghi et al., 2005; Carnaghi & Yzerbyt, 2006), we decided to address stereotype change more directly by looking at the impact of the social context on the way perceivers deal with the information that is specific to the deviant. Indeed, it stands to reason that if a deviant group member is appraised in a context in which the information clashes more with the assumed stereotype of the reference group of perceivers, this target should end up being subtyped more strongly and should have less of an impact on the perceivers' views. Evidence in support of this hypothesis would go a long way to support our socially situated view of stereotype change in that it is not information that triggers some cognitive processes but triggers its larger meaning in light of the social context. Several studies were conducted to examine this issue (Carnaghi & Yzerbyt, 2005, in press).

In the first study (Carnaghi & Yzerbyt, in press, Exp.1), we again confronted participants with the prospect of meeting with a negative or a positive audience and conveying their impressions about a deviant member of a group. This time, we did not provide specific information about the views of the group, but capitalized instead on our participants' knowledge regarding two obvious reference groups. One reference group was the group of students and the other was an equal opportunity organization active on campus at the time of the study. Importantly, pretests indicated that students evaluated these two groups in equally positive terms. However, whereas students were generally believed to hold rather derogatory beliefs about homosexuals, the opposite was true of the members of the equal opportunity organization. This careful choice of reference groups allowed us to present information about the same moderately positive homosexual target in both conditions and to expect a number of distinct reactions. The first hypothesis was that participants would much less readily conclude that they had been confronted with a subtype when the prospective audience was comprised of members of the equal opportunity organization rather than other students. We also expected participants' stereotypical beliefs to become more positive in the first than in the second case. For both audiences, we predicted that we would see some level of overlap between participants' views about homosexuals at the end of the study and the assumed stereotype of the audience as measured at the outset of the study.

After having been informed about the audience they would later be confronted with, participants were given information about a moderately positive disconfirming member of the group of homosexuals. The dependent measures involved participants' assumed stereotypes of the audience, their impressions of the target, their perceptions of the degree of typicality of the target, and their personal stereotype about the group of homosexuals. Finally, participants were asked to indicate the extent to which they were in favor of homosexual relationships. Clearly, we expected the positive disconfirming homosexual to be seen as less (versus more) representative of the group when the prospective audience was thought to hold a negative (versus positive) view about homosexuals in general. In addition, we hoped that participants' expressions of stereotypical beliefs would be more positive when the audience was believed to hold a positive, as opposed to a negative, view toward homosexuals. This meant that we expected to see some overlap between the assumed stereotypes of the audience concerning homosexuals and the personal stereotypes about the same group.

As expected, the view of homosexuals that was thought to prevail among students was less flattering than the stereotype believed to exist among members of the equal opportunity organization. Also, the target was seen to be counterstereotypical and more positive than negative. Interestingly, the impression of the target was not different in the two conditions. In contrast, but in line with predictions, the target was seen as significantly less typical among the students than the equal opportunity organization. The difference in pattern between the impression data and the typicality data is not unprecedented in the subtyping literature (Kunda & Oleson, 1995, 1997; Yzerbyt et al., 1999), and it strongly suggests that it is not so much what we see but how we interpret it in relation to the stereotype that is affected by the prospective audience.

In order to examine the personal stereotypes of the participants, we computed a negative stereotyping score and found that homosexuals in general were rated more negatively in the student audience condition than in the equal opportunity audience condition. As it turned out, we found that the assumed stereotypes of the audience and the personal stereotypes were equally overlapping in the two audience conditions. A more specific analysis within subject correlations between the ratings given for the assumed stereotypes of the audience and the personal stereotypes gave way to the same absence of difference between conditions. In other words, in both conditions, participants seem to have taken the assumed stereotypes of the audience as a critical standard of judgment and, as a result, ended up seeing the disconfirming positive target as less typical in the negative audience condition, espousing the views of their audience. In line with what one would expect, participants in the student condition reported being less in favor of homosexual relationships that the rest of the participants.

Although the two audiences used in this study had been tested to be equivalent in terms of likeability and status, one might object that they are not strictly equivalent, especially in terms of participants' membership statuses. This limitation notwithstanding, this study provides intriguing evidence regarding the impact of referent groups on information processing.

Same Stereotype but Different Audiences

In order to further ascertain the argument concerning the socially situated nature of stereotype change and subtyping, we conducted several follow-up studies (Carnaghi & Yzerbyt, 2005, in press; Yzerbyt & Carnaghi, 2005) in which we kept constant the content of the stereotypes of the audience and varied instead the nature of the audience. This manipulation can be seen as the mirror image of the previous study. With it, we should be able to determine whether participants shape their judgments to suit the stereotypes held by the audience, mainly because such a reaction is individually profitable, in terms of gaining prestige or avoiding sanctions, or mainly because it allows them to affirm what is normative from the perspective of the (referent) in-group.

In one of these (Carnaghi & Yzerbyt, 2005), participants expected to meet with members of an in-group (e.g., students of the University of Louvain at Louvain-la-Neuve, the French-speaking campus of the University of Louvain) or outgroup audience (e.g., students of the University of Leuven, the Dutch-speaking campus of the University of Louvain). The stereotypes of the audience were held constant across conditions: Participants were always informed that the audience considered homosexuals as not very artistic or creative. As for the deviant group member, all participants were confronted with a moderately artistic and creative homosexual man. Again, we predicted that participants' perceptions of typicality of a stereotype-disconfirming member would be influenced by the stereotypes of the audience. However, this time, we did not simply expect participants to embrace the stereotypes of the audience equally easily in the two conditions. Specifically, we hoped to see participants react to the deviant with more skepticism when the latter clashed with an in-group stereotype than when the latter clashed with an out-group stereotype. As a consequence, the deviant target should be seen as much less typical when participants learned that they later would communicate their judgments to an in-group rather than out-group audience. We also expected the relationships between participants and their audiences to influence their endorsement of the stereotype of the audience. We thus anticipated that participants would consider homosexuals in general as less artistic and less creative in the in-group than in the out-group audience condition.

Results proved most supportive indeed. Whereas participants had the same impression of the target regardless of experimental condition, they more readily considered the target as a deviant group member when they recognized the audience as a self-inclusive group than when the audience was an out-group.

Said otherwise, participants perceived the target as much less typical of the larger group of homosexuals when he violated the stereotype thought to prevail among an in-group rather than an out-group audience. Looking at the stereotype of the group at the end of the experiment, participants judged the group of homosexuals as less artistic when they expected to later communicate their judgment to an in-group rather than to an out-group audience. Interestingly, our audience manipulation did not affect participants' ratings concerning stereotypical items that were not an explicit part of the stereotypes of the audience, confirming the highly specific use of the consensus information by our participants. In conclusion, these data reveal that participants are more likely to conform to the audience stereotype when the audience is an in-group rather than an out-group. As a result, they not only tended to perceive the disconfirming target as less typical, but they also tended to perceive the rest of the group as more in line with the stereotypes of the audience.

In another study (Yzerbyt & Carnaghi, 2005, Exp. 1), we adopted a somewhat different strategy and examined whether people's evaluations of a disconfirming member of a stereotyped group would be influenced by the ability to prototype an in-group audience. Specifically, we hypothesized that the higher the perceived ability to prototype an in-group audience, the stronger the expectation of agreement would be. We further expected that the stereotypical views of the audience would come across as more extreme in the high than in the low prototypical audience condition. Finally, we predicted that the target would be contrasted away from the assumed stereotype of the audience more in the high than in the low prototypical audience condition.

Concretely, when participants arrived at the laboratory, they received the general instructions for the study, along with a small portrait of the audience. They were told that the audience comprised several students like them who had written some sort of identification passport in order to introduce themselves. The identification passport included six behaviors. Depending on the experimental condition and based on pretest work, the behaviors were either very or not very prototypical of students in general. After participants had indicated what, in their opinions, were the assumed stereotypes about homosexuals of the audience, they then received the description of a homosexual man. The specific portrait comprised statements that disconfirmed the stereotypes of homosexuals (e.g., he hates movies about love stories, but he is very fond of action movies), as well as statements that confirmed the stereotype of heterosexuals (e.g., he works hard as a construction worker, and he rarely feels tired). Participants then conveyed their impressions about the target using the same 12 personality traits that they had used to rate the assumed stereotypes of the audience.

A series of manipulation check items confirmed that the high prototypical audience was seen as more representative of the in-group than the low prototypical audience. As for the main findings, when participants expected to meet with a prototypical audience, the target was evaluated further away from the stereotypes. In other words, compared to low prototypical audience participants, high prototypical audience participants were significantly more likely to see the deviant as an atypical member of the group of homosexuals.

A most interesting and important message emerges from these two studies. As a matter of fact, the pattern of findings nicely echoes other research showing that the validity of a persuasive message is largely determined by the membership of its source (Abrams & Hogg, 1990; Clark & Maass, 1988; David & Turner, 1996; Hogg & Turner, 1987; Mackie, 1986). We found that our participants were more influenced by in-group than by out-group sources. They also proved to be more sensitive to high prototypical in-group sources than to low prototypical in-group sources. If the results of the our initial studies might indeed be interpreted in terms of a surveillance effect, such as the tendency to tailor one's communication in order to avoid sanctions from the audience (Reicher & Levine, 1994a, 1994b; Tetlock, Skitka, & Boettger, 1989), the results of this follow-up work allow us to question such an interpretation. In particular, the study in which either an in-group or out-group audience was used indicates that perceivers are sometimes ready to take some distance from their prospective audiences. This pattern clearly runs against the idea that all communication has to be cooperative and that the audience-tuning effect is just reflective of the communicator's attempt to find common ground with the receiver. Because social identity concerns are also at work in the context of these studies, the stereotype eventually held by our participants about the group was more likely to diverge from the one held by the audience when the audience was an out-group rather than an in-group.

A Cognitive and/or a Social Account

The present set of studies allows us to critically appraise a purely cognitive account of our findings. Indeed, one could argue that participants in the various conditions that were created in our initial studies examined the evidence that was presented to them under circumstances in which strikingly different stereotypes had been activated. It is therefore hardly surprising that participants reacted differently to the information that was given to them. For instance, participants in the second study presented above (Carnaghi & Yzerbyt, 2006) were found to devote more time to whatever information about the deviant that ran counter to the stereotypes of their prospective audiences. This pattern can be seen as showing that the evocation of (the stereotype of) the audience functions as a catalyst; we could also say a prime, that prompts a certain reference point or a knowledge structure. This informational interpretation of data is all the more reasonable that we explicitly communicated the content of the stereotypes of the audience to our participants before they were confronted with the target information.

There are not one but two versions of a priming account of the data. The first account considers that any evidence for the intervention of a cognitively salient reference point strongly questions a socially situated account of stereotype change. In other words, because perceivers appraise information from the vantage point of some salient knowledge structure, there is no need to take into account the potential role of more distal social factors. This viewpoint would have us disregard altogether the social significance of the knowledge structure or prime that is being activated.

A second, perhaps less imperialistic, view on the role of cognitive factors, indeed one that takes into account the social meaning of the primed stereotype, holds that the specific knowledge structure that is activated upon mentioning a particular audience is appraised in a way that preserves its social significance. For instance, coming back to the fourth study presented above (Carnaghi & Yzerbyt, 2005), we had participants confronted with one of two audiences. These two audiences were said to hold the exact same views about the stereotyped group. However, whereas the audience was believed to be an in-group in one condition, it was thought to be an out-group in the other condition.

Clearly, to the extent that the knowledge structure made salient in participants' minds is the same in these two conditions, the finding that participants perceive the deviant target as a more or less typical member of the group in the two conditions requires that one complements the knowledge structure with additional information that incorporates the relational aspect of the situation. Specifically, information about the deviant target is assimilated to or contrasted away from the stereotype of the audience not only as a function of the sheer gap between the target information and the stereotype, as was observed in our initial studies, but also by taking into account the identity of the audience. This second approach is no less cognitive than the first one. Simply, it considers that social factors moderate people's reactions to the knowledge structure that is being primed when evoking the views of the audience. Such a socially situated view of cognition nicely converges with other research efforts stressing the need to take into account both the relational and informational features of a situation (Smeesters, Warlop, Van Avermaet, Corneille, & Yzerbyt, 2003; Smeesters, Yzerbyt, Corneille, Warlop, & Van Avermaet, 2005).

The Management of Inconsistency

The above studies provide intriguing evidence that people handle information differently as a function of the audience. This differential treatment is responsible for the divergent consequences in terms of judgments of typicality and stereotypical views of the target group. Obviously, however, we need more information regarding whether and how the audience influences the way participants process the information that concerns a member of a stereotyped group. We did this in one recent study (Yzerbyt & Carnaghi, 2005, Exp. 2) in which we also wanted to investigate the consequence of this process on the later accessibility of the stereotypical constructs.

Again, participants expected to meet with an in-group audience that varied in terms of its prototyping. The target was now chosen to be an American man who partially confirmed and partially disconfirmed the stereotypes of Americans. Given that there was no obvious contrasting category, we decided to refer only to American stereotypical traits in the judgment materials. We hypothesized that the higher the perceived prototyping of the audience the stronger the expectation of agreement would be. In order to gain a better appreciation of the direction of the influence of the audience, we also included a no-audience control condition.

As in our initial studies, we secured a measure of attention allocation and stimuli interpretation by recording the time participants took to read the description of the target. This was done in the hope that participants would generally spend more time in order to process the information in the experimental conditions than in the control condition and that they would take longer processing behavioral information about negative than about positive traits. More importantly, we expected that participants would spend more time processing disconfirming rather than confirming information. We further predicted the presence of a significant interaction between the status of the behavioral information and prototyping the audience. Specifically, we predicted that participants would manifest greater processing efforts aimed at dismissing disconfirming evidence when they believe that they would later meet with a high prototypical rather than with a low prototypical in-group audience. We hoped this pattern to be moderated by the valence of the stereotypical traits implied by the behavioral information. Indeed, pretest work had indicated that the attitude of the student population toward the American group was rather negative and students had been found to characterize this group more strongly on negative than on positive dimensions (Costarelli, 2000). Therefore, we hoped that participants' preferential focus on disconfirming information as a function of prototyping the audience would be more marked for negative than for positive stereotypical traits.

The main ambition, however, of the present study was that we wanted more definitive evidence for the cognitive process assumed to take place during the presentation of the information. To this end, we also included a lexical decision task at the end of the presentation of the information. Our conjecture is that perceivers activate the stereotype of the out-group as a contrasting reference point, as a standard of comparison, in order to define the deviant as an exception to the rule. We therefore expected to find evidence of increased accessibility of the stereotypical traits that participants presumably tried to maintain even in the face of counterstereotypical information. Again, we anticipated that this phenomenon would be more pronounced in the high prototypical audience than in the low prototypical audience condition and would show up in the case of negative stereotypical traits but less so or not at all for positive stereotypical traits.

After learning about their prospective audiences, a highly prototypical or much less prototypical group of students depending on conditions, participants read information about the target in the form of eight behaviors displayed one at a time on the computer screen. The target was an ambiguous member of the group as he partly confirmed and partly disconfirmed participants' prior beliefs about Americans. Four behaviors exemplified four traits pretested as stereotypical of Americans in general and four disconfirmed four stereotypical traits. Each subset of four traits comprised two positive and two negative traits. Any effect related to the particular selection of behaviors included in the experimental materials was controlled by preparing four versions of the target's description in which a different set of stereotypical traits were confirmed or disconfirmed in the behaviors. Participants paced themselves through the behavioral information, pressing the space bar when they felt ready to examine the next behavior. The time spent reading each behavior served as our online measure of attention allocation and stimuli interpretation.

After having conveyed their impression about the target using the eight personality traits that had been confirmed or disconfirmed by the behavioral information, participants performed our key lexical decision task. The experimental trials of the lexical decision task comprised 22 personality traits and 22 nonwords which were paired for length. Eight of these 22 traits were those that had been confirmed or disconfirmed in the target description. The time that participants took in order to correctly identify these eight traits was used as a measure of accessibility.

The data pertaining to reading time largely confirmed our earlier findings. As one would expect, participants in the no-audience condition globally took less time than their audience counterparts. Moreover, the no-audience participants did not react differently to disconfirming and confirming behaviors. A different pattern emerged in the experimental conditions where participants took more time to handle the disconfirming behaviors. Moreover, participants' tendencies to devote more attention to the disconfirming rather than the confirming behaviors was much more pronounced in the high rather than in the low prototypical audience condition. Finally, in line with the negative stereotype prevailing in the larger student population, the deeper processing of disconfirming relative to confirming behaviors observed in the high prototypical audience condition was much more pronounced for those behaviors that clashed the negative rather than the positive side of the stereotype.

The data for the lexical decision task revealed no significant effects for the positive traits. For the negative traits, we found a most interesting pattern. Indeed, participants in the high prototypical audience condition were faster at recognizing negative traits that had been associated with stereotype-disconfirming behavioral information than their low prototypical counterparts. The same comparison for reaction times to traits that had been associated with stereotype-confirming information did not reveal any significant effect.

Together, the data from the reading times and lexical decisions are most informative, especially when it comes to those participants confronted with a high prototypical audience. Apparently, these participants were particularly prone to spending time when presented with unexpected positive (as compared to negative) behavioral evidence from a member of a largely derogated group. Moreover, the negative traits that were being questioned by this positive behavior of the target, although never explicitly mentioned in the materials, were recognized very fast indeed on a later lexical decision task. This pattern strongly suggests that participants in this high prototypical audience condition indeed activated the stereotypical traits when confronted with contradicting evidence.

Such a finding goes a long way to inform us about the information processing at work when people meet a deviant member of a stereotyped group. It underlines the nature of the cognitive work allowing perceivers to fence off group members that come across as being out of the ordinary. From what we see in this last study, it may thus well be that the consequence of this inferential work, aimed at discounting the deviant member, has the paradoxical effect of making the corresponding stereotypical features of the target group even more accessible and salient. One potential consequence of this process is to strengthen the association between the category and the stereotypical features.

FROM STEREOTYPE CHANGE TO OTHER PHENOMENA

Building upon recent social cognition work that acknowledges perceivers' attachments to their stereotypical views of other groups (Kunda & Oleson, 1995; Yzerbyt et al., 1999), we proposed that one key element in the perpetuation or change of stereotypes is that such beliefs play a role in allowing people to be considered decent representatives of their group. As a consequence, the extent to which perceivers think that specific stereotypical beliefs are shared by other members of their group will influence the way people process the incoming information. This will be especially the case when the prospect of interaction with members of the in-group is being stressed and the identity of the audience is such that they are thought to be highly prototypical members of the group. Our reasoning is also related to recent work in the domain of stereotype change that used the idea of consensus validation of personal beliefs in an attempt to alter people's social beliefs (Haslam et al., 1996; Sechrist & Stangor, 2001; Stangor et al., 2001; Wittenbrink & Henly, 1996).

Because perceivers are preoccupied with the social significance of their beliefs and that such concerns are likely to play a key role in matters of stereotype change and stereotype maintenance, they will likely capitalize on the assumed beliefs and the identity of a prospective audience to orient their assessments of the target. Whereas they may distance themselves from an audience that they do not recognize as valid, they will invest substantial cognitive energy to handle information that seemingly clashes with the assumed opinions of a self-inclusive audience. A straightforward strategy to investigate issues of this sort was to compare the way perceivers come to process information and issue judgments about target people depending on the nature of the audience they expect to meet.

The present research program clearly emphasizes the socially situated nature of the cognitive processes involved in the maintenance or modification of stereotypical beliefs. In several studies, we show that, compared to people who receive information with no specific social concerns on their minds, people expecting to later meet with an audience tailor their appraisals of the information so as to clarify their positions in the social landscape. We found that the same information could give way to an increased or decreased mode of processing time as a function of its meaning not so much in light of people's own views, but in light of their assumptions about the ambient norms. That is to say, perceivers were ready to mobilize their cognitive resources but only when confronted with information that clashed against the stereotypes held by the audience (Carnaghi et al., 2005; Carnaghi & Yzerbyt, 2005, 2006, in press; Yzerbyt & Carnaghi, 2005). As for perceptions of the typicality of a disconfirming target, data clearly confirms that participants take very seriously any information that runs counter to the stereotypes of the audience. Indeed, perceivers view the target as a deviant member of the target group only when the obtained information is at odds with the group representation that is shared within a self-inclusive audience.

We also provide evidence that the same information regarding a deviant target fares very differently as a function of the nature of the audience who affirms its stereotype. As our measures of stereotype endorsement (Carnaghi & Yzerbyt, 2005, in press) and stereotype accessibility (Yzerbyt & Carnaghi, 2005) revealed, the consequence of the subtyping process is the preservation of the stereotype assumed to prevail among in-group members. Finally, our work innovated in that it links individual cognitive processes and social factors and allowed us to overcome the limitations typically found in the social influence perspective or in the individual-based cognitive approach.

At a theoretical level, the goal of the present research was thus to transcend the dichotomy between the informational model and the social perspective by recasting an important cognitive process (e.g., subtyping) into a meaningful social context. At a more practical level, several lessons can be learned as far as stereotype change is concerned. It would seem that a critical determinant of stereotype change will be the larger social context within which the information about the individual target member is encountered. Perceivers will likely dismiss target information that clashes with those stereotypical beliefs assumed to prevail in the in-group. This means that one should facilitate change on the basis of target information by altering people's assumptions about the in-group norms. In contrast, perceivers will generally dismiss target information that seems at odds with whatever views are believed to have wide currency among in-group members. Of course, because people belong to several in-groups, some of which may hold rather different views about the target group, it would be profitable to actualize the in-group which allows the best integration of the information about the target member. An alternative strategy rests on manipulating the beliefs thought to exist among out-group members. Indeed, one should be able to facilitate stereotype change by presenting target evidence in a context where this information diverges from those stereotypes that are strongly associated with an out-group.

We mentioned earlier the relevance of the work conducted in the framework of the communication game and of the accountability hypothesis. Turning from an interpersonal to a group communication context, theorists working in the tradition of social identity theory (SIT; Tajfel & Turner, 1979) and self-categorization theory (SCT; Turner, 1991) also examined how individuals may be affected by their group memberships in a communication setting (Reicher, Spears, & Postmes, 1995; see also Barreto & Ellemers, 2003). For these authors, the group communication context was regulated by a cognitive as well as a strategic dimension. The cognitive dimension refers to the particular category that is made contextually salient in the communication setting. In line with SCT, once individuals perceive themselves as members of a given category, they tend to actively compare their viewpoints with the beliefs of the other members of the same category. This contextually driven comparison process leads people to determine the group norm (e.g., in-group prototype) and, presumably, to assign the norm to the self. As a result, individuals' perceptions and behaviors tend to be in-group normative. In other words, when some social identity is being activated, group members feel pressure to actively reach a consensus with the other members of their group on relevant issues. This process transforms an idiosyncratic perception about the social environment into a shared and subjectively valid point of view on social reality (Hogg, 1987; Turner, 1991).

As for the strategic dimension of the group communication context, a number of studies indicate that people are not only concerned with their individual reputation but that they also care about how others see their social selves (Barreto, Spears, Ellemers, & Shahinper, 2003; Branscombe, Ellemers, Spears, & Doosje, 1999). Beyond a mere passive reaction to the group norm, people may also actively bring external perceptions of themselves in line with expectations. In fact, communicational settings may lead people to switch from being a mere target of group pressure to being an agent of influence (Reicher, Spears, & Postmes, 1995; Spears & Lea, 1994). The confrontation with an audience provides people with an ideal opportunity not only to think of themselves as a group member but also to secure acknowledgement of their depersonalized self-views from others.

For instance, people are generally inclined to present themselves as group members when the group has a desirable social standing and could function as a referent group. In this case, people are likely to align their messages to the norm advocated by the group as an audience either because associating with a referent group could be seen as personally profitable (Ellemers, 1993; Barreto

& Ellemers, 2000) or because behaving in accordance with the group-based expectations may prevent them from being sanctioned (Reicher & Levine, 1994a, 1994b; Marques, Yzerbyt, & Leyens, 1988). However, as we showed in our studies as well, communicators do not conform to every audience (Carnaghi & Yzerbyt, 2005, press). Indeed, when confronted with an out-group audience, and even though communicators may take into account out-group norms in their messages in order to avoid their public violations (Reicher & Levine, 1994a, 1994b), they nevertheless tend to express what is normative for their own groups (Barreto & Ellemers, 2003).

The significance of a socially situated view of information processing is far from limited to the issue of stereotype change. In fact, it would seem that much progress made in recent years with respect to our understanding of perceivers' reactions toward other groups derives precisely from the acknowledgement that they are not only individuals but that they are also members of social groups. This means that the way social perceivers appraise their environment, be it information about members of stereotyped groups or a multitude of other daily events, cannot be fully appreciated if one minimizes, or even worse obliterates, the issue of social embedment. This perspective has been as helpful to reexamine the issue of stereotype change as it has contributed to shed new light on the issue of intergroup emotions. Like others (Mackie, Devos, & Smith, 2000), we have been able to show the role of social factors in the emergence of emotional reactions (Dumont, Yzerbyt, Wigboldus, & Gordijn, 2003; Gordijn, Wigboldus, & Yzerbyt, 2001; Yzerbyt, Dumont, Wigboldus, Gordijn, 2003; for a review, see Yzerbyt, Dumont, Mathieu, Gordijn, & Wigboldus, 2006). By casting people's emotional experiences in more social terms and taking advantage of the advances made by appraisal theorists, the field has been able to go beyond the rather individualistic and simplistic view of prejudice. As much as Lewin taught us to pay attention to both the person and the situation, we think that cognitive processes and emotional phenomena have their roots in people's social motivations as much as in their cognitive apparatus (Yzerbyt, 2006). It is our opinion that the same cross-fertilization can take place by mixing more individualistic approaches adopted by social cognition researchers and more social perspectives be they proposed by social identity theorists or others. The lesson is that more attention should be paid to the interplay of people's social concerns and their cognitive processes when it comes to changing views about other groups. This, in our view, is a fascinating lesson of a socially situated view of stereotype change.

CONCLUSION

Why do our daily contacts with Arab shop owners not generalize to the rest of the group? Why is that we are so pleased about the work relationship with an obese colleague and yet remain reluctant to see obese people in general as courageous and dynamic? Research about stereotypes and intergroup relations has long shown that exposure to stereotype-disconfirming information is far from being a sufficient condition to change people's preexisting beliefs. Social perceivers may well modify their attitude toward a specific positive member of a negatively stereotyped group, but they usually fail to generalize their constructive experience to the group as a whole (Rothbart & John, 1985; Stephan & Stephan, 1985).

Over the last two decades, a variety of efforts have delineated the conditions under which encounters with unexpected information about a member of a stigmatized group may translate into a more accurate and possibly more positive representation of the rest of the group. With a few exceptions, the work on this important issue ignores the fact that people are not isolated information processors but find themselves in the midst of complex and significant social networks. Still, there is little doubt that the processing of information about a specific individual, particularly when this person is a member of a stigmatized social category, cannot be conducted in total ignorance of the social insertion of the perceivers. In other words, the a priori knowledge of other people's opinion about social groups and the particular relation with these others influences the appraisal of the information concerning a particular group member.

The current endeavor was guided by our conviction that the tendency to subtype or to generalize a deviant will depend on the assumptions made by perceivers regarding the views held by their social environments in general and their immediate audiences in particular. The clear signal emanating from our work is that policy makers would do well to take into account the social context of information acquisition if one wishes to alter people's beliefs.

ACKNOWLEDGMENTS

The research presented in this chapter was funded by grant ARC 01/06-270 C from the Communauté Française de Belgique.

REFERENCES

Abrams, D., & Hogg, M. A. (1988). Comments on the motivational status of self-esteem in social identity and intergroup discrimination. *European Journal of Social Psychology, 18*, 317–334.

Abrams, D., & Hogg, M. A. (1990). Social identification, self-categorization, and social influence. In W. Stroebe & M. Hewstone (Eds.), *European Review of Social Psychology, 1*, 195–228.

Abrams, D., Wetherell, M. S., Cochrane, S., Hogg, M. A., & Turner, J. C. (1990). Knowing what to think by knowing who you are: Self categorization and the nature of norm formation, conformity, and group polarization. *British Journal of Social Psychology, 29*, 97–119.

Allport, G. W. (1954). *The nature of prejudice.* Cambridge, MA: Addison-Wesley.

Asch, S. E. (1940). Studies in the principles of judgments and attitudes: II. Determination of judgments by group and by ego standards. *Journal of Social Psychology, 12,* 433–465.

Asch, S. E. (1951). Effects of group pressure upon the modification and distortion of judgments. In H. Guetzkow (Ed.), *Groups, leadership and men; research in human relations* (pp. 177–190). Pittsburgh: Carnegie Press.

Asch, S. E. (1952). *Social psychology.* Englewood Cliffs, NJ: Prentice-Hall.

Barreto, M., & Ellemers, N. (2000). You can't always do what you want: Social identity and self-presentation determinants of the choice to work for a low status group. *Personality and Social Psychology Bulletin, 26,* 891–906.

Barreto, M., & Ellemers, N. (2003). The effect of being categorised: The interplay between internal and external social identities. *European Review of Social Psychology, 14,* 139–170.

Barreto, M., Spears, R., Ellemers, N., & Shahinper, K. (2003). Who wants to know? The effect of audience on identity expression among minority group members. *British Journal of Social Psychology, 42,* 299–318.

Bless, H., Schwarz, N., Bodenhausen, G. V., & Thiel, L. (2001). Personalized versus generalized benefits of stereotype disconfirmation: Trade-offs in the evaluation of atypical exemplars and their social groups. *Journal of Experimental Social Psychology, 37,* 386–397.

Branscombe, N. R., Ellemers, N., Spears, R., & Doosje, B. (1999). The context and the content of social identity threat. In N. Ellemers, R. Spears, & B. Doosje (Eds.), *Social identity: Context, commitment, content* (pp. 35–58). Oxford: Basil Blackwell.

Carnaghi, A., & Yzerbyt, V. Y. (2005). Subtyping in a social context: How the audience shapes stereotype change. *Unpublished data.* Catholic University of Louvain

Carnaghi, A., & Yzerbyt, V. Y. (2006). Social consensus and the encoding of consistent and inconsistent information: When one's future audience orients information processing. *European Journal of Social Psychology, 36,* 199–210.

Carnaghi, A., Yzerbyt, V. Y., Cadinu M., & Mahaux, N. (2005). Tell me who you are and I will tell you what I think: Stereotyping processes in a justification context. *Italian Journal of Psychology, 1,* 91–110.

Carnaghi, A., & Yzerbyt, V. Y. (in press). Subtyping and social consensus: the role of the audience in the maintenance of stereotypical beliefs. *European Journal of Social Psychology.*

Cialdini, R. B., Levy, A., Herman, C. P., & Evenbeck, S. (1973). Attitudinal politics: The strategy of moderation. *Journal of Personality and Social Psychology, 25,* 100–108.

Cialdini, R. B., Levy, A., Herman, C. P., & Evenbeck, S. (1973). Attitudinal politics: The strategy of moderation. *Journal of Personality and Social Psychology, 25,* 100–108.

Cialdini, R. B. (1988). *Influence: Science and practice* (2nd edition). Glenview, IL: Scott, Foresman and Co.

Clark, R. D., & Maass, A. (1988). The role of social categorization and perceived source credibility in minority influence. *European Journal of Social Psychology, 18,* 381–394.

Costarelli, S. (2000). Odi et Amo: ambivalenza attitudinale nei contesti inter-gruppo. *Unpublished doctoral dissertation,* University of Bologna, Italy.

Coull, A., Yzerbyt, V. Y., Castano, E., Paladino, M. P., & Leemans, V. (2001). Protecting the in-group: Motivated allocation of cognitive resources in the presence of threatening in-group members. *Group Processes and Intergroup Relations, 4,* 327–339.

David, B., & Turner, J. C. (1996). Studies in self-categorization and minority conversion: Is being a member of the outgroup an advantage. *British Journal of Social Psychology, 35,* 179–201.

Deutsch, M., & Gerard, H. B. (1955). A study of normative and informational social influences upon individual judgment. *Journal of Abnormal and Social Psychology, 51,* 629–636.

Dovidio, J. F., Glick, P., & Rudman, L. (2005). *On the nature of prejudice: Fifty years after Allport.* Oxford, UK: Blackwell.

Dumont, M., Yzerbyt, V. Y., Wigboldus, D., & Gordijn, E. (2003). Social categorization and fear reactions to the September 11 th terrorist attacks. *Personality and Social Psychology Bulletin, 29,* 1509–1520.

Ellemers, N. (1993). The influence of socio-structural variables on identity management strategies. *European Review of Social Psychology, 4,* 27–57.

Fiske, S. T. (1980). Attention and weight in person perception: The impact of negative and extreme behaviour. *Journal of Personality and Social Psychology, 38,* 889–906.

Fiske, S. T. (1998). Stereotyping, prejudice, and discrimination. In D. T. Gilbert, S. T. Fiske, & G. Lindzey (Eds.), *The Handbook of Social Psychology* (4th ed., Vol. 2, pp. 357–411). New York: McGraw-Hill.

Fiske, S. T. (2000). Stereotyping, prejudice, and discrimination at the seam between the centuries: evolution, culture, mind, and brain. *European Journal of Social Psychology, 30,* 299–322.

Gordijn, E., Wigboldus, D., & Yzerbyt, V. Y. (2001). Emotional consequences of categorizing victims of negative outgroup behavior as ingroup or outgroup. *Group Processes and Intergroup Relations, 4,* 317–326.

Haslam, S. A., Oakes, P. J., Reynolds, K. J., & Turner, J. C. (1999). Social identity salience and the emergence of stereotype consensus. *Personality & Social Psychology Bulletin, 25,* 809–818.

Hewstone, M., Hassebrauck, M., Wirth, A., & Waenke, M. (2000). Pattern of disconfirming information and processing instructions as determinants of stereotype change. *British Journal of Social Psychology, 39,* 399–411.

Higgins, E. T., McCann, C. D., & Fondacaro, R. (1982). The "communication game": Goal-directed encoding and cognitive consequences. *Social Cognition, 1,* 21–37.

Higgins, E. T., & McCann, C. D. (1984). Social encoding and subsequent attitudes, impressions, and memory: "Context-driven" and motivational aspects of processing. *Journal of Personality and Social Psychology, 47,* 26–39.

Higgins, E. T., Rholes, W. S., & Jones, C. R. (1977). Category accessibility and impression formation. *Journal of Experimental Social Psychology, 13,* 141–154.

Hogg, M. A., & Turner, J.C. (1987). Intergroup behaviour, self-stereotyping and the salience of social categories. *British Journal of Social-Psychology, 26,* 325–340.

Johnston, L., & Hewstone, M. (1992). Cognitive models of stereotype change: (3) Subtyping and the perceived typicality of disconfirming group members. *Journal of Experimental Social Psychology, 28,* 360–386.

Judd, C. M., & Park, B. (1993). Definition and assessment of accuracy in social stereotypes. *Psychological Review, 100,* 109–28.

Kashima, Y. (2000). Maintaining cultural stereotypes in the serial reproduction of narratives. *Personality and Social Psychology Bulletin, 26,* 594–604.

Kunda, Z., & Oleson, K. C. (1995). Maintaining stereotypes in the face of disconfirmation: Constructing grounds for subtyping deviants. *Journal of Personality and Social Psychology, 68,* 565–79.

Kunda, Z., & Oleson, K. C. (1997). When exceptions prove the rule: How extremity of deviance determines the impact of deviant examples on stereotypes. *Journal of Personality and Social Psychology, 72,* 965–79.

Lerner, J. L., & Tetlock, P. E. (1999). Accounting for the effects of accountability. *Psychological Bulletin, 125,* 255–275.

Leyens, J.-P., Yzerbyt, V. Y., & Schadron, G. (1994). *Stereotypes and Social Cognition.* London: Sage.

Lyons, A., & Kashima, Y. (2003). How are stereotypes maintained through communication? The influence of stereotype sharedness. *Journal of Personality and Social Psychology, 85,* 989–1005.

Mackie, D. M. (1986). Social identification effects in group polarization. *Journal of Personality and Social Psychology, 50,* 720–728.

Mackie, D. M., Devos, T., & Smith, E. R. (2000). Intergroup emotions: Explaining offensive action tendencies in an intergroup context. *Journal of Personality and Social Psychology, 79,* 602–616.

Marques, J. M., Yzerbyt, V. Y., & Leyens, J. P. (1988). The "Black Sheep effect": Extremity of judgment towards ingroup members as a function of group identification. *European Journal of Social Psychology, 1,* 1–16.

Maurer, K. L., Park, B., & Rothbart, M. (1995). Subtyping versus subgrouping processes in stereotype representation. *Journal of Personality and Social Psychology, 69,* 812–824.

Moreno, K. N., & Bodenhausen, G. V. (1999). Resisting stereotype change: The role of motivation and attentional capacity in defending social belief. *Group Processes and Intergroup relations, 2,* 5–16.

Moscovici, S. (1976). *Social Influence and Social Change.* New York: Academic Press.

Park, B., & Judd, C. M. (1990). Measures and model of perceived group variability. *Journal of Personality and Social Psychology, 59,* 173–191.

Park, B., Wolsko, C., & Judd, C. M. (2001). Measurement of subtyping in stereotype change. *Journal of Experimental Social Psychology, 37,* 325–332.

Pennington, J., & Schlenker, B. R. (1999). Accountability for consequential decisions: Justifying ethical judgments to audiences. *Personality and Social Psychology Bulletin, 25,* 1067–1081.

Quinn, A., & Schlenker, B. R. (2002). Can accountability produce independence? Goals as determinants of the impact of accountability on conformity. *Personality and Social Psychology Bulletin, 28,* 472–83.

Reicher, S., & Levine, M. (1994a). Deindividuation, power relations between groups and the expression of social identity: The effects of visibility to the out-group. *British Journal of Social Psychology, 33,* 145–163.

Reicher, S., & Levine, M. (1994b). On the consequences of deindividuation manipulations for the strategic considerations of the self: Identifiability and the presentation of social identity. *European Journal of Social Psychology, 24,* 511–524.

Reicher, S. D., Spears, R., & Postmes, T. (1995). A social identity model of deindividuation phenomena. *European Review of Social Psychology, 6,* 161–198.

Rothbart, M., & John, O. P. (1985). Social categorization and behavioral episodes: A cognitive analysis of the effects of intergroup contact. *Journal of Social Issues, 41,* 81–104.

Rothbart, M., & Lewis, S. (1988). Inferring category attributes from exemplar attributes. Geometric shapes and social categories. *Journal of Personality and Social Psychology, 55,* 861–872.

Ruscher, J. B., & Hammer, E. Y. (1996). Choosing to sever or maintain association induces biased impression formation. *Journal of Personality and Social Psychology, 70,* 701–712.

Ruscher, J. B., Fiske, S. T., & Schnake, S. B. (2000). The motivated tactician's juggling act: Compatible vs. incompatible impression goals. *British Journal of Social Psychology, 39,* 241–256.

Ruscher, J. B., Hammer, E. Y., & Hammer, E. D. (1996). Forming shared impressions through conversation: An adaptation of the continuum model. *Personality and Social Psychology Bulletin, 22,* 705–720.

Schneider, D. J. (2004). *The psychology of stereotyping.* New York: The Guilford Press.

Sechrist, G. B., & Stangor, C. (2001). Perceived consensus influences intergroup behavior and stereotype accessibility. *Journal of Personality and Social Psychology, 80,* 645–654.

Sherif, M. (1966). *In common predicament: Social psychology of intergroup conflict and cooperation.* Boston: Houghton-Mifflin.

Sherman, J. W., Stroessner, S. J., Conrey, F. R., & Azam, O. A. (2005). Prejudice and stereotype maintenance processes: Attention, attribution, and individuation. *Journal of Personality and Social Psychology, 89,* 607–622.

Smeesters, D., Warlop, L., Van Avermaet, E., Corneille, O., & Yzerbyt, V. Y. (2003). Do not prime hawks with doves: The interplay of construct activation and consistency of social value orientation on cooperative behavior. *Journal of Personality and Social Psychology, 84,* 972–987.

Smeesters, D., Yzerbyt, V., Corneille, O., Warlop, L., & Van Avermaet, E. (2006). *On prisoners and dictators: The role of other-self focus, social value orientation, and stereotype primes in shaping cooperative behavior.* Manuscript submitted for publication.

Spears, R., & Lea, M. (1994). Panacea or panopticon: The hidden power in computer-mediated communication. *Communication Research, 21,* 427–459.

Stangor, C., Sechrist, G. B., & Jost, J. T. (2001). Changing racial beliefs by providing consensus information. *Personality and Social Psychology Bulletin, 27,* 486–496.

Stephan, W. G., & Stephan, C. W. (1985). Intergroup anxiety. *Journal of Social Issues, 41,* 157–175.

Tajfel, H., & Turner, J. C. (1979). An integrative theory of intergroup relations, in W. G. Austin & S. Worchel (Eds), *The psychology of intergroup relations.* Monterey, CA: Brooks-Cole.

Tetlock, P. E., Armor, D., & Peterson, R. S. (1994). The slavery debate in antebellum America: Cognitive style, value conflict, and the limits of compromise. *Journal of Personality and Social Psychology, 66,* 115–126.

Tetlock, P. E., & Lerner, J. F. (1999). The social contingency model: Identifying empirical and normative boundary conditions on the error-and-bias portrait of human nature. In Y. Trope (Ed.), *Dual-process theories in social psychology* (pp. 571–585).

Tetlock, P. E., Skitka L., & Boettger, R. (1989). Social and cognitive strategies for coping with accountability: Conformity, complexity and bolstering. *Journal of Personality and Social Psychology, 57,* 632–640.

Turner, J. C. (1991). *Social influence.* Milton Keynes: Open University Press.

Weber, R., & Crocker, J. (1983). Cognitive processes in the revision of stereotypic beliefs. *Journal of Personality and Social Psychology, 45,* 961–977.

Wilder, D. A. (1986). Intergroup contact: The typical member and the exception to the rule. *Journal of Experimental Social Psychology, 20,* 177–194.

Wittenbrink, B., & Henly, J. R. (1996). Creating social reality: Informational social influence and the content of stereotypic beliefs. *Personality and Social Psychology Bulletin, 22,* 598–610.

Yzerbyt, V. Y. (2006). From subtle cues to profound influences: The impact of changing identities on emotions and behaviors. In P. A. M. van Lange (Ed.), *Bridging social psychology: Benefits of transdisciplinary approaches,* (pp. 391–396). Mahwah: Erlbaum.

Yzerbyt, V. Y., & Carnaghi, A. (2005). *Social consensus and the maintenance of stereotypic beliefs: Knowing whom you'll talk to affects what you do with the information.* Manuscript submitted for publication,

Yzerbyt, V. Y., & Corneille, O. (2005). Cognitive process: Reality constraints and integrity concerns in social perception. Catholic University of Louvain at Louvain-la-Neuve, Belgium. In J. F. Dovidio, P. Glick, & L. Rudman (Eds.), *On the nature of prejudice: 50 years after Allport.* London, UK: Blackwell.

Yzerbyt, V. Y., Coull, A., & Rocher, S. J. (1999). Fencing off the deviant: the role of cognitive resources in the maintenance of stereotypes. *Journal of Personality and Social Psychology, 77,* 449–62.

Yzerbyt, V. Y., Dumont, M., Mathieu, B., Gordijn, E., & Wigboldus, D. (2006). Social comparison and group-based emotions. In S. Guimond (Ed.), *Social comparison processes and levels of analysis: Understanding cognition, intergroup relations, and culture* (pp. 174–205). Cambridge, UK: Cambridge University Press.

Yzerbyt, V. Y., Dumont, M., Wigboldus, D., & Gordijn, E. (2003). I feel for us: The impact of categorization and identification on emotions and action tendencies. *British Journal of Social Psychology, 42,* 533–549.

Zajonc, R. B. (1960). The process of cognitive tuning in communication. *Journal of Abnormal and Social Psychology, 61,* 159–167.

Chapter 4

Cultural Dynamics of Stereotypes: Social Network Processes and the Perpetuation of Stereotypes

Anthony Lyons
University of Newcastle upon Tyne, United Kingdom

Anna Clark
Free University Amsterdam, The Netherlands

Yoshihisa Kashima
The University of Melbourne, Australia

Tim Kurz
University of Newcastle upon Tyne, United Kingdom

Culturally shared beliefs, values, and practices are *sine qua non* of social life; it is a truism to say that society cannot exist without culture. Yet, shared beliefs and ideas can be at the heart of many social issues and problems as well. Whether it be inequality, prejudice, intergroup conflict, terrorism, or other social issues or problem, such phenomena would hardly be a problem or even exist at all if not for the beliefs and ideas that spread and perpetuate within particular groups or communities. Stereotypes are a classic example. Stereotypes are typically shared within a society (e.g., Katz & Braly, 1933), and tend to perpetuate over time (e.g., Schaller, Conway, & Tanchuk, 2002) even when evidence clearly demonstrates that they are often highly inaccurate (e.g., Kunda & Oleson, 1995; Richards & Hewstone, 2001). Although there may be some aspects of stereotypes that are genetically coded (e.g., Hirschfeld, 1996), their specific contents are likely to be socially learned. Stereotypes spread through communities from one individual to another as community members learn the stereotypes of a group, either through conversations or other forms of communication, such as the mass media (van Dijk, 1987), or a general diffusion of information. In other words, stereotypes are prevalent in a large group of people, relatively stable over time, and often transmitted from person to person by social learning. These properties make stereotypes a cultural phenomenon (e.g., Lyons & Kashima, 2001).

The idea that information diffusion is central to cultural dynamics is not new. In the early 20th century, anthropologists such as Graebner, Schmidt, Smith, and Perry postulated that much of existing human cultures resulted from diffusion of cultural knowledge and practices. More recently, researchers such as Dawkins (1976/1989; also see Aunger, 2002; Blackmore, 1999), Cavalli-Sforza and Feldman (1981), Boyd and Richerson (1985), and Sperber (1996) put forward different forms of diffusionist theories of culture. In social psychology too, researchers such as Kashima (2000), Schaller, Conway, and Tanchuk (2002), and Heath, Bell and Sternberg (2001) began to explore what type of information is likely to diffuse through social networks. In this chapter, we draw on our program of research to shed greater light on the factors likely to increase or decrease the chances of particular information diffusing through social networks, especially information that is consistent or inconsistent with cultural stereotypes. Depending on the content of the information that is most frequently and widely circulated about a social group, a certain *information environment* may be constituted by the diffused information (e.g., Fiedler, 2000; Kashima, Woolcock, & Kashima, 2000). If stereotype-consistent (SC) information is more prevalent in the information environment than stereotype-inconsistent (SI) information, the stereotype is likely to be maintained. But why would SC information be preferentially transmitted over SI information?

It is our contention that specific features of social networks play an important role in determining the extent to which stereotype-relevant information diffuses through the network. Specifically, we suggest there are two major contributors. The first involves the *relational* processes that occur as people try to form new network ties and maintain or enhance existing ones. In other words, people are likely to be selective in what they communicate and how they communicate depending on whether they are trying, for example, to establish a tie with a stranger or operating within an existing tie. The second is the network *structure*, of which there are two main elements. One is *network composition*, that is, the type of people that make up a network in terms of their backgrounds, knowledge, and so on. The other is *network configuration*, that is, the pattern of network ties that connect people. For instance, a network can be centralized, where only one or a few people have direct ties with most others in the network, or decentralized, where most or all people have direct ties with each other (Wasserman & Galaskiewicz, 1994). Arguably, relational processes and structural features of social networks play a significant role in driving the cultural dynamics of stereotypes, namely, the formation, maintenance, and potential transformation of culturally shared stereotypes.

STEREOTYPES, COMMUNICATION, AND SOCIAL NETWORKS

Let us develop our argument more fully. As we outlined previously, our contention is that, in order to understand stereotypes as culturally shared beliefs and to understand the cultural dynamics of stereotypes, it is critically important to consider the processes of communication and social networks. This is because communication is one mechanism likely to account for the high level of *stereotype sharedness*, a feature that makes stereotypes a cultural phenomenon. Although individuals' similar experiences with those who belong to stereotyped groups may account for the sharedness of stereotypes in some cases, through having formed similar conclusions about the group's characteristics, this direct contact hypothesis is limited in its power to explain the level of stereotype sharedness we observe today. People often have stereotypes of groups with which they have little or no contact. And even though the pictures that people portray of social groups tend to be rather homogeneous in nature (e.g., Ostrom & Sedikides, 1992), any group is bound to have a large variation in its members' characteristics (Allport, 1954; Leyens, Yzerbyt, & Schadron, 1994). So despite occasions in which individuals do form group impressions through direct contact with members of stereotyped groups (e.g., see Dovidio, Gaertner, & Kawakami, 2003), it is highly unlikely that this process alone can explain the level of sharedness that many stereotypes attain, which can sometimes span entire nations of people or even international communities.

This leaves one prominent possibility: *communication*. Both interpersonal communication and the mass media are powerful communication channels for transmitting stereotypes. The media's capacity to reach many people in a single transmission makes it a potentially powerful form for spreading and perpetuating stereotypes; however, media effects are not always strong and are often moderated by a number of variables (e.g., Perse, 2001). One of the factors that can strengthen a mass medium's effect on individuals' beliefs, attitudes, and behavior is the *interpersonal communication* from the people around them, such as friends and family (Katz & Lazarsfeld, 1955; Lazarsfeld, Berelson, & Gaudet, 1948). In other words, stereotypes may be effectively transmitted and *adopted*, when they are communicated from those whom people typically interact with (for similar arguments, see Haslam, Turner, Oakes, McGarty, & Reynolds, 1998; Klein, Tindale, & Brauer, this volume). We believe that interpersonal communication is a powerful medium for communicating stereotypes in such a way that they are likely to be perpetually reproduced in the society. Indeed, communicating about particular groups, or the individuals from such groups, takes up a considerable proportion of conversation time between almost any set of individuals (e.g., Dunbar, Marriott, & Duncan, 1997; Keller-man & Palomares, 2004).

Thus, one of the key factors leading to the cultural sharing of stereotypes is the diffusion of information through social networks. A social network con-sists of relationships among individuals who have some ongoing interaction with each other (Scott, 2000). This can range from an acquaintance, with whom one interacts only infrequently, or a close friend or family member, with whom interaction is frequent. Individuals who interact, whether frequently or infrequently, are said to have a *direct tie* between each other. A direct tie may be strong or weak. Granovetter (1973, p. 1361; also see 1982) defined strength of a tie as "a . . . combination of the amount of time, the emotional intensity, the intimacy (mutual confiding), and the reciprocal services which character-ize the tie." *Strong ties* are typically held between close friends, involve strong reciprocal commitments, and imply frequent interactions. *Weak ties* exist be-tween casual acquaintances who, whilst perhaps not knowing each other well, are on speaking terms with each other. Such ties would typically involve small talk, brief chats, and casual conversation rather than the more intimate forms of interaction that is more common where strong ties are involved. In either case, information may be transmitted along a direct tie. However, the people who make up a social network (e.g., colleagues in a work setting) can also have *indirect ties*, in which one person might never directly interact with another per-son, but they may each have a direct tie with a third individual. In this case, information can travel between them via the third person. Thus, networks con-sist of a combination of direct and indirect ties between individuals.

The need to form and maintain a social network is likely to be a significant so-cial motive (e.g., Fiske, 2004). Although some have argued that any one indi-vidual may only be able to maintain a social network of up to approximately 150 people (Dunbar, 1996), generally developing and increasing a network brings many benefits, one of which is an increase in access to resources or so-cial capital (see Lin, 2001). Social capital can comprise any kind of aid, from advice and emotional support to borrowing objects or lending a hand with a job or task. In this way, the social capital that an individual has access to through the development and maintenance of a social network help him or her in achieving personal goals. In addition, through the ties that connect people, in-formation can flow through a social network to a potentially enormous popula-tion. Although researchers often designate particular boundaries for a social network, such as the network within a particular workplace (Krackhardt & Brass, 1994) or a neighborhood (e.g., Weenig & Midden, 1991), such networks rarely exist in isolation. They are likely to be interconnected with each other as we will discuss later in this chapter. In this way, a stereotype or stereotype-relevant information can potentially be transmitted from one person to another until no more ties exist for further propagation, at which point all individuals within en-tire national groups or even international groups may have been exposed to it.

However, it is unlikely that all stereotypes or stereotype-relevant information will diffuse through networks so extensively. Indeed, a lot of information may not even survive communication between just a few ties. Bartlett (1932) demonstrated this very convincingly with his classic experiment of serial reproduction. In many of his experiments, Cambridge undergraduates read an Amerindian story, *War of the Ghosts,* and retold it from one person to another, through several ties along a chain. Clearly, this is a form of social network, albeit simple, which consists of a chain of network ties. Much of the original information was lost in the first communication, with only a relatively small proportion retained after several transmissions. Allport and Postman (1947) also demonstrated a similar effect when they examined the communication of rumors (for equally similar findings, also see Gauld & Stephenson, 1967; Gilovich, 1987; Hafeez-Zaidi, 1958; Haque & Sabir, 1975). Given this, one might question why one piece of information spread throughout social networks and not another?

Therefore, in order to answer the question of why stereotypes spread and perpetuate—a central question in the cultural dynamics of stereotypes—it is critical to examine *how* and *why* particular information is more likely to be communicated through the various small and large social networks connecting the individuals in a community. In the next section, we argue that one of the most critical factors is that of relational processes, the process of forming, maintaining, and transforming interpersonal relationships or network ties.

RELATIONAL PROCESSES AND DIFFUSION
OF STEREOTYPE-RELEVANT INFORMATION

A central part of establishing social networks is interpersonal communication. Through the telling of stories and jokes, the recounting of one's daily experiences, and the gossiping about others, people share information, beliefs and opinions, and perhaps even develop a shared view of the world. At the same time, communication fulfils important functions to regulate social relationships between individuals. In this sense, interpersonal communication and relational processes are mutually constitutive. In this section, we argue that processes of social networking, and therefore the formation and maintenance of relationships, has a strong influence on the extent to which SC or SI information are communicated through social networks.

Communication, Grounding and Regulation
of Social Relationships

Communication is a collaborative process (e.g., Clark, 1996a; Clark & Brennan, 1991; for a review, see Kashima, Klein, & Clark, 1996b). According to Clark's grounding model, communicators engage in communication on the basis of *common ground*. This represents the knowledge that the communicators assume to be mutually shared on the basis of their past experience of interaction with each other (*personal common ground*; e.g., when you are talking with your friend), or their mutual group membership (*communal common ground*: e.g., living in the same city, speaking the same language). Communicators jointly strive to establish a mutual understanding of new information, through a collaborative process that Clark called *grounding*. The grounding process consists of at least two phases: (a) one communicator's presentation and (b) another's acceptance. When one presents information (e.g., "Gary had a trouble with the police again"), another may accept it easily (e.g., "Oh, again!"), or with further queries or elaboration (e.g., "What? Does he have a criminal record? He sure doesn't look like it . . .").

As a number of research traditions in social psychology have pointed out (Bartlett, 1932; Freyd, 1983; McIntyre et al., 2004; Moscovici, 1984; Semin, 2000; Vygotsky, 1978), novel information is understood via successful integration or assimilation into existing, meaningful structures. Communication is no exception. Whether a presentation is easily accepted, and therefore grounded, depends in part on how consistent the presented information is relative to the preexisting shared knowledge or common ground between the communicators. As Grice's (1975) maxim of quantity suggests, communicators are encouraged to provide new information that is unknown to their communication partners. Yet, Grice's other maxims suggest communication should be relevant and should not be obscure. If information is *too* new, it runs the risk of being obscure and irrelevant (Kashima, Klein, & Clark, in press, called this informativeness-groundability dilemma). This speaks to the inherent tension between what is known and unknown that provides the impetus and creative tension for communication. Communication should entail a new and unique rendition of a topic, but is constrained by the necessity that it needs to be understood via existing knowledge.

The tension between the known and unknown, however, is not purely a matter of information transmission; rather, it may have significant implications for the interpersonal relationship between the communicators. On the one hand, if the communicators are motivated to create interpersonally affirming experiences of understanding and agreeing with each other, they may jeopardize these experiences by communicating new and unknown information, which may be obscure and hard to understand. On the other hand, by communicating relatively known, but easily understood information, they may be able to have an experience of smooth and pleasant interpersonal interaction. It was Goffman (1959) who argued that communication partners work cooperatively to maintain each other's "face," namely, a person's needs and wants in interaction. Because interpersonal communication is collaborative, its successful execution may strengthen the interpersonal tie by attending to the communicators' faces, but disruption to the process may weaken it.

This line of reasoning suggests that communication is not only about grounding information efficiently and successfully, but also about forming and maintaining social relationships or social network ties (for a review of related ideas, see Kashima, Klein, & Clark, in press). In ensuring that the conversation goes smoothly and easily, communicators are also attending to their relationships. Communicators who experience a pleasant and smoothly flowing conversation create a greater sense of closeness; failing to do so would have a negative effect on building and maintaining intimacy. In other words, the process of grounding involves people coming to agree on mutual knowledge, which may provide a sense of sharing, togetherness, and common understanding. In this sense, it is likely that the grounding of information in communication and the regulation of interpersonal relationships are often closely linked.

A case in point is gossip, whose communicative content is thought to have important social regulatory functions (Dunbar, 1996; Baumeister, Zhang, & Vohs, 2004). In gossiping, people are not only spending time together and thus bolstering social connection, they are also conveying information about each other, about other members of their society, and about social norms. Baumeister and colleagues have argued that, as such, gossip is akin to social and cultural learning and thus plays an important role in the regulation of relationships. Indeed, it was noted that the content that is often contained within the form of gossip is frequently unquestioned by communicators. That is, gossip is often grounded immediately, with fewer challenges by an audience than other types of communication (Eder & Enke, 1991), perhaps therefore pointing to a predominant function of promoting feelings of social connectedness between people.

Therefore, common ground, information perceived to be shared among communicators, is important not only for gauging what information is likely to be already known versus new, but also to carry a message of interpersonal relationships. Brown and Levinson (1987) argued that claiming common ground in communication is a major strategy of positive politeness, which is a series of conversational moves that recognise the partner's needs and wants in a way that shows they represent a commonality, such as a commonality of knowledge, attitudes, interests, goals, and in-group membership. Brown and Levinson outline three major methods of claiming common ground: (a) to show a sharedness of interests, wants and goals in order to convey that their communication partner "*is admirable and interesting*" (p. 107), (b) to stress common membership or "in-group" identity, thus sharing needs and wants on this basis, and (c) to claim a common perspective in terms of knowledge, attitudes, and opinions. In many ways, these linguistic strategies are similar to intimate language usage, in that intimacy and friendship are conveyed through sharedness and similarity between the communicators: "Positive-politeness utterances are used as a kind of metaphorical extension of intimacy, to imply common ground or sharing of wants to a limited extent even between strangers who perceive themselves, for the purposes of the interaction, as somehow similar" (Brown & Levinson, 1987, p. 108).

Regulation of Social Relationships and Diffusion of Stereotype-Relevant Information

The upshot of the foregoing argument is that certain types of information might be more likely to be communicated partly because these types are more likely to result in the communicators' feelings of agreement and closeness; information that is linked to common ground, or shared knowledge, is more likely to promote positive interpersonal relationships. Communication of stereotype-relevant information is no exception. Communicators are likely to assume that a cultural stereotype is already known to both communicators and therefore constitutes part of their common ground. SC information is likely to be already shared and likely to promote interpersonal closeness; however, SI information is likely to be new and unknown, and interpersonally risky. In line with this, Ruscher and Duval (1998) showed that communicators indeed regarded stereotypical information as more likely to elicit agreement in conversation. In a similar vein, Clark (2005) asked communicators to rate SC and SI information in terms of how easily shared it would be with a fellow university student in conversation and how easily understood it would be by a fellow university student. Communicators generally perceived that SC information was more shareable, and also predicted that it would be more easily understood by another university student.

People are indeed correct about their perceptions that SC information is more easily shared than SI information. Kashima, Lyons, McIntyre, and Clark (submitted) had participants in five-person communication chains engage in conversation about a stereotype target. In the first conversation of the chain, one communicator had read an original story about the target and was asked to communicate it to the other communicator. The second conversation then occurred between the second communicator in the first conversation and a third, naïve communicator, and so on. The resulting conversations were coded for how SC and SI information was grounded. The presentation of SC information in conversation did not receive a great deal of response from the listener; the speaker was able to continue under the assumption of mutual understanding. In contrast, the listener was more likely to react directly and immediately to the speaker's presentation of SI information, suggesting that in this situation, some collaboration was required to effectively ground the information.

This line of reasoning suggests that communicators would be more likely to mention SC information than SI information, especially if they are motivated to establish a sense of agreement and social connectedness between one another. In support of this, Ruscher, Hammer, and Hammer (1996) demonstrated that when dyads work under an explicit consensus-seeking motivation, they spend more time discussing SC than SI information, and express more spontaneous agreement when discussing the SC information. More to the point, Ruscher, Cralley, and O'Farrell (2005) argued that feelings of closeness between newly acquainted dyads likely increases motivation to get along, a communication goal which, in turn, should increase attention to shared information that will easily facilitate consensual impressions, and in turn, increase a sense of closeness. University students who did not know each other were manipulated to have either high or low feelings of interpersonal closeness. The participants then heard a description of a stereotyped target that included SC and SI information. Analyses of the dyads' subsequent conversation about this target showed that closer dyads spent more time discussing SC information, agreed more when discussing SC information and formed more stereotypic impressions than did less close dyads. The authors noted the profound implications this has for the many social situations where newly formed groups are asked to make decisions (such as a jury, expert panels). We echo this concern and in particular for the case where biased communication between dyads impacts on the extent to which SC and SI information are then diffused through the networks in which they belong.

Similarly, using Bartlett's (1932) serial reproduction paradigms, in which stimulus information is transmitted from one person to another, Kashima and Lyons (Kashima, 2000; Lyons & Kashima, 2001, 2003) showed that SC information is more likely than SI information to remain in the transmitted story (SC bias). Clark (2005; see Clark & Kashima, under review) examined whether the SC bias in serial reproductions can be explained in terms of the *social connectivity* of information, namely, the extent to which communicators perceived the inclusion of the particular information in a shared message would be socially engaging, give an impression of them being friendly and likeable, and generally contribute to building a positive relationship between the communicators. In particular, Clark asked her participants to read a story about a stereotyped target containing SC and SI information and then communicate the story to a fellow university student. After the communication, she had her participants rate the SC and SI information in terms of social connectivity, which was measured in terms of the extent to which communicating the information would "help to establish a connection or social bond with a communication partner," and would "appear friendly" to a communication partner. Results showed that information perceived as more socially connective was also perceived as more communicable and was actually communicated more in the message to fellow students. Social connectivity was predicted by the stereotype consistency of the stereotype information, such that more consistent information was perceived to be more socially connective. Path analysis revealed that social connectivity ratings fully mediated the relationship between stereotype consistency and actual communication.

Strength of Network Ties and Diffusion
of Stereotype-Relevant Information

If indeed the social connectivity of information plays a significant role in interpersonal communication, and if information more consistent with shared knowledge or common ground is more socially connective, then, the interpersonal relationship, or social network tie, between the communicators is likely to influence the diffusion dynamics of SC and SI information. In this regard, it is useful to consider the strength of a tie (Granovetter, 1973) between the communicators. Although information may traverse both strong and weak ties, different types of information are more or less likely to diffuse depending on the strength of a tie. In the context of organizational communication, Hansen (1999) argued that simple information highly codified within a society may easily travel through weak ties, whereas complex information that requires prolonged training or repeated interactions may need strong ties to diffuse. In terms of stereotype-relevant information, SC information is highly codified, which requires little effort to transmit. Stereotype-inconsistent information is more complex and typically requires greater effort to communicate effectively.

So although much of the research presented so far points to the notion that closer dyads, with relatively strong ties, are more likely to communicate SC rather than SI information, it is worth noting the potential for an interesting paradox in which considerably strong ties, or particularly high levels of closeness (e.g., close friends), might lead to more SI information being communicated compared to weaker ties. Indeed, this suggestion has some empirical support from a study by Ruscher, Santuzzi, and Hammer (2003), who examined how dyads with different degrees of closeness communicate stereotype-relevant information. Close dyads (e.g., close friends) are likely to enjoy a luxury of breadth and depth of common ground and familiarity with communicative strategies that allow greater freedom in what can be expressed, and what can be disagreed upon without risk to the relationship. For this reason, close friends should be good at forming shared impressions as well as being able to share and tolerate idiosyncratic opinions. Ruscher et al. referred to this as "complex impressions," which are characterized by a range of information integrated into a coherent unit. They examined communication of SC and stereotype irrelevant items under an explicit consensus-seeking goal. Findings showed that relationship closeness was associated with a greater ease of forming shared impressions, greater ease in expressing different opinions and disagreement, and greater achieved impression complexity. Thus it seems that close dyads can integrate a more diverse range of information and rely less on the shared stereotype.

However, this study only examined SC and stereotype-irrelevant information, so it remains to be tested whether the same findings would hold for explicitly stereotype-inconsistent information. Nonetheless, there is some suggestive evidence that SI information may be more likely to circulate through strong ties. McIntyre et al. (2004) reported that a serial reproduction chain, which consisted of friends, transmitted SI information more than would usually be expected from serial reproduction chains made of strangers or casual acquaintances.

So far, we have considered social network ties involving positive interpersonal relationships. In contrast to situations involving close dyads who are committed to ongoing relationships, there may be situations where communicators may be motivated to increase the distance between them (e.g., where two people do not like each other) and therefore deliberately avoid using information that is easy to ground or which contributes to a feeling of connectedness and friendliness. Whether such a situation could promote the use of SI information over SC information could also be an important area for future investigation.

Some Concluding Comments on Relational Features of Social Networks

A central motive for any communicator is to establish and maintain a social network around him or her. Thus, communicators are likely to favor information that will most likely help them achieve this goal. In general it seems that since SC information is more likely to achieve this goal and is perceived as such, messages contain more SC information than SI information.

It is possible that SI information has a social "cost," to the extent that it does not particularly facilitate feelings of closeness due to incongruence with common ground, and the communication of it may therefore be a risky strategy in terms of the conversational management of social relationships. Despite this, it might also be possible that the communication of SI information is better communicated between particularly strong ties or very close dyads, where greater freedom may exist for expressing new and complex information without impacting negatively on the relationship.

It is important to emphasize both informational and relational aspects of interpersonal communication in the cultural dynamics of stereotypes. Although there are a number of contemporary cultural diffusionist theories (e.g., Boyd & Richerson, 1985; Cavalli-Sforza & Feldman, 1981; Dawkins, 1976; Sperber, 1996), most of them regard cultural transmission of information from the perspective of information transfer. Perhaps with the exception of Sperber and Wilson (1986), all the theories take the view that cultural transmission is akin to epidemiological reproductions of information. Although Sperber and Wilson view the collaborative nature of communication processes seriously, they do not fully recognize the relational aspect of social communication. It is our contention that the relational processes inherent in interpersonal communication are central to the process of cultural dynamics in general, and the cultural dynamics of stereotypes in particular, with various consequences for the diffusion of stereotype-relevant information through social networks.

STRUCTURAL FEATURES OF NETWORKS AND
DIFFUSION OF STEREOTYPE-RELEVANT INFORMATION

Although particular types of information are likely to be emphasized and communicated when people are engaged in establishing and maintaining network ties, it is also likely that the structural features of the network itself will influence the diffusion of information. A host of studies have demonstrated that this is indeed the case. For example, the extent to which particular types of information spread through a network is often influenced by network *configuration*, such as the strength of network ties, the density of the network, and so on (e.g., Djelic, 2004). But apart from network configuration, it is also the case that the *composition* of a network can influence the extent of diffusion. That is, various characteristics of the individuals who belong to a network can affect the likelihood of particular information diffusing through the network (e.g., Weenig & Midden, 1991; Nieuwbeerta & Flap, 2000; Visser & Mirabile, 2004). This section examines the structural features of networks and how they may affect the diffusion of stereotype-relevant information. We will first examine network composition before turning to a discussion of network configuration.

Network Composition

Social networks often consist of people with *similar* characteristics, which is commonly referred to as *homophily* in networks. There is a tendency for people to form network ties with others who are similar, and the resultant homogeneity of people connected by social networks is a major feature of many networks (McPherson, Smith-Lovin, & Cook, 2001). Indeed, a large body of literature has revealed that people who share similar characteristics are more likely to have ties to people who are similar rather than dissimilar (e.g., Blau, Blum, & Schwartz, 1982; Coleman, 1958; Marsden, 1988). The type of dimensions on which people judge themselves to be similar or dissimilar are wide-ranging, including race (e.g., Marsden, 1987), gender (Eder & Hallinan, 1978), age (e.g., Verbrugge, 1977), education (e.g., Marsden, 1987), attitudes, and values, and many other dimensions. Whilst some social networks allow members little or no choice in deciding whom to form ties with, such as family and the workplace, even within these contexts the extent to which people develop stronger or weaker ties with others is considerably influenced by tendencies toward homophily (McPherson, et al., 2001).

One further feature of social networks is the presence of an *interdependence* between the members. In other words, the information that one person communicates to another undoubtedly constrains or influences what that person then communicates to a third person, thus shaping the content of what is ultimately diffused through the network. Indeed, Bartlett's (1932) early experiments using the method of serial reproduction demonstrated this very clearly. Once information was omitted or transformed in some way by one person in a communication chain, it rarely reverted back to the original content further along the chain. Apart from the first person in a chain, people were not exposed to the original set of information and therefore depended entirely on the content of the information reproduced by the person before them and how they reproduced it. This is often the case in real-world settings, where information in the form of rumors, news stories, or gossip is circulated through a network in which many members have no access to the original event or source from which the information originated.

As a result of this, a failure to reproduce a particular set or type of information by a small subset of network members can potentially result in most or all other members failing to receive that information. The only way for information to be diffused throughout a network is for a large majority of people in that network to communicate it to one another. This requires a high level of homophily that results in members of a network sharing a similar tendency to transmit particular types of information to one another. Given that network ties often do develop between people who share similar characteristics, the actual composition of that network (e.g., the shared background of the people and/or the beliefs, values, and ideas that they share) may determine exactly what types of information are most likely to successfully diffuse through the network.

The previous section in this chapter pointed out that SC information is sometimes more likely to be communicated than SI information because of the function it serves in establishing network ties. However, the extent to which this information successfully diffuses throughout an entire network is likely to depend on the extent to which people share characteristics that give them a *similar* tendency to focus on SC rather than SI information. Without this, that is, a high level of heterogeneity in a network, SI information could diffuse through a network just as much as SC information. As a result of widespread exposure to evidence that undermines stereotypes, the long-term maintenance of stereotypes may not occur. Weber and Crocker (1983), for instance, demonstrated that when people are exposed to a certain amount of SI information, they do, in fact, change their stereotypes. This is even the case when the SI information is highly dispersed (e.g., Hewstone, Hassebrauck, Wirth, & Waenke, 2000). That is, even if exposure to a small amount of SI information occurs among a number of members of a stereotyped group, stereotype change can and often does occur. So, for stereotypes to be maintained, a social network requires a certain degree of sharedness of various qualities of characteristics, at least to the extent that a consistent bias toward transmitting SC rather than SI information occurs among network members.

Investigating how the composition of a social network, particularly in terms of shared characteristics among network members, influences the diffusion of SC and SI information is the main focus of this section. However, before exploring empirical and other work, it is first necessary to distinguish between two types of network homophily. According to Lazarsfeld and Merton (1954; see also McPherson et al., 2001), there are at least two main types of homophily: (a) *status homophily* and (b) *value homophily*. Status homophily refers to the situation in which people form network ties with those who have a similar status or position in society to themselves, or a similar demographic background. Thus, characteristics such as ethnicity, age, gender, occupation, education, socio-economic status, and generally low- and high-status groups fall within this category. Value homophily, on the other hand, points to the various internal states that often play a part in attracting people to one another. This includes beliefs, values, attitudes, interests, and so on. Due to the fact that value homophily actually includes various cognitions other than values, it will be hereafter referred to as *cognitive homophily*.

These two types of homophily are not mutually exclusive. Although network ties may at times form on the basis of status homophily (e.g., developing ties with people of your home country when living in a foreign country), some degree of cognitive homophily is always likely to emerge in some form or another when ties are being maintained over time. In other words, as people continue to interact, they often begin to develop and share similar beliefs, ideas, values, and so on (e.g., Clark & Brennan, 1991; Krauss & Fussell, 1996), which can at times have the effect of further strengthening the tie and solidifying the network. This is indeed a process of social influence; that is, they not only develop a basic level of common ground (see Clark, 1996) by becoming mutually knowledgeable of each other's beliefs and values, but tend toward forming *similar* beliefs and values. This is closely related to Hardin and Higgins' (1996) notion of *shared reality*, and their general thesis that people are inherently motivated to either interact with those who share similar perceptions of the world or to influence those around them to share similar perceptions (also see Wittenbaum & Stasser, 1998). This may not only serve to enhance a feeling of connectedness with others (see previous section in this chapter), but often helps people to gain a sense of verification or confirmation that their perceptions of the world are valid and accurate (see Kashima, Klein, & Clark, in press).

In terms of understanding how network composition specifically affects the diffusion of SC and SI information, the main focus should be on the assessment of the extent to which particular forms of cognitive homophily (e.g., shared beliefs in the stereotypes) are present. Even if a network consists of people who share common demographic statuses (e.g., age, ethnicity) or social identities, the most fundamental question for researchers interested in the communication of SC and SI information is whether they share similar aims, beliefs, values, and other tendencies. How they collectively remember and interpret a set of stereotype-relevant information and their collective aims or other tendencies when communicating ultimately determines the extent to which particular information either succeeds or fails to diffuse through a network. For this reason, the following section focuses on the role of particular forms of cognitive homophily (or the lack thereof) in the extent to which SC and SI information diffuse through social networks.

Cognitive homophily and the diffusion of stereotype-relevant information. As suggested earlier, network ties can be *established* on the basis of cognitive homophily; that is, through an awareness of shared beliefs and interests, or such sharedness might develop after ties have been created for other reasons (e.g., status homophily). Whatever the route to cognitive homophily in social networks, extensive research in a variety of disciplines or fields of interest has demonstrated that many networks are relatively homogeneous when it comes to things such as shared beliefs, ideas, values, and attitudes. For instance, work on group norms has highlighted that not only do groups tend to develop shared beliefs and values, but the sharedness of these are often critical for groups to function coherently and efficiently (Kaplan & Miller, 1987), as well as promote feelings of solidarity (Wheelan, 1994). But perhaps even more important, depending on the content of the beliefs, values, and so on, that people do in fact share, the content of specific information that they choose to communicate to one another is greatly influenced (Clark, 1996; also see Stasser & Titus, 1987).

In recent times, a growing amount of research has explored how the sharedness of stereotypes plays a role in the diffusion of stereotype-relevant information through social networks (e.g., Lyons & Kashima, 2003; Clark & Kashima, under review; also see Visser & Mirabile, 2004, for a study on attitude-relevant information and the effect of attitude homogeneous and heterogeneous networks). In one such study, Lyons and Kashima (2001) used a stereotype-relevant story about an Australian Rules Football Player to demonstrate how such information becomes increasingly congruent with shared stereotypes when communicated through networks. In their study, participants formed four-person chains, and following the method of serial reproduction, they communicated the story from memory, from one person to another, along the chains. More SC than SI information was diffused through the network. In line with Bartlett's (1932) research, much of the SI information was, in fact, lost early in the chains, never to be recovered again. The end result was a story that rapidly became, and subsequently remained, stereotype consistent as it circulated through the chains. Moreover, in a similar study, Kashima (2000) even found that in cases where SI information is communicated more than SC information early in a chain, much of it still fails to ultimately diffuse through the network.

Apart from a general pattern in which more SC than SI information diffuses through social networks, Lyons and Kashima (2001) also found that *specific* items of SC information were especially likely to be communicated, with the story then transforming in one particular direction. In other words, a tendency to spread specific content was shared by most or all network members, which would have resulted in a very distinct impression of the story character being conveyed. A likely explanation for this was the presence of a highly developed level of sharedness, such that specific stereotypes were widely shared between network members and perhaps also other ideas and thoughts about the specific items of information that were worth retaining or omitting from the story. In fact, a follow-up study involving students from the same population (e.g., first-year psychology students) used in Lyons and Kashima's (2001) study revealed that students shared a general belief in the relevant stereotypes about football players (Lyons, 2002), even to the extent that *all* students were observed to believe some of the stereotypes (e.g., aggressive, loud).

Given this, it is indeed likely that a network that is composed mostly of people who share similar stereotypes plays a large role in driving the diffusion of SC rather than SI information through the network. As a demonstration of this, Lyons and Kashima (2003, Study 1; also see Klein, Jacobs, Gemoets, Licata, & Lambert, 2003) examined the extent to which the diffusion of SC information depends on network members believing similar stereotypes. In their study, stereotype-like descriptions of a novel group were used to manipulate the level of homogeneity of group beliefs within a series of networks. Similar to the studies discussed above, participants formed four-person chains. In one condition, all participants in the chains believed the same set of stereotypes about the target group (stereotype homogeneity). In a second condition, half the participants in a chain believed one set of stereotypes and the other half believed a different set (stereotype heterogeneity). When a story about a member of the target group was circulated through the chains, much of the information in the story that was consistent with the stereotypes believed in the stereotype-homogeneity condition was diffused through the chain and little inconsistent information survived. However, in the stereotype heterogeneity condition, no particular information was any more or less likely to diffuse through the chain.

Not only does this and the other previously discussed studies highlight the role of cognitive homophily, in this case, network ties have shared stereotypes, as crucial for the diffusion of SC information through a network, they also point to another interesting possibility. That is, there may be a point at which SC information fails to diffuse through a network when the composition of the network is such that a critical number or proportion of members do not believe the stereotypes. Although the study reported by Lyons and Kashima (2003) suggests that having at least half of network members not sharing a belief in a set of stereotypes is sufficient to prevent more SC than SI information diffusing through the network, a particular threshold (or critical mass) might even be lower than this on average (see Granovetter, 1973). According to Valente (1996), a threshold can usually be determined in any network, which is a point at which information is communicated sufficiently widely for its diffusion to then accelerate and spread to most or all other network members. If thresholds can be found or predicted for particular networks (perhaps based on the extent of particular forms of cognitive homophily) in which SI information is communicated to an extent that it then diffuses throughout a network, then this may inform strategies for changing stereotypes or preventing stereotype maintenance. In other words, due to the interdependence inherent in social networks, changing the stereotypic beliefs of only a particular number of individuals in a network may be sufficient for the SC bias to ultimately collapse, resulting in a greater flow of SI information. With increased exposure to evidence that disconfirms their stereotypes, network members may be less likely to maintain their stereotypes in the long run, and the process of stereotype change might begin.

It is worth noting, however, that a sharedness of stereotypic beliefs is only one of the factors in a social network that can potentially facilitate the diffusion of SC rather than SI information. For instance, the extent to which network members expect that individuals of stereotyped groups can vary in their characteristics may influence the extent to which they acknowledge and communicate SI information. In other words, even though members of a network might share a belief in the stereotypes of a group, they could nevertheless believe that there are "exceptions to the rule" such that SI information about some individuals from the group would be tolerated, believed to be true and accurate (see Lyons & Kashima, 2003), and transmitted to others in the network. Indeed, past research has shown that people are more likely to consider SI information when forming or re-evaluating their stereotypes when they believe that groups are not entirely homogeneous in their characteristics (Linville, Fisher, & Salovey, 1989). So, if a network consists of many people with such beliefs, SI information might better diffuse through the network than if this form and level of shared tendency was not present.

Providing some support for this notion, Lyons and Douglas (in preparation) examined the communication of information about a variety of target people from a particular region of the United Kingdom and found that the biased communication of SC over SI information was more likely to be displayed by participants who held a belief that groups and individuals in general are relatively fixed in their qualities and thus unchangeable. Individuals who also scored low on the personality dimension of *openness* were more likely to favour communicating SC information and omitting SI information. Meanwhile, participants who scored high on *need for cognitive closure* (e.g., the need for quick, complete answers to any questions; see Kruglanski & Webster, 1996) were also most likely to exhibit a bias toward disseminating SC information. Consequently, the extent to which a social network is composed of people with such beliefs and dispositions may also influence the extent to which SC information diffuses through the network more than SI information. Where a high level of homophily exists for any of these, SC information is likely to diffuse more successfully than SI information, although once again, the actual level of sharedness (or threshold) required before the SC advantage is lost is an important question for future research.

Despite the role played by beliefs about individual and group changeability and individual dispositions, the level of cognitive homophily with respect to shared stereotypic beliefs undoubtedly plays a large role in the diffusion of SC and SI information through a network. However, this implies that people communicate according to their own beliefs, such that if they believe particular stereotypes, then they transmit more SC than SI information. This is not always the case. Higgins and his colleagues have shown, for instance, that people often tailor their communication to suit the beliefs (or other requirements) of their audience, such as omitting positive information about a target person when the audience is known to dislike him or her (e.g., Higgins, 1981; Higgins & McCann, 1984). Related more closely to stereotypes, Ruscher (2001) has also demonstrated that the extent to which people communicate more or less SC and SI information is often influenced by their perception of the audience's beliefs and knowledge.

What the research on audience tailoring generally points to is that another form of cognitive homophily that could facilitate the diffusion of SC rather than SI information is that of shared beliefs about what other network members believe. In other words, if many members of a network believe that most others in their network believe a set of stereotypes, then they may be even more inclined to favour communicating SC information. This notion is actually captured by Clark's (1996) notion of *communal common ground* (also see Kashima, Klein, & Clark, in press), in which people within a community either know or believe that others in their community share particular beliefs, knowledge, attitudes, values, and so on. Clark (1996; Clark & Brennan, 1991) further suggests that people who share such a common ground often tailor communication in such a way that reinforces the common ground. In the case of shared stereotypes, the reasons for this are potentially varied and complex, with research so far uncovering multiple processes, such as enhancing feelings of social connectedness (Clark & Kashima, under review; also see previous section in this chapter), a need for efficient and coherent communication (Lyons & Kashima, in press), and desires to communicating truthfully (Lyons & Kashima, 2003). Regardless of the reasons, the extent to which a network is composed of people who share a belief that others in the network believe a set of stereotypes may influence the diffusion of SC and SI information.

To test this possibility, Lyons and Kashima (2003, Study 3) assembled first-year psychology students into communication chains. In half of the chains, students were led to believe that most other students in their year level did not believe a set of stereotypes about a novel group. In the other half, students were led to believe that most other students did believe the stereotypes. When a story about a member of the group was communicated along the chains, SC information was transmitted more than SI information only when students believed that their peers believed the stereotypes. When students expected that their peers did not believe the stereotypes, the advantage of SC information was lost. The study clearly demonstrated that this form of cognitive homophily, whereby members share a belief that others (who may or may not necessarily be network members) believe the stereotypes of a group, can be an important factor in the successful diffusion of SC information. If a certain number of network members believe otherwise, a tendency seems to exist for the SC bias to collapse. Thus, cognitive homophily that involves actual shared beliefs about a target group (and other shared dispositional or perceptual tendencies) may not always be sufficient for SC information to diffuse more successfully through a network than SI information. However, it would appear that when a network also consists of many people who believe that others share a belief in the stereotypes, then the chances of SC information being diffused through the network increases substantially.

In all, particular forms of cognitive homophily, such as shared stereotypic beliefs, shared beliefs about the beliefs of others, shared beliefs about the changeability of human characteristics and dispositions, amongst others, are likely to play a large role in determining the extent to which SC or SI information diffuse throughout a network. Where SC information diffuses more widely, stereotypes are likely to spread and be maintained over time. Although yet to be explored in any great depth, some reduction in the level of cognitive homophily in a network (for particular and relevant forms of shared beliefs and tendencies) could have the effect of reducing SC biases, and thus perhaps sowing the seeds for stereotype change.

Configuration of Social Networks and Distribution of Stereotypic Beliefs

Not only the composition, but also configuration of a social network can affect the spread of stereotype-relevant information; consequently, network configurations can affect people's beliefs in cultural stereotypes within the network. In order to illustrate this point, we extrapolate from the foregoing discussions to argue that the diffusion dynamics due to network configuration can explain *pluralistic ignorance* (e.g., Miller & McFarland, 1991; Prentice & Miller, 1993) about stereotypes. This is the tendency of people to believe that the general public holds stronger stereotypes than those held by themselves or their close friends (e.g., Bowen & Bourgeois, 2001); in so doing, they are ignorant about the fact that most people hold views similar to their own. To put it differently, we develop a network-process explanation of pluralistic ignorance, according to which erroneous perceptions of the general public may form in the absence of cognitive or motivational biases, but due to the availability of SC and SI information in social networks that take a certain global configuration.

More specifically, in the first section, we examine the general question about how a network of interpersonal relationships develops over time, and what sort of global structure is likely to ensue. In other words, we examine the development of social networks and consider its global consequences (e.g.,

Pattison & Robins, 2002). Concepts used in social network analysis are briefly introduced and used to analyze the global structure of large-scale social networks in society. We then turn to the more specific question: Once a certain global structure is established in social networks, does it have implications for the diffusion of stereotypes? In answering this question, we explore how particular social network configurations may influence the diffusion of stereotype-relevant information within those networks and how this can shed light on the phenomenon of pluralistic ignorance.

Local network configuration and its global consequences. People do not form their interpersonal relationships completely freely; the pattern of friendships and acquaintanceships is locally constrained, and some local configurations of network ties are more likely than others. To illustrate this point, let us consider a simple case. Suppose that a person has network ties to other people. Following the standard terminology in social network analysis, let us call a *2-star* the case in which this person has two network ties to two others, B and C, where there is no direct tie between B and C. The open triangles in Fig. 4–1 illustrate a 2-star. More generally, in the *k-star* configuration, one person has *k* ties to other people who have no ties to each other; a 2-star then bridges two people; a 3-star bridges three people, etc.

In the case of a 2-star, Heider's (1958) *balance theory* suggests that if person A befriends B and C, B and C are also likely to become friends to each other. To put it differently, the current network configuration of an open triangle

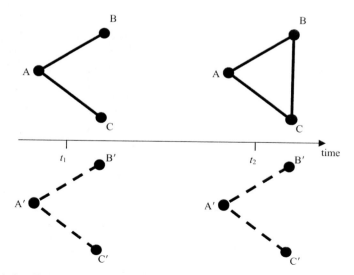

FIGURE 4–1.   Evolution of a 2-Star Social Network.
Note: Circles indicate individuals; solid lines represent strong ties, whereas broken lines are weak ties.

(t_1 above the time line in Fig. 4–1) is more likely to be transformed into a closed triangle (t_2 above the time line in Fig. 4–1). Obviously, there are a number of factors that may hinder this process; e.g., B and C may live far away, the interest shared by A and B (e.g., playing football) may be incompatible with that shared by A and C (e.g., poetry reading), B and C may belong to different social categories based on such characteristics as status and ethnicity. One such factor is the strength of ties. Granovetter (1973) argued that when A has strong ties (solid lines in Fig. 4–1) with B and C, then B and C are likely to form a tie; however, if they are weak ties (broken lines in Fig. 4–1), there may not be a strong tendency for a closure and an open triangle made up of weak ties may remain open.

These processes lead to the formation of (a) closely knit, highly clustered social networks in which everyone has a strong tie, or *bond*, with most of the others, and (b) weak ties that may potentially connect, or *bridge* (Harary, Norman, & Cartwright, 1965), such clustered networks (e.g., Friedkin, 1982), suggesting the importance of these two configurations of networks when theorizing the diffusion dynamics of stereotype-relevant information. Fig. 4–2 presents schematic pictures of the *clustered* and *bridging* networks. In clustered networks, which involve strong ties, social influence is likely to be strong, resulting in a high level of cognitive homophily. First, strong ties may exert both normative and informational social influences as people are likely to comply with their close friends and trust their opinions (e.g., Marsden & Friedkin, 1993; Meyer, 1994; also see Latané & L'Herrou, 1996, for an account of how social influence and network structure lead to clustering of attitudes in particular areas of a network). Furthermore, people who are bonded together may regard themselves as a highly cohesive entity (Campbell, 1958), or a *group*,

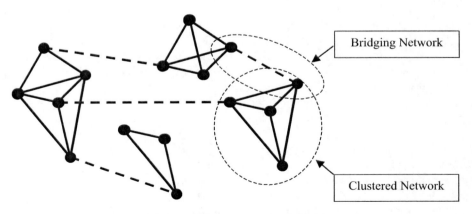

FIGURE 4–2.   A Small World Network with Bonds and Bridges.
Note: Circles represent individuals; solid lines are strong ties, and broken lines are weak ties.

rather than a sheer aggregate of individuals. Turner (1987) argues that this could result in a third form of social influence, referent informational social influence, which stems from people's appropriation of a group norm as their own *modus operandi.*

On the other hand, bridging networks may facilitate the diffusion of information that is easy to communicate. Consider the following argument: When people who are connected by weak ties meet, their common ground tends to be a fairly large communal one. They would not engage in conversations about matters of deep personal importance, but rather would exchange gossip, largely innocuous social commentaries, and information that is publicly available (e.g., new products among managers, published research findings among scientists). Information that does not require a great deal of explanation and background knowledge can travel efficiently through bridging networks. In a sense, the position that bridges clustered networks is highly central (e.g., Freeman, 1979; Friedkin, 1991) and is likely to play an important role in the efficient flow of information.

Bonding and bridging social network structures can provide different types of social benefits to the network members, and therefore supply different kinds of *social capital* (e.g., Coleman, 1988; see Field, 2003). On the one hand, clustered networks can not only provide social support when in need of help, but also generate trust among its members because any untrustworthy actions can easily be monitored and sanctioned (Coleman, 1988). In this way, a clustered network can increase the likelihood of behaviors that benefit its members. On the other hand, bridging networks can give access to resources that are unavailable to people from their clustered networks. Burt (2001) argued that people who occupy positions that bridge clustered networks can access valuable resources and control the flow of information. For those who broker between people, this structure can give a great advantage in gaining benefits.

The local processes of strong tie closure and weak tie bridging can produce a certain global social network structure. Milgram (1967) has termed this phenomenon a *small world*, in which highly clustered networks are bridged by sparse connections among them (see Fig. 4–2). According to Watts (1999; Watts & Strogatz, 1998), a small world is characterized by a high level of clustering among people and a relatively short average path length (e.g., a small number of links between two people in a network on the average). Pattison, Robins, and their colleagues (Pattison & Robins, 2002; Robins, Pattison, & Woolcock, 2005) showed that the prevalence of both closure and bridging can generate a small world structure in this sense. Based on their neighborhood-based model of social network analysis, they manipulated the likelihood of forming closed triangles and bridging ties (2-stars) in computer simulation experiments, and showed that when these local configurations are likely (but a 3-star is unlikely), a small world structure was likely to emerge at the global level.

The upshot of a small world is that such global configurations require relatively short steps for one person to reach another in the society. Milgram and his colleagues' (1967; Korte & Milgram, 1970; Travers & Milgram, 1969) empirical research suggests that the United StatesI in the 1960s was indeed akin to a small world. As depicted in the play, *Six Degrees of Separation* (Guare, 1990), the median number of intermediaries required for someone in Wichita, Kansas or Omaha, Nebraska to send a letter to another in Boston was five (Milgram). In a larger study where 196 residents in Nebraska sent letters to a target person in Boston, Korte and Milgram reported that the mean number of intermediaries was 5.2. It is worth noting that the majority of letters did not actually reach the final destination (only 28%, or 44 out of 160, made it in the 1967 study; 21%, or 42 out of 196, in the 1969 study). In addition, this rate fell even further when the starting person and the person at the final destination were of difference ethnic backgrounds: 33% when a White person sent a letter to a White person, but only 13% when a White person sent a letter to a Black person (Korte & Milgram). Nonetheless, those letters that made it needed only 5.5 for White-to-White and only 5.9 for White-to-Black chains to traverse the length of the United States from Los Angeles to New York (Korte & Milgram). If our society does, in fact, have the characteristics of a small world, what are its implications for the distribution of stereotypic beliefs in the society?

Network configuration, diffusion dynamics, and distribution of stereotypes. The local configuration of a social network may affect the flow of information. In particular, bridging networks may be good at transmitting simple information; whereas clustered networks may fare well in sharing complex information. By simple and complex information, we mean the *communicability* of information; that is, the extent to which the information is easy or difficult to communicate between people (Schaller, Conway, & Tanchuk, 2002). Bridging networks are likely to communicate information through "small talk" and brief conversations, which are good for transmitting communicable information. In contrast, bonding networks transmit information through extended conversations and repeated interactions, allowing for less communicable information to be transmitted due to the increased opportunity for multiple attempts and elaborate grounding processes.

The communication network research of the 1950s and 1960s (e.g., Bavelas, 1950; Leavitt, 1951) provides empirical support for this proposition. In these studies, the network structure was manipulated by permitting certain positions to be able to communicate with each other but denying communications to others, and the speed and accuracy of solving problems and the members' satisfaction were examined. Provided that the task performance depended primarily on the efficiency with which relevant information was transmitted across the network, Shaw's (1964; also see 1954) influential review of this literature can be interpreted as suggesting that the flow of simple information was more efficient in centralized networks than in decentralized networks, however, complex information was better transmitted in decentralized than centralized networks. Although configurations of decentralized networks vary, one of the prototypical forms was a highly clustered network in which all positions were connected to each other.

The local configuration of a social network may affect the distribution of stereotypic beliefs because it may influence the flow of stereotype-relevant information. Kashima et al. (manuscript in preparation) examined the effects of communicability on the distribution of stereotypes within clustered and centralized communication networks. They provided some participants with behavioral descriptions of two groups, such that the groups differed on their perceived levels of warmth and competence. A pilot study confirmed that information about warmth was more communicable than information about competence. In one condition, only one person had the original information, and this person then communicated to three others separately, thus forming a *centralized* 3-star network. In the other condition, two people had the original information, each of whom communicated to another person. In this condition, however, they changed their conversation partners, and each person spoke with everyone else in the end, thus forming a completely *clustered* network. In two experiments, it was found that people formed stronger stereotypes on the more communicable warmth dimension in the centralized network, but stronger stereotypes on the less communicable competence dimension in the clustered network.

A similar case can be made with regard to stereotype-relevant information. As discussed previously, information that is consistent with cultural stereotypes (SC information) is likely to be more socially connective and communicable than information inconsistent with them (SI information). Therefore, in bridging networks consisting of weak ties, SC information is likely to be efficiently transmitted. In other words, information that comes into a clustered network through bridges of weak ties is more likely to be SC than SI information. By contrast, clustered networks could transmit and retain the less communicable SI information, which may then be shared within the network, thus potentially weakening the stereotypes within clustered networks. Recall that people who are close to each other, namely, those who are connected by strong ties, are more likely able to communicate more complex information, which may include more SI information. This may produce a gap between people's perceptions of the stereotypes held by the general public and those held by themselves and their immediate social circles (e.g., members of the clustered network). That is, people might think their close friends and they themselves do not hold as strong a stereotype, or at least more complex views about social groups, as the general public. In fact, this appears to be the case as the research in pluralistic ignorance attests (Prentice & Miller, 1993; Tam, Lau, & Chiu, 2004). In particular, Bowen and Bourgeois (2001) found that student participants perceived the "average college student's" attitudes towards lesbian, gay, and bisexual students to be more negative compared to their own attitudes and those of their friends.

CONCLUSION

Recent research in the communication of stereotypes and stereotype-relevant information within social networks has demonstrated that communication processes may play a major part in the spread and perpetuation of social stereotypes. However, further research is required to properly unpack the potentially complex and multifaceted processes that can lead to the diffusion of both SC and SI information through social networks. The current research reported within the literature could be interpreted as painting a rather contradictory picture in terms of research findings, with some research, for example, arguing that SC biases are driven by a motivation to communicate truthfully and other studies suggesting that social connectedness goals are highly important. In reality, it is likely that, rather than representing a contradiction, such findings may simply reflect the extent to which current research has only just begun to scratch the surface of a very complex set of social psychological processes that come into play at any one time or in any one situation to result in greater or lesser amounts of SC and SI information being communicated. The aim behind this chapter was therefore to begin the process of piecing together some of the many potential factors involved, from the microlevel processes involved in establishing and maintaining relationships to the macrolevel processes of social network structures within which all instances of communication of stereotype-relevant information take place.

Although we have sought to describe many possible factors that are likely to influence the extent to which SC and SI information are communicated and ultimately diffuse through social networks, we have not yet reached the point of determining which of these factors are likely to predominate at any one time or exactly how they combine to produce particular outcomes. This is, however, a focus for future research. Indeed, the potential exists for an enormous amount of research that probes more deeply into understanding how and why stereotypes are communicated in particular contexts, ranging from the relational aspects of communication right up to broader analyses of small and large social-network structures and the distribution of information within these. Such investigations may not only allow for a deeper understanding of how stereotypes ultimately spread and perpetuate over time, but may also help to generate greater insight into the cultural dynamics processes through which many other culturally shared beliefs and attitudes spread and perpetuate.

On this general note, it is also worth mentioning that although many of the arguments and research presented in this chapter point toward a situation in which the relational and structural aspects of social networks are geared toward perpetuating existing stereotypes, stereotype change can and does occur from time to time. For instance, the Princeton Trilogy (Katz & Braly, 1933; Gilbert, 1951; Karlins, Coffman, & Walters, 1969) demonstrated how particular generations of Princeton University students shared many stereotypes of some common groups, but tended to share different stereotypes of these groups from one generation to the next. Clearly, new stereotypes and/or SI information spreads through social networks under certain conditions, along with the demise of previously shared stereotypes. There are likely to be many factors behind this, which require exploration through further research. As an example of one possibility already alluded to in this chapter but worth re-iterating, is the degree of closeness between members of a network. Although having common ground for particular stereotypes is often likely to promote the diffusion of SC rather than SI information, and especially when people are actively building and/or enhancing a relationship with another network member, when people are particularly close, SI information might have a greater chance of diffusing through a network. That is, with high levels of intimacy and a strong or deep common ground around stereotypes, more idiosyncratic information (e.g., SI) is perhaps better tolerated. After all, such information is more likely to be interesting and a prompt for discussion than SC information (McIntyre et al., 2004). Indeed, part of understanding how social-network processes contribute to perpetuating stereotypes is also understanding how they might encourage stereotype change. Given that many stereotypes do eventually change, it is possible that social networks contain particular processes or "forces" that counter the tendency towards stereotype maintenance, and if so, these need to be explicated through further research.

In all, there is clearly much potential for new and exciting research that locates stereotypes in the context of social networks. Admittedly, however, this chapter is by no means exhaustive in terms of highlighting all the possible theoretical and operational issues that may concern those studying stereotyping from a communication perspective. For example, it is worth considering what the overall goal of such research should be. Exactly what hypothetical situation are we hoping to bring about in society as a result of our studies into stereotype communication processes? Much of the research reviewed in this chapter implicitly constructs the communication of more SI information and less SC information as being the "ideal" situation that one should be striving to promote (although see Ruscher et al., 2003 for an exception). Indeed, contemporary models of stereotype change (e.g., Kashima, Woolcock, & Kashima, 2000; Queller & Smith, 2002) tend to focus on the importance of individuals becoming exposed to "counter-stereotypical" instances or information. Such models, as a result, tend to conceptualize SC and SI information as being at opposing ends of a linear dimension of various characteristics/behaviors. For example, SC information relating to "femininity" might be conceptualized as a female behaving submissively, with SI information being conceptualized as a female behaving assertively. The aim, within such a framework, then becomes to attempt to prevent individuals from "falling prey" to a bias toward the communication and perception of females-as-submissive over females-as-assertive.

One could alternatively argue, however, that the social ill-effects of peoples' reliance upon and use of stereotypes is perhaps more the result of a bias toward *all* information relating to stereotypes of social groups (be it "consistent" *or* "inconsistent"). So, for example, it is the extent to which the dimension of assertiveness-submissiveness is considered conversationally *relevant* in relation to gender that gives such gender stereotypes their social "power." When conceptualizing the social communication process in this manner, it becomes potentially problematic to view an ideal state of affairs as being one in which more SI than SC information (or even an equal amount of the two) is being communicated. After all, it is possible that a focus on predominantly SI information in a narrative about a group member could actually *also* serve to reinforce the stereotype of the group as a whole in a similar way as would a focus on SC information (e.g., by highlighting the unusualness of SI information). So apart from examining the frequency of SC versus SI items of information that are communicated, an important focus should also be the extent to which stereotypical *dimensions* (e.g. assertiveness-submissiveness) are drawn upon and made relevant in communications about a member of a social group (e.g., women) in comparison to other stereotype-irrelevant information. This is something worth considering in future research on the communication of stereotypes, especially when it comes to understanding and theorizing how stereotypes might change through communication processes.

Another issue that the stereotype communication literature would be ill advised to ignore is the extent to which stereotypes of social groups are often highly ideologically, politically, and value laden. The stereotype communication literature has generally adopted the position that stereotypes of various social groups or categories of persons are essentially theoretically synonymous. For example, stereotypes of occupational groups (or even novel/fictional groups) are often theorised and operationalized as being theoretically synonymous with those relating to categories such as gender, ethnicity and class. However, following Ruscher, Cralley and O'Farrell (2005), we would suggest that the extent to which social categorizations are value-laden may have a large impact on the ways in which people communicate about members of social groups. For example, consider the argument outlined earlier in this chapter regarding the importance of stereotype communication in the building of social relationships. One must also consider that the communication of stereotypes (particularly negative ones) of many socially disadvantaged or disempowered groups (e.g., ethnic minorities, women, the poor) may be seen in some contexts as violating social norms of equality and egalitarianism. In such instances, the communication of SC information may actually serve to *damage*, rather than build, social relationships. Future research would be well advised to consider how such ideological elements may impact upon the communication of stereotypes relating to various social groups in various communicative contexts.

In this chapter we have attempted to provide a conceptual overview of the literature relating to the spread and maintenance of social stereotypes within social networks. We have considered a variety of features that may be seen to influence the diffusion of stereotypes through networks, such as the *relational* processes inherent in the formation and maintenance of network ties and the *composition* and *configuration* of the social network. Our intention, in doing so, was to demonstrate the importance of conceptualizing and examining stereotype formation, maintenance, and change at the level of social networks, and how this can add to our overall understanding of the cultural dynamics of stereotypes. We hope that our review of this literature may stimulate others in the stereotypes field to explore this exciting new area of research.

REFERENCES

Allport, G. W., & Postman, L. F. (1947). *The psychology of rumor.* New York: H. Holt.
Allport, G. W. (1954). *The nature of prejudice.* New York: Addison-Wesley.
Aunger, R. (2002). *The electric meme: A new theory of how we think.* New York: Free Press.
Bartlett, F. C. (1932). *Remembering: A study in experimental and social psychology.* Cambridge: Cambridge University Press.
Baumeister, R. F., Zhang, L., & Vohs, K. D. (2004). Gossip as cultural learning. *Review of General Psychology, 8,* 111–121.
Bavelas, A. (1950). Communication patterns in task-oriented groups. *Journal of the Acoustical Society of America, 22,* 725–730.
Blackmore, S. J. (1999). *The meme machine.* Oxford, UK: Oxford University Press.
Blau, P. M., Blum, T. C., & Schwartz, J. E. (1982). Heterogeneity and intermarriage. *American Sociological Review, 47,* 45–62.
Bowen, A. M., & Bourgeois, M. J. (2001). Attitudes toward lesbian, gay, and bisexual college students: The contribution of pluralistic ignorance, dynamic social impact, and contact theories. *Journal of American College Health, 50,* 91–96.
Boyd, R., & Richerson, P. J. (1985). *Culture and the evolutionary process.* Chicago, IL: University of Chicago Press.
Brown, P., & Levinson, S. C. (1987). Politeness: Some universals in language useage. Cambridge: Cambridge University Press.
Burt, R. S. (2001). Structural holes versus network closure as social capital. In N. Lin, K. Cook, & R. S. Burt (Eds.), *Social capital: Theory and research* (pp. 31–56). Hawthorne, NY: Aldine de Gruyter.
Campbell, D. T. (1958). Common fate, similarity, and other indices of the status of aggregates of persons as social entities. *Behavioral Science, 3,* 14–25.
Cavalli-Sforza, L. L., & Feldman, M. W. (1981). *Cultural transmission and evolution.* Princeton: Princeton University Press.
Clark, A. E. (2005). Coordinating on common ground: How stereotype sharedness contributes to the maintenance of stereotypes in communication. Unpublished doctoral dissertation, University of Melbourne, Australia.
Clark, A. E., & Kashima, Y. (under review). Stereotype maintenance in communication: The role of social connectivity in communication.
Clark, H. H., & Brennan, S. E. (1991). Grounding in communication. In Resnick, L., Levine, J., & Teasley, S. (Eds.), *Perspectives on socially shared cognition.* Washington, DC: American Psychological Association.

Clark, H. H. (1996a). Communities, commonalities, and communication. In Gumperz, J. J. & Levinson, S. C. (Eds.), *Rethinking linguistic relativity* (pp. 324–355). Cambridge, UK: Cambridge University Press.

Clark, H. H. (1996b). *Using language.* NY: Cambridge University Press.

Coleman, J. (1958). Relational analysis: The study of social organizations with survey methods. *Human Organizations, 17,* 28–36.

Coleman, J. S. (1988). Social capital in the creation of human capital. *American Journal of Sociology, 94,* 95–120.

Dawkins, R. (1976/1989). *The selfish gene.* Oxford, UK: Oxford University Press.

Djelic, M. L. (2004). Social networks and country-to-country transfer: Dense and weak ties in the diffusion of knowledge. *Socio-Economic Review, 2,* 341–370.

Dovidio, J. F., Gaertner, S. L., & Kawakami, K. (2003). Intergroup contact: the past, present, and the future, *Group Processes and Intergroup Relations, 6,* 5–20.

Dunbar, R. I. M. (1996). *Grooming, gossip and the evolution of language.* London, England: Faber and Faber.

Dunbar, R. I. M., Marriott, A., & Duncan, N. D. C. (1997). Human conversational behavior. *Human Nature, 8,* 231–246.

Eder, D., & Hallinan, M. T. (1978). Sex differences in children's friendships. *American Sociological Review, 43,* 237–250.

Eder, D., & Enke, J. L. (1991). The structure of gossip: Opportunities and constraints on collective expressions among adolescents. *American Sociological Review, 56,* 494–508.

Fiedler, K. (2000). Beware of samples! A cognitive-ecological sampling approach to judgment biases. *Psychological Review, 107,* 659–676.

Field, J. (2003). *Social capital.* London, England: Routledge.

Fiske, S. T. (2004). *Social beings: A core motives approach to social psychology.* Hoboken, NJ: John Wiley & Sons.

Freeman, L. C. (1979). Centrality in social networks conceptual clarification. *Social Networks, 1,* 215–239.

Freyd, J. J. (1983). Shareability: The social psychology of epistemology. *Cognitive Science, 7,* 191–210.

Friedkin, N. E. (1982). Information flow through strong and weak ties in intraorganizational social networks. *Social Networks, 3,* 273–285.

Friedkin, N. E. (1991). Theoretical foundations for centrality measures. *American Journal of Sociology, 96,* 1478–1504.

Gauld, A., & Stephenson, G. M. (1967). Some experiments relating to Bartlett's theory of remembering. *British Journal of Psychology, 58,* 39–49.

Gilbert, G. M. (1951). Stereotype persistence and change among college students. *Journal of Personality and Social Psychology, 46,* 245–254.

Gilovich, T. (1987). Secondhand information and social judgment. *Journal of Experimental Social Psychology, 23,* 59–74.

Goffman, E. (1959). *The presentation of self in everyday life.* Garden city, NY: Doubleday.

Granovetter, M. (1973). The strength of weak ties. *American Journal of Sociology, 78,* 1360–1380.

Granovetter, M. (1982). The strength of weak ties: A network theory revisited. In P. V. Marsden & N. Lin (Eds.), *Social structure and network analysis* (pp. 105–130). Beverly Hills, CA: Sage.

Grice, H. P. (1975). Logic and conversation. In P. Cole & J. L. Morgan (Eds.), *Syntax and semantics: Speech acts.* NY: Academic Press.

Guare, J. (1990). *Six degrees of separation.* New York, NY: Random House.

Hafeez-Zaidi, S. M. (1958). An experimental study of distortion in rumour. *The Indian Journal of Social Work, 19,* 211–215.

Hansen, M. T. (1999). The search-transfer problem: The role of weak ties in sharing knowledge across organization subunits. *Administrative Science Quarterly, 44,* 82–111.

Haque, A., & Sabir, M. (1975). The image of the Indian army and its effects on social remembering. *Pakistan Journal of Psychology, 8,* 55–61.

Harary, F., Norman, R. Z., & Cartwright, D. (1965). Structural models: An introduction to the theory of directed graphs. Hoboken, NJ: John Wiley & Sons.

Hardin, C., & Higgins, E. T. (1996). Shared reality: How social verification makes the subjective objective. In R. M. Sorrentino & E. T. Higgins (Eds.), *Handbook of motivation and cognition: Foundations of social behavior.* NY: Guilford Press.

Haslam, S. A., Turner, J. C., Oakes, P. J., McGarty, C., & Reynolds, K. J. (1998). The group as a basis for emergent stereotype consensus. In M. Hewstone (Ed.), *European review of social psychology, Vol. 8* (pp. 203–239). Chichester, UK: John Wiley & Sons.

Heath, C., Bell, C., & Sternberg, E. (2001). Emotional selection in memes: The case of urban legends. *Journal of Personality and Social Psychology, 81,* 1028–1041.

Heider, F. (1958). *The psychology of interpersonal relations.* Hoboken, NJ: John Wiley & Sons.

Hewstone, M., Hassebrauck, M., Wirth, A., & Waenke, M. (2000). Pattern of disconfirming information and processing instructions as determinants of stereotype change. *British Journal of Social Psychology, 39,* 399–411.

Higgins, E. T., & McCann, C. D. (1984). Social encoding and subsequent attitudes, impressions, and memory: "Context-driven" and motivational aspects of processing. *Journal of Personality and Social Psychology, 47,* 26–39.

Higgins, E. T. (1981). The "communication game": Implications for social cognition and persuasion. In E. T. Higgins, C. P. Herman, & M. P. Zanna (Eds.), *The Ontario Symposium* (Vol. 1, pp. 343–392). Hillsdale, NJ: Erlbaum.

Hirschfeld, L. A. (1996). *Race in the making: Cognition, culture, and the child's construction of human kinds.* Cambridge, MA: MIT Press.

Huston, T. L., & Levinger, G. (1978). Interpersonal attraction and relationships. *Annual Review of Psychology, 29,* 115–156.

Kaplan, M. F., & Miller, C. E. (1987). Group decision making and normative versus informational influence: Effects of type of issue and assigned decision rule. *Journal of Personality and Social Psychology, 53,* 306–313.

Karlins, M., Coffman, T. L., & Walters, G. (1969). On the fading of social stereotypes: Studies in three generations of college students. *Journal of Personality and Social Psychology, 13,* 1–16.

Kashima, Y. (2000). Maintaining cultural stereotypes in the serial reproduction of narratives. *Personality and Social Psychology Bulletin, 26,* 594–604.

Kashima, Y., Klein, O., & Clark, A. E. (in press). *Grounding: Sharing information in social interaction.*

Kashima, Y., Lyons, A., McIntyre, A. M., & Clark, A. E. (under review). *Bartlett, serial reproduction, and social psychology of cultural dynamics.* Manuscript submitted for publication.

Kashima, Y., Robins, G., Kashima, E., Tindale, R. S., Lyons, A., & Bain, P. (2007). *Communication and essentialism: Grounding the shared reality of a social category.*

Kashima, Y., Woolcock, J., & Kashima, E. (2000). Group impressions as dynamic configurations: The tensor model of group impression formation and change. *Psychological Review, 107,* 914–942.

Katz, D., & Braly, K. (1933). Racial stereotypes of one hundred college students. *Journal of Abnormal and Social Psychology, 28,* 280–290.

Katz, E., & Lazarsfeld, P. F. (1955). *Personal influence: The part played by people in the flow of mass communications.* New York, NT: Free Press.

Kellermann, K., & Palomares, N. A. (2004). Topical profiling: Emergent, co-occurring, and relationally defining topics in talk. *Journal of Language and Social Psychology, 23*, 308–337.

Klein, O., Jacobs, A., Gemoets, S., Licata, L., & Lambert, S. M. (2003). Hidden profiles and the consensualization of social stereotypes: How information distribution affects stereotype content and sharedness. *European Journal of Social Psychology, 33*(6), 755–777.

Klein, O., Tindale, S., & Brauer, M. (this volume). The consensualization of stereotypes in small groups. In Y. Kashima, K. Fiedler, & P. Freytag (Eds.), *Stereotype dynamics: language-based approaches to stereotype formation, maintenance, and transformation.* Mahwah, NJ: Lawrence Erlbaum.

Korte, C., & Milgram, S. (1970). Acquaintance networks between social groups: Application of the small world method. *Journal of Personality and Social Psychology, 15*, 101–108.

Krackhardt, D., & Brass, D. J. (1994). Intraorganizational networks: The micro side. In S. Wasserman & J. Galaskiewicz (Eds.), *Advances in social network analysis: Research in the social and behavioral sciences* (pp. 207–229). Thousand Oaks, California: Sage.

Krauss, R. M., & Fussell, S. R. (1996). Social psychological models of interpersonal communication. In E. T. Higgins & A. W. Kruglanski (Eds.), *Social psychology: Handbook of basic principles* (pp. 55–701). NY: Guilford Press.

Kruglanski, A. W., & Webster, D. M. (1996). Motivated closing of the mind: "Seizing" and "freezing". *Psychological Review, 103*, 263–283.

Kunda, Z., & Oleson, K. C. (1995). Maintaining stereotypes in the face of disconfirmation: Constructing grounds for subtyping deviants. *Journal of Personality and Social Psychology, 68*, 565–579.

Latané, B., & L'Herrou, T. (1996). Spatial clustering in the conformity game: Dynamic social impact in electronic groups. *Journal of Personality and Social Psychology, 70*, 1218–1230.

Lazarsfeld, P., Berelson, B., & Gaudet, H. (1948). *The people's choice.* New York, NY: Columbia University Press.

Lazarsfeld, P. F., & Merton, R. H. (1954). Friendship as a social process: A substantive and methodological analysis. In M. Berger (Ed.), *Freedom and control in modern society* (pp. 18–66). New York, NY: Van Nostrand.

Leavitt, H. J. (1951). Some effects of certain communication patterns on group performance. *Journal of Abnormal and Social Psychology, 46*, 38–50.

Leyens, J. P., Yzerbyt, V., & Schadron, G. (1994). *Stereotypes and social cognition.* Thousand Oaks, CA: Sage Publications.

Lin, N. (2001). Social Capital: A theory of social structure and action. New York: Cambridge University Press.

Linville, P. W., Fisher, G. W., & Salovey, P. (1989). Perceived distributions of the characteristics of ingroup and outgroup members. *Journal of Personality and Social Psychology, 57*, 165–188.

Lyons, A., & Douglas, S. (2007). *The role of individual differences in the communication of stereotypes.* Manuscript in preparation.

Lyons, A. (2002). *Maintaining Stereotypes in Communication: The Role of Communication Processes and the Shared Nature of Stereotypes.* Unpublished Doctoral Dissertation.

Lyons, A., & Kashima, Y. (2007). Maintaining stereotypes in communication: Investigating memory biases and coherence-seeking in storytelling. *Asian Journal of Social Psychology.*

Lyons, A., & Kashima, Y. (2001). The reproduction of culture: Communication processes tend to maintain cultural stereotypes. *Social Cognition, 19*, 372–394.

Lyons, A., & Kashima, Y. (2003). How are stereotypes maintained through communication? The influence of stereotype sharedness. *Journal of Personality and Social Psychology, 85*, 989–1005.

Marsden, P. V. (1987). Core discussion networks of Americans. *American Sociological Review, 52*, 122–313.

Marsden, P. V. (1988). Homogeneity in confiding relations. *Social Networks, 10*, 57–76.

Marsden, P. V., & Friedkin, N. E. (1993). Network studies of social influence. *Sociological Methods and Research, 22*, 127–151.

McIntyre, A., Lyons, A., Clark, A. E., & Kashima, Y. (2004). The microgensis of culture: Serial reproduction as an experimental simulation of cultural dynamics. In M. Schaller & C. S. Crandall (Eds.), *The psychological foundations of culture.* Mahwah, NJ: LEA.

McPherson, M., Smith-Lovin, L., & Cook, J. M. (2001). Birds of a feather: Homophily in social networks. *Annual Review of Sociology, 27*, 415–444.

Meyer, G. W. (1994). Social information processing and social networks: A test of social influence mechanisms. *Human Relations, 47*, 1013–1047.

Milgram, S. (1967). The small-world problem. *Psychology Today, 1*, 61–67.

Miller, D. T., & McFarland, C. (1987). Pluralistic ignorance: When similarity is interpreted as dissimilarity. *Journal of Personality and Social Psychology, 53*, 298–305.

Moscovici, S. (1984). The phenomenon of social representations. In R. M. Farr & S. Moscovici (Eds.), *Social Representations.* Cambridge, England: Cambridge University Press.

Nieuwbeerta, P., & Flap, H. (2000). Crosscutting social circles and political choice: Effects of person network composition on voting behavior in The Netherlands. *Social Networks, 22*, 313–335.

Ostrom, T. M., & Sedikides, C. (1992). Out-group homogeneity effects in natural and minimal groups. *Psychological Bulletin, 112*, 536–552.

Pattison, P. (1994). Social cognition in context: Some applications of social network analysis. In S. Wasserman & J. Galaskiewicz (Eds.), Advances in social network analysis: Research in the social and behavioral sciences (pp. 79–109). Thousand Oaks, California: Sage.

Pattison, P., & Robins, G. (2002). Neighborhood-based models for social networks. *Sociological Methodology, 32*, 301–337.

Perse, E. M. (2001). *Media effects and society.* Mahwah, NJ: Lawrence Erlbaum.

Pool, I., & Kochen, M. (1978). Contacts and influence. *Social Networks, 1*, 1–48.

Prendice, D. A., & Miller, D. T. (1993). Pluralistic ignorance and alcohol use on campus: Some consequences of misperceiving the social norm. *Journal of Personality and Social Psychology, 64*, 243–256.

Queller, S., & Smith, E. R. (2002). Subtyping versus bookkeeping in stereotype learning and change: Connectionist simulations and empirical findings. *Journal of Personality and Social Psychology, 82*, 300–313.

Richards, Z., & Hewstone, M. (2001). Subtyping and subgrouping: Processes for the prevention and promotion of stereotype change. *Personality and Social Psychology Review, 5*, 52–73.

Robins, G., Pattison, P., & Woolcock, J. (2005). Small and other worlds: Global network structures from local processes. *American Journal of Sociology, 110*, 894–936.

Ruscher, J. B. (2001). *Prejudiced communication: A social psychological perspective.* New York, US: Guilford Press.

Ruscher, J. B., Cralley, E. L., & O'Farrell, K. J. (2005). How newly acquainted dyads develop shared stereotypic impressions through conversation. *Group Processes and Intergroup Relations, 8*(3), 259–270.

Ruscher, J. B., & Duval, L. L. (1998). Multiple communicators with unique target information transmit less stereotypic impressions. *Journal of Personality and Social Psychology, 74,* 324–344.

Ruscher, J. B., & Hammer, E. D. (1994). Revising disrupted impressions through conversations. *Journal of Personality and Social Psychology, 66*(3), 530–541.

Ruscher, J. B., Hammer, E. Y., & Hammer, E. D. (1996). Forming shared impressions through conversation: An adaptation of the continuum model. *Personality and Social Psychology Bulletin, 22,* 705–720.

Ruscher, J. B., Santuzzi, A. M., & Hammer, E. Y. (2003). Shared impression formation in the cognitively interdependent dyad. *British Journal of Social Psychology, 42,* 411–425.

Schaller, M., Conway, L. G., & Tanchuk, T. L. (2002). Selective pressures on the once and future conents of ethnic stereotypes: Effects of the communicability of traits. *Journal of Personality and Social Psychology, 82*(6), 861–877.

Scott, J. (2000). *Social network analysis: A handbook (2nd ed.).* Thousand Oaks, California: Sage.

Semin, G. R. (2000). Agenda 2000: Communication: Language as an implementational device for cognition. *European Journal of Social Psychology, 30,* 595–612.

Shaw, M. E. (1954). Some effects of problem complexity upon problem solution efficiency in different communication nets. *Journal of Experimental Psychology, 48,* 211–217.

Shaw, M. E. (1964). Communication networks. *Advances in Experimental Social Psychology, 1,* 111–147.

Sperber, D., & Wilson, D. (1986). *Relevance: Communication and cognition.* Cambridge, MA: Harvard University Press.

Sperber, D. (1996). *Explaining culture.* Oxford, UK: Blackwell.

Stasser, G., & Titus, W. (1987). Effects of information load and percentage of shared information on the dissemination of unshared information during group discussion. *Journal of Personality and Social Psychology, 53,* 81–93.

Tam, K.-P., Lau, I. Y.-M., & Chiu, C.-Y. (2004). Biases in the perceived prevalence and motives of severe acute respiratory syndrome prevention behaviors among Chinese high school students in Hong Kong. *Asian Journal of Social Psychology, 7,* 67–81.

Travers, J., & Milgram, S. (1969). An experimental study of the small world problem. *Sociometry, 32,* 425–443.

Turner, J. C. (1987). *Rediscovering the social group: A self-categorization theory.* Oxford, UK: Blackwell.

Valente, T. W. (1996). Social network thresholds in the diffusion of innovations. *Social Networks, 18,* 69–89.

van Dijk, T. A. (1987). *Communicating racism: Ethnic prejudice in thought and talk.* London, England: Sage.

Verbrugge, L. M. (1977). The structure of adult friendship choices. *Social Forces, 56,* 576–597.

Visser, P. S., & Mirabile, R. R. (2004). Attitudes in the social context: The impact of social network composition on individual-level attitude strength. *Journal of Personality and Social Psychology, 87,* 779–795.

Vygotsky, L. S. (1978). *Mind in society: The development of higher psychological processes.* Cambridge, MA: Harvard University Press.

Watts, D. J., & Strogatz, S. H. (1998). Collective dynamics of 'small-world' networks. *Nature, 393,* 440–442.

Watts, D. J. (1999). *Small worlds: The dynamics of networks between order and randomness.* Princeton, NJ: Princeton University Press.

Wasserman, S., & Galaskiewicz, J. (1994). Advances in social network analysis: Research in the social and behavioral sciences. Thousand Oaks, California: Sage.

Weber, R., & Crocker, J. (1983). Cognitive processes in the revision of stereotypic beliefs. *Journal of Personality and Social Psychology, 45,* 961–977.

Weenig, M. W. & Midden, C. J. (1991). Communication network influences on information diffusion and persuasion. *Journal of Personality and Social Psychology, 61,* 734–742.

Weenig, M. W. H., & Midden, C. J. H. (1991). Communication network influences on information diffusion and persuasion. *Journal of Personality and Social Psychology, 61,* 734–742.

Wheelan, S. A. (1994). *Group processes: A developmental perspective.* Boston, MA: Allyn & Bacon.

Wittenbaum, G. M., & Stasser, G. (1998). The re-evaluation of information during group discussion. *Group Processes and Intergroup Relations, 1,* 21–34.

Part 2

SYMBOLIC MEDIATION AND STEREOTYPING

Chapter 5

A Semiotic Approach to Understanding the Role of Communication in Stereotyping

Klaus Fiedler, Matthias Bluemke, Peter Freytag, Christian Unkelbach, and Sabine Koch
University of Heidelberg, Germany

Some psychological assumptions appear so common and natural that they rarely become the target of theoretical reflection. Let us take as a starting point the common gender stereotype that women tend to be more emotional than men. Traditionally, to demonstrate that such a stereotype can bias social perception, participants would typically be exposed to carefully selected stimulus information to show no difference in the emotionality of men and women and, yet, judgments would reflect more emotionality attributed to female than male target persons. In journals and textbooks of social cognition, stereotype effects are commonly explained within the heuristics and biases framework, that is, in terms of restricted mental resources and processing motivation. In the given example, one might explain the belief that women are more emotional than men in terms of Kahneman and Tversky's (1972) representativeness heuristic. Emotionality is more representative of females than of males. Alternatively, researchers may draw on the notion of illusory correlations based on the expectancy that femininity and emotionality belong together (Camerer, 1988; Chapman & Chapman, 1967; Hamilton & Rose, 1980) or based on the similarity of the two concepts (cf. Fiedler, 2000; Shweder, 1977, 1982). In still another role-theoretical framework (Eagly, 1987; Hoffman & Hurst, 1990), perceived gender differences in emotionality can be explained in terms of the social roles played by women and men.

A puzzling and intriguing question—which is not fully resolved when referring to heuristics, expectancies, roles, or similarities as explanatory devices—is why these influences can be stronger than reality. How is it possible that the stereotypes arising from heuristics, expectancies, or role constraints emerge and persist in the absence of supporting evidence, and sometimes even in spite of contrary evidence? Answers to this fundamental question can be classified as belonging to one of two classes: (a) motivational or (b) cognitive. On one hand, *motivational* accounts attribute stereotypical biases to a desire to confirm one's expectancies, which may be stronger than the motive to assess the world accurately (Chaiken, 1987; Kunda, 1990). On the other hand, *cognitive* approaches posit that stereotypes (like other biases) result from resource limitations that prevent people from systematic or exhaustive information processing. Having missed or forgotten part of the evidence on female and male emotionality, the resulting uncertainty promotes stereotype-based inferences.

Thus, what psychologists have in mind when they interpret stereotypes as a reflection of heuristics, expectancies, illusory correlations, or social roles is that individuals either *want* to use these error-prone devices (motivational) or *need* to resort to them, due to resource limitations. The purpose of the present chapter is to supplement these two common notions with another theoretical perspective, which is much less common but nevertheless suggests a universal source of stereotyping. This alternative approach assumes that stereotypes and other biases can originate in the sign systems used to transmit information on particular variables (such as gender and emotionality), quite independently of an individual's motives and mental resources. We suggest the term *semiotic* to denote this approach.

OUTLINE OF A SEMIOTIC APPROACH
TO STEREOTYPING

A semiotic approach is in no way in conflict, or incompatible, with cognitive and motivational approaches, but it adds a radically distinct component. Particularly, it points to origins of stereotyping that are located outside the individual, in sign systems used for information transmission. Cognition (e.g., beliefs) refers to knowledge acquired in past and present processes; whereas motivation (e.g., desires) refers to needs in the present and goals in the future of the individual. Both are properties located *within* the individual. In contrast, the aim of a semiotic approach is to illuminate the crucial role of information transmitters used for communication *between* individuals, as distinct from feeling and thinking within individuals. As subjective experience is communicated between people, they have to use sign systems. The inherent properties of available sign systems can, to a considerable extent, determine the outcome of interpersonal communication, as eventually reflected in stereotypes and socially shared beliefs.

Verbal language is certainly the most refined sign system, but by no means the only one. For another example, involving nonverbal signs, let us assume that body language affords a sign system including six cues to communicate femininity and emotionality: (a) enhanced eye contact, (b) reactivity, (c) affective voice, (d) verbosity, (e) expressiveness, and (f) flushing (see Fig. 5–1). Assume further that all six cues can take on but two values: (a) present and (b) absent. After appropriate inversions of all six cue dimensions, the degree of femininity increases with the number of present (rather than absent) cues. Now consider the mapping rule for the other attribute linked to femininity in the stereotype, emotionality. Again, the degree of emotionality seems to increase, because the two traits are confounded through the sign system used for information transmission (see Fig. 5–1). An actor who expresses femininity through such a sign system will very likely appear quite emotional as well. For a person to express masculinity and emotionality at the same time, or for a prototypically feminine person to appear nonemotional may be much harder, if not impossible. Even when that person is completely unknown, ruling out prior beliefs and sentiments, and even when communication partners are unbiased and accuracy motivated, the strong overlap within the sign system between the patterns denoting femininity and emotionality will hardly give them a chance to disentangle the two variables.

The crucial property of the eight-cue transmitter system that serves to foster a gender stereotype in this example is *cue overlap*, which is a well-known source of artifacts in psychometrics. Two personality traits (e.g., leadership ability and extraversion) that are in fact independent may appear to be highly correlated if the questionnaires used to measure both traits are based on overlapping item sets, creating an artificial source of common variance (cf. Burke, Brief, & George, 1993; Hurrell, Nelson, & Simmons, 1998; Watson & Pennebaker, 1989).

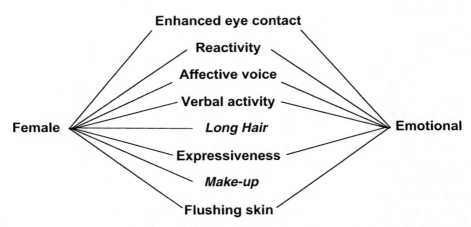

FIGURE 5–1.   Overlapping cue representation of (female) gender and emotionality.

Erroneous diagnostic inferences in such cases must not be attributed to test users' motives or cognitive biases, but to immanent properties of test instruments. Note that questionnaire tests are sign systems used to transmit personality information for diagnostic purposes; the cues of these sign systems are the test items.

More generally, by "sign system" we refer to any set of cues that can be used to encode and decode a message. The cues, which make up a sign system, can be words, gestures, idioms, grammatical forms, phonetic voice features, or more complex attributes such as logical constructions, text styles, or extended propositions (like test items). The assumption is not that any single cue system provides an exhaustive description of the whole miracle of communication. Rather, any sign system can only elucidate that aspect of a communication that a researcher wants to analyze—just as all scientific models only explain an aspect but never the full phenomenon to be explained.

All cue systems analyzed within the present studies consist of lists or profiles of n words or simple phrases. Communications are represented as vectors of cue values across a profile (e.g., an n-element vector of 1 and 0 values denoting the presence or absence of n words, or word classes). Just as persons can be described in terms of their n trait values in a semantic differential, or in terms of their responses to n items in a personality test, social communications in general can be represented by n-element vectors describing the occurrence, frequency, or intensity of n cues in the communication. Even when communications appear in prosaic style or in complex grammatical structures (as in a personal review), it is possible to count the occurrence rate of different function words or substance words in the text, to assess the reference to a specific profile of emotions, the number of references to persons and groups, or the occurrence of specific mistakes or flaws.

Although such additive n-element profiles, defined over a specific sign system, do not describe the whole communication in all its rich details, they can be used to test specific hypotheses about how the communication exerts its influence. For example, the crucial information conveyed in a personal review lies in the occurrence of certain critical abilities and social attributes, while many stylistic and prosaic aspects of the review text can be largely ignored. In a similar vein, communications about stock market, sports teams, consumer products, political candidates, or job applicants can be reduced to n-item profiles capturing share values, performance ratings, traits, symptoms, or interview responses typically transmitted in a standardized format. Put differently, our definition of sign systems is quite unrestrictive. Sign systems can vary in breadth (from specific words to all words of the lexicon), in abstractness level (from phonemes and lexemes to types of story structure), in sign type (from arbitrary symbols to cues that resemble their referent), or in origin (from symbols reflecting the communicator's choice to cues reflecting the researcher's focus). It is our contention that the contribution of sign-system overlap to stereotype maintenance will generalize across different kinds of sign systems.

A BACK-TRANSLATION PARADIGM

Empirical investigations of semiotic influences on social stereotypes require their own specific methods. Traditional methods in stereotype research include typicality ratings (e.g., Corneille & Judd, 1999; Hewstone & Hamberger, 2000; Rosch & Mervis, 1975; Rothbart & Lewis, 1988), subtyping (Hewstone & Lord, 1998; Kunda & Oleson, 1995; Weber & Crocker, 1983), priming (Fazio, Jackson, Dunton, & Williams, 1995; Wittenbrink, Judd, & Park, 1997), or implicit association tests (Karpinski & Hilton, 2001).

The basic methodological tool for capturing semiotic influences is *back translation*, a method quite common in ethnology and intercultural research, but hardly ever used in social-cognition experiments. The back-translation task involves (a) the translation of a well-defined set of input information onto a sign system and (b) the subsequent back translation from that sign system into the output information. For example, a job candidate's performance is translated onto a test profile from which the candidate's performance can then be recoded again. The properties of the sign systems (e.g., the tests or cue dimensions it contains) can be manipulated experimentally. When different sign systems applied to the same performance input (e.g., different test batteries) produce systematic differences in the back-translated inferences about the candidate's performance, such a bias must reflect the properties of the sign system. In this case, we have compelling evidence for the role of extra-individual, semiotic influences on social-information transmission.

The back-translation paradigm appears to be intuitively appealing and plausible. For instance, translating an American political contract to Chinese and then back into American English may not leave the contract unchanged. The properties of the sign systems (e.g., the English and Chinese language) will change the content and to some extent the meaning of the contract. It would be hard to believe that such processes of back translation should not also have a systematic influence on the genesis and communication of social stereotypes. Accordingly, let us now turn to a first experimental demonstration of our semiotic approach within the back-translation paradigm. To illustrate the process by which overlapping cues support stereotypical beliefs, we use the same example as in the introduction, the common belief that women are more emotional than men.

ESTABLISHING THE SEMIOTIC MEDIATION
OF STEREOTYPICAL INFERENCES

The first experiment serves to illustrate the basic methodology of the back-translation paradigm. The study consisted of three parts, the first of which was a pilot test. Twelve graduate students rated various prominent persons (e.g., actors, singers, politicians, and athletes) for their perceived degree of femininity and emotionality using separate rating scales. Selecting six exemplars for each combination of gender (male vs. female) and emotionality (low vs. high), a set of 24 target persons was created, establishing the same differences in emotionality for male and female targets. Thus, the correlation between gender and emotionality in the stimulus material was zero. If anything, the central tendency of the selected males' emotionality was slightly higher than that of the selected females.

In the second part of the experiment, communicators were asked to encode the target persons' personality using a cue profile, such that recipients of their communication would be able to decode the gender and emotionality of the persons described. This was indeed the task, in the third part, of recipients who were presented with the cue profiles produced by the communicators. The recipients' task was to back-translate the cue profiles into the two variables defining the gender stereotype; that is, to reproduce the targets' gender and emotionality. The aim was to demonstrate that even though the stimulus materials had been carefully selected to involve no gender differences in emotionality, the recipients' inferences of gender and emotionality would be markedly correlated. To the extent that the cues offered by the sign system for the encoding of gender and emotionality would overlap greatly, the sign system used for communication forces recipients to make correlated inferences of the two attributes.

The primary goal of this first experiment is to demonstrate how the back-translation paradigm works and how sign systems used as transmitters can induce stereotypical inferences. We did not yet include a manipulation of specific properties of the sign systems. The sign system chosen was only intended to be representative of ordinary language, that is, to cover linguistic terms commonly used as predicates in descriptions of social behavior. Specifically, two sign systems were compared, representing two prominent language levels for describing people and their behaviors: 24 common trait adjectives or 24 common action verbs (Table 5–1). The selection of the two sign systems was based on previous work on the linguistic category model (Fiedler, Semin, Finkenauer, & Berkel, 1995; Semin & Fiedler, 1988). The first 12 items in each profile represented matched pairs of adjectives and action verbs, referring to most common episodes of social behavior (e.g., aggressive—to attack; helpful—to help). The remaining 12 (nonmatched) items in each profile were the most frequently used terms at each language level, as determined by Fiedler et al. (1995). Together, the two profiles can be considered to be quite representative of the predicates used in natural language to describe people and their behavior in general. In principal, then, they should be suitable for encoding gender and emotionality. We wondered, however, whether these two sign systems would also allow recipients to reproduce the target persons' values on the critical attributes and whether their back-translated gender and emotionality values would reflect the zero correlation built into the stimulus material.

TABLE 5–1.
Trait Adjectives and Action Verbs Used for Sign Systems

German Terms		English Translation	Original
Action Verbs	Trait Adjectives	Action Verbs	Trait Adjectives
attack	aggressive	angreifen	aggressiv
spy	distrustful	nachspionieren	misstrauisch
ridicule	contemptuous	verspotten	geringschaetzig
avoid	timid	vermeiden	furchtsam
reject	hostile	zurueckweisen	feindselig
dispute	jealous	streitig machen	eifersuechtig
renounce	selfless	verzichten	uneigennuetzig
praise	acknowledging	loben	anerkennend
agree	tolerant	zustimmen	tolerant
reconcile	agreeable	sich versoehnen	vertraeglich
look after	sociable	sich kuemmern	gesellig
conform to	respectful	sich richten nach	ehrfuerchtig
disturb	faithful	stoeren	treu
flee	nice	fliehen	lieb
delight	friendly	erfreuen	freundlich
surprise	impudent	ueberraschen	unverschaemt
harm	vicious	schaden	boese
save	indifferent	retten	gleichgueltig
convince	strict	ueberzeugen	streng
help	thankful	helfen	dankbar
explain	sad	etwas erklaeren	traurig
compel	just	andere noetigen	gerecht
allow	dependent	erlauben	abhaengig
defend	funny	verteidigen	lustig

In the second phase of the experiment, then, the 24 targets were presented to ten communicators. Half of the communicators used the verb profile, and the other half used the adjective profile. The back translation of the 240 profiles created in this fashion was later accomplished by 30 recipients, each of whom received eight adjective profiles and eight action-verb profiles. Instructions to encoders emphasized that the need to encode the target persons in such a way that recipients could make correct inferences from the target profiles. They were told to describe the targets only on applicable traits or verbs (on graphical scales), ignoring nonapplicable attributes. Conversely, decoders knew that communicators had constructed the profiles with the intention to be understood. On each decoding trial, the target described in a profile first had to be classified as either male or female before the recipient had to rate the target on five traits: (a) emotionality, (b) objectivity, (c) tact, (d) ambition, and (e) vulnerability.

A check on the gender and emotionality manipulation revealed that encoders actually perceived the four subsets of stimulus persons (emotional females, emotional males, unemotional females, unemotional males) as intended. Encoder ratings thus corroborated the assumption that emotionality was perceived independently of target gender. Did communicators encode the differences between targets systematically? For a check, we computed the agreement between encoders in discriminating between the targets separately for all 24 cue dimensions, using an index of the reliability with which a given cue was used consensually (cf. Rosenthal, 1987). This index, which can vary between 0 and 1 like any other reliability index, exceeded .60 for 15 out of the 24 action-verb cues and for 22 out of the 24 trait adjective cues. Thus, most cues were utilized systematically across judges, providing the basis for above-chance communication and decoding.

It was expected that the original independence of gender and emotionality should be lost, however, due to the overlapping cue mapping rules for gender and emotionality. As a consequence, back-translated gender and emotionality should be substantially correlated. Put differently, communicators should use similar, overlapping cues to encode female gender and emotionality, and recipients should utilize these overlapping cues to make similar gender and emotionality inferences. As a consequence, the resulting attribute inferences should be correlated across the 24 targets.

Let us first examine the overlap in the encoded profiles. To assess the extent to which the same cues were similarly utilized for decoding gender and emotionality, we calculated for each cue (a) the correlation between its value and the average recipient inference of gender and (b) the correlation between its value and the average recipient inference of emotionality. These matched pairs of correlations (assessing the role of a cue in gender and emotionality inferences) were then correlated across all cues. This correlation amounted to 0.91 for the verb profiles and to 0.62 for the adjective profiles. This provides strong support for the assumption that the cue patterns for encoding gender and emotionality were indeed highly overlapping.

The crucial question is whether these overlapping cue patterns actually led to stereotypical correlations after back translation. Indeed, the correlations between the 24 pairs of back-translated gender and emotionality inferences were systematically positive, supporting the gender stereotype that femininity co-occurs with high emotionality. For verb cues, the average correlation was $r = .24$, and for adjective cues, the average correlation was $r = .23$.

This illusory correlation between gender and emotionality ratings did not occur in isolation but generalized to an entire pattern of stereotypical correlations between gender classifications and all other trait ratings (summarized in Table 5–2). Typically female trait inferences (emotional, tactful, vulnerable) came along with the classification of profiles as female, whereas typically male

Q3]

TABLE 5–2.
Average Correlations Between Recipients' Inferences of Female Gender
and Five Related Traits

	Emotionality	Objectivity	Tactfulness	Ambition	Vulnerability
Gender	0.24*	−0.09	0.22*	−0.36*	0.34*
Emotionality		−0.13	0.15	−0.08	0.33
Objectivity			0.25	0.11	−0.02
Tactfulness		Action-verb Cues		−0.28	0.35
Ambition					−0.29
Gender	0.23*	0.03	0.29*	−0.28*	0.35*
Emotionality		−0.17	0.03	0.05	0.47
Objectivity			0.52	−0.06	−0.09
Tactfulness		Trait-adjective Cues		−0.31	0.26
Ambition					−0.18

Note. Those correlations with gender that are significantly different from zero (by *t*-test, $\alpha <$ 0.01) are marked with an asterisk.

trait inferences (objective, ambitious) accompanied profiles considered male. Both cue systems (action verbs and adjectives) produced a similar degree of confusion.

To summarize, this first illustration of the back-translation method shows that the communication of two stereotypically associated attributes, gender and emotionality, which create overlapping cue patterns in linguistic sign systems, is intrinsically confounded. Inferences of one attribute, gender, were not independent of inferences of the other attribute, emotionality. This simple demonstration has obvious implications for stereotyping that have been largely neglected in previous theories. Stereotypes may reflect, to an unknown degree, the transmission of social information through sign systems that are mainly designed to convey meaning and coherence, rather than making strict distinctions. And even though cue systems may vary in the degree to which they support the biased encoding of stereotype-related information, there is no reason why such a simple principle should not contribute to the genesis, and persistence, of stereotypes.

Although the semiotic principle seems simple, it is not trivial. For one thing, a glance at the adjectives and verbs listed in Table 5–1 reveals that the cue systems afford various opportunities to disentangle gender and emotionality. More importantly, however, we have to realize that the stereotype would have not appeared if the information had not been translated back and forth. The effect—call it trivial or not—reflects the impact of the sign system rather than any motivated tendencies or capacity limitations in the human participants.

In fact, our participants were highly accuracy-motivated. Ironically, however, the highly systematic fashion in which they utilized the different cue systems had the effect of facilitating the stereotype-consistent attribute inferences, rather than preventing them, as one might have expected from a heuristics-and-biases perspective.

MANIPULATING THE PROPERTIES OF SIGN SYSTEMS

Nevertheless, the initial study only provides a first step in our semiotic approach. Thus far, we have only seen that transmitting descriptions of men and women through linguistic sign systems can foster the stereotype that female gender comes along with high emotionality, although the input information was carefully chosen to avoid such gender differences. Yet, we do not know for sure that cue overlap was responsible for the stereotype shift, simply because we did not manipulate the cue-overlap factor. We cannot fully exclude that the back-translation task merely created noise or uncertainty that recipients resolved with normal guessing strategies. Having just classified a target as female, they may have guessed under uncertainty that her emotionality must be quite high. Thus, we need to consider conditions under which (nonoverlapping) sign systems do not lead to correlated decoding inferences, in spite of guessing demands.

Moreover, we need to demonstrate the mediational role of specific cues more cogently. Given as many as 24 cues but only 16 target profiles in the first study, and in the absence of specific assumptions about the role of particular cues, it was not possible to conduct a mediational analysis of the cues' regression weights. For a more stringent test of the impact of specific cues, we need to reduce the number of cues and manipulate the inclusion of specific, overlapping versus nonoverlapping, cues in the sign system.

This was accomplished in another experiment that followed the same basic plan but differed from the initial study in some crucial respects. First, the gender-emotionality relation was replaced by another topic, namely, the naive personality theory that dominance and self-confidence are correlated. Within this stereotype, specific cue systems can be manipulated more easily than in the gender-emotionality domain. Moreover, the naïve theory linking self-confidence to dominance is less charged with ideological and emotional surplus value than the gender-emotionality topic. Second, we replaced the prominent target persons with sketches of unknown, synthetic target persons to rule out prior knowledge about specific target persons. The new targets consisted of black-and-white photographs of ordinary people, along with some biographical dummy information and, importantly, a list of pretested traits to indicate the two stereotypically related attributes: self-confident (S) and/or dominance (D). Again, the S and D were uncorrelated across the series of target persons, as manipulated by the traits ascribed to the targets. More precisely, independence was accomplished in two different ways. In the first half of the stimulus series, the stimulus information included an equal number of six targets from each combination of S (present vs. absent) and D (present vs. absent), making a total of 24 target persons. In the second half of the stimulus series, neither S-related traits nor D-related traits would ever be ascribed to any of the 24 target persons. Note that under the latter conditions, S is uncorrelated with D in a radical fashion, that is, through null information rather than equal frequencies of S-D pairings.

Third, and crucially, the composition of the sign system was manipulated. Participants had to encode their impressions of the 48 target persons using a profile that covered 12 behavioral cues. Subsets of the cues of the sign system profiles were manipulated. In a *separable condition*, the profile included three cues distinctively related to S (but not to D), three cues distinctively related to D (but not S), and six filler cues that were unrelated to both S and D (marked by an asterisk in Fig. 5–2). In the *overlapping condition*, the profile included the same six fillers, but the S cues were not exclusively related to S but to D as well, just as the D cues were not exclusively related to D but also to S. This sign system did not lend itself to separate, independent encoding of S-related and D-related information. Rather, the transmission of the attributes was confounded due to overlapping cues.

Decoder participants whose task is to infer the degree of S and D from the target cue profiles should find S and D more related when given overlapping rather than separable cues (see below). Furthermore, this prediction should not only hold for the first half of the stimulus series (where stimulus information varied for S and D) but also for the second half (where there was no stimulus information for S and D). Even when the sign system is not fed with relevant input at all, the inherent semiotic properties of the sign system alone should generate an illusory relationship between S and D—provided the sign system entails overlapping rather than separable cues.

To be sure, such a distinct pattern could not be due to guessing under uncertainty alone, because any tendency of recipients to guess similar values on S and D inferences (due to the semantic similarity of "dominance" and self-confidence") should generalize across separable and overlapping conditions. Any systematic difference between conditions could only reflect the sign-system manipulation. In addition, convergent findings for the first and second half of the stimulus series would suggest that the whole communication process need not be intended to convey, or even be concerned with, information about S and D. Sign systems can mimic an illusory relationship even for attributes that are neither present in the reference targets nor ever meant by communicators. Thus, the second half of the stimulus series is particularly well suited to establishing the independence of semiotically mediated stereotype effects from traditional cognitive and motivational approaches.

In the encoding phase, 32 participants were presented with pictures and brief personality sketches of 48 target persons encoded into the 12-cue profile. In the decoding phase, other participants rated the persons described in these

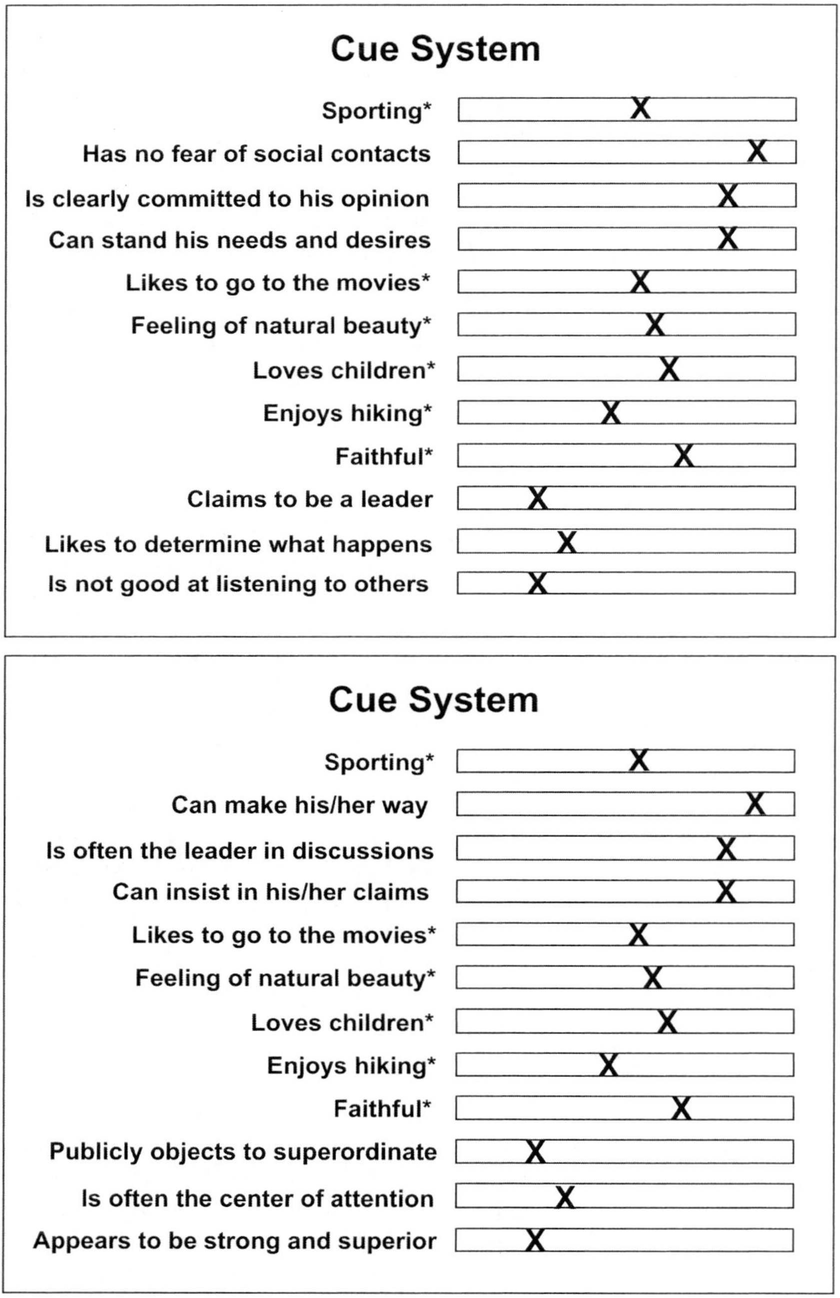

Cue System

Sporting*	X	
Has no fear of social contacts		X
Is clearly committed to his opinion		X
Can stand his needs and desires		X
Likes to go to the movies*	X	
Feeling of natural beauty*	X	
Loves children*	X	
Enjoys hiking*	X	
Faithful*	X	
Claims to be a leader	X	
Likes to determine what happens	X	
Is not good at listening to others	X	

Cue System

Sporting*	X	
Can make his/her way		X
Is often the leader in discussions		X
Can insist in his/her claims		X
Likes to go to the movies*	X	
Feeling of natural beauty*	X	
Loves children*	X	
Enjoys hiking*	X	
Faithful*	X	
Publicly objects to superordinate	X	
Is often the center of attention	X	
Appears to be strong and superior	X	

FIGURE 5–2. Cue systems designed for the communication self confidence (cues 2–4) and dominance (cues 10–12) in the separable condition (top) and in the overlapping condition (bottom), respectively.

profile series for self-confidence (S) and dominance (D). Half of the participants (in both phases) were assigned to each of the two levels of the variable *sign system* (separable vs. overlapping cues). In addition, the *informativeness* of personality sketches was varied within participants (informative vs. uninformative). The first half of the personality sketches contained traits relevant to S (self-confident, steadfast, showing solidarity, and funny) and to D (dominant, rigorous, strict, and predominant), along with neutral traits (conscientious, neat, noble, and polite). However, the presence and absence of S traits was uncorrelated with the presence versus absence of D traits. The second half never contained information relevant to S and D (last 24 sketches).

A new group of judges rated the extent to which a large number of behavioral cues can be considered indicators of S and D (on seven-point scales from $1 = $ not at all to $7 = $ completely). Six separable cues were selected. One set of three cues was representative of S but not of D, whereas the other set of three cues was representative of D but not of S. Further, six overlapping cues were selected that referred to a similar degree to S and D. The exact wording of the cues used in separable and overlapping profiles can be taken from the top and bottom parts of Fig. 5–2, respectively. The complete profiles consisted of 12 behaviors. In the separable condition, the triple of cues relevant to the assessment of S appeared in positions 2, 3, and 4, while the triple of cues relevant to the assessment D appeared in positions 10, 11, and 12. In the overlap condition, these cues were replaced by triples of overlapping cues indicative of both S and D. The remaining six cues were filler items representing neutral behaviors (see Fig. 5–2).

Encoders received a booklet with the 48 sketches (24 male targets and 24 females). They had to rate each target regarding all 12 cues, using graphical scales labeled "doesn't apply at all" and "applies completely." Depending on the between-participants factor, the six cues pertaining to S and D did either overlap or were separable. Only the first 24 personality sketches were informative with respect to the key concepts S and D. The remaining 24 sketches contained no trait adjectives related to S or D, representing the empty condition. Decoding participants received a booklet with all profiles constructed by one encoding participant, either from the separable or the overlapping condition; they provided their S and D inferences on graphical rating scales.

Based on the encoding data, mean S and D scores were defined as the average rating of the cues in positions 2, 3, and 4 (pertinent to S in the separable condition) and the average rating of cues in positions 10, 11, and 12 (pertinent to D in the separable condition). The same triples were averaged in the overlap condition. We then computed, within each participant, the correlation between these two scores (for S and D triples) across profiles, thereby assessing the degree to which an S-D contingency was already encoded into the cue profiles. For the decoding analysis, we computed the correlation between each judge's S and D ratings, across all profiles. In addition, coefficients of cue utilization were computed, that is, the regression weights indicating the weight given to the critical cues when making decoding inferences of S and D. All analyses were conducted separately for the informative and the uninformative part of the stimulus series.

Before we turn to the back-translation results, it is first important to establish the premise that overlapping and separable cues were actually utilized as intended. Thus, we factor-analyzed the cue intercorrelations. In the separable condition, the factor analysis of the 12 cues across all 768 profiles (16 encoders $\times$ 48 targets) resulted in two dominant factors. The first triple of cues (e.g, the separable S cues) received the highest loadings (.75, .77, and .66) on the first factor. The second triple of cues (e.g., the separable D cues) received maximal loadings on the second factor (.44, .74, and .68). In the factor analysis of the overlapping cue system, very high loadings were obtained on the first factor for all six cues relevant to the assessment of both S and D (ranging from .80 to .90).

Functional separation of S and D cues in the separable condition is also apparent in the cue intercorrelations (averaged-over encoders). The mean cue intercorrelation *within the two triples* amounts to .41, as compared with a mean correlation *between the two triples* of .12. The difference is highly significant. In the overlapping condition, the mean intercorrelation within the two triples ($r = .75$) was significantly higher than the mean intercorrelation between triples ($r = .64$), when pooling across all 16 judges. Thus, despite the overlap, the two triples of cues can be distinguished functionally, presumably due to their adjacent profile positions (e.g., 2, 3, and 4 vs. 10, 11, and 12). Moreover, the between-triple correlation was much higher in the overlapping condition ($r = .71$) than in the separable condition ($r = .12$), reflecting the intended difference in separability.

Let us now consider the back-translation outcomes. For each decoder, the S and D inferences were correlated across the 24 profiles (of each subset, informative and uninformative), providing a suitable summary index for the tendency of the cue system to induce an illusory S-D relation. The theoretical predictions were clearly borne out. Correlations between S and D inferences were much higher for overlapping than for separable cues. This difference was not only obtained for the 24 profiles of the informative part of the stimulus series (mean $r = .75$ vs. $r = .34$ for overlapping and separable cues, respectively), but also for the uninformative part of the stimulus series, ($r = .64$ vs. $r = .27$). Thus, regardless of whether the original information was relevant to S and D or not, an overlapping sign system that confounds the representation of S and D produced strong illusory dependencies between S and D. These illusory correlations were much higher than in the separable condition, although in this condition, S and D inferences were also correlated, presumably reflecting normal expectancy effects.

To demonstrate that inferences were systematically determined by the profiles encoded in the overlap and separable conditions, we conducted regression analyses within each decoder across the 24 profiles. Decoders' S or D inferences served as the criterion and the average cue values in the two triples of critical cues served as predictors. Fig. 5–3 gives the resulting regression weights, averaged across all decoders.

Consider first the regression weights for the prediction of S inferences. In the separable condition, much more weight was given to the first triple of cues (mean β = 0.63 for informative profiles) than to the second triple of cues (β = 0.01) when inferring S. In the overlapping condition, in contrast, S inferences were influenced not only by the first triple (β = 0.32) but also by the second triple (β = 0.47). Thus, S inferences were driven only by S cues in the separable condition, but by S and D cues in the overlapping condition. The same pattern was found for the uninformative profiles.

The regression weights for the prediction of D inferences also demonstrated that the D cues in the second triple (mean β = 0.50) received higher weights than the S cues in the first triple (β = 0.21) in the separable condition, although the difference was less clear-cut compared to the S inferences. In the overlap condition, the second triple (β = 0.48) contributed only slightly more to D inferences than the first triple (β = 0.37). Again, this pattern was obtained consistently for both for informative and uninformative profiles.

Altogether, the results from this study replicated and extended the demonstration that merely transmitting social information through a linguistic sign system can create a strong stereotypic relationship between personality attributes. This phenomenon was even shown to extend to a "surrealistic" condition in which the input information was irrelevant to the two attributes in question. As the illusory correlation between decoders' S and D inferences were clearly elevated in the overlapping condition, an account in terms of guessing

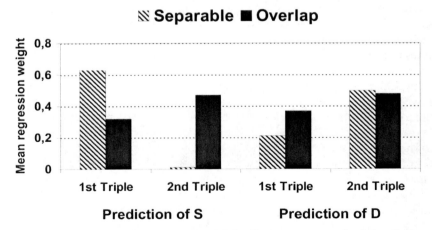

FIGURE 5–3.   Mean regression weights of the first versus second triple of relevant cues in S and D inferences. In the separable condition, the first triple was composed of non-overlapping S cues only and the second triple was composed of non-overlapping D cues only.

under uncertainty (e.g., similar responses on semantically related attributes, S and D) can be ruled out.

Regression analyses further elucidated the two-stage encoding and decoding process through which properties of the cue system determined stereotypical inferences. Given a separable cue system, encoders actually encoded S and D information into distinct cue subsets. Consequently, decoders who received such information were able to back translate S and D information separately. In the overlapping condition, in contrast, encoders did not sufficiently discriminate between S and D, leaving little chance for decoders to distinguish between S and D. This cue-mediated process is clearly evident from the individual regression weights.

CONTROLLING THE ENCODING STAGE OF COMMUNICATION

In another study we skipped the encoding step and manipulated the cue profiles experimentally. In this way, it was possible to disentangle stereotypical decoding inferences from encoding effects. In the experiment just reported, stereotypical correlations were already present in the encoded profiles. Thus, decoders were already fed with confounded information. The aim of the following study was to isolate semiotic influences during the decoding stage, controlling for the cue correlations in the encoded profiles.

We therefore constructed the profiles synthetically rather than leaving it up to encoders, using the same criterial attributes (S and D) and cue systems as in the preceding experiment. Given synthetic profiles, it was possible to manipulate the specific correlations between S cues and D cues that were built into the profiles. An overlapping sign system should produce strong correlations between decoders' S and D inferences, diverging from the actual correlation between the two triples of cues. In contrast, separable cues should enable decoders to recognize the actual strength of the correlation between S and D. Accordingly, we manipulated the strength of the actual correlation that held between S and D, in addition to the use of separable versus overlapping cue systems.

Across 25 target profiles, the intercorrelations among the 12 behavioral cues were manipulated using an algorithm that allows for the construction of specific patterns of intercorrelation (cf. Kaiser & Dickman, 1962). All correlations involving filler cues were set close to zero, all correlations *within* the two critical cue triples were always rather high (on average .79), and all correlations *between* individual cues belonging to different triples were either zero, for the independent condition, or around .50 in the correlated condition. The resulting correlation between the sum of S cues (first-triple cues) and the sum of D cues (second-triple cues) was either $r = 0$ (in the independent condition or $r = .58$ in the correlated condition.

Using a marriage-broker cover story, participants were told that behavioral cue profiles had been assessed for all clients and that the two attributes, S and D, were central for partner mediation. Instructions emphasized either the need to clearly *distinguish* S and D or the importance to *assess the joint occurrence* of S and D. After this explication of the problem context, participants were given a choice between the overlapping cue system and the separable cue system, whatever they deemed more appropriate for the task at hand. The 60 participants were randomly assigned to four experimental groups resulting from the orthogonal pairing of actual S-D correlation (.00 vs. .58) and instruction (distinguish vs. assess joint occurrence of S and D).

Thus, rather than manipulating separable versus overlapping cues directly, the assignment of a cue system was left up to participants' free choice, calling for their own metacognitive insights into semiotic constraints. To the extent that participants understand the dangers of an overlapping cue system, metacognitively, they should avoid them, especially when instructions emphasize the need to distinguish S from D. For several reasons, though, we did not expect such metacognitive insight to be particularly high. First, it is well known that introspective control over multiple-cue judgments is typically rather low (Fiedler & Walka, 1993; Goldberg, 1968; Hammond & Summers, 1972). Second, the process of cue selection is more likely determined by rules of semantic consistency than by rule-based reasoning. Meaningfully related cues might be preferred to unrelated cues, creating a tendency to choose overlapping rather than separable cues. And third, as Kahneman and Tversky (1973) noted, human judges are not sensitive to the advantage of orthogonal over redundant predictors. Instead they trust more in meaningfully intercorrelated cues that raise an illusion of consistency and validity.

Three measures of the stereotypical relation between S and D were included. First, judges rated the contingency they had seen between S and D directly on a graphical scale. Second, frequency-based correlations were computed from frequency estimates of how many profiles out of 25 had been (a) high in S as well as D, (b) high in S and low in D, (c) low in S as well as D, and (d) high in D and low in S. And, third, the dependent measure of most interest was the correlation between each decoder's S and D inferences from the 25 profiles.

Would participants recognize the advantage of separable sign systems? In fact, the proportion of participants who preferred overlapping cues was 37 out of 60. This proportion was virtually the same in both instruction conditions, (18/30 and 19/30). Regardless of whether integration or separation of S and D was emphasized as task-relevant, the advantage of separable cues was not recognized. For further analyses, then, we no longer relied on the instruction manipulation but on the partition of participants into those who chose separable versus overlapping cues, in addition to the actual contingency factor ($r = .00$ vs. .58).

The mean contingency measures are summarized in Table 5–3, transformed linearly to comparable scales. The first measure pertains to the correlation between each participant's judgments of S and D judgments across all profiles. For a frequency-based correlation measure, we used the coefficient $r = ((a + d) - (b + c))/(a + b) + (b + c)$, which is less vulnerable to small-cell frequencies than the commonly used phi coefficient. For comparison purposes, the graphical ratings were also transformed linearly to a range from -1 to $+1$.

A general bias to perceive a positive S-D contingency was most evident for direct judgments. The correlations based on S and D ratings (.12) and the frequency-based correlations (.16) in the separable independent condition did not differ significantly from zero. For all other conditions, strong illusory contingencies were obtained. Thus, two conditions must be met to detect attribute independence; cues must be separable *and* the actual correlation must be zero. The planned contrast between the separable independent condition and all other conditions was significant for the online measure, the frequency-based measure, but not for direct judgments, which exhibit a general bias toward the semantic relatedness of S and D.

To render the decoding process transparent, two regression analyses were computed within each decoder, using S and D online judgments as criteria and three predictors: the sum score for the first triple of critical cues (e.g., the S cues of the separable condition), the sum for the second triple of critical cues (e.g., the D cues of the separable condition), and the scatter of each profile's filler elements (for a crude measure of other distinct profile elements). The mean regression weights are given in Table 5–4. In the separable condition, S ratings were solely determined by the first triple of cues (mean $\beta = .80$ and .86, for independent and correlated conditions, respectively), and D judgments were solely determined by the second triple of cues ($\beta = .77$ and .87), with negligible regression weights for other predictors. In contrast, in the overlap condition, both cue sets received intermediate weights (see Table 5–4) in the

TABLE 5–3.
Mean Perceived Correlation as a Function of Experimental Condition

	Dependent Variable		
Condition	Online Measure	Frequency-Based	Direct Rating
Separable Independent	.12	.16	.40*
Separable Correlated	.37*	.50*	.47*
Overlapping Independent	.26*	.49*	.43*
Overlapping Correlated	.44*	.55*	.57*

Note. Direct contingency ratings are linearly transformed to the same range as correlation coefficients (-1 to $+1$). An asterisk indicates means that are significantly greater than 0 (by t test, alpha = .05).

TABLE 5–4.
Mean Regression Weights in Different Experimental Conditions

	Prediction of S Judgments			Prediction of D Judgments		
	β_S	β_D	R	β_S	β_D	R
Separable Independent	.80*	−.02	.84*	.08	.77*	.79*
Separable Correlated	.86*	−.11	.83*	−.03	.87*	.86*
Overlapping Independent	.25*	.46*	.64*	.53*	.32*	.71*
Overlapping Correlated	Could not be esitmated, due to collinearity					

Note. Statistics marked by an asterisk are significantly greater than 0 by *t*-test (alpha = .05) across participants.

prediction of both S (mean β = .25 and .46, for the first and second triple) and D (mean β = .53 and .32). (The regression weights for the correlated condition could not be estimated, due to extreme collinearity). The systematic utilization of cues is evident in rather high multiple correlations in all conditions (mean *R* ranging from .71 to .86).

The results of this experiment confirm our suspicion that judges have little meta-cognitive understanding for the constraints of overlapping (vs. separable) sign systems, as operationalized with our profiles. They rather preferred redundant cues that convey a sense of internal consistency. Once they had chosen an overlapping cue system, however, they had little chance to disentangle the stereotypical attributes that were confounded in the cue system. Altogether, the results of all three pioneer studies reported in this chapter provide converging evidence for the notion that stereotypical inferences can be mediated by the semiotic properties of the sign systems used for communication, independently of prior expectancies, intentions, or heuristic guessing strategies.

CONCLUSION

The semiotic approach we have depicted in the present chapter has several theoretical and practical implications. First, the back-translation paradigm appears to have face validity for the transmission of social knowledge in real life. The greatest part of stereotype learning is not based on direct experience with persons or groups but on indirect, second-hand information conveyed on TV, in newspapers, advertising, movies, novels, fairy tales, jokes, pictures, and conversation with other people. Accordingly, stereotype researchers have recently suggested methods and research tools for capturing the role of communication in stereotyping. These methods include the analysis of implicit quantifiers inherent in different trait terms (Gidron, Koehler, & Tversky, 1993; Hampson, John, & Goldberg, 1986; Rothbart & Park, 1986; Semin & Fiedler, 1991), the representation of behavior at different levels of abstraction (Semin & Fiedler, 1988, 1991; Vallacher & Wegner, 1987), linguistic discrimination of in-group and out-group (Maass, 1999; Wigboldus, Semin, & Spears, 2000), the serial reproduction of narratives (Kashima, 2000), and the consensus of inferences from "thin slices" of social information (Ambady & Rosenthal, 1992; Borkenau & Liebler, 1993; Kenny, 1991; Levesque & Kenny, 1993). The back-translation method employed for the present investigation would appear to add another useful paradigm for the study of communication approaches to stereotyping.

Granting a theoretical role for semiotic mediation, one prominent goal of future research would be the description of the very cue systems (e.g., language, body language, emblems, personality traits), which mediate social cognition. Just as in the area of lying and lie detection, where cues to deception have been studied and validated in metaanalyses (Zuckerman et al., 1981), Brunswik's (1956) lens model affords a framework to illuminate the cues or sign systems serving as carriers of stereotype communication. The import of new multimedia tools into social psychology should facilitate the registration and analysis of cue systems in different sensory modalities.

We believe that our semiotic approach not only reiterates the well-known role played by semantic factors in social inferences, but also offers a distinct, clearly spelled-out alternative algorithm by which semiotic overlap is turned into stereotypical correlations. The analogy required to understand the semiotic algorithm is not between a stereotype and a personality tester, whose beliefs and wishful thinking prevent him from measuring personality traits objectively. Rather, the analogy points to psychometric tests of overlapping item contents that preclude an independent measurement of distal traits, even in fully unbiased, accuracy-motivated testers.

ACKNOWLEDGMENTS

Helpful comments on an earlier draft of this paper by Galen Bodenhausen and Herbert Bless are gratefully acknowledged.

REFERENCES

Ambady, N., & Rosenthal, R. (1992). Thin slices of expressive behavior as predictors of interpersonal consequences: A meta-analysis. *Psychological Bulletin, 111*, 256–274.
Borkenau, P., & Liebler, A. (1993). Convergence of stranger ratings of personality and intelligence with self ratings, partner ratings, and measured intelligence. *Journal of Personality and Social Psychology, 65*, 546–553.
Brunswik, E. (1956). *Perception and the representative design of experiments.* Berkeley: University of California Press.
Burke, M. J., Brief, A. P., & George, J. M. (1993). The role of negative affectivity in understanding relations between self-reports of stressors and strains: A comment on the applied psychology literature. *Journal of Applied Psychology, 78*, 402–412.

Camerer, C. (1988). Illusory correlations in perceptions and predictions of organizational traits. *Journal of Behavioral Decision Making, 1,* 77–94.

Chaiken, S. (1987). The heuristic model of persuasion. In M. P. Zanna, J. M. Olson, & P. C. Herman (Eds.), *Social influence: The Ontario Symposium* (Vol. 5, pp. 3–39). Hillsdale, NJ: Erlbaum.

Chapman, L. J., & Chapman, J. P. (1967). Genesis of popular but erroneous psychodiagnostic observations. *Journal of Abnormal Psychology, 72,* 193–204.

Conger, A. J., & Jackson, D. N. (1972). Suppressor variables, prediction and the interpretation of psychological relationships. *Educational and Psychological Measurement, 32,* 579–599.

Eagly, A. H. (1987). *Sex differences in social behavior: A social-role interpretation.* Hillsdale, NJ: Lawrence Erlbaum.

Fazio, R. H., Jackson, J. R., Dunton, B. C., & Williams, C. J. (1995). Variability in automatic activation as an unobtrusive measure of racial attitudes: A bona fide pipeline? *Journal of Personality and Social Psychology, 69,* 1013–1027.

Fiedler, K. (1996). Explaining and simulating judgment biases as an aggregation phenomenon in probabilistic, multiple-cue environments. *Psychological Review, 103,* 193–214.

Fiedler, K., Blümke, M., & Koch, S. (2001). Vicarious functioning and cue utilization in the communication of stereotypes. Unpublished manuscript, University of Heidelberg.

Fiedler, K., & Walka, I. (1993). Training lie detectors to use nonverbal cues instead of global heuristics. *Human Communication Research, 20,* 199–223.

Gidron, D., Koehler, D. J., & Tversky, A. (1993). Implicit quantification of personality traits. *Personality and Social Psychology Bulletin, 19,* 594–604.

Gigerenzer, G., & Goldstein, D. G. (1996). Reasoning the fast and frugal way: Models of bounded rationality. *Psychological Review, 103,* 650–669.

Gigerenzer, G., Hoffrage, U., & Kleinbölting, H. (1991). Probabilistic mental models: A Brunswikian theory of confidence. *Psychological Review, 98,* 506–528.

Gigerenzer, G., Todd, P. M., & the ABC Research Group. (1999). *Simple heuristics that make us smart.* New York: Oxford University Press.

Hamilton, D. L., & Rose, R. L. (1980). Illusory correlation and the maintenance of stereotypic beliefs. *Journal of Personality and Social Psychology, 39,* 832–845.

Hammond, K. R., & Summers, D. A. (1972). Cognitive control. *Psychological Review, 79,* 58–67.

Hampson, S. E., John, O. P., & Goldberg, L. R. (1986). Category breadth and hierarchical structure in personality: Studies of asymmetries in judgments of trait implications. *Journal of Personality and Social Psychology, 51,* 37–54.

Hewstone, M., & Hamberger, J. (2000). Perceived variability and stereotype change. *Journal of Experimental Social Psychology, 36,* 103–124.

Hewstone, M., & Lord, C. G. (1998). Changing intergroup cognitions and intergroup behavior: The role of typicality. In C. Sedikides, J. Schopler, & C. Insko (Eds.), *Intergroup cognition and intergroup behavior* (pp. 367–392). Mahwah, NJ: Lawrence Erlbaum.

Hoffman, C., & Hurst, N. (1990). Gender stereotypes or rationalization? *Journal of Personality and Social Psychology, 58,* 197–208.

Hurrell, J. J., Nelson, D. L., & Simmons, B. L. (1998). Measuring job stressors and strains: Where we have been, where we are, and where we need to go. *Journal of Occupational Psychology, 3,* 368–389.

Kahneman, D., & Tversky, A. (1972). Subjective probability: A judgment of representativeness. *Cognitive Psychology, 3,* 430–454.

Kahneman, D., & Tversky, A. (1973). On the psychology of prediction. *Psychological Review, 80,* 237–251.

Kaiser, H. F., & Dickman, K. (1962). Sample and population score matrices and sample correlation matrices from an arbitrary population correlation matrix. *Psychometrika, 27,* 179–182.

Karpinski, A., & Hilton, J. L. (2001). Attitudes and the Implicit Association Test. *Journal of Personality and Social Psychology, 81,* 361–372.

Kashima, Y. (2000). Maintaining cultural stereotypes in the serial reproduction of narratives. *Personality and Social Psychology Bulletin, 26,* 594–604.

Kenny, D. A. (1991). A general model of consensus and accuracy in interpersonal perception. *Psychological Review, 98,* 155–163.

Kunda, Z. (1990). The case for motivated reasoning. *Psychological Bulletin, 108,* 480–498.

Kunda, Z., & Oleson, K. C. (1995). Maintaining stereotypes in the face of disconfirmation: Constructing grounds for subtyping deviants. *Journal of Personality and Social Psychology, 68,* 565–579.

Levesque, M. J., & Kenny, D. A. (1993). Accuracy of behavioral predictions at zero acquaintance: A social relations analysis. *Journal of Personality and Social Psychology, 65,* 1178–1187.

Maass, A. (1999). Linguistic intergroup bias: Stereotype perpetuation through language. *Advances in Experimental Social Psychology, 31,* 79–121.

Rosch, E., & Mervis, C. B. (1975). Family resemblances: Studies in the internal structures of categories. *Cognitive Psychology, 7,* 573–605.

Rosenthal, R. (1987). *Judgment studies: Design, analysis, and meta-analysis.* Cambridge, MA: Cambridge University Press.

Rothbart, M., & Lewis, S. (1988). Inferring category attributes from exemplar attributes: Geometric shapes and social categories. *Journal of Personality and Social Psychology, 55,* 861–872.

Rothbart, M., & Park, B. (1986). On the confirmability and disconfirmability of trait concepts. *Journal of Personality and Social Psychology, 50,* 131–142.

Semin, G. R., & Fiedler, K. (1988). The cognitive functions of linguistic categories in describing persons: Social cognition and language. *Journal of Personality and Social Psychology, 54,* 558–567.

Semin, G. R., & Fiedler, K. (1991). The linguistic-category model, its bases, applications, and range. *European Review of Social Psychology, 2,* 1–30.

Shweder, R. A. (1977). Likeness and likelihood in everyday thought: Magical thinking in judgments about personality. *Current Anthropology, 18,* 637–658.

Shweder, R. A. (1982). Fact and artifact in trait perception: The systematic distortion hypothesis. In B. A. Maher & B. Maher (Eds.), *Progress in personality research, Vol. 2* (pp. 65–101). New York: Academic Press.

Tversky, A. (1977). Features of similarity. *Psychological Review, 84,* 327–352.

Tversky, A., & Gati, I. (1978). Studies of similarity. In E. Rosch & B. B. Lloyd (Eds.), *Cognition and categorization* (pp. 79–98). Hillsdale, NJ: Lawrence Erlbaum.

Watson, D., & Pennebaker, J. W. (1989). Health complaints, stress, and distress: Exploring the central role of negative affectivity. *Psychological Review, 96,* 234–254.

Weber, R., & Crocker, J. (1983). Cognitive processes in the revision of stereotypic beliefs. *Journal of Personality and Social Psychology, 45,* 961–977.

Wigboldus, D. H. J., Semin, G. R., & Spears, R. (2000). How do we communicate stereotypes? Linguistic bases and inferential consequences. *Journal of Personality and Social Psychology, 78,* 5–18.

Wittenbrink, B., Judd, C. M., & Park, B. (1997). Evidence for racial prejudice at the implicit level and its relationship with questionnaire measures. *Journal of Personality and Social Psychology, 72,* 262–274.

Zuckerman, M., DePaulo, B. M., & Rosenthal, R. (1981). Verbal and nonverbal communication of deception. *Advances in experimental social psychology, 14,* 1–59.

Chapter 6

Derogatory Language in Intergroup Context: Are "Gay" and "Fag" Synonymous?

Andrea Carnaghi
University of Trieste

Anne Maass
University of Padova

In October 2004, the Italian Minister for Italians Abroad, Mirko Tremaglia, commented the defeat of Rocco Buttiglione at the European Parliament by publicly stating: "Poor Europe. The fags are in the majority." Unsurprisingly, his statement solicited a wave of protests. Would the reaction have been the same had Tremaglia used a neutral term such as "gay" or "homosexual"? Most likely, the outrage against Tremaglia's claim had little to do with the content of his statement (however inaccurate and polemic), but rather with the disparaging and offensive nature of the group label (*fag*) used in his utterance.

Although derogatory group labels such as *fag* would be considered highly inappropriate in most democratic societies (particularly when pronounced by high-level public servants), such terms are more common than one may expect. For instance, the reader of this chapter may want to generate all derogatory labels reserved to homosexuals in his or her native language. This exercise will likely lead the reader to discover a surprisingly large repertoire of ethno- or, more accurately, homophaulisms. The pervasiveness of epithets emerges very clearly from Irving Allen's (1983a, 1983b, 1984) lexical analyses of defamatory terms describing minority groups, as well as from recent collections of ethnic slurs available on the web.[1] Derogatory group labels refer to a wide range of characteristics. Some derogatory group labels simply represent abbreviations (*abo* for Aboriginal, *balkie* for Balkan immigrant), while others refer to physical characteristics (*redneck* for farmer in the Southern United States, *big nose* for Jew, *blinkie* for blind person, *10% off* for minority groups practicing circumcision, *sickle cell* for Black); to geo-political facts (*51st stater* for Canadians, *stani* for immigrants from central Asian countries ending in -stan); or to first names either common among a given ethnic group or associated with a particular historical figure or event (*Charlie* for Vietnamese, *Adolf* for Germans, *Jim* for Blacks, *Joe* for Americans; see Allen, 1983b). Also, many derogatory group labels include animal (*kiwi* for New Zealander) or food metaphors (*kraut* for German, *baguette* for French, *apple* for American Indian), as well as sexual allusions (see Allen, 1984). Interestingly, the derogatory lexicon is particularly rich with respect to targets with multiple minority membership, such as ethnic minority females or people belonging to religious *and* ethnic minorities (*Jewop* for Jewish Italians, *Jewxican* for Mexican Jews, *sister* for Black female, *Black velvet* for Aboriginal prostitute, *African queen* for Black gay male).

Although derogatory group labels can, assuming that the process is universal, in principle, refer to any kind of social category, including sexual, racial, ethnic, religious, or national groups, they are not equally distributed across groups, but vary systematically with relative size and status. In particular, analyses of archival data by Mullen and collaborators suggest that derogatory terms referring to immigrant groups tend to become more complex and less negatively valenced as the relative size and familiarity of the group increases (Mullen & Johnson, 1993, 1995; Mullen, Rozell, & Johnson, 2000, 2001). This suggests that the availability and valence of derogatory group labels provide a rough index of the status of ethnic minorities in a given society.

Although there is a wide range of derogatory group labels, they tend to share two important features. First, group labels are only considered derogatory when they are used with the clear intent to harm the minority target, as illustrated by Tremaglia's discourse cited at the beginning of this chapter. The same label may take on a very different meaning when used by members of the target group. For instance, a speech act in which an African American refers to another as "nigger" would generally not be considered harmful speech. Second, unlike other forms of discriminatory speech, derogatory group labels are typically used in intragroup speech acts in which members of the majority group communicate among each other. In other words, derogatory labels such as *nigger* or *fag* are more likely to be used when talking *about* than when talking *to* members of the respective minority group (see Graumann, 1995).

---

[1] For instance, the reader may want to consult one of the following Web sites: http://www.answers.com/topic/list-of-ethnic-slurs; http://gyral.blackshell.com/names.html; http://www.rsdb.org.

Although the prevalence of derogatory group labels is well-established, surprisingly little is known about the cognitive and affective consequences that such discriminatory speech has on the listener. The main question addressed in the present paper is whether terms like *African American* vs. *nigger* or *homosexual* vs. *fag* are synonymous. Technically, neutral vs. derogatory word pairs are equivalent as they refer to the same object—or in our case, to the same social group; yet they are not equivalent in valence or in social acceptability. This raises the interesting question of whether derogatory terms are semantically interchangeable with neutral category labels, considering that they describe the same object, or whether they produce distinct effects in the listener's mind.

To date, only few studies have investigated the impact of derogatory ethnic labels on the evaluation of minority targets (Greenberg & Pyszczynski, 1985; Kirkland, Greenberg, & Pyszczynski, 1987; Simon & Greenberg, 1996). The first to hypothesize that overhearing of derogatory labels may activate negative feelings and beliefs regarding the target group were Greenberg and Pyszczynski (1985), who conducted an experiment in which White Americans were exposed to a debate between a White and a Black person who, respectively, won or lost the debate. Subsequently, participants overheard a comment from one of the "evaluators" (in reality, a confederate) who criticized the Black target either in an ethically offensive way (e.g., "there's no way that nigger won the debate") or in an ethically neutral manner (e.g., "there's no way that pro debater won the debate"). In line with hypotheses, the Black debater was perceived as less skilled when he had been the target of a derogatory ethnic label (*nigger*) than when criticized on ethically neutral grounds (*pro debater*).

A subsequent study by Kirkland and colleagues (1987) showed that the negative evaluation even generalizes to other people who are indirectly associated to the target of the slur. In a fictitious jury trial, either a Black or a White defense attorney defended a White client. When the defense attorney was Black, participants overheard either a critical comment that was ethically offensive (a racial slur such as "God, Mike, I don't believe it. That nigger doesn't know shit") or one that was offensive, but not on ethnic grounds (e.g., "God, Mike, I don't believe it. That shyster doesn't know shit"). In line with previous findings (Greenberg et al., 1985), the Black attorney was evaluated more negatively when labeled in an ethnically derogatory (rather than ethnically neutral) fashion. Interestingly, the White client was also considered more negatively and received harsher verdicts when defended by a Black attorney who was the target of the derogatory ethnic criticism, suggesting that the effects of the derogatory ethnic label extend to other people who are indirectly associated with the minority target.

A limit of this set of studies is that, in both studies, the derogatory ethnic label (*nigger*) was compared to a label that made no reference to ethnicity (*pro debater* or *shyster*), but not to a neutral label describing the same group (*Black, African American*). Thus, it remains unclear whether the derogatory ethnic label (*nigger*) triggered negative evaluations because of its derogatory nature or because of its reference to a negatively valued ethnic group (*Blacks*). Simon and Greenberg (1996) have tried to respond to this criticism by conducting a study in which participants were exposed to either a derogatory ethnic label (*nigger*) or to a neutral ethnic label (*Black*). In an additional control condition, participants were not presented with any critical remark about the minority target. Differently from the previous studies, these authors also assessed the level of prejudice toward African Americans, dividing participants into three distinct groups: namely, (a) pro-Black, (b) anti-Black, and (c) ambivalent. Results indicated that the Black target person was evaluated more positively in the no-criticism control condition than in the experimental conditions; however, the neutral and the derogatory ethnic label conditions did *not* differ from each other. Moreover, the evaluation of the target across conditions was moderated by participants' level of prejudice. Pro-Black participants reported the same evaluation of the target regardless of experimental condition. Anti-Black participants disparaged the target much more in the experimental conditions than in the no-criticism control condition, however, without distinction between the derogatory and the neutral ethnic label condition. Finally, ambivalent participants expressed a similar evaluation of the target in the control and in the neutral ethnic label conditions, while their evaluation of the target was much more flattering in the derogatory ethnic label condition. In sum, there was absolutely no evidence that the derogatory ethnic label (*nigger*) would trigger a more negative evaluation than the nonderogatory ethnic label (*Black*). If anything, there was a tendency to evaluate the target of the derogatory ethnic label relatively more positively, although this was limited to participants with ambivalent attitudes.

To our knowledge, to date there is no evidence in the literature that derogatory group labels such as *fag* or *nigger* would trigger affective reactions, evaluations, or cognitive representations that are any different from those triggered by corresponding neutral labels such as *homosexual* or *Black*. This would suggest that derogatory group labels are indeed synonyms of neutral category terms, and that political-correctness norms—those that discourage the use of derogatory terms—are superfluous.

However, before drawing such conclusions, it may be worthwhile to investigate this issue more carefully. Indeed, there are reasons to believe that prior research may not be entirely conclusive. First of all, all previous studies have employed explicit measures—such as evaluations of the target person—that allow a great degree of intentional control. It is possible that derogatory group labels trigger spontaneous negative reactions, but that these may not necessarily show on explicit measures. Since explicit attitude measures are open to intentional control, people may find it relatively easy to hide such thoughts even if the derogatory label may initially have activated a negative image of the minority group. Simon and Greenberg's (1996) finding that people with ambiguous attitudes toward Blacks actually evaluated the target more positively when labeled as *nigger* rather than *Black* would argue in favor of such a controlled compensation mechanism. Thus, although derogatory group labels do not seem to trigger more negative explicit evaluations, this does not prove that they may not affect people on an implicit or automatic level.

Second, previous studies on ethnophaulisms did not clearly distinguish between stereotypic content and valence. If participants in Greenberg and Pyszczynski's (1985) and Kirkland et al.'s (1987) studies evaluated the argumentative competency of the Black debater or attorney negatively, this may either reflect their stereotypic views ("Blacks have poor verbal skills") or their negative affective reaction. As convincingly argued by Wittenbrink, Judd, and Park (1997, 2001), valence and stereotypicality are two distinct dimensions of implicit prejudice that may combine in an interactive fashion. Disambiguating these two aspects is particularly critical in the case of derogatory group labels, as it remains to be seen whether, compared to neutral labels, they activate (a) different stereotypic content, (b) different affective reactions, or (c) a combination of both. It is conceivable that the stereotypic content activated by derogatory and neutral labels is identical for the simple reason that both labels refer to the same group; yet derogatory labels may evoke more negative associations, regardless of stereotypicality. Alternatively, and in line with Wittenbrink et al.'s work, one may envisage an interactive pattern such that derogatory labels specifically activate that part of the group stereotype that is negative in content. For instance, whereas the term *gay* may activate anything that is stereotypical of homosexuals, be it positive or negative, the term *fag* may only activate the negative subportion of the stereotype (for example, *effeminate*, but not *artistic*).

OVERVIEW OF OUR RESEARCH PROGRAM

Our own research project intended to investigate these issues, pursuing four major goals. First, it aimed at investigating the implicit effects of derogatory vs. neutral labels referring to the same social group and at identifying their distinct impact on stereotypic content and valence. In other words, we asked whether derogatory group labels, compared to neutral labels, trigger more stereotypical or more negative images of the minority target, or both. Throughout this research project, we relied on different paradigms in order to tap the cognitive, affective, and motor consequences of the exposure to derogatory group terms. We will initially address the relation between derogatory group labels and the evaluative reactions they could entail, and subsequently focus on the relation between derogatory labels and attitudes toward a given group with respect to its distinct aspects—namely, stereotypic content and valence.

Our second aim was to understand whether derogatory group labels would exert a similar influence on majority members and on those that belong to the minority group that is the target of the slur. Thus, we tested whether neutral vs. derogatory labels concerning sexual orientation may differ in terms of explicit judgments, as well as automatic activation of stereotype and prejudice depending on the sexual orientation of the perceivers.

The third aim was to test whether the language used (neutral vs. deroga-tory) may not only modify the perception of the specific target group, but also the broader context in which the event is embedded. More specifically, we investigated an entirely new hypothesis: that derogatory group labels, com-pared to neutral category labels, may motivate people to construe the situation in terms of intergroup rather than interindividual relations.

Four, previous studies have failed to disentangle the pure cognitive (or af-fective) effects of being exposed to a derogatory label from those triggered by a public context of discrimination. As a matter of fact, all studies have pre-sented participants with a specific experimental situation: A derogatory term was stated by another person (generally an ingroup member) toward an indi-vidual target. Previous studies in the social influence domain have repeatedly shown that when people find themselves in a context that condones deroga-tory acts toward a minority group, they are more likely to display discrimina-tory acts toward the same group (Crandall, Eshleman, & O'Brein, 2002; Lam-bert et al., 2003); however, it has also been shown that when discrimination toward outgroup members is normatively sanctioned, people overtly take dis-tance from the agent of discrimination and display more egalitarian reactions toward these members (Castelli, Arcuri, & Zogmaister, 2003). Therefore, it is still unclear whether the lack of any effect of the derogatory labels on partici-pants' reactions is due to a sort of cognitive isomorphism between category and derogatory labels or to participants' tendency to avoid any form of com-pliance with the source of discrimination.

Although we are aware that variations in the contextual norm of 'political correctness' or in the membership of the speaker using the derogatory term will have important effects on the audience's reactions (Hornsey, Trembath, & Gunthorpe, 2004), in the current research program we are strictly focusing on the effect elicited by the derogatory labels per se while ignoring the im-portance of other (relevant) social factors.

Derogatory Group Labels and Their Relation to Automatic Stereotype and Prejudice

The first set of studies investigated the participants' associations in reaction to category *vs.* derogatory labels referring to homosexuals as a group. This question was addressed by means of three different unobtrusive measures of implicit attitude, namely, (a) a free association task, (b) an approach-avoid-ance measure, and (c) a semantic priming procedure. In this way, we expected to circumvent the possibility that participants may have employed a controlled strategy while reporting their reactions (Simon & Greenberg, 1996).

The first study (Carnaghi, Maass, Bianchi, Castelli & Brentel, 2005; pilot study) was intended to provide initial evidence for the hypothesis that category (e.g., *homosexual*) vs. derogatory group labels (e.g., *fag*) would trigger differentially valenced semantic associations. To attain this aim, we conducted a study in which participants were told that we were interested in the way people produce free associations. Specifically, participants were presented with a series of stimulus words, which were comprised of several words irrelevant to sexual orientation terms (e.g., *sun, crapper*[2]). Importantly, the list also included one term referring to homosexuals which, depending on the experimental condition, was either a neutral category label (e.g., *homosexual*) or a derogatory label (e.g., *fag*). Participants were asked to spontaneously report the first three concepts that came to their mind and, at the end of the experiment, to judge the valence of each word they had previously reported.

Data analysis revealed that the first association was much more positive when following a neutral prime word (*homosexual* or *gay*) than when following a derogatory prime word (*queer* or *fag*). Moreover, we conducted a content analysis, classifying participants' responses in six a priori defined categories: (a) slurs, (b) stereotype-relevant words, (c) discrimination-related words, (d) negative feelings, (e) sexual-intercourse-related words, and (f) references to the speakers' discriminative intent; however, our content analyses revealed no difference between prime words.

Taken together, these data suggest that the first associations that come into people's minds when confronted with a neutral vs. derogatory group label differ clearly in valence, but not in terms of semantic content. Regardless of the specific meaning of the association, neutral prime words triggered much more positive associations than derogatory prime words.

In the second study (Carnaghi & Maass, 2006), we tested whether derogatory group labels compared to category labels would elicit automatic behavioural responses indicative of differential target evaluation, namely the Implicit Approach-Avoidance Task (i.e., IAAT; Castelli, Zogmaister, Smith, & Arcuri, 2004; Chen & Bargh, 1999; Duckworth, Bargh, Garcia, & Chaiken, 2002; Vaes, Paladino, Castelli, & Leyens, 2003; Wentura, Rothermund, & Bak, 2000). This paradigm is based on the theoretical assumption that the evaluative component of an attitudinal object is also comprised of the behavioral representation associated with that object, which is typically compatible with approach or avoidance movements. Confirming this assumption, several studies (Castelli et al., 2004; Chen & Bargh, 1999; Duckworth et al., 2002; Solarz, 1960; Vaes et al., 2003; Wentura et al., 2000) have shown that approach-like movements are faster for positive than negative attitudinal objects, whereas avoidance-like movements are faster for negative than positive objects (Solarz, 1960; Chen & Bargh, 1999; Duckworth et al., 2002).

In line with these findings, we intended to test whether derogatory labels, such as *fag*, would trigger automatic evaluations any different from those

---

[2]A few slang words (e.g, *crapper*) were included in the list to make sure that the derogatory label (*fag* or *queer*) was not the only one deviating from the official language use that is typical of psychology experiments.

elicited by corresponding neutral labels, such as *gay*. We therefore conducted a study in which students were told that they were participating in a classification task. Participants were seated in front of a computer monitor and informed that they had to judge a small sample of items that appeared on the screen. Specifically, they were told that the item could be either social groups, such as *Africans*, or nonsocial groups, such as *Bottles*. Importantly, among the labels referring to social groups were two neutral category group labels—namely, *gay* and *Southerner*—and two corresponding derogatory group labels—namely, *fag* and *terrone* (derogatory term for Southern Italian).[3]

Following the procedure outlined by Castelli et al. (2004), the task consisted of two sessions. In the first session, participants were asked to use the approach key (avoidance key) for items related to social groups, and to use the avoidance key (approach key) for items related to nonsocial groups. In the second session, participants were provided with the same items, but the response set was reversed. Participants provided their answers through a modified standard keyboard in which one key button (e.g., approach key) was closer than the other one (e.g., avoidance key) to the to-be-classified items. The time participants took to approach or avoid each item constituted our dependent variables.

Results showed that participants were much faster at approaching category group labels (e.g., *gay, Southerner*) than derogatory group labels (e.g., *fag, terrone*), whereas no difference emerged between category and derogatory group labels in the avoidance movement.

Although these two studies provide consistent evidence for the idea that derogatory and neutral category labels elicit different affective reactions, they failed to analyze the relationship between derogatory labels and attitude toward a given group with respect to its distinct aspects—namely stereotypic content and valence. The third experiment (Carnaghi et al., 2005) addressed this issue.

Following the procedure outlined by Wittenbrink and colleagues (1997, 2001), we used a semantic priming paradigm. Specifically, a prime was subliminally presented, followed by a target stimulus requiring a word/nonword decision. Primes comprised two neutral category labels (e.g., *gay, homosexual*), two derogatory labels (e.g., *fag, fairy*), and two nonsense labels (e.g., *secadftg* and *gruiteo*). The target words included six traits stereotypical of gays, six counterstereotypical traits, and six that were irrelevant to the group in question. Moreover, in line with previous research (Wittenbrink et al., 1997, 2001), half of the traits in each category were positive and half were negative.

On the basis of the previous literature, we advanced two competing hypotheses. First, we expected that both neutral and derogatory labels would activate those semantic concepts that are stereotypically associated with gays—that is, regardless of type of prime (neutral or derogatory), participants should react faster to stereotypical than to counterstereotypical or irrelevant target words; however, compared to category labels, derogatory labels would be less

---

[3]In Italian, the term *terrone* is a derogatory label describing Southern Italians.

likely to activate flattering associations and more likely to activate negative association related to the group. Thus, we expected our participants to react more quickly to positive targets (and more slowly to negative targets) when primed by neutral category rather than by derogatory labels.

Alternatively, a second prediction was advanced, mimicking the findings by Wittenbrink et al. (1997). According to this idea, neutral and derogatory primes may activate different subsets of the gay stereotype. Derogatory labels should mainly activate negative stereotypical information, whereas neutral labels were expected to activate negative and positive stereotypes in a more balanced fashion. No differences were expected for counterstereotypical and irrelevant stimuli.

The analyses of participants' reaction times supported the former hypothesis, showing that participants, regardless of type of label, reacted faster to stereotypical than to counterstereotypical and irrelevant targets. Apparently, both labels activated the stereotype of the group, and they did so to a similar extent. In other words, category and derogatory labels were equally likely to activate the semantic concepts that are stereotypically associated with gays.

In line with our hypothesis, however, participants showed a greater facilitation for positive targets when preceded by a category prime than when preceded by a derogatory prime. Moreover, participants tended to show a greater facilitation for negative targets when preceded by a derogatory prime, but no facilitation was found when negative targets were preceded by a category prime. Importantly, this pattern was not modified by the stereotypicality of the target words, indicating that neutral and derogatory primes did not activate different subsets of the gay stereotype.

Together, these results suggest that derogatory group labels differ from neutral group labels, mainly with respect to the valence of the associations they are able to trigger. Thus, it is not so much the ability to activate stereotypical content but the tendency to activate less positive and, at least in part, more negative associations that distinguish derogatory from neutral group labels.

Derogatory Group Labels: What Are Their Effects on Minority Members?

The second issue investigated in the current research program was the question of whether derogatory group labels affect minority members belonging to the target group in the same way as they affect majority members. In particular, we wanted to compare the explicit and implicit reactions of heterosexuals and homosexuals to derogatory and category group labels.

In the first study (Carnaghi & Maass, in press), we used an explicit measure in order to verify whether heterosexuals and homosexuals differed in terms of perceived harmfulness of derogatory group labels such as *fag* and *fairy*. Although we are unaware of any previous study investigating this issue, it is highly relevant to understand whether these two groups conceived the labels in question as equally derogatory. Depending on the literature one takes into account, several alternative hypotheses may be advanced.

First, since emotional reactions of anger are more likely to emerge when perceivers see the target of an offensive action as a part of their own group (Smith, 1999; Dumont, Yzerbyt, Wigboldus, & Gordijn, 2003; Yzerbyt, Dumont, Wigboldus, & Gordijn, 2003), one would expect homosexuals (e.g., the target of the derogatory labels in our studies) to evaluate derogatory group labels, such as *fag*, as much more harmful than heterosexuals do.

Second, as the stereotype held by a dominant group toward a stigmatized minority group massively permeates mass media (Wilson & Gutierrez, 1985), and since representation of groups are transmitted and reproduced throughout interpersonal communication (Giles, 1977; Van Dijk, 1987), people normally learn the different and disparaging way they can label a stigmatized group regardless of whether they are personally part of the group that is the target of such derogatory terms. In other words, the "cultural stereotype" of homosexuals, as well as the derogatory labels associated with that group, may be just as accessible to homosexuals as it is to heterosexuals (Devine, 1989; Devine & Baker, 1991). As stated provocatively by the journalist Titti De Simone during a public speech at the Milan Gay Pride parade: "*after all, also us homosexuals have been educated to be heterosexuals.*" Therefore, one may expect heterosexuals and homosexuals to provide very similar judgments about the harmfulness of derogatory group labels.

A third possibility is that homosexuals, being part of the target group, may no longer conceive terms such as *fag* as negative. Since the ingroup is generally evaluated positively, it is possible that any reference to that group, even when framed in disparaging terms, takes on a positive meaning. Indeed, it is well known that many minority groups import derogatory language, originally created by hostile majority groups, into minority speech, thereby changing the implicit valence of such terms. For instance, the term *nigger*, arguably the most influential and controversial insult in the English language, frequently appears in Black speech as a way of referring, in an ironic or even affectionate way, to the ingroup (Kennedy, 2002). Thus, one may not exclude a third possibility: namely, that derogatory terms are perceived as less offensive by gays than by heterosexuals.

In order to test these hypotheses, we (Carnaghi & Maass, in press) conducted a study in which participants were presented with a series of disparaging and neutral words. Specifically, items comprised two derogatory group labels concerning homosexuals (*fag* and *fairy*), two neutral category labels regarding the same group (*gay* and *homosexual*), two highly offensive ("hard") slurs unrelated to homosexuality (*coglione* and *stronzo*[4]), and two soft slurs unrelated to homosexuality (*sciocco* and *stupido*[5]). Participants were told to indicate the extent to which they perceived each of the listed items as offensive (*of-*

---

[4]Roughly equivalent to the word *asshole.*

[5]Roughly equivalent to the word *stupid.*

fensivo) words by means of a 7-point Likert scale ranging from 1 ("not at all offensive") to 7 ("totally offensive").

The results clearly show that both heterosexuals and homosexuals considered the derogatory group label the most offensive, followed by the hard slur, the light slur, and, least harmful, the neutral category label. Curiously, however, even the benign category labels were not considered entirely harmless. Important for our aim, gays and heterosexuals did not differ reliably in their explicit judgment of the different labels, although gays tended to consider both the neutral category labels and the derogatory labels referring to the ingroup as slightly *less* offensive.

In conclusion, this study has shown that heterosexuals and homosexuals are equally aware of the harmful and offensive flavor of derogatory group labels. In other words, the majority group and those that are potentially the target of such a slur both hold an accurate perception of the sense of offense the speaker wants to elicit when using such terms. Thus, when asked to express a reasoned opinion at the explicit level, both groups are equally aware of the offense the target may suffer when confronted with such a slur.

In a follow-up study (Carnaghi & Maass, 2005a, in press), we intended to directly compare homosexuals' and heterosexuals' automatic activation of stereotype and prejudice in response to being exposed to a derogatory vs. neutral category group label concerning gays as a group. Again, in order to try to avoid perceivers' sensitivity to social desirability or normative pressure, we decided to pursue this aim by means of an unobtrusive measure of implicit attitude, namely a subliminal semantic prime paradigm.

Participants performed a lexical decision task and were subliminally presented with a prime, followed by a target stimulus requiring a word/nonword decision (Wittenbrink et al., 1997, 2001). Primes comprised two neutral category labels (e.g., *gay, homosexual*) and two derogatory labels (e.g., *fag, fairy*). Moreover, the target words included eight traits stereotypical of gays, eight counterstereotypical traits, and eight traits that were irrelevant to the group in question. Furthermore, half of the traits in each category were positive and half negative.

Since heterosexuals and homosexuals both hold an accurate and rather similar perception of the harmfulness of derogatory group labels concerning gays, one may hypothesize that participants, regardless of their sexual orientation, would react faster to positively valenced targets, but slower to negatively valenced targets, when following a neutral group label rather than a derogatory prime; however, since emotional reactions are more likely to emerge when an offense is directed at the ingroup members rather than the outgroup members, one could argue that this pattern of results would be displayed more strongly by homosexuals than by heterosexuals. Alternatively, for the reasons outlined earlier, any reference to the ingroup, even if of disparaging nature, may solicit a positive automatic reaction in the homosexual minority group.

Our data tend to support the latter hypothesis. Heterosexual participants were faster at reacting to positive targets when following a category prime rather than a derogatory prime, while no difference between primes was found on negative targets. In contrast, this interaction did not emerge among homosexual participants who, regardless of type of prime, displayed faster reaction times for positive than negative targets. Together, these two studies suggest distinct reactions at the implicit and the explicit level. At the explicit level, heterosexuals and homosexuals rate derogatory group levels approximately equally offensive, but their automatic reactions are quite distinct. Whereas heterosexuals are negatively affected by derogatory group labels (which tend to inhibit positive associations), homosexuals showed positive reactions to any label referring to the ingroup, be it a neutral, politically correct label or a disparaging label. This suggests, somewhat counterintuitively, that the use of derogatory terms may have more severe (automatic) consequences for members of the majority group that for those that are the target of the slur.

Do Derogatory Group Labels Make an Iintergroup Context More Salient than Neutral Category Labels?

The last question addressed in our research program was whether derogatory group labels may not only affect the perception of the specific target person or group, but also have more general implications for the way the situation is construed. In our opinion, a given derogatory label may well motivate people to reframe an individual into the prototypic instance of his or her social category, thereby mentally converting an interpersonal setting into an intergroup situation.

The current endeavor was guided by our conviction that the overhearing of derogatory group labels compared to neutral group labels could make intergroup concepts more cognitively available. Stated otherwise, we intended to verify whether the exposure to a derogatory group label, such as *fag*, would activate intergroup related concepts to a greater extent than the corresponding neutral category term (*gay*).

To test this hypothesis, we (Carnaghi & Maass, 2005) used a semantic priming paradigm in which a prime was subliminally presented, followed by a target stimulus requiring a word/no-word decision (Wittenbrink et al., 1997, 2001). Primes comprised two neutral labels (e.g., *gay* and *homosexual*) and two derogatory labels (e.g., *fag* and *fairy*). A pretest conducted on a small sample of the experimental population allowed us to include attributes as the target stimuli, that orthogonally varied in valence (positive vs. negative) as well as in their reference to intergroup context (relevant vs. irrelevant). For example, *cooperation* and *antagonism* denote, respectively, positive and negative terms referring to an intergroup context, whereas *holiday* and *vomit* represent positive and negative terms unrelated to group relations.

In support of our hypothesis, reaction times tended to be shorter for targets related to intergroup relations when following a derogatory rather than a category prime, whereas no difference between primes was found for targets that are irrelevant to the question of intergroup relations. In other words, the use of derogatory group labels, compared to category labels, appears to make intergroup related concepts much more accessible.

In this study we also analyzed whether participants' levels of Social Dominance Orientation (SDO) would moderate the just mentioned effect. Since individuals with high levels of SDO are particularly prone to perceive societies as a hierarchical group-based system (Pratto, Sidanius, Stallworth, & Malle, 2000; Sidanius & Pratto, 1999), we suspected that these individuals would be more responsive to the effects of derogatory group labels. This prediction is in line with a previous study by Pratto and Shih (2000) that tested the effect of intergroup labels on prejudice. These authors showed that the higher the salience of an intergroup context, the higher the likelihood for high SDO individuals to display *outgroup derogation* (e.g., salience of intergroup context ⇒ outgroup derogation). On the basis of these results, the current study intended to analyze the reverse causal relation, namely the effect of *derogatory outgroup labels* on the accessibility of intergroup related constructs (e.g., outgroup derogation ⇒ salience of intergroup context). Hence, we hypothesized that prejudice cues, such as derogatory group labels, would lead high, but not low SDO, participants to display greater accessibility of inter-group related constructs.

As can be seen in Fig. 6–1, participants with low levels of SDO reacted in similar ways to intergroup relevant and irrelevant targets, regardless of the type of prime they had been exposed to. In contrast, participants with high levels of SDO were much faster to react to intergroup-relevant targets when they followed a derogatory rather than a category prime. At the same time, they tended to react much slower to irrelevant targets when they followed a derogatory rather than a category prime. These results clearly suggest that individuals who chronically "support group-based hierarchy and the domination of inferior groups by superior groups" (Pratto et al., 2001) activated to a greater extent

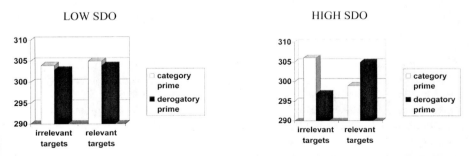

FIGURE 6–1. Response latency for terms relevant vs. irrelevant to intergroup relations as a function of neutral vs. derogatory primes and level of SDO in Carnaghi and Maass (2005b).

concepts related to the inter-group context when a prejudiced cue, such as a derogatory group label, was present in their environment.

CONCLUSION

Together, the findings of our research project suggest that ethno- or homo-phaulisms such as *nigger* or *fag* are by no means synonymous to their respective official terms *Black* or *homosexual*. Although previous research on explicit evaluations had observed no detrimental effects of disparaging group labels (Simon & Greenberg, 1996), our findings suggest that such discriminatory language exerts strong and reliable effects at the *automatic* level. Compared to neutral labels, derogatory group labels triggered more negative associations (Carnaghi et al., 2005), decreased the likelihood of approach-like motor reactions (Carnaghi & Maass, 2006), and activated semantically positive, but inhibited semantically negative content (Carnaghi et al., 2005). Importantly, the latter study also suggested that derogatory group labels tend to elicit more hostile, but no more stereotypical, thoughts about the target group. Thus, disparaging labels do not activate the stereotype any more than do neutral labels, nor do they specifically activate the negative subportion of the stereotype. In other words, the difference between neutral and derogatory labels lies exclusively in the valence of what comes to mind. An interesting question to be investigated by future studies deals with the moderating role of perceivers' (explicit) prejudice on the priming effects triggered by category and derogatory labels. Previous studies (Devine, 1989) on this issue have shown that participants, who had been primed with stereotypical (e.g., *athletic, lazy*) and derogatory (e.g., *nigger*) labels, ineluctably applied their stereotypical negative knowledge concerning African American to a member of this group. Importantly, this priming effect was found regardless the participants' levels of prejudice toward the group in question. In sharp contrast, Lepore and Brown (1997, 1999) showed that high- and low-prejudice participants primed with stereotypical and derogatory labels formed a comparably negative impression of a target person when immediately asked to judge a target but not when a time delay was interposed between the priming procedure and the judgment task. In this latter case, only high-prejudice participants still showed evidence for target stereotyping. Therefore, whereas stereotypical and derogatory labels make negative stereotypes temporarily accessible to both high- and low-prejudice individuals, negative stereotypical features keep on exerting their effects only for high-prejudice individuals, who likely have those features chronically activated. Given this state of affairs, it is theoretically and empirically important to test whether category labels, such as *gay*, automatically activate differently valenced representations of the group in people's mind as a function of their prejudice level, whereas derogatory labels, such as *fag*, may equally exert their deleterious effects on participants' affective reactions regardless of their explicit level of prejudice.

Another relevant issue to be investigated by future studies concerns the subsequent consequences for people's behaviors toward the target of the slur. Work by Simon and Greenberg (1996) suggests that people are able to engage in compensatory mechanisms that may mask their automatically activated negative reactions, yet we suspect that this is not always the case. Whereas some behaviors, such as expressing verbal evaluations, allow a great degree of intentional control, others, such as emitting nonverbal cues or managing interpersonal distance, may escape people's control and, hence, may well mirror the hostile reaction that is automatically activated by the derogatory label.

Importantly, our subsequent studies (Carnaghi & Maass, in press) also suggest that majority members are more strongly affected by derogatory language than those belonging to the group that is the target of the discriminatory language. This finding is somewhat counterintuitive, but becomes highly relevant when one considers that most disparaging speech takes place in within-majority discourse. In other words, derogatory labels seem to have their greatest impact exactly in the setting in which they are most likely to be used.

Finally, the last study (Carnaghi & Maass 2005) provides preliminary evidence that derogatory group labels may not only affect the way people feel about the target group and its members, but also how they construe the general setting. Indeed, these first results suggest that people exposed to derogatory group labels are more likely to conceive the situation in terms of intergroup relations. Although the exact processes remain to be investigated, one could hypothesize that derogatory group labels are likely to activate a specific and circumscribed subgroup of the outgroup as a whole. Therefore, compared to the (more general) category label, it is conceivable that a more specific and homogeneous [sub-]group representation of gays was elicited by the derogatory terms—namely, *fag*. If this was the case, it may also be possible that a variation in the participants' representation of their own group took place. In other words, the prime of a derogatory label could accentuate the intragroup similarity, both for the outgroup and the ingroup, and exacerbate the intergroup differentiation, thus increasing the salience of an intergroup context. Since the above reasoning relies on conjectural hypotheses, further research should address the effect of derogatory group labels both on the representation of the outgroup, which is the target of slur, and of the ingroup.

The fact that intergroup constructs became highly available in people's minds suggests that they are put in an intergroup mindset that is qualitatively different from that of people exposed to neutral labels. If supported by future research, this may have important implications as it opens the possibility that derogatory group labels have the power to trigger all the well-known psychological processes that are generally associated with intergroup settings.

Although our research is still in its initial stage, it suggests quite clearly that derogatory labels are much more influential than earlier work had suggested. Even though the effects may not always become apparent at an explicit, controlled level, derogatory labels seem to exert a hidden, yet powerful, influence that is reflected in greater hostility and in a greater propensity to construe the situation in terms of intergroup relations.

REFERENCES

Allen, I. L. (1983a). *The language of ethnic conflict: Social organization and lexical culture.* Columbia University Press: New York.

Allen, I. L. (1983b). Personal names that became ethnical epithets. *Names, 31*, 307–317.

Allen, I. L. (1984). Male sex roles and epithets for ethnic women in American slang. *Sex Roles, 11*, 43–50.

Carnaghi, A., & Maass, A. (2005). Category vs. derogatory group label and their effect on the activation of intergroup context. *Unpublished Manuscript.*

Carnaghi, A., & Maass, A. (2006). Effetti delle etichette denigratorie sulle risposte comportamentali [The effect of derogatory labels on behavioral responses]. *Psicologia Sociale, 1,* 121–132

Carnaghi, A., Maass, A. (in press). In-group and Out-group perspectives in the use of derogatory group label: gay vs. fag. *Journal of Language and Social Psychology.*

Carnaghi, A., Maass, A., Bianchi, M. B., Castelli, L., & Brentel, M. (2005). *Gay or fag? On the cognitive and affective consequences of derogatory group labels.* Manuscript submitted for publication.

Castelli, L., Arcuri, L., & Zogmaister, C. (2003). Perceiving ingroup members who use stereotypes: Implicit conformity and similarity. *European Journal of Social Psychology, 33*, 163–175.

Castelli, L., Zogmaister, C., Smith, E. R., & Arcuri, L. (2004). On the automatic evaluation of social exemplar. *Journal of Personality and Social Psychology, 86*, 373–387.

Crandall, C. S., Eshleman, A., & O'Brein, L. (2002). Social norms and suppression of prejudice: The struggle for internalization. *Journal of Personality and Social Psychology, 82*, 359–378.

Chen, M., & Bargh, J. A. (1999). Consequences of automatic evaluation: Immediate behavioral predispositions to approach or avoid the stimulus. *Personality and Social Psychology Bulletin, 25*, 215–224.

Devine, P. G. (1989). Stereotypes and prejudice: Their automatic and controlled components. *Journal of Personality and Social Psychology, 56*, 5–18.

Devine, P. G., & Baker, S. M. (1991). Measurement of racial stereotype subtyping. *Personality and Social Psychology Bulletin, 17*, 44–50.

Duckworth, K. L., Bargh, J. A., Garcia, M., & Chaiken, S. (2002). The automatic evaluation of novel stimuli. *Psychological Science, 13*, 513–519.

Dumont, M., Yzerbyt, V. Y., Wigboldus, D., & Gordijn, E. H. (2003). Social categorization and free reactions to the September 11th terrorist attacks. *Personality and Social Psychology Bulletin, 29*, 1509–20.

Giles, H. (1977). *Language and ethnic relations.* New Tork: Accademic Press.

Greenberg, J., & Pyszczynski, T. (1985). The effect of overheard ethnic slur on evaluations of the target: How to spread a social disease. *Journal of Experimental Social Psychology, 21*, 61–72.

Graumann, C. F. (1995). Discriminatory discourse. *Pattern of Prejudice, 29*, 69–83.

Hornsey, M. J., Trembath, M., & Gunthorpe, S. (2004). 'You can criticize because you care': Identity attachment, constructiveness, and the intergroup sensitivity effect. *European Journal of Social Psychology, 34*, 499–518.

Kennedy, K. (2002). *Nigger. The strange career of a troublesome word.* New York: Pantheon Books.

Kirkland, S. L., Greenberg, J., & Pyszczynski, T. (1987). Further evidence of the deleterious effects of overheard derogatory ethnic labels: Derogation beyond the target. *Personality and Social Psychology Bulletin, 13*, 216–227.
Lambert, A. J., Payne, B. K., Jacoby, L. L., Shaffer, L. M., Chasteen, A. L., & Khan, S. R.
(2003). Stereotypes as dominant responses: On the "social facilitation" of prejudice in anticipated public contexts. *Journal of Personality and Social Psychology, 84*,
277–295.
Lepore, L., & Brown, R. (1997). Category activation and stereotype accessibility: Is prejudice inevitable? *Journal of Personality and Social Psychology, 72*, 275–287.
Lepore, L., & Brown, R. (1999). Exploring automatic stereotype activation: A challenge
to the inevitability of prejudice. In D. Abrams & M. Hogg (Eds.), *Social Identity
and Social Cognition*. Oxford: Blackwell Publisher.
Mullen, B., & Johnson, C. (1993). Cognitive representation in ethnophaulisms as a
function of group size: the phenomenology of being in a group. *Personality and
Social Psychology Bulletin, 19*, 296–304.
Mullen, B., & Johnson, C. (1995). Cognitive representation in ethnophaulisms and
illusory correlation in stereotyping. *Personality and Social Psychology Bulletin, 21*,
420–433.
Mullen, B., Rozell, D., & Johnson, C. (2000). Ethnophaulisms for ethnic immigrant
groups: Cognitive representation of 'the Minority' and 'The Foreigner.' *Group
Processes and Intergroup Relations, 3*, 5–24.
Mullen, B., Rozell D., & Johnson, C. (2001). Ethnophaulisms for ethnic immigrant
groups: The contributions of group size and familiarity. *European Journal of Social
Psychology, 31*, 231–246.
Pratto, F., & Shih, M. (2000). Social dominance orientation and group context in
implicit group prejudice. *Psychological Science, 11*, 515–518.
Pratto, F., Sidanius, J., Stallworth, L. M., & Malle, B. F. (2001). Social dominance ori-
entation: A personality variable predicting social and political attitudes. In
D. Abrams & M. A. Hogg (Eds.), *Intergroup relations: Essential readings* (pp. 30–59).
New York: Psychology Press.
Sidanius, J., & Pratto, F. (1999). Social dominance: An intergroup theory of social hier-
archy and oppression. New York: Cambridge University Press.
Simon, L., & Greenberg, J. (1996). Further progress in understanding the effects of
derogatory ethnic labels: The role of preexisting attitudes toward the targeted
group. *Personality and Social Psychology Bulletin, 12*, 1195–1204.
Smith, E. R. (1999). Affective and cognitive implications of a group becoming a part
of the self: New models of prejudice and of the self-concept. In D. Abrams & M. A.
Hogg (Eds.), *Social identity and social cognition* (pp.183–196). Malden: Blackwell
Publishers
Solarz, A. (1960). Latency of instrumental responses as a function of compatibility
with the meaning of eliciting verbal signs. *Journal of Experimental Psychology, 59*,
239–245.
Van Dijk, T. A. (1987). *Communicating racism: Ethnic prejudice in thought and talk*. Thousand Oaks: Sage Publications,
Vaes, J., Paladino, M. P., Castelli, L., & Leyens, J. P. (2003). On the behavioral consequences of infrahumanization: The implicit role of uniquely human emotions in intergroup relations. *Journal of Personality and Social Psychology, 85*,
1016–1034.
Wentura, D., Rothermund, K., & Bak, P. (2000). Automatic vigilance: The attention-
grabbing power of approach- and avoidance-related social information. *Journal of
Personality and Social Psychology, 78*, 1024–1037.
Wilson, C. C., & Gutierrez, F. F. (1985). *Race, multiculturalism, and the media: From mass
to class communication*. Thousand Oaks: Sage Publications.

Wittenbrink, B., Judd, C. M., & Park, B. (1997). Evidence for racial prejudice at the implicit level and its relationship with questionnaire measures. *Journal of Personality and Social Psychology, 72,* 262–274.

Wittenbrink, B., Judd, C. M., & Park, B. (2001). Evaluative versus conceptual judgment in automatic stereotyping and prejudice. *Journal of Experimental Social Psychology, 37,* 244–252.

Yzerbyt, V. Y., Dumont, M., Wigboldus, D., & Gordijn, H. E. (2003). I feel for us: The impact of categorization and identification on emotions and action tendencies. *British Journal of Social Psychology, 42,* 533–549.

Chapter 7

Dynamics of Sex-Role Stereotypes

Sabine Sczesny and Janine Bosak
University of Bern, Switzerland

Amanda B. Diekman
Miami University

Jean M. Twenge
San Diego State University

Differences between men and women have gained much attention, particularly in the popular media. Following the *differences hypothesis*, women and men are expected to be significantly different psychologically. In contrast, following the *similarities hypothesis*, women and men are expected to be similar on most psychological variables. Results from a recent review of 46 meta-analyses by Hyde (2005) support the gender-similarities hypothesis. Nevertheless, research has consistently demonstrated the remarkably different beliefs that people hold about men and women. In these group stereotypes men are believed to be more agentic, e.g., competitive and individualistic, whereas women are assumed to be more expressive and communal, e.g., kind and nurturing (e.g., Diekman & Eagly, 2000). People's highly elaborated set of associations concerning men and women appears to be cross-culturally valid (Best & Thomas, 2003; Williams & Best, 1990a). In addition, gender differences also exist in self-perception (e.g., Costa, Terracciano, & McCrae, 2001). Men describe themselves as more agentic than women, whereas women see themselves as higher in communion than men (e.g., Bem, 1974; Spence & Buckner, 2000).

Moreover, gender stereotypes are not only beliefs about the attributes, roles, and behaviors that characterize men and women in terms of *descriptive norms*; they also include consensual expectations about the qualities that men and women ought to have or ideally would posses in terms of *prescriptive norms* (e.g., Burgess & Borgida, 1999; Cialdini & Trost, 1998; Prentice & Carranza, 2002). Research on expectations that perceivers share about the ideal men and women (e.g., Spence & Helmreich, 1978; Williams & Best, 1990b) or the beliefs that men and women hold about their ideal selves (Wood, Christensen, Hebl, & Rothgerber, 1997) supports the assumption that people approve that women are communal and men are agentic.

From a socio-cultural perspective, the characteristics ascribed to men and women are related to the social roles that members of each sex occupy. Specifically, social role theory (Eagly, 1987; Eagly, Wood, & Diekman, 2000) maintains that gender stereotype contents are derived from observations of women and men in sex-typical domestic and occupational roles. Consistent with the principle of correspondence bias (Gilbert, 1998; Gilbert & Malone, 1995), social perceivers infer that there is a correspondence between the behaviors people are engaged in and their psychological characteristics. Thus, the assertive, task-oriented behaviors required by men's typical occupations and authority roles favor inferences that men are especially agentic. Similarly, the person-oriented, nurturing behavior required by women in their female-typical occupations, domestic roles, or child care roles may lead people to reason that women possess communal characteristics (e.g., Eagly & Steffen, 1984). Moreover, the descriptive aspect of gender stereotypes that follows from perceivers' correspondent inferences might foster prescriptive norms for men and women. For example, Hall and Carter (1999) found that as behaviors are predominantly performed by one sex in actuality (as assessed by meta-analytic data), people also judge these behaviors increasingly appropriate for one sex only. These stereotypical expectancies are especially powerful in that they affect men's and women's self-perceptions and behavior (e.g., Snyder, 1981). Behavioral confirmation of other people's sex-stereotypical expectancies (see the review by Geis, 1993) and individual's self-regulatory processes (e.g., Wood et al., 1977) might contribute to men's and women's sex-stereotypical self-concepts and behavior. As a growing body of evidence suggests, personality traits change along with societies. For example, as American society has grown less conformist, the need for social approval has decreased (Twenge & Im, in press), and self-esteem has risen as self-focus is encouraged from childhood (Twenge & Campbell, 2001; for a review, see Twenge, 2006). Furthermore, as modern life became more isolating and challenging, anxiety and depression increased (Klerman & Weissman, 1989; Lewinsohn, Rohde, Seeley, & Fischer, 1993; Twenge, 2000).

Thus, *beliefs about women's and men's characteristics* are assumed to be related to how the group has been or will be positioned in the social structure over time; analogously, *sex-stereotyped personality traits of women and men* are likely to change along with their societal roles (Eagly, 1987). Men and women are trained for different roles in life and then move on to perform those roles; thus, when their roles change, so should gender-role attitudes and the expectations for girls and boys.

In general, stereotypical beliefs about men and women might not only stem from differences in actually observed role behavior, but also from interpersonal communication and the mass media. People as well as the media communicate sex-stereotypical expectations with regard to gender-appropriate behavior and roles for men and women (e.g., Deaux & Kite, 1993) and this might lead individuals to confirm these expectations (for behavioral confirmation, see Geis, 1993). Moreover, when talking about role occupants, people tend to explain or even rationalize the role distribution in conversation, and this may amplify gender stereotypes based on the role distribution. For example, Hoffman and Hurst (1990) provided participants with descriptions of two fictitious groups that were portrayed as either child-raisers or city-workers. When asked to discuss a possible explanation for the observed role distribution participants often referred to personality differences of such group members that ". . . might occupy the particular roles that they do, due to their personalities. . . . Patient, kind, understanding, etc., would be characteristics you would want in a child-raiser, and a city-worker you would wish to be determined, energetic, etc." (p. 202). In sum, communication plays an important role in providing people with information about the differing roles of men and women and its underlying rationales. Communication thus contributes to the maintenance and dynamics of sex-role stereotypes.

CHANGE AND STABILITY IN THE SOCIAL ROLES OF MEN AND WOMEN

In many Western societies, the positions of men and women have shown divergent trends since the mid-20th century. In short, women's roles have shown greater change than those of men, particularly in women's entry into male-dominated roles. To exemplify these changes in Western societies, we refer to information on the United States.

In the United States, 32.7% of all women participated in the workforce in 1948. Since then, women's participation has increased to 59.2% in 2004 (U.S. Department of Labor, 2005), and this trend is expected to continue in the future (Fullerton, 1999). Women have also entered other formerly male-dominated roles, including academia (Kite et al., 2001), and are increasingly choosing majors such as business, medicine, and law (Astin, Oseguera, Sax, & Korn, 2002). The changes of women's status over the 20th century in the United States have been curvilinear rather than linear, as illustrated by the following data (see Twenge, 2001, for details):

> Women's status increased prior to and during World War II, decreased postwar, and then increased after the late 1960s. For example, women's age at first marriage was actually higher in 1940 (21.5 years) than 1960 (20.3 years);

Women did not marry on average at 21.5 years of age again until 1979. Thus women married younger in 1978 than in 1940, indicating that the change in women's status was not linear. Despite the image of Free Love Baby Boomers, women in the 1970s married very young by historical standards. By 2000, however, the median age at first marriage for women was 25—an all-time high. The number of college degrees earned by women also followed a curvilinear pattern (U.S. Bureau of Census, 1925–2005) as illustrated in Fig. 7–1. In 1920, 34% of college degrees went to women; 40% in 1930; 41% in 1940; 32% in 1952; and 35% in 1960. The percentage of college degrees awarded to women does not reach the 1940 number of 41% again until 1965. Thus, a smaller percentage of college degrees was awarded to women during the 1950s and early 1960s than during the 1930s. By the late 1980s women earned the majority of college degrees (57% in 2005). This pattern also appears in the percentage of doctorates granted to women, which was 15% in 1930 but dropped to 9% by 1955. It did not reach the 1930 figure of 15% again until 1972. Thus women earned a higher percentage of doctorates in 1930 than they did in 1970. By 2003, women earned 48% of doctorates, demonstrating the rapid pace of change over 30 years. Furthermore, we can observe a rise of female leaders in the United States in the last decades: The proportion of female managers has risen

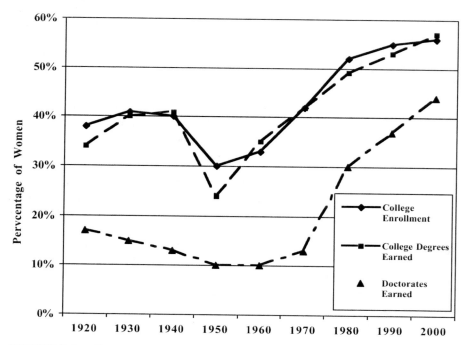

FIGURE 7–1. Percentage of Enrollment and Degrees Earned by Women in the United States from 1920 to Now in Decades.

from only 18% in 1972 to 46% in 2001 (U.S. Bureau of Labor Statistics, 1982, 2002).[1]

However, some aspects of women's roles show stability. Most prominent is women's retention of primary responsibility for caretaking roles. Women are more likely than men to care for children or elderly parents (Cancian & Olinker, 2000). Time-diary data that compared women's time use from 1965 to 1998 showed that women maintained similar amounts of time with children as a primary activity (Bianchi, 2000). Moreover, when women do enter the paid labor force, they often work in jobs that involve caretaking or communal characteristics to some extent (e.g., nurse) (Cejka & Eagly, 1999). Finally, only few women hold powerful positions with high levels of authority in the workplace. For example, women are still a rarity in top management positions of the Fortune 500 companies, holding only 1% of Chief Executive Officer (CEO) positions (Catalyst, 2002).

Men's roles in the United States have shown more stability over this period of time. Men's participation rate in the paid labor force has declined only slightly over the 20th century: in 1948 86.6% of all men were employed in the labor force, in 2004 73.3% (U.S. Department of Labor, 2005). Men's reports of time allocation also reflect less time with children (as a primary activity) than do women's (Bianchi, 2000). Although men increased their time with children from 1965 to 1998, women's time with children continued to be greater. Men's largest increase was for time spent with children in any activity, which rose from 2.8 to 3.8 hours per day; in contrast, women's time with children in any activity remained stable at 5.3 to 5.5 hours per day.

PRESENT RESEARCH QUESTIONS

The aim of this chapter is to contribute to answering the following three questions by reviewing some of our own research: (a) Are such socio-cultural changes in fact accompanied by perceptions of changes in the stereotypes of men and women? (see section "Dynamic Gender Stereotypes"). (b) Do women's and men's personalities actually change along with societies? (see section "Changes in Sex-Stereotyped Personality Traits over Time"), and (c) Do changes in the social roles of women and men correspond to changes in sex-stereotypic beliefs

---

[1]In general, it is important to note that these percentages have to be interpreted carefully as the reference set is not always provided or clear. For example, output-bound statistics such as the finding that the number of female managers has risen from only 18% in 1972 to 46% in 2001 in the United States is not related in the statistics to the numbers/percentages of male and female competitors for leadership roles. Such statistics are very rare (as an example for such data sets: see the statistics for medical school admission, Association of American Medical Colleges, 2004).

about female and male leaders and to changes in their leadership-specific personality traits (see section "Changes in Sex-Role Stereotyping of Leadership").

DYNAMIC GENDER STEREOTYPES

Although most work on stereotypes focuses on the ways in which they restrict social change, evidence suggests that people's beliefs about groups can also include visions of change from the group's past to the future. These beliefs about change have been termed *dynamic stereotypes* (Diekman & Eagly, 2000). Thus, stereotypes do not solely focus on a group's present-day characteristics, but they might include beliefs about the group's past or future characteristics as well. Since the roles of women in particular have changed in recent decades in Western societies, as previously noted, gender groups are especially useful for exploring dynamic stereotypes.

On the basis of this actual change and stability in roles over time, beliefs about women were predicted to be more dynamic, whereas beliefs about men were expected to be more stable (e.g., Diekman & Eagly, 2000; Diekman, Goodfriend, & Goodwin, 2004). Based on the changes in their roles just described, women were expected to be perceived as gaining male-stereotypic traits from the past to the future, while retaining their high levels of female-stereotypic traits. In addition, men were expected to be perceived as retaining their relatively high levels of male-stereotypic traits and lower levels of female-stereotypic traits from the past to the future.

Evidence for Dynamic Stereotypes

To investigate these predictions, participants' beliefs about men and women of different time periods were examined. In the typical procedure (e.g., Diekman & Eagly, 2000), participants are asked to consider the average man or the average woman in a specified time period (e.g., 1950, 2050). For beliefs about the present day, no time period is specified. Participants then rate the target individual's likelihood of possessing different characteristics. For example, in the initial studies participants rated the target individual's likelihood of possessing each of several traits, which reflected six dimensions of gender stereotypes (Cejka & Eagly, 1999): (a) masculine personality, (b) masculine cognitive, (c) masculine physical, (d) feminine personality, (e) feminine cognitive, and (f) feminine physical. Finally, participants estimate the distribution of men and women into different domestic and occupational roles (e.g., homemaker, lawyer) in their specified time period. These role estimates comprise a measure of *societal role nontraditionalism* that reflects the percentage of roles occupied by the nontraditional sex (e.g., female auto mechanics, men who care for children).

Findings across several studies have upheld the prediction that beliefs about women in particular are dynamic (Diekman & Eagly, 2000). This pattern is illustrated in Fig. 7–2. In general, people believe that women have increased and will continue to increase in their male-stereotypic characteristics. Women are also expected to retain a high level of female-stereotypic characteristics from the past to the future. In contrast to the perceived dynamism of women, men are generally projected to remain stable in their higher levels of male-

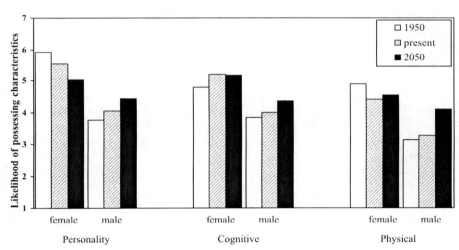

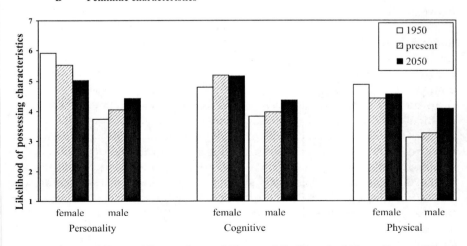

FIGURE 7–2. Effects of Target Sex and Year on Likelihood of Masculine and Feminine Characteristics (Data are from Diekman & Eagly, 2000, Experiment 1).

stereotypic characteristics and lower levels of female-stereotypic characteristics. Although college student samples sometimes predict an increase in men's feminine sex-typed personality traits over time, data collected from adult samples reflect a projection of stability.

Social role theory predicts that to the extent that individuals occupy the same social structure and perceive that structure similarly, their beliefs about men and women should be fairly consensual. Upholding this prediction, these basic findings—that people perceive women as adopting counter-stereotypic traits to a greater extent than men are—have been replicated across a wide range of participant characteristics. Similar patterns have been found for male and female participants, older and younger adults, and private versus public university students (Diekman & Eagly, 2000). In addition, participant characteristics such as ethnicity, political orientation, or religious attendance have shown no systematic effects on their stereotypic beliefs (Diekman, Goodfriend, & Evans, 2005).

A critical prediction of the social-role perspective is that these dynamic stereotypes are rooted in projections about the social structure, rather than general optimism on the part of participants. Certainly, the projection of women's greater assumption of highly valued agentic traits might reflect mere optimism about the future. A test of this optimism explanation was carried out by asking participants to rate past, present, or future men or women's negative gender stereotypic traits, including negative masculine sex-typed personality attributes (e.g., egotistical, aggressive) and negative female-stereotypic attributes (e.g., whiny, gullible) (Spence, Helmreich, & Holahan, 1979). Consistent with social-role predictions and inconsistent with the optimism prediction, individuals projected women to increase in their negative as well as their positive masculine characteristics (Diekman & Eagly, 2000; Diekman et al., 2004). In addition, more detailed analysis of the negative femininity ratings revealed different patterns of change for the unmitigated communion versus verbal passive-aggression components of negative femininity. Participants projected a decline in women's tendency to show unmitigated communion, but an increase in their tendency to show verbal passive aggression (Diekman et al., 2004).

In addition to personality traits, other aspects of women and men's characteristics have also revealed projections of change and stability over time. Beliefs about women's power also reflect dynamism: Women, more than men, were projected to have gained and continue to gain in individual, occupational, economic, political, and relational power from the past to the future (Diekman et al., 2004). However, these projections were also tempered with some realism: The highest ratings of future power were reported for individual and relational power, rather than the more structural elements of power. Beliefs about men and women's commitment to marriage relationships also show dynamism over time (Goodfriend, Diekman, & Truax, 2006). Consistent with the investment model (Rusbult, Martz, & Agnew, 1998), as women's perceived role nontraditionalism increased from the past to the future, participants projected that women had more alternatives regarding relationships, less satisfaction, less investment, and less commitment to marital relationships. In contrast, these variables were perceived as more stable for men.

The Basis of Dynamic Stereotypes in Social Roles

Various forms of evidence support the social role theory prediction that dynamic stereotypes are based in beliefs about the distribution of men and women into social roles. First, several studies have used path analyses to demonstrate that the relationship between year and women's adoption of male-stereotypic characteristics is mediated by perceived role nontraditionalism (Diekman & Eagly, 2000; Diekman et al., 2004) as illustrated in Fig. 7–3. As individuals perceive the division of labor to become more gender-equal, they perceive women to adopt more male-stereotypic characteristics (see also section "Changes in Sex-Role Stereotypes of Leadership").

Experimental findings also contribute to the body of evidence pointing to the basis of dynamic stereotypes in social roles. In one study (Diekman & Eagly, 2000, Experiment 5), participants were asked to imagine a particular division of labor in the future: a traditional division of labor, an equal division of labor, or a division of labor similar to that of today. As expected, participants in the gender-equal condition were most likely to project individuals to have counter-stereotypic characteristics. In contrast, participants in the traditional condition were least likely to project individuals to have counter-stereotypic characteristics.

In another experiment (Diekman & Goodfriend, 2006, Experiment 3), participants read a brief scenario about roles in a novel society. This scenario de-

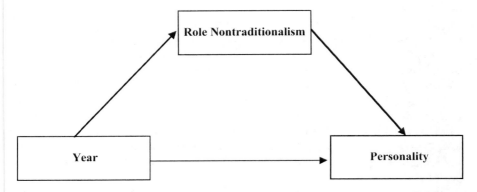

FIGURE 7–3. Mediation of the Relationship between Year and Adoption of Gender-Stereotypic Personality Characteristics by Perceived Role Traditionalism.

scribed how the government of this society had initiated programs to move the economy in a particular direction. Participants were randomly assigned to read about a government that encouraged either a business competition system or a caretaking system. Afterwards, participants rated the extent to which either agentic or communal traits would be prevalent in the population in 15 years, as well as how useful, or valuable these traits would be. As predicted, participants in the caretaking condition inferred that communion was more prevalent, useful, and valuable; likewise, participants in the business-competition condition inferred that agency was more prevalent, useful and valuable. In addition, evidence for proscriptive stereotypes also emerged: In the caretaking condition, agentic characteristics were perceived as less prevalent, useful, and valuable, and in the business competition condition, communal characteristics were perceived as less prevalent, useful, and valuable.

Another vein of evidence providing support for the basis of dynamic stereotypes in social roles comes from cross-cultural data. Dynamic stereotypes are predicted to correspond to the profile of role change that has occurred within the local national context. Thus, to the extent that countries experience different role change, the dynamic stereotypes should vary across countries. These hypotheses were investigated in studies that compared data from the United States to data from Latin America (Diekman, Eagly, Mladinic, & Ferreira, 2005) and from Germany (Wilde & Diekman, 2005). In Latin America, role changes for women have been similar to those in the United States: Over recent decades, women have increasingly assumed formerly male-dominated roles. However, other important social transitions for citizens of Brazil and Chile have been the transition from an agrarian society to a capitalist society, and the transition from dictatorship to democracy. These transitions likely foster male-stereotypic traits, such as independence and agency, that are more positively valued in capitalistic and democratic societies relative to communal, agrarian societies (e.g., Bellah et al., 1996; Hernandez & Iyengar, 2001). Because these transitions affect both male and female citizens, any changes in related traits would be expected to apply to both male and female individuals. Comparisons between the United States and Latin American countries (Diekman, Eagly, et al., 2005) found both similarities and differences in dynamic stereotypes. Similar to the United States, participants in Brazil and Chile predicted women to adopt male-stereotyped traits over time. In contrast to the United States, Latin American participants also projected men to adopt higher levels of masculine personality and cognitive characteristics over time, whereas in the United States, participants projected stability for men. As noted above, this projected increase in male-stereotypic qualities for both sexes is due to the fact that in Chile and Brazil, men as well as women have experienced role transitions.

An investigation of dynamic stereotypes in Germany also revealed theoretically meaningful differences within an overall context of similarity (Wilde & Diekman, 2005). Like women in the United States, German women have experienced rapid role change since World War II; thus, they were predicted to increase in their male-stereotypic characteristics. However, the roles of German and United States women also diverged in the period immediately after the war. Although the post-World War II period in the United States was an extremely prosperous time that marked a return to gender conventionality, this period was much more difficult in Germany. The population had a relative decrease in the male-female ratio because of the devastation of the war, and thus women had to assume male-typical roles. As a consequence, dynamic stereotypes of women in these two countries showed similarity in the present and future, but differences in the past. Consistent with their different roles, women of the past in Germany were perceived as more likely to possess positive masculine personality traits (e.g., courageous, daring) than their U.S. counterparts. In addition, they were ascribed with lower levels of feminine physical traits (e.g., beautiful, pretty), which aligns with the physical nature of their roles, and higher levels of negative feminine personality characteristics (e.g., whiny, complaining), perhaps because of their dissatisfaction in the postwar period.

Altogether the present research demonstrates that perceivers believe the attributes of women in particular to be dynamic. Survey data, experimental findings, and results from cross-cultural studies show a high consensus in that the stereotype of women is particularly dynamic, with women being perceived as increasing in masculine personality traits. In contrast, the stereotype content of men was projected to be relatively stable across time, with men retaining their masculine qualities and only slightly increasing in feminine traits. Moreover, consistent with the social role theory, perceptions of change appear to be rooted in people's observations of changes in the social roles, that is, an increase of women in formerly male-dominated roles. Change in social roles can thus lead perceivers to believe that the personality of women adapts to their new roles.

CHANGES IN SEX-STEREOTYPED
PERSONALITY TRAITS OVER TIME

In the following section, we will address the question of whether men's and women's sex-stereotyped personality traits change in correspondence with shifts in their social roles. In the United States, more girls have grown up with working mothers as role models since the 1970s, which leads to girls' higher scores on measures of stereotypically masculine traits (Gilroy, Talierco, & Steinbacher, 1981). The anticipation of work roles may lead to more agentic traits as well, because employed women are higher in these traits (e.g., Clarey & Sanford, 1982; Wertheim, Widom, & Wortzel, 1978). More girls have also participated in sports over the last few decades, which is also linked to higher scores on measures of stereotypically masculine traits (Butcher, 1989; Fletcher, 1971). Overall, the striking changes in women's status and roles over the century suggest that women's traits might show substantial birth cohort differences. Based on the U.S.-data presented above (which show a curvilinear pattern between the 1930s and the 1990s), women's traits should become more "masculine" or agentic between the 1930s and the 1940s, less agentic during the postwar years, and more agentic again after the late 1960s. In contrast, since men's roles have not undergone such radical shifts as women's roles, men's traits are projected to stay relatively stable.

Evidence for Changes in Sex-Stereotyped Personality Traits

In order to investigate whether the influence of social change in men's and women's sex-stereotyped traits over the 20th century applies to sex-stereotypical traits, Twenge used a method called *cross-temporal metaanalysis* in two studies (Twenge, 1997, 2001). In such metaanalyses, the main statistic is the correlation between the mean scores and the year in which the data were collected. A significant positive correlation means that a trait has increased over time, while a significant negative correlation means that a trait has decreased over time. The percentage of variance explained by birth cohort can be determined using the regression equation,[2] calculating the difference between the scores at the earliest and latest year and using the average standard deviation reported for individual samples. Means on measures can also be matched with social indicators (e.g., the median age at first marriage for women, the percentage of college degrees going to women) from the corresponding years to determine how the trait covaries with aspects of the social environment.

For both studies described here, a database search was conducted and articles were located that report mean scores from personality scales that had been used over several decades. The analyses included five measures of assertiveness/dominance (the Bernreuter Dominance Scale, the dominance scale from the California Psychological Inventory, nDom from the Edwards Personal Preference Scale, the College Self-Expression Scale, and the Rathus Assertiveness Schedule) and two measures of sex-stereotypical traits (the Bem Sex-Role Inventory and the Personal Attributes Questionnaire). Data of samples from the United States were analyzed, since most findings located came from the United States: The data on assertiveness and dominance (one type of "masculine" trait) are available from the 1930s to the 1990s (Twenge, 2001), and the data on sex-stereotyped traits ("masculine" and "feminine" traits) is available from the early 1970s to the 1990s (Twenge, 1997).

---

[2]This is more accurate than estimating the variance from the correlation. Because the datapoints come from samples instead of individuals, the correlations are stronger than they would be if all individuals from the samples were included. Using the regression equation avoids committing this "ecological fallacy" for the variance estimate.

Changes in Assertiveness

Twenge (2001) examined changes in men's and women's assertiveness on the five scales (including data from more than 52,000 students). The results showed that college women's assertiveness followed the same pattern as their status and roles: it increased between the 1930s and World War II, decreased postwar, and increased again after the late 1960s. This pattern replicated in samples of high-school girls as well. Within each era, the shifts in assertiveness averaged .44 standard deviations; overall, birth cohort explained about 14% of the variance in women's assertiveness. Women's assertiveness scores were correlated with historical statistics matched for each year, including median age at first marriage, labor force participation, and educational attainment. In contrast, college men's scores on assertiveness did not show significant birth cohort changes (though men's scores on the College Self-Expression Scale did increase from 1968 to 1993). During the most recent time period, sex differences in assertiveness decreased from a male advantage of .40 standard deviations in 1968 to no difference $= -.07$ standard deviations in 1993. Thus assertiveness, once a solid sex difference favoring men, is now a personality trait with no discernible differences between men and women. Thus, as women's roles have changed, their personalities have reflected the traits needed for these new roles (Eagly, 1987).

Further Changes in Sex-Stereotyped Traits

The Bem Sex-Role Inventory and the Personal Attributes Questionnaire, both written in the early 1970s, measure personality traits that have historically been stereotyped as "masculine" or "feminine." Cross-temporal metaanalysis on both of these scales were performed, with data from 1973 through 1994 (including data from more than 28,000 individuals) (Twenge, 1997).

Women's scores on agency/masculinity (both the BSRI-M and PAQ-M) increased significantly over time. The change was so linear that the correlation between women's BSRI-M scores and the year of data collection was .73. The magnitude of the change was also large: .80 SDs on the BSRI-M, about 14% of the variance (similar to the variance explained by birth cohort in assertiveness scores). The sex difference on both masculinity measures also decreased over time, showing that men's and women's scores on stereotypically masculine traits grew more similar as time passed in the 1970s, 1980s, and 1990s. There were no significant changes in communion/femininity for women on either scale (although women's PAQ-F scores show a positive, though not significant, correlation with year). Thus young women strongly increased their self-endorsement of stereotypically masculine traits between the 1970s and the 1990s, without any decrease in their endorsement of stereotypically feminine traits. This nicely mirrors the social change in women's roles during this era, when women entered higher education and work roles in striking numbers, yet did not significantly alter their home and parenting roles. Changes in men's sex-stereotyped traits were inconsistent between the two measures. Men endorsed significantly more stereotypically feminine traits and more stereotypically masculine traits with time on the BSRI, but not on the PAQ.

Taken together, the present research illustrates that men's and women's personalities actually change in accordance with the social roles that they occupy in society. In particular, the data reflect that women's scores on masculine sex-typed traits (such as assertiveness) correspond with their new roles. Corresponding to the stability of the social roles occupied by men, hardly any remarkable changes in their self-reported personality traits were observed. Women's and girl's sex-stereotypical traits have varied over time, apparently in response to their roles in society. Women's assertiveness rose during eras when their status was increasing, such as before World War II and after the late 1960s. When their status was decreasing after World War II, their assertiveness also decreased. The striking upswing in women's and girls' sports participation, education, and work roles after the early 1970s led to an equally striking change in women's personalities. Women are now just as assertive as men, and score very similar to men on measures of so-called masculine traits. "Masculine" traits like dominance and assertiveness now show so few sex differences that they have clearly outlived their label. Thus, social change does not only affect people's beliefs about the sexes but also becomes internalized in women's self-perceptions of personality traits.

CHANGES IN SEX-ROLE STEREOTYPING OF LEADERSHIP

The attribution of leadership abilities is one domain in which sex stereotypes were shown to be particularly influential (Heilman, 2001; Sczesny, & Kühnen, 2004).) Traits attributed to managers elicited a significantly higher correlation with the description of a typical man than with the description of a typical woman. This think-manager-think-male stereotype was confirmed in many studies in the last decades (Powell, Butterfield, & Parent, 2002; Schein, 1973, 1975; Willemsen, 2002).

Recent research by Sczesny, Bosak, and colleagues assessed whether changes in the social roles of women and men within societies (see section "Change and Stability in the Social Roles of Men and Women") correspond to changes in sex-stereotypic beliefs about women and men in leadership roles and in their leadership-specific personality traits (Sczesny, 2003a; 2003b; Sczesny, Bosak, Neff, & Schyns, 2004; Sczesny, 2005). The authors expected that when the distribution of women and men into roles within a society is similar (with respect to gender equality and leadership participation; e.g., Wirth, 2001) and work-related values are less masculine-typed (e.g., Hofstede, 1998), no or small/modest differences between female leaders and leaders-in-general (e.g., no gender specification) should be observable. When the sex distribution within a society is more in line with traditional sex-role stereotypes, however, larger differences between female leaders and leaders-in-general should be observable.

Analogously, in societies in which the gender equality is higher and/or work-related values are more masculine typed, women are expected to describe themselves as similarly agentic as men. The fact that women perform most of caretaking and nurturing roles—at home and in the workforce—in most societies should correspond with higher levels of communion among women compared to men. Since typical roles for men (e.g., breadwinner, authority roles) promote agentic qualities and men have not acquired feminine sex-typed roles to the same extent as women have entered male-dominated occupations in most societies, men are expected to ascribe high levels of agency and low levels of communion to themselves.

Evidence for Changes in Sex Stereotypes of Leadership

Sczesny and colleagues investigated such cultural variations of sex-role stereotyping of leadership (Sczesny, 2003a, 2003b; Sczesny et al., 2004; the studies included data of 900 participants). They studied samples from Australia, Germany, and India (business students and executives). The selection of these countries was based on several indicators[3] (for details see Sczesny et al., 2004). Participant's task was to estimate the percentage to which one of three stimulus groups, that is, (a) executives in general (no gender specification), (b) male executives, or (c) female executives, possesses communal, person-oriented and agentic, task-oriented leadership-specific personality traits.[4] Descriptive norms were measured by asking what percentage of all executives in general (female executives/male executives) possess this characteristic. Participants also rated the importance of these characteristics for the respective stimulus group. Prescriptive norms were measured by asking about the importance of each

---

[3]Australia and Germany seem to be quite similar regarding their achieved high gender equality compared to India (see the gender-related development index and the gender empowerment measure; Wirth, 2001, reporting data of the Human Development Report of the United Nations of 1999). Despite this fact, Australia and Germany differ with respect to values relevant in the context of work (see Hofstede, 1998). Based on these indicators, Germany and Australia are similar regarding gender equality and leadership participation: Both countries show a less different distribution of women and men into social roles than India. Australia and India are similar in their lesser masculinity of work-related values compared to Germany.

[4]Such leadership characteristics are associated with gender stereotypes (Cann & Siegfried, 1990): a 'masculine typed' task-oriented dimension (initiating structure) and a 'feminine typed' person-oriented dimension (consideration). Person-oriented traits are, for example, dependable and just. Task-oriented traits are, for example, decisive and planning ahead.

characteristic to the role of the executive (female executive/male executive). Furthermore, other groups of participants described themselves on the two types of traits and their importance for themselves. In these self-description groups, participants indicated whether they possessed the given characteristics or not and how important the characteristics were to them.

Perception of Leadership Traits

A better fit of male executives with executives in general than of female executives was found in one of five samples only (among German business students; Sczesny, 2003a). Only this finding is in line with results of previous research (see Schein, 2001). German executives (Sczesny, 2003b) and Australian, German, and Indian students (Sczesny et al., 2004) also showed a less gender-stereotypic view of leadership compared to previous findings. Nevertheless, an interculturally shared view of a feminine-specific leadership competence (Friedel-Howe, 1993) was observed: Women were assumed to possess a higher social competence (person orientation) than men (contrary to the similar self-views of women and men with respect to person-oriented traits). Neither the descriptive nor the prescriptive norms among women and men seem to be influenced by the think-manager-think-male stereotype. The many cultural similarities probably indicate a homogeneity of the management context in the investigated countries. Thus, female management students in India may be socialized in the same way as female management students in other countries and may differ more from other female subgroups within their own country. Nevertheless, a recent meta-analysis of the "think manager-think-male" phenomenon indicated that—when comparing women and men (e.g., without a role specification as managers) with managers (without gender specification)—managers were rated as more similar to men than to women in all investigated countries, although this effect is decreasing over time in the United States (Koenig, Eagly, Mitchell, Bosak, & Ristikari, 2005).

The results indicate impressive changes in the traditionally masculine sex-typed domain of leadership with regard to people's perceptions of female leaders. Across countries, female leaders are perceived as possessing and expected to possess agentic traits to the same extent as leaders in general, while retaining their positively valued feminine-typed qualities. Thus, an increase of women in leadership is mirrored in perceivers' belief systems about female leaders.

Self-Description of Women and Men

In the present studies, the self-description of women and men indicates that women and men in all three countries reported actual and desired task- and person-oriented traits to a similar extent. Only German female students reported more person-oriented traits than male students (Sczesny, 2003a) and German female executives emphasized the importance of person-oriented characteristics for themselves (Sczesny, 2003b). These German women are probably trying to handle the dilemma of either "being too feminine or too masculine" (Eagly & Karau, 2002) by at least partly fulfilling gender-stereotypic expectancies. Altogether the findings on the self-description reflect the recently observed changes in the self-images of women in masculine-typed global personality traits and assertiveness (Twenge, 1997; 2001). The observed change in men's self-view of person-oriented traits was not expected. One possible explanation is that not only task orientation but also person orientation was valued as important for leadership in all three countries. About 50% of executives in general were assumed to possess person-oriented traits, and in Australia and India person-oriented traits were assessed even as more important for leadership than task-oriented traits (reflecting work cultures less pronounced in masculinity in both countries; Hofstede, 1998).

The results demonstrate fundamental changes not only in women's but also in men's self-perception in all three countries with regard to leadership traits. These changes in people's self-view correspond to recent changes in leadership context: an increased proportion of female leaders (e.g., Eagly, 2003) and the demand for person-oriented (feminine sex-typed) leadership skills (e.g., Van Engen, Van der Leeden, & Willemsen, 2001). Thus, women's change in self-description might especially go along with the *descriptive* changes (e.g., increased percentage of female leaders) in management; whereas men's recent endorsement of person-oriented traits reflects the new, desired mode of management (*prescriptive* aspect). Nevertheless, it is important to note that the changes observed in men's and women's self-image might be influenced by the motivation to meet the ideal self or the assumed leadership requirements, that is, wishful thinking, and might not show actual manifestations.

DISCUSSION

Consistent with a social-cultural perspective, our research shows that an increase of women in formerly male-dominated social roles in the last decades is accompanied by people's perceptions of greater agency in women, and by women ascribing more agentic traits to themselves. Respective changes are even observed in the masculine sex-typed domain of leadership, indicating less sex-stereotypic beliefs about female leaders and less pronounced sex differences in leadership-specific personality traits. In contrast to the dynamics of women's roles, men's roles have been rather stable. Nonetheless, some changes in sex-stereotypic beliefs about men and their self-reported personality traits toward greater communion were observed.

It is important to note that our research reflects a full array of research methodologies, comprising experimental, survey, and meta-analytical research. Also, different types of samples such as college-student samples, community samples, and expert samples (e.g., business students, executives) were drawn to investigate the research questions. Moreover, the research encompasses cross-cultural data (Australia, Brazil, Chile, Germany, India, United States). Nevertheless, most of the data comes from U.S. samples. Thus, the insights gained from the present research should be validated with samples from countries with different societal backgrounds. Such data would allow cross-cultural comparisons of corresponding changes in people's belief systems about the sexes and changes in individual's self-view.

The present research findings rely on explicit measures (e.g., rating scales). Such measures appear to be appropriate to assess people's (changing) beliefs of men and women. Nevertheless, they are vulnerable to demand characteristics (Diekman & Eagly, 2000). Social desirability and self-presentational concerns are thus likely to influence perceivers' responses on explicit measures. However, demand characteristics do not appear to have affected the findings on people's perception of women and men in the past, the present, and the future. Although asking about a past or future year could have suggested to participants to respond in terms of change characteristics for both sexes, the findings of stability for male targets suggest that this explanation cannot account fully for the findings. Participants reported changes in personality predominantly for women based on their assumed change in women's roles (e.g., Diekman & Eagly, 2000; Diekman, Goodfriend, & Goodwin, 2004). Participant's ratings of an increase in roles agency cannot be traced back to general optimism: Even when participants rated negatively valued gender-stereotypic traits, they projected women to assume role-congruent negative attributes to a greater extent in the future.

With respect to the self-reported personality traits, it is not possible to rule out that the present data are affected by demand characteristics. Despite the increase in women's self-reports of agency in general, there is still evidence of women's self-limiting behavior, especially in masculine-typed areas (e.g., Hannover & Bettge, 1993; Sieverding, 2003). For example, Sieverding (2003) assessed achievement-related self-evaluations in a simulated job interview in which women compared to men showed a significant under-evaluation of their performance although they did not differ in their actual performance from men. These findings suggest that behavioral measures (e.g., frequency estimates of behavior, probability of performing a certain behavior) might be a better method to assess whether changes in people's self-views have occurred (which should then be reflected in their behavior) than self-reports on trait-rating scales which are of abstract nature and might be influenced by self-presentational concerns.

Finally, the present data give us some hints regarding the question of cause and effect indicating that change in the content of sex stereotypes seems to be rooted in people's observations of changes in the social roles of women and men (see section "The Basis of Dynamic Stereotypes in Social Roles"). Nevertheless, in the future more experimental and longitudinal research is needed, which examines the mutual influence of both factors and the mechanisms (e.g., increased proportion of female leaders) that might mediate changes in people's belief systems and in their personalities as well.

ASPECTS OF FUTURE CHANGE

One implication of beliefs that encompass malleability is that change in the future may be perceived more positively. According to the role-congruity perspective, traits that align with valued social roles garner positive evaluation (Diekman & Eagly, in press; Eagly & Diekman, 2005). Support for these predictions applied to dynamic stereotypes comes from studies in which student participants evaluated the cross-temporal trends of change and stability for men and women (Diekman & Goodfriend, 2006). In these studies, the dynamic stereotype of women was generally positively evaluated. As women were projected to gain in male-stereotypic traits, their holding of these traits was more positively evaluated. In addition, to the extent that participants perceived roles as becoming more equal, they positively evaluated women's dynamism and negatively evaluated men's stability. Moreover, the expectation of role equality predicted positive evaluation of women's agency in the future, even when controlling for traditional gender role ideology (e.g., hostile, benevolent, or modern sexism; Diekman, Goodfriend, & Evans, 2005). In a changing role system, then, approval goes to those who are modifying their characteristics.

Even though the dynamic stereotype of women is positively evaluated in general, people might react negatively toward a woman who actually enacts agentic behavior. These negative reactions stem from the prescriptive norms associated with the present female gender role. In accordance with the existing female gender role, women should behave in a female-stereotypical, communal manner. Women who fail to do so and rather manifest male-stereotypical, agentic traits violate standards for their gender and may thus be unfavorably evaluated, in particular by those who endorse traditional gender roles (*see role congruity theory*, Eagly & Karau, 2002). For example, Heilman and colleagues (1995) found that female managers were perceived as more hostile (e.g., more devious, selfish) and less rational (e.g., less logical, objective) than male managers, even though both sexes were described as successful in their leadership behavior. In sum, women tend to be penalized when performing agentic behavior incongruent with their female gender role (e.g., Rudman & Glick, 1999).

In contrast to the dynamic stereotype of women, the stereotype of men appears to be relatively static. People perceived men to retain their agentic qualities and to acquire only slightly communal traits. Which conditions would contribute to a dynamic in the male stereotype encompassing greater communion? If men were observed to perform typically feminine roles and behaviors (e.g., homemaker, nurse, child care) perceivers would assume men to have acquired the communal characteristics necessary for these activities. Even though men have increased their time with children over the last decades (see section "Dynamic Gender Stereotypes"), men might engage in qualitatively different activities (e.g., playing outdoors) with their children and perform less of the typical communal behaviors (e.g., feeding, dressing) compared to women. Furthermore, men have entered female-dominated occupations to a much lesser extent than women have entered male-dominated occupations (Reskin & Roos, 1990). This minor change of men with regard to communal characteristics and female-stereotyped roles might stem from the fact that in patriarchal societies rewards such as prestige and high wages are associated with occupations that favor masculine, agentic characteristics. For example, Glick (1991) found that the more occupations are thought to require masculine-typed personality traits the more they were associated with higher prestige and earnings. Moreover, men who assume a female-dominated role that is incongruent with the male gender role might be denied the highly valued agentic qualities and even regarded negatively due to the violation of traditional gender norms (see *role congruity theory*, Eagly & Karau, 2002; *sub-typing as a softie*, Eckes, 1994). Nevertheless, even though men still do not endorse more communal traits in general such as affectionate or sympathetic (e.g., Twenge, 1997), recent research has shown that in a work-related context, men assign as many "soft skills" or person-oriented leadership traits such as team-builder, communicative, or encouraging to themselves as women do (e.g., Sczesny et al., 2004; Taris & Bok, 1998). Men appear to approve of these feminine sex-typed characteristics as the recent trend in management theory and management practice emphasizes the person-oriented qualities as important to success in leadership roles (van Engen, van der Leeden, & Willemsen, 2001).

In line with the social role theory some models of group perception also suggest that in the long run the objective distribution of information that is encountered by a cognitive system will be mirrored by respective judgments, that is, these models also indicate that information about role distribution in groups should be reflected in people's perceptions of their members (Fiedler, 1996; Kashima, Woolcock, & Kashima, 2000). However, based on these models there are at least several other mechanisms reasonable that could produce biases that might represent cognitive and motivational barriers for change in gender stereotypes: (a) biased sampling of information—although statistical data on women's and men's role distribution in society may suggest no sex differences, the information that is learned by an individual may be biased for various reasons including the biased transmission of information by other people and mass media; (b) small sample of information—if one does not have a lot of information, biases such as illusory correlations may emerge, that is, perceivers may overestimate the frequency with which distinctive variables co-occur (Hamilton & Gifford, 1976). For example, when women in leadership positions behave in a relatively uncommon, negative way (e.g., bashing of a subordinate), perceivers might see women as disproportionately likely to behave negatively although the proportion of men who behave negatively is the same as the proportion of women; (c) noncognitive sources of biases—such biases due to emotions and motivations might, for example, lead people to disapprove of change in men's and women's roles and their respective traits. People might seek to justify existing social systems by believing that groups such as women and men deserve their place in the social hierarchy (Jost & Banaji, 1994).

CONCLUSION

The observed change in women's self-view toward greater agency is fundamental in that this part of the self-concept has been shown to be associated with career motivation and career success (Abele, 2000; 2003). For example, in a recent study on management students' self-reports of how suitable they felt for an advertised leadership position, women felt less competent for the leadership position than men (Bosak & Sczesny, under review). However, self-reported agency mediated this effect indicating that men and women judge themselves as similarly suitable for the leadership position when their agency is taken into consideration. Thus, women's increasing adoption of male-dominated occupations will lead to greater agency, and successful performance in these roles will engender an increase in agentic traits (see the *reciprocal impact model*, Abele, 2003). Similarly, if men adopted female-dominated roles and occupations, we would expect men to acquire communion to a greater degree and men's successful fulfillment of these roles should foster an increase in communal traits. The extent to which change in men's roles and change in beliefs about men and/or men's self-view will occur can be expected to depend on the status of female-dominated roles within the society and the respective norms that approve or disapprove of certain traits and behaviors in men.

As noted in much research on self-fulfilling prophecies (Geis, 1993), the power of stereotypes is that they can shape reality. If individuals expect women and men to be different in the future than they are today, those expectations themselves might help to create that reality. Recent evidence suggests that even briefly imagining women of the future, as compared to women of the past, shifts implicit gender associations to be less stereotypic (Johnston & Diekman, 2006). To the extent that the future is an activated state, individuals might react to others on the basis of the future stereotype rather than the present-day stereotype. Similarly individuals might behave in a way confirming their self-image in the future. The beliefs about the future, whether they are accurate or not, can thus be very influential with regard to current-day beliefs and behavior. Furthermore interpersonal interaction (between peers or between parents and children) that communicates these beliefs as well as media representations of egalitarian roles of men and women might thus contribute significantly to a reduction in sex-role stereotyping (Ochman, 1996; Thompson & Zerbinos, 1995).

From a social psychological perspective, the way in which the sexes are represented in the grammatical structure of different languages can contribute to the formation, persistence, and dynamics of gender stereotypes (for an overview: see Stahlberg, Braun, Irmen, & Sczesny, 2007): Research on masculine generics has indicated that far-reaching consequences can result from the degrees of "female invisibility" (e.g., lexically "male" expressions: *brotherhood of men, forefathers*; or referring back to other pronoun: *Everyone should do his best*). For example, public polls may lead to different results when gender-fair expressions rather than masculine generics are used. Apart from generics, sex stereotypes are also communicated via other language mechanisms, for example, through specific words that are used to describe men and women or male and female achievement. Communication can thus exert a powerful influence with regard to changing the contents of sex-role stereotypes.

REFERENCES

Association of American Medical Colleges (2004): *Applicants, Accepted Applicants, and Matriculants by Sex*. Retrieved May 7, 2006, from http://www.aamc.org/data/facts/2004/2004summary.htm.

Abele, A. E. (2000). Gender gaps in early career development of university graduates: Why are women less successful than men? *European Bulletin of Social Psychology, 12*(3), 22–37.

Abele, A. E. (2003). The dynamics of masculine-agentic and feminine-communal traits: Findings from a prospective study. *Journal of Personality and Social Psychology, 85*, 768–776.

Astin, A. W., Oseguera, L., Sax, L. J., & Korn, W. S. (2002). *The American freshman: Thirty-five year trends 1966–2001*. Los Angeles: Higher Education Research Institute, UCLA.

Bellah, R. N., Madsen, R., Sullivan, W. M., Siwdler, A., & Tipton, S. M. (1996). *Habits of the heart: Individualism and commitment in American life*. Berkeley: University of California Press.

Bem, S. L. (1974). The measurement of psychological androgyny. *Journal of Consulting and Clinical Psychology, 31*, 634–643.

Best, D. L., & Thomas, J. J. (2003). Cultural diversity and cross-cultural perspectives. In A. H. Eagly, A. E. Beall & R. J. Sternberg (Eds.), *The Psychology of Gender* (pp. 296–327). New York: Guilford.

Bianchi, S. M. (2000). Maternal employment and time with children: Dramatic change or surprising continuity? *Demography, 37*, 401–414.

Bosak, J., & Sczesny, S. (2007). *Am I the right candidate?—Still a matter of sex? Self-ascribed fit of women and men to a leadership position*. Unpublished manuscript.

Burgess, D., & Borgida, E. (1999). Who women are, who women should be: Descriptive and prescriptive gender stereotyping in sex discrimination. *Psychology, Public Policy, and Law, 5*, 665–692.

Butcher, J. E. (1989). Adolescent girls' sex role development: Relationship with sports participation, self-esteem, and age at menarche. *Sex Roles, 20*, 575–593

Cancian, F. M., & Olinker, S. J. (2000). *Caring and gender*. Thousand Oaks, CA: Pine Forge.

Cann, A., & Siegfried, W. D. (1990). Gender stereotypes and dimensions of effective leader behavior. *Sex Roles, 23*, 413–419.

Catalyst (2002). *Fact sheet: Women CEOs*. Retrieved October 6, 2002, from http://www.catalystwomen.org/press_room/factsheets/fact_women_ceos.htm

Catalyst. (2002, November 19). Catalyst census marks gains in numbers of women corporate officers in America's largest 500 companies [press release]. Retrieved December 12, 2003, from http://www.catalystwomen.org/press_room/press_releases/2002_cote.htm

Cejka, M. A., & Eagly, A. H. (1999). Gender-stereotypic images of occupations correspond to the sex segregation of employment. *Personality and Social Psychology Bulletin, 25*, 413–423.

Cialdini, R. B., & Trost, M. R. (1998). Social influence: Social norms, conformity, and compliance. In D. T. Gilbert, S. T. Fiske, & G. Lindzey (Eds.), *The Handbook of Social Psychology* (4th ed., Vol. 2, pp. 151–192). Boston: McGraw-Hill.

Clarey, J. H., & Sanford, A. (1982). Female career preference and androgyny. *Vocational Guidance Quarterly, 30*, 258–264.

Costa, P. T., Terracciano, A., & McCrae, R. R. (2001). Gender differences in personality traits across cultures: Robust and suprising findings. *Journal of Personality and Social Psychology, 81*, 322–331.

Deaux, K., & Kite, M. (1993). Gender stereotypes. In F. L. Denmark & M. A. Paludi (Eds.), *Psychology of women: A handbook of issues and theories.* (pp. 107–139). Westport, CT: Greenwood Press/Greenwood Publishing Group, Inc.

Diekman, A. B., & Eagly, A. H. (2000). Stereotypes as dynamic constructs: Women and men of the past, present, and future. *Personality and Social Psychology Bulletin, 26*, 1171–1188.

Diekman, A. B., & Eagly, A. H. (2007). Of men, women, and motivation: A role congruity account. In J. Shah & W. L. Gardner (Eds.), *Handbook of Motivational Science.* New York: Guilford.

Diekman, A. B., Eagly, A. H., Mladinic, A., & Ferreira, M. C. (2005). Dynamic stereotypes about women and men in Latin America and the United States. *Journal of Cross-Cultural Psychology, 36*, 209–226.

Diekman, A. B., & Goodfriend, W. (2006). Rolling with the changes: A role congruity perspective on gender norms. *Psychology of Women Quarterly, 77*, 350–383

Diekman, A. B., Goodfriend, W., & Evans, C. (2005). The influence of role beliefs on stereotype content: An individual-difference approach. Unpublished manuscript.

Diekman, A. B., Goodfriend, W., & Goodwin, S. (2004). Dynamic stereotypes of power: Perceived change and stability in gender hierarchies. *Sex Roles, 50*, 201–215.

Eagly, A. H. (1987). *Sex differences in social behavior: A social-role interpretation*. Hillsdale, NJ: Erlbaum.

Eagly, A. H. (2003). The rise of female leaders. *Zeitschrift für Sozialpsychologie, 34*, 123–132.

Eagly, A. H., & Diekman, A. B. (2005). What is the problem? Prejudice as an attitude-in-context. In J. F. Dovidio, P. Glick, & L. A. Rudman (Eds.), *On the nature of prejudice: Fifty years after Allport* (pp. 19–35). Malden, MA: Blackwell.

Eagly, A. H., & Karau, S. J. (2002). Role congruity theory of prejudice toward female leaders. *Psychological Review, 109*, 573–598.

Eagly, A. H., & Steffen, V. J. (1984). Gender stereotypes stem from the distribution of women and men into social roles. *Journal of Personality and Social Psychology, 46*, 735–754.

Eagly, A. H., Wood, W., & Diekman, A. B. (2000). Social role theory of sex differences and similarities: A current appraisal. In T. Eckes & H. M. Trautner (Eds.), *The developmental social psychology of gender* (pp. 123–174). Mahwah, NJ: Erlbaum.

Eckes, T. (1994). Explorations in gender cognition: Content and structure of female and male subtypes. *Social Cognition, 12*, 37–60.

Fiedler, K. (1996). Explaining and simulating judgment biases as an aggregation phenomenon in probabilistic, multiple-cue environments. *Psychological Review, 103*, 193–214.

Fletcher, R. (1971). Relationships between personality traits and high school activity participation. *Psychology: A Journal of Human Behavior, 8*(4), 40–43.

Friedel-Howe, H. (1993). Frauen und Führung: Mythen und Fakten [Women and leadership: myths and facts]. In L. V. Rosenstiel (Hrsg.), Führung von Mitarbeitern: Handbuch für erfolgreiches Personalmanagement [Leadership: Handbook for successful human resource management] Stuttgart: Schäffer-Poeschel.

Fullerton, H. N., Jr. (1999). Labor force participation: 75 years of change, 1950–98 and 1998–2025. *Monthly Labor Review, 122*, 3–12.

Geis, F. L. (1993). Self-fulfilling prophecies: A social psychological view of gender. In A. E. Beall & R. J. Sternberg (Eds.), *The psychology of gender* (pp. 9–54). New York: Guilford.

Gilbert, D. T. (1998). Ordinary personology. In D. T. Gilbert, S. T. Fiske, & G. Lindzey (Eds.), *The handbook of social psychology* (4th ed., Vol. 2, pp. 89–150). New York: McGraw-Hill.

Gilbert, D. T., & Malone, P. S. (1995). The correspondence bias. *Psychological Bulletin, 117*, 21–38.

Gilroy, F. D., Talierco, T. M., & Steinbacher, R. (1981). Impact of maternal employment on daughters' sex-role orientation and fear of success. *Psychological Reports, 49*, 963–968.

Glick, P. (1991). Trait-based and sex-based discrimination in occupational prestige, occupational salary, and hiring. *Sex Roles, 25*, 351–378.

Goodfriend, W., Diekman, A. B., & Truax, A. L. (2006). Relationships in context: Dynamic gender stereotypes and romantic relationships. Unpublished manuscript, Boise State University, Boise, ID.

Hall, J. A., & Carter, J. D. (1999). Gender-stereotype accuracy as an individual difference. *Journal of Personality and Social Psychology, 77*, 350–359.

Hamilton, D. L., & Gifford, R. K. (1976). Illusory correlation in interpersonal perception: A cognitive basis of stereotypic judgments. *Journal of Experimental Social Psychology, 12*, 392–407.

Hannover, B., & Bettge, S. H. (1993). Mädchen und Technik [Girls and technology]. Göttingen: Hogrefe.

Heilman, M. E. (2001). Description and prescription: How gender stereotypes prevent women's ascent up the organizational ladder. *Journal of Social Issues, 57*, 657–674.

Heilman, M. E., Block, C. J., & Martell, R. F. (1995). Sex stereotypes: Do they influence perceptions of managers? *Journal of Social Behavior and Personality, 10*, 237–252

Hernandez, M., & Iyengar, S. S. (2001). What drives whom? A cultural perspective on human agency. *Social Cognition, 19*, 269–294.

Hofstede, G. (1998). *Masculinity and femininity: The taboo dimension of national cultures.* Thousand Oaks: CA: Sage.

Hoffman, C., & Hurst, N. (1990). Gender stereotypes: Perception or Rationalization? *Journal of Personality and Social Psychology, 58*, 197–208.

Hyde, J. S. (2005). The gender similarities hypothesis. *American Psychologist, 60*, 581–592.

Johnston, A. M., & Diekman, A. B. (2006). Effects of dynamic stereotypes on present-day beliefs. Paper presented at the Midwestern Psychological Association, Chicago, IL.

Jost, J. T., & Banaji, M. (1994). The role of stereotyping in system justification and the production of false consciousness. *British Journal of Social Psychology, 22*, 1–27.

Kashima, Y., Woolcock, J., & Kashima, E. S. (2000). Group impressions as dynamic configurations: The tensor product model of group impression formation and change. *Psychological Review, 107*, 914–942.

Koenig, A. M., Eagly, A. H., Mitchell, A. A., Bosak, J., & Ristikari, T. I. (2005). The "think manager-think male" phenomenon: A meta-analysis. Presentation at the annual meeting of the Midwestern Psychological Association, Chicago, IL.

Kite, M. E., Russo, N. F., Brehm, S. S., Fouad, N. A., Hall, C. C. I., Hyde, J. S., et al. (2001). Women psychologists in academe: Mixed progress, unwarranted complacency. *American Psychologist, 56,* 1080–1098.

Klerman, G. L., & Weissman, M . M. (1989). Increasing rates of depression. *Journal of the American Medical Association, 261,* 2229–2235.

Lewinsohn, P., Rohde, P., Seeley, J., & Fischer, S. (1993). Age-cohort changes in the lifetime occurrence of depression and other mental disorders. *Journal of Abnormal Psychology, 102,* 110–120.

Ochman, J. M. (1996). The effects of nongender-role stereotyped, same-sex role models in storybooks on the self-esteem of children in grade three. *Sex Roles, 35,* 315–336.

Powell, G. N., Butterfield, D. A., & Parent, J. D. (2002). Gender and managerial stereotypes: Have the times changed? *Journal of Management, 28,* 177–193.

Prentice, D. A., & Carranza, E. (2002). What women should be, shouldn't be, are allowed to be, and don't have to be: The contents of prescriptive gender stereotypes. *Psychology of Women Quarterly, 26,* 269–281.

Reskin, B. F., & Roos, P. A. (1990). *Job queues, gender queues: Explaining women's inroads into male occupations.* Philadelphia: Temple University Press.

Rudman, L. A., & Glick, P. (1999). Feminized management and backlash toward agentic women: The hidden costs to women of a kinder, gentler image of middle managers. *Journal of Personality and Social Psychology, 77,* 1004–1010.

Rusbult, C. E., Martz, J. M., & Agnew, C. R. (1998). The Investment Model Scale: Measuring commitment level, satisfaction level, quality of alternatives, and investment size. *Personal Relationships, 5,* 357–391.

Schein, V. E. (1973). The relationship between sex-role stereotypes and requisite management characteristics. *Journal of Applied Psychology, 57,* 95–100.

Schein, V. E. (1975). Relations between sex-role stereotypes and requisite management characteristics among female managers. *Journal of Applied Psychology, 60,* 340–344.

Schein, V. E. (2001). A global look at psychological barriers to women's progress in management. *Journal of Social Issues, 57,* 675–688.

Sczesny, S. (2003a). A closer look beneath the surface: Various facets of the think-manager-think-male stereotype. *Sex Roles, 49,* 353–363.

Sczesny, S. (2003b). Führungskompetenz: Selbst- und Fremdwahrnehmung weiblicher und männlicher Führungskräfte [The perception of leadership competence by female and male leaders]. *Zeitschrift für Sozialpsychologie, 34,* 133–145.

Sczesny, S. (2005). Gender stereotypes and implicit leadership theories. In B. Schyns & J. R. Meindl (Eds.), *Implicit leadership theories: Essays and explorations* (pp. 159–172). Greenwich, CT: Information Age Publishing.

Sczesny, S., Bosak, J., Neff, D., & Schyns, B. (2004). Gender stereotypes and the attribution of leadership traits: A cross-cultural comparison. *Sex Roles, 51,* 631–645.

Sczesny, S., & Kühnen, U. (2004). Meta-cognition about biological sex and gender-stereotypic physical appearance: Consequences for the assessment of leadership competence. *Personality and Social Psychology Bulletin, 30,* 13–21.

Sieverding, M. (2003). Frauen unterschätzen sich: Selbstbeurteilungs-Biases in einer simulierten Bewerbungssituation [Women Underevaluate Themselves: Self-Evaluation-Biases in a Simulated Job Interview]. *Zeitschrift für Sozialpsychologie, 34,* 147–160.

Snyder, M. (1981). On the self-perpetuating nature of stereotypes about women and men. *Journal of Experimental Social Psychology, 18,* 277–291.

Spence, J. T., & Buckner, C. E. (2000). Instrumental and expressive traits, trait stereo-types, and sexist attitudes. *Psychology of Women Quarterly, 24,* 44–62.
Spence, J. T., & Helmreich, R. L. (1978). *Masculinity and femininity: Their psychological dimensions, correlates, and antecedents.* Austin: University of Texas Press.
Spence, J. T., Helmreich, R. L., & Holahan, C. K. (1979). Negative and positive com-ponents of psychological masculinity and femininity and their relationships to self-reports of neurotic and acting out behaviors. *Journal of Personality and Social Psy-chology, 37,* 1673–1682.
Stahlberg, D., Braun, F., Irmen, L., & Sczesny, S. (2007). Representation of the sexes in language. In K Fiedler (Ed.), *Social communication. A volume in the series Frontiers of Social Psychology* (pp. 163–187) (Series Editors: A. W. Kruglanski & J. P. Forgas). New York: Psychology Press.
Taris, T. W., & Bok, I. A. (1998). On gender specificity of personal characteristics in per-sonnel advertisements: A study among future applicants. *The Journal of Psychology, 132,* 593–610.
Thompson, T. L., & Zerbinos, E. (1995). Gender roles in animated cartoons: Has the picture changed in 20 years? *Sex Roles, 32,* 651–673.
Twenge, J. M. (1997). Changes in masculine and feminine traits over time: A meta-analysis. *Sex Roles, 36,* 305–325.
Twenge, J. M. (2000). The age of anxiety? Birth cohort change in anxiety and neuroti-cism, 1952–1993. *Journal of Personality and Social Psychology, 79,* 1007–1021.
Twenge, J. M. (2001). Changes in women's assertiveness in response to status and roles: A cross-temporal meta-analysis, 1931–1993. *Journal of Personality and Social Psychol-ogy, 81,* 133–145.
Twenge, J. M. (2006). *Generation Me: Why today's young Americans are more confident, assertive, entitled—and more miserable than ever before.* New York: Free Press.
Twenge, J. M., & Campbell, W. K. (2001). Age and birth cohort differences in self-esteem: A cross-temporal meta-analysis. *Personality and Social Psychology Review, 5,* 321–344.
Twenge, J. M., & Im, C. (in press). Changes in the need for social approval, 1958–2001. *Journal of Research in Personality.*
U.S. Bureau of the Census, Statistical Abstract of the United States. Various years, 1925–2005. Washington, DC: U.S. Government Printing Office.
U.S. Bureau of Labor Statistics (1982). Labor force statistics derived from the current population survey: A databook (Vol. 1: Bulletin 2096). Washington, DC: U.S. Department of Labor.
U.S. Bureau of Labor Statistics (2002). Household data: Annual averages (Table 11: Employed persons by detailed occupation, sex, race, and Hispanic origin). Retrieved March 10, 2003, from http://www.bls.gov/cps/cpsaat11.pdf.
U.S. Department of Labor (2005). Labor force statistics from the current population survey. Retrieved October 21, 2005, from http://data.bls.gov/cgi-bin/srgate (Bureau of Labor Statistics database, series IDs LNU01300001 and LNU01300002)
Van Engen, M. L., van der Leeden, R., & Willemsen, T. M. (2001). Gender, context and leadership styles: A field study. *Journal of Occupational and Organizational Psy-chology, 74,* 581–598.
Wertheim, E. G., Widom, C. S., & Wortzel, L. H. (1978). Multivariate analysis of male and female professional career choice correlates. *Journal of Applied Psychology, 63,* 234–242.
Wilde, A., & Diekman, A. B. (2005). Cross-cultural similarities and differences in dynamic stereotypes: A comparison between Germany and the United States. *Psy-chology of Women Quarterly, 29,* 188–196.

Willemsen, T. M. (2002). Gender typing of the successful manager: A stereotype reconsidered. *Sex Roles, 46,* 385–391.

Williams, J. E., & Best, D. L. (1990a). *Measuring sex stereotypes. A multination study.* Newbury Park, CA: Sage.

Williams, J. E., & Best, D. L. (1990b). *Sex and psyche: Gender and self viewed cross-culturally.* Newbury Park, CA: Sage.

Wirth, L. (2001). *Breaking through the glass ceiling: Women in management.* Geneva, Switzerland: International Labor Office.

Wood, W., Christensen, P. N., Hebl, M. R., & Rothgerber, H. (1997). Conformity to sex-typed norms, affect, and the self-concept. *Journal of Personality and Social Psychology, 73,* 523–535.

Part 3

STEREOTYPE AND LANGUAGE USE

Chapter 8

A Model of Biased Language Use

Clemens P. J. Wenneker
University of Amsterdam, The Netherlands

Daniël H. J. Wigboldus
Radboud University Nijmegen, The Netherlands

Prejudiced communication is everywhere (Ruscher, 2001). Not only does it rear its ugly head explicitly, for instance in the case of sexist jokes, but it may also show up in much more implicit ways. Research on biased language use has demonstrated that people show subtle linguistic biases as a function of prejudiced thoughts, stereotypes, and expectancies (for overviews see Maass, 1999; Wigboldus & Douglas, 2007). For instance, it has been demonstrated that positive in-group and negative out-group behaviors are described at a higher level of linguistic abstraction (e.g., "The in-group member is intelligent," "The out-group member is stupid") than positive out-group and negative in-group behaviors (e.g., "The out-group member gave the right answer to the question," "The in-group member gave the wrong answer to the question"). This form of biased language use is named "the linguistic intergroup bias" (LIB; Maass, Salvi, Arcuri, & Semin, 1989). Research into this fascinating phenomenon has been very fruitful over the past two decades or so.

In this chapter, we will start with a brief overview of this line of research. Subsequently, the main focus will be on processes underlying this biased language use. It has been convincingly argued and demonstrated that processes during retrieval and communication of information have a major impact on biased language use (see Douglas, Sutton, & McGarty, in press). We argue that, in addition to processes taking place at the time of the actual communication of information, the way information originally gets encoded into memory may also influence the level of language abstraction of communication. Based on these two routes to biased language use we put forward the biased language model (BLM).

BIASED LANGUAGE USE

The first research on LIB was conducted in the context of Italian horse races (Maass et al., 1989). In these races, different sections of a city compete with each other. Not surprisingly, in-group identification during these races is high. In one of the studies, participants were shown cartoons depicting positive behaviors (e.g., interrupting the race in order to help an injured member of the opposed team) and negative behaviors (e.g., secretly drugging a horse of the competing team) performed by in-group or out-group members. Subsequently, participants were asked to choose from four options increasing in linguistic abstraction the description that they thought best described the behavior depicted in each cartoon. It was found that positive behaviors performed by an in-group member and negative behaviors performed by an out-group member were described more abstractly than negative behaviors performed by an in-group member and positive behaviors performed by an out-group member (a LIB effect).

The descriptions that participants could choose from were based on the linguistic category model (LCM; Semin & Fiedler, 1988, 1991, 1992). The LCM distinguishes between different linguistic categories, with different cognitive functions. In its original form, the LCM consists of four categories differing in linguistic abstraction (Semin & Fiedler, 1988). Descriptive action verbs (DAV) constitute the most concrete category, and give an objective, valence neutral description of specific behaviors (e.g., "The doctor embraces the old man"). Interpretative action verbs (IAV) give a more general description of a behavior, generalizing across specific behaviors (e.g., "The doctor helps the old man"). The next category of the linguistic category model is constituted by state verbs (SV). These verbs do not refer to a specific behavior, but describe a state, and generalize across specific events (e.g., "The doctor likes the old man"). The most abstract category consists of adjectives (ADJ). These do not refer to a specific behavior, but only to the subject, thus generalizing across specific objects (e.g. "The doctor is friendly").

Semin and Fiedler (1988, 1991, 1992) found that linguistic abstraction is an important dimension underlying these different categories. They asked participants to rate a representative sample of all four categories, summing up to 72 verbs and adjectives. Participants indicated that the more abstract the category, the greater the temporal stability of the information was, the more information was given about the subject, the less information was given about the situation, the less information could be objectively verified, and the more one could disagree with the information. Subsequent research demonstrated that the more abstract a description, the more likely that a subject's behaviors would be repeated in the future (Maass et al., 1989). In summary, the more abstract a description, the more is revealed about the person, the more concrete a description, the more is revealed about the situation.

It is important to note that any behavior may be described in a semantically correct way using each of the four linguistic categories of the LCM. Take for instance the doctor and the old man in our example. From a semantic point of view, all four descriptions may provide a sensible description of a scene in which a doctor embraces an old man. However, due to the differences in level of abstraction, the impact on a recipient will differ greatly as a function of the specific linguistic category that is used to describe this scene. Language and social cognition thus may influence each other bidirectionally (see Semin, 2000). On the one hand communicators may use the linguistic tools that are most useful for the communicative act at hand. On the other hand, recipients of these communications will be influenced in their perceptions and thoughts by the specific linguistic tools used by communicators. This dialectical interplay between language and social cognition has been demonstrated convincingly in research on the LIB.

Two explanations for the LIB have been advanced (Maass, Milesi, Zabbini, & Stahlberg, 1995). The first explanation is based on social identity theory (Tajfel & Turner, 1979, 1986) and proposes that in an intergroup context people will try to defend and enhance their in-group identities (the in-group protection hypothesis). This goal is served by describing positive in-group behavior and negative out-group behavior more abstractly than negative in-group behavior and positive out-group behavior. The second proposed explanation is more cognitive and is based on the idea that expectancies guide language production (the differential expectancy view). Thus, expectancy confirming behaviors are described more abstractly than expectancy disconfirming behaviors. This explains the LIB effect, because, in general, people expect more positive and less negative behavior from an in-group member than from an out-group member (Howard & Rothbart, 1980). For this reason, in many situations both proposed explanations yield the same predictions, the exceptions being circumstances in which one expects a certain negative behavior from an in-group member or a certain positive behavior from an out-group member.

Maass et al. (1995) used the latter expectations to pit the two explanations against each other in a single design. Results supported the differential expectancy view: Regardless of the valence of the behaviors and the group membership of the actor, expected behaviors were described more abstractly than unexpected behaviors. Apparently, differential expectancies are sufficient to produce biased language use. Subsequently, the question became whether Maass et al. (1995) found no support for the in-group protection hypothesis because it was not viable or because participants were just not motivated enough to demonstrate an intergroup bias in this specific intergroup context. Maass, Ceccarelli, and Rudin (1996) proposed that "in highly competitive, hostile, or in-group threatening situations . . . motivational considerations may become relevant and even override cognitive mechanisms" (p. 513). They manipulated in-group hostility and found support for the in-group protection hypothesis in addition to an effect based on differential expectancies. In the increased hostility condition, but not in the reduced hostility condition, positive behaviors of an in-group member and negative behaviors of an out-group member were described more abstractly than negative behaviors of an in-group member and positive behaviors of an out-group member, independent of the stereotypic expectancy. The conclusion is that when people are motivated enough, they can adjust their language use and show a bias in language abstraction, resulting in a LIB effect, in addition to and independent of an effect based on differential expectancies.

To summarize, the in-group protection mechanism seems especially important in an in-group threatening setting, whereas the cognitive mechanism seems to be a more general one. Of interest, the cognitive mechanism seems to operate not only at an intergroup level, but also at an interpersonal level (Maass et al., 1995; Wigboldus, Semin, & Spears, 2006). For instance, Wigboldus et al. (2006) asked participants to think about a good friend and to write two stories about this friend, one in which the friend behaved as expected, and one in which the friend behaved unexpectedly. These stories were coded for their mean level of linguistic abstraction using the LCM. Results showed that expected behaviors were described more abstractly than unexpected behaviors. The phenomenon that, in general, regardless of valence or intergroup context, expected behavior is described more abstractly than unexpected behavior, is now commonly referred to as the linguistic expectancy bias (LEB; Maass, 1999; Wigboldus, Semin, & Spears, 2000).

By now, support for the LIB and LEB has been found in different languages (e.g., Dutch, English, German, and Italian) in numerous experiments, field studies, and analyses of mass media, and exploring different intergroup settings and stereotypes (for overviews see Maass, 1999; Wigboldus & Douglas, 2007). Importantly, evidence for both linguistic biases has been found using the multiple-choice format described above, as well as using more open methods in which participants generate and communicate their own stories which are coded according to the LCM.

The Impact of Biased Language Use

We noted earlier that the LCM supposes a bidirectional relationship between language and cognition. The LIB and LEB demonstrate that communicators use language strategically when describing relevant behaviors. Importantly, research has demonstrated that this biased language use indeed influences subsequent inferences made by recipients (e.g., Maass et al., 1989; Wigboldus et al., 2000; Wigboldus et al., 2006). For example, Wigboldus et al. (2000) asked participants to write stories in which either a male or female friend behaved in a typically male or female way. Half of the stories thus described stereotype-consistent behaviors (e.g., a male friend behaving in a typically male way or a female friend behaving in a typically female way). The other half described stereotype-inconsistent behaviors (e.g., a male friend behaving in a typically female way or a female friend behaving in a typically male way). After a filler task, participants switched computers, and read and judged the stories written by another participant on a scale that was developed to measure the extent to which behaviors in the stories were dispositionally versus situationally attributed. Results demonstrated that the stories written by communicators exhibited a LEB effect. When coded with the LCM, stereotype-consistent stories had a higher mean level of linguistic abstraction than stereotype-inconsistent stories. Furthermore, results demonstrated that recipients made stronger dispositional (and weaker situational) attributions for stereotype-consistent than for stereotype-inconsistent stories. Importantly, these differences in dispositional inferences were mediated by differences in linguistic abstraction of the stories.

A weakness of this study is that both communicators and recipients shared the cultural stereotypes that were used. Moreover, all recipients had served as communicators themselves in an earlier phase of the experiment. Thus, the recipients were aware of the extent to which the stories that they received were consistent with the stereotypes. Therefore, in principle, the recipients may have made dispositional attributions about stereotype consistent behaviors and situational attributions about stereotype inconsistent behaviors, not because of the level of linguistic abstraction, but because they knew the behaviors were stereotype consistent or inconsistent. Only when expectancies are manipulated at an individual level instead of a group level, independent recipients, who do not know the actor in a message, will not know whether the message is consistent with expectations. After all, when you do not know an actor, you cannot predict what to expect of this person. As a result, the explicit content of a message will not provide any clues about whether the behavior is expected of the actor. A more stringent test of the mediation hypothesis outlined by Wigboldus et al. (2000) thus is obtained when expectancy consistency is manipulated at an individual level.

Wigboldus et al. (2006) did exactly this. In their study, participants functioned either as communicators or recipients. Communicators were asked to communicate an expected and unexpected story about a good friend in their own words. A set of independent participants functioned as recipients of these messages. Recipients' attributions about the actor in the message were measured. Care was taken to ensure that recipients did not know how these messages originated, and thus could not infer from the explicit content to what extent a message described expected or unexpected behavior of an actor. In line with the LEB phenomenon, communicators described expectancy consistent behavior at a higher level of abstraction than expectancy inconsistent behavior. Moreover, this LEB effect influenced recipients' dispositional inferences in an expectancy confirming way. That is, stronger dispositional inferences for expected messages than for unexpected messages were found. Importantly, this effect was mediated by the level of linguistic abstraction of the messages.

In summary, in line with the original LIB model put forward by Maass and colleagues (1989), research has demonstrated that existing stereotypes produce biased language, which in turn contributes to the (interpersonal) transmission and maintenance of stereotypical views. Whereas the original LIB model focuses on language use in an intergroup context, the LEB model pertains to linguistically biased descriptions of expected and unexpected behaviors in general. This can be due to stereotypical expectancies as well as differential expectancies at an individual level.

Processes Underlying Biased Language Use

What psychological processes underlie this biased language use? This question was partly answered by Maass and colleagues (1995). They wondered what the mechanisms underlying the LIB were, and found that in-group protection as well as differential expectancies could cause this effect, with the latter resulting in the LEB. Recently, from two different points of view, new advancements have been made regarding the processes underlying biased language use.

First, research on language abstraction has evolved from intrapersonal research focused on mechanisms underlying linguistic biases to more interpersonal research focused on language abstraction as a communicative tool (e.g., Semin, 2000). Some have even proposed that having a communicative purpose is a necessary condition for the emergence of biased language use (Semin, Gil de Montes, & Valencia, 2003). A prime example of this approach is the research performed by Douglas and colleagues (for an overview, see their chapter in this volume). Her research convincingly demonstrates that communication goals can produce biased language use (e.g., Douglas & Sutton, 2003; Fiedler, Bluemke, Friese, & Hofmann, 2003). For example, Douglas and Sutton (2003) showed participants cartoons of actors behaving positively and negatively. Participants were asked to choose from four descriptions (increasing in linguistic abstraction according to the LCM) the one that they found the most appropriate. In addition, participants received a positive or negative communication goal. Specifically, they were explicitly asked to portray the actor in a favorable way (positive communication goal) or in an unfavorable way (negative communication goal). Participants with a positive communication goal chose more abstract positive descriptions and more concrete negative descriptions than participants with a negative communication goal. This demonstrates that people can use linguistic abstraction as a tool to attain a desired communication goal. Communication goals that are activated during the communication of information thus will influence language use.

Second, research on the effects of stereotypes on encoding processes in general (e.g., von Hippel, Sekaquaptewa, & Vargas, 1995) and on spontaneous trait inferences in particular (Wigboldus, Dijksterhuis, & van Knippenberg, 2003; Wigboldus, Sherman, Franzese, & van Knippenberg, 2004) recently has led to research into the effects of encoding on the LIB and the LEB (Wenneker, Wigboldus, & Spears, 2005). Wenneker et al. (2005) demonstrated that a LIB effect was present only when communicators knew about the group membership of the actor they had to describe before they received the behavioral information they were asked to communicate in their own words. When they heard about the group membership after they received the behavioral information (but before they communicated), no LIB effect was found in their communications. Presumably, the way they encoded the original behavioral information was affected by the group membership of the actor when they knew this group membership beforehand, resulting in a LIB effect. Learning about the actor's group membership afterwards did not change the original encoding and therefore no LIB effect was found under these conditions. This study demonstrates that differences in the encoding of information can be sufficient for a LIB effect to occur.

Where does this leave us? On the one hand, research demonstrates that communication goals activated at the communication of information affect linguistic biases. On the other hand, encoding processes may affect linguistic biases without any communication goals present. In our view, there are two important moments when biased processing may lead to biased language use (see Fig. 8–1). First, biased processing may take place during the encoding of information into memory. This process initially defines the representation of the behavior in the individual mind. That is, information may be stored more concretely or more abstractly during the (conceptual) encoding stage. For example, when observing the two men fighting in public, a bystander may store this information more abstractly into memory when she knows the fighters are skinheads (e.g., "They are skinheads thus violent"). When subsequently asked to describe the scene, the bystander will retrieve this abstract information from memory, which may result in biased language use.

Second, biased processing may take place during the retrieval and communication of information. Consider the example of the two men fighting in public again. Based on the goals activated at the moment of communication a bystander may adjust the level of linguistic abstraction of the message

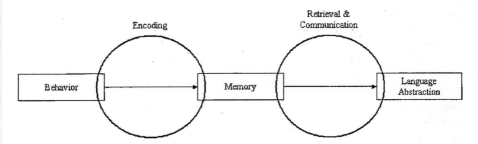

FIGURE 8–1. Processes underlying biased language use.

(e.g., Douglas & Sutton, 2003). For example, if a bystander wants to portray one fighter as positively as possible because this is a friend, she is likely to use concrete language to describe this person's negative behavior, whereas she might describe the same behavior more abstractly if the aim is to portray a negative image of the fighter. Importantly, in our view, processes at encoding and processes at retrieval and communication do not exclude each other, but constitute two independent routes that may influence language use.

In the following, empirical evidence for both routes to biased language use will be described in more detail. A comprehensive overview of research on the effects of communication goals on biased language use is provided by Douglas et al. (in press), our main focus therefore will be on the effect that biased encoding processes have on biased language use.

ENCODING EFFECTS

Encoding is defined mostly as the process by which information is stored as mental concepts into memory (e.g., Baron & Byrne, 2003), and became a front stage concept in psychology with the extensive research on the encoding specificity principle (see Tulving & Thomson, 1973). According to this principle, information can be encoded in different ways into memory (depending on the context), and how information can be retrieved from memory depends on how it is encoded. For example, the word *animal* is better remembered with the cue something friendly than with the cue something ferocious when it is encoded in the sentence, "The camper petted the animal," while the reverse is true when it is encoded in the sentence, "The camper escaped from the animal" (Barclay, Bransford, Franks, McCarrell, & Nitsch, 1974).

Our use of the term *encoding* adheres to the broad definition of storing information into memory. In the original LIB paper by Maass and colleagues encoding is defined in a more general way "as the translation of language-free (visually presented) information into a linguistic code" (1989, Footnote 1, p. 981). To be able to distinguish encoding from translating into language the information stored in memory, we will use terms such as retrieval and communication to refer to the translation of concepts from memory into words (see Wigboldus & Douglas, 2007). We use encoding strictly for storing information into memory.

When one looks into the concept of encoding in more detail, a first and broad distinction can be made between more perceptual and more conceptual encoding (for an overview see von Hippel et al., 1995). With respect to biased perceptual encoding, research shows for example how group influence (e.g., minority versus majority influence) may cause a conversion in the perception of the afterimage of a blue color (Moscovici & Personnaz, 1980, 1991). Participants were given a suggestion that the colored stimulus was green rather than blue. The results showed that this suggestion had an influence on the after-

image color participants reported. Another example is given by research showing how expectancies can lead people to hear complete words along with a
cough, while actually a phoneme was replaced by the cough (Samuel, 1981).
An example of the effects of stereotypes on perceptual encoding can be found
in a clever and appealing series of studies by Correll, Park, Judd, and Wittenbrink (2002). They had White as well as African American participants playing a videogame, in which they showed a White or African American target
holding either a gun or a harmless object (e.g., a cell phone). Participants
had to decide as quickly as possible whether to shoot the target. When holding
a gun, both the White and African American participants were faster in deciding to shoot the target when he was an African American than when he
was a White. On the other hand, when the target held a harmless object, they
were faster in deciding not to shoot him when he was a White than when he
was an African American. Of importance, this so-called "shooter bias" was
higher for participants that endorsed the stereotype more, but was not related
to the level of prejudice. Presumably, based on the expectancies resulting from
activated stereotypes, participants encoded the scene perceptually differently
depending on the race of the target.

A primary example of biased conceptual encoding is the finding that, in general, unexpected behavior is better recalled than expected behavior (the "memory incongruency effect"; see Stangor & McMillan, 1992). For instance, in a classical study, Hastie and Kumar (1979) asked participants to form an impression
of a target person by reading aloud eight traits, all (almost) synonymous to each
other (e.g., implying intelligence) and 20 behavioral descriptions. The descriptions included congruent behaviors (e.g., "won the chess tournament"), incongruent behaviors (e.g., "made the same mistake three times"), and neutral
behaviors (e.g., "took the elevator to the third floor"). When subsequently
asked to freely recall as many behaviors as possible, participants recalled significantly more incongruent behaviors than congruent or neutral behaviors.

Stressing the fact that these effects result from biased encoding, subsequent
research has shown that this incongruency effect is found only when an expectancy is induced before the information is presented. When an expectancy is
induced after the presentation of information, the inconsistent information is
remembered worse than the consistent information (e.g., Dijksterhuis & Van
Knippenberg, 1995; Van Knippenberg & Dijksterhuis, 1996). Varying the stage
at which expectancies are cued (before or after the information) is a common
way to disentangle encoding from retrieval effects (e.g., Rothbart, Evans, &
Fulero, 1979; Snyder & Uranowitz, 1978). Because all participants have the same
information available at recall, one can estimate the effect of encoding by sub-
tracting the amount of recall when expectancies were active only at retrieval
from the amount of recall when expectancies were active both at encoding and
retrieval. The generally accepted explanation for the memory incongruency effect is that people process incongruent information more elaborately, because
they have to make sense of the incongruent information (for an overview see

Roese & Sherman, in press). When expectancies are activated after the encoding of information, the information has already been processed.

Another example of biased conceptual encoding that is highly relevant for our current purposes is research on the effects of stereotypes on spontaneous trait inferences (STIs; Stewart, Weeks, & Lupfer, 2003; Wigboldus et al., 2003). A STI is the spontaneous inference of a trait that is not presented, but is (strongly) implied by a presented behavior (for an overview see Uleman, Newman, & Moskowitz, 1996). Wigboldus et al. (2003) investigated the effects of stereotypes on STIs with the probe-recognition paradigm (McKoon & Ratcliff, 1986; Uleman, Hon, Roman, & Moskowitz, 1996). Participants are presented with sentences. After each sentence, a probe word appears and participants have to indicate as quickly as possible whether this probe word was part of the preceding sentence or not. The idea behind this interference paradigm is that participants will take more time to indicate that a probe word was not part of the preceding sentence when this probe word was implied by the sentence. In the case of STIs, the sentences are descriptions of concrete behaviors (e.g., "X hits the saleswoman") and the probe words are traits (e.g., "aggressive"). In the case of a STI, participants will take more time to indicate that the trait probe was not part of the preceding trait-implying sentence.

Wigboldus et al. (2003) presented participants with stereotype-consistent as well as stereotype-inconsistent category behavior combinations within a probe-recognition paradigm. Whether a behavior was stereotype consistent or stereotype inconsistent was dependent on a category label that described the actor. Importantly, this category label was presented either before, or after the behavioral sentence was presented. When a stereotype-inconsistent category label (e.g., "girl") preceded a sentence (e.g., "X hits the saleswoman"), weaker spontaneous trait inferences were made than when a stereotype-consistent category label (e.g., "skinhead") preceded the same sentence. That is, participants took longer to indicate that the implied trait (e.g., "aggressive") was not part of the preceding sentence when an inconsistent category label was presented right before the sentence. In line with Dijksterhuis and van Knippenberg (1995, 1996), Wigboldus et al. (2003) argued that the category label temporarily inhibits access to category-inconsistent traits. In the case of inconsistent category-behavior combinations, this means that the implied trait is temporarily less accessible. As a result, the STI is not made. Interestingly, when a category label followed a sentence, no differences were found in response times to the trait probes as a function of the stereotype consistency of the category labels. In other words, when the behavioral sentence preceded the category information, the spontaneous abstract trait inference was always made, independent of the stereotype consistency of the category label that was presented after the sentence (but before the trait probe, of course). This finding fits the idea that once the original behavior is encoded, the category label exerts much less influence. This pattern of findings was found with subliminal as well as supraliminal category label presentation.

These results demonstrate that activation of stereotypes during encoding is of influence on spontaneous trait inferences, in contrast to the activation of stereotypes during retrieval. As will be apparent in the next section, trait inferences can be compared to the activation of the most abstract level of the LCM. In fact, a STI is the spontaneous activation of the most abstract level of the LCM on the basis of behavioral information (the lowest level of linguistic abstraction in the LCM). This research therefore supports the idea that biased encoding can result in biased language use.

ENCODING AND BIASED LANGUAGE USE

Although it has been assumed that biased language use is primarily a result of biased encoding of information (see, Maass et al., 1989; von Hippel et al., 1995), this was never demonstrated in the past. In fact, it was the research paradigm used to study the LIB and LEB that precluded an investigation of the separate effects of encoding and retrieval of information on biased language use. That is, in most research to date, participants were asked to describe a picture, either by describing the behavior in the picture in their own words or by choosing the most appropriate description out of a set of four. The group membership of the actor is manipulated in the picture, or presented beforehand. In both cases, no distinction can be made between processes operating at encoding and processes operating at retrieval and communication. Moreover, because pictures are described on the spot, with the picture still in front of the participants, no information needs to be retrieved from memory, and encoding effects therefore may not operate. Recently, we have put forward a thesis that biased encoding of behavioral information is a sufficient cause of LIB or LEB effects, and that a communicative intent or purpose is not a necessary requirement for their emergence (Wenneker et al., 2005).

In a first study (Wenneker et al., 2005), we investigated whether biased encoding of information can be a sufficient condition for the emergence of a LEB effect. Participants were asked to communicate in their own words a story in which the actor behaved consistently and inconsistently with stereotypes. Importantly, half of the participants received information about the category membership of the actor before they heard the story, the other half of the participants after they heard the story. More specifically, all participants heard a story via headphones about a man named Robert behaving in an intelligent and sociable way. Robert engaged in a total of four intelligent and four sociable concrete behaviors. For example, "Robert tells funny stories" (sociable) and "Robert answers every questions he gets correctly while playing Trivial Pursuit" (intelligent). Furthermore, to prevent priming of a concrete abstraction level, Robert was described at an abstract level as well (as "sociable" and "talkative" on the one hand, and "intelligent" and "smart" on the other). After a long filler task, participants continued the experiment. They were prompted to relate the story they had heard in their own words to an un-specified participant in a future study, by typing it into the computer. Impor-tantly, all participants received extra information about Robert in the form of a short story. In this extra story, it was explained that Robert was either a chess master or a hairdresser. Note that the intelligent behaviors in the story that participants had to communicate were consistent with the chess master stereotype and inconsistent with the hairdresser stereotype. The reverse is true for the sociable behaviors. Importantly, the timing of the category label presentation was manipulated. Half of the participants received the category label information just before they heard the story containing the behaviors, while the other half of the participants received the category label informa-tion after they heard the story and after the half hour filler, but just before they had to communicate in their own words the story they had heard.

In line with the LEB, we expected participants to relate the stereotype-consistent behaviors in the story more abstractly than the stereotype-inconsistent behaviors. Moreover, we expected this effect to be more pronounced when the category label was presented before participants heard the story than when the category label was presented after participants heard the story, demonstrat-ing an encoding effect. Participants' related stories were coded according to the LCM. The results confirmed our hypotheses and supported the idea that biased encoding of information can be a sufficient cause for the emergence of a LEB effect. At the moment participants were asked to communicate the story in their own words, all participants were in possession of the same infor-mation about the actor (behavior and category label). However, only when participants had received the category label before hearing and processing the story, were stereotype-consistent behaviors described at a higher level of lin-guistic abstraction than stereotype-inconsistent behaviors. When participants received the category label afterwards, no LEB effect emerged.

In a similar vein, we performed a second study with which we aimed to repli-cate the encoding effect, but this time with the LIB. Participants again were re-quired to relate a story. This time a female actor behaved positively and nega-tively. Examples of these behaviors are "She shows the tourists the way" (positive) and "She calls him names" (negative). The female actor was de-scribed abstractly as well, namely as "nice" and "friendly" on the one hand, and "not sympathetic" and "antisocial" on the other. Similar to the LEB study, half of the participants received information about the group membership of the actor before they heard the story and half of the participants after they heard the story. This extra information was embedded in an in-group threatening story. As noted above, Maass et al. (1996) have shown that LIB effects can be enhanced by identity threat, so we presented all participants with in-group threatening information. Specifically, the actor was described as either an un-dergraduate (bachelor) student of the University of Amsterdam (the in-group for our participants) or a student of a nearby university of professional educa-tion (the out-group). The in-group threatening information emphasized the loss of status for university students in the Netherlands, as a result of the recent decision by the Dutch government that not only students of universities but also students of universities of professional education may earn a bachelor's degree after three years.

Again results supported our encoding predictions. Although, in general, positive behaviors were described less abstractly than negative behaviors, this effect was more pronounced for an out-group actor than for an in-group actor. Importantly, this relative LIB effect occurred only when participants learned about the group membership of the actor beforehand, and not when participants learned about the group membership of the actor after they received the behavioral information. The results of this study thus suggest that biased encoding of information can be a sufficient cause for the emergence of a LIB effect too, and replicate the findings of the LEB study.

Taken together, these studies emphasize that how information is encoded into memory can in itself produce biased language use. Processes occurring during the actual communication thus are not a prerequisite for biased language use. Of course, some communication was still involved in these studies. After all, all participants were asked to communicate information. Our point is that in the current studies biased encoding must have been responsible for the LIB and LEB effect given that the communicative act was the same in all conditions. As noted earlier, we certainly do not want to imply that biased language use may only result from biased encoding. On the contrary, there is overwhelming evidence that processes during retrieval and communication, such as receiver effects (Fiedler et al., 2003; Wigboldus, Spears, & Semin, 2005) or activated communication goals (Douglas & Sutton, 2003; Semin et al., 2003) have strong effects on biased language use.

RETRIEVAL AND COMMUNICATION EFFECTS

In a recent overview of research into language, stereotypes and intergroup relations, Wigboldus and Douglas (2007) describe several motives, communication goals and other external factors that may influence biased language use during retrieval and communication. We have already seen that motives such as in-group identity threat may lead to enhanced LIB effects (Maass et al., 1996). Also, a situationally induced need for closure may increase biased language use (Webster, Kruglanski, & Pattison, 1997). So, language abstraction can be sensitive to the motivational state of the communicator at the moment of communication. In a similar vein, social roles may influence biased language use. Research by Schmid and colleagues (Schmid & Fiedler, 1996, 1998; Schmid, Fiedler, Englich, Ehrenberger, & Semin, 1996) demonstrates that the motives inherent in the social roles of defense and prosecution lawyers influence their linguistic choices. That is, more concrete language is used to describe the behavior of the defendant by the defense lawyer who has a motive to establish the innocence of a defendant, thus deflecting blame from the defendant. The prosecution lawyers' motive to establish the defendant's guilt leads them to use more abstract language, implying personal responsibility for the defendant's actions. Interestingly, these results seem to indicate that individuals can exert a certain level of control over their use of language abstraction, even though they may not be consciously aware that they are doing so.

Another recent line of research has demonstrated that recipient characteristics may influence biased language use. That is, at the moment of communication, communicators may attune the level of linguistic abstraction of their message on the basis of the characteristics of the recipient of their message. For example, Rubini and Sigall (2002) found that participants, whose goal was to be liked by recipients, presented their own political views more abstractly when communicating with an agreeing audience than with a mixed audience. In a similar vein, Douglas and McGarty (2001, 2002) found that communicators' use of language abstraction may be influenced by their motivation to please their audiences. Wigboldus et al. (2005) found that the group membership of the recipient (whether this is an in-group or an out-group member) may influence the occurrence of a LEB effect in recipients' messages. Interestingly, recipient effects such as these have been found to be able to completely reverse a LEB effect (e.g., Fiedler et al., 2003; Wigboldus et al., 2005). For instance, Wigboldus et al. (2005) found that when communicators described expected and unexpected information about an in-group target to an in-group recipient, unexpected information was described more abstractly than expected information. Presumably, the expected can be taken for granted when communicating with in-group members about in-group members. Under these conditions it is the unexpected that is more diagnostic and as a result gets emphasized by using abstract terms (also see Fiedler et al., 2003). More examples and a more elaborate discussion of recipient effects and biased language use can be found in Douglas et al. (in press) in this volume.

Finally, research by Douglas and Sutton (2003) demonstrated that communication goals may influence language abstraction and even may override a LEB effect. As we described earlier, when communicators were explicitly asked to portray an actor in a favorable way (positive communication goal) or in an unfavorable way (negative communication goal), communicators with a positive communication goal chose more abstract positive descriptions and more concrete negative descriptions than participants with a negative communication goal. This demonstrates that people can use linguistic abstraction as a tool to attain a desired communication goal. Interestingly, these effects have been found to override the usual LEB effect. That is, in addition to the communication goal manipulation, participants were asked to think of the actor as either their best friend, or their worst enemy. In the absence of a communication goal instruction, the friend versus enemy manipulation resulted in the usual LIB/LEB effect. Positive behaviors of friends and negative behaviors of enemies were described more abstractly than negative behaviors of friends and positive behaviors of enemies. However, when a communication goal was given, this LEB effect disappeared. That is, independent of whether the actor was a friend or an enemy, when explicitly asked to portray the actor in a positive way, communicators used more abstract language to describe positive behaviors than negative behaviors. In the case of a negative communication goal, the reverse was found (Douglas & Sutton, 2003).

Consequently, the following question becomes relevant: Under what circumstances is abstract language use influenced by the way the information was originally encoded? The findings by Douglas and Sutton (2003) indicate that encoding effects may be completely overridden by communication goals activated at the moment of communication. However, does this mean that the original encoding gets overwritten? Or is it overwhelmed only temporarily? Recent research (Wenneker et al., 2005) demonstrated that the orginal encoding of information does not dissappear. That is, although people will recode information linguistically to attain a certain interpersonal goal, the original encoding may still exert its own influence under the right circumstance. We argue that this will be the case especially when cognitive capacity is limited. After all, when constructing a message, communicators not only have to take into account their current communication goals, they also have to correct for the way the information was originally encoded. In general, correcting first impressions such as these takes up cognitive resources and is much harder to perform when cognitive capacity is taxed (e.g., Gilbert, 2002). Especially under these low capacity conditions, communicators who are busy with creating a message that fits their current communication goal will be less able to correct for the way the information was originally encoded.

In two studies, we tested this hypothesis by asking participants to relate expected and unexpected information to another participant. The expectancy of the information was based on an impression formation goal (e.g., participants were asked to form a positive or negative impression of an actor) or a category label (e.g., participants learned about a category membership of an actor that was stereotype consistent or inconsistent with the behaviors in the story). In all cases, the information about the actor was presented before the behavioral information. As a result, at the moment of encoding, all participants knew which behaviors were to be expected and which were unexpected for this particular actor. This in itself should lead to a LEB effect based on biased encoding. Additionally, at the moment of communication, participants received a communication goal instruction and were asked to portray the target person in the information they had received in a positive or in a negative way. In general, this explicit communication goal also was expected to influence the level of language abstraction used (see Douglas & Sutton, 2003). Finally, half of the participants were put under time pressure or all participants were asked to write down the story for a second time, which was quite annoying for them and resulted in participants spending significantly less time on writing down the story again. Results demonstrated that in all conditions the communication goal had a huge effect. In fact, this effect was so strong that it overwhelmed the encoding effect when participants were not under time pressure or were communicating the story for the first time. In line with earlier findings (see Douglas & Sutton, 2003), no evidence for a LEB effect based on the expectancy of the information was found under these conditions. However, under time pressure or when writing the story for a second time (taking less time to do so), participants did demonstrate a LEB effect based on the original encoding of the information. Under these conditions of low cognitive capacity, participants did not seem to be able to correct for the way they originally encoded the information. It seems that when communicators have enough cognitive capacity to correct for the original encoding of information they can easily do so and tailor their message completely to their current communicative needs. However, when cognitive resource is sparse, the way the to-be-communicated information was originally encoded pops up again in the communicator's messages and influences the level of linguistic abstraction used.

In summary, strong effects of motives, recipient characteristics and communication goals on language abstraction have been found to occur at the retrieval and communication phase. These effects may, temporarily, overwhelm encoding effects. Under the right circumstances, however, encoding effects may show up again in biased language use.

An interesting question is to what extent these effects are due to conscious or nonconscious processing. In general, it is found that participants are not aware of their biased language use in the form of a LIB or LEB effect (Maass et al., 1999; Franco & Maass, 1996, 1999). Moreover, linguistic biases such as the LIB have been found to be related to implicit measures of prejudice and not explicit ones (von Hippel, Sekaquaptewa, & Vargas, 1997). The LIB thus is considered an implicit indicator of prejudice. On the other hand, explicit communication goal effects as the ones described above are the result of explicit motives that participants are aware of. As noted by Douglas and Sutton (2003), although participants in their research may have been aware of the communication goal, they probably were unaware that they attained this goal using biased language abstraction. In the following we will get back on this interesting issue.

THE BIASED LANGUAGE MODEL

As noted before, we think that there are two important moments in the communication process where biased processing may lead to biased language use, namely during encoding and during retrieval and communication (see Fig. 8–1). These two processes lead to two independent influences on language abstraction. Our conceptualization of two different processes that operate independently of each other can be linked to general theorizing about the more automatic or associative and the more controlled or systematic dual processes that underlie thought and behavior (for overviews see Chaiken & Trope, 1999;

Smith & DeCoster, 2000). Importantly, however, we do not think that there is a simple one-on-one relationship between automatic or associative processes and encoding effects on the one hand and controlled or systematic processes and retrieval and communication effects on the other hand.

Smith and DeCoster (2000) summarized the general ideas underlying dual-process models and link the two process modes to two memory systems: A slow-learning memory system that accumulates long-term knowledge, and a fast-learning memory system that can record new experiences in a specific context. The associative processing mode is based on the properties of the slow-learning memory system in which general representations of the typical properties of the world are stored in an associative fashion. This mode operates automatically and preconsciously. The rule-based processing mode uses symbolically represented rules that are structured by language and logic, and is based on both the slow-learning memory system and the fast-learning memory system. This mode operates optionally when one has the motivation and cognitive capacity.

Building on this work we would like to sketch a dual-process model underlying biased language use with respect to language abstraction (see Fig. 8–2). It has to be noted that this model outlines the major influences on the level of language abstraction used when communicating behavioral information. This means that the model deals with how information is encoded and subsequently communicated, and not which information. An important assumption under-

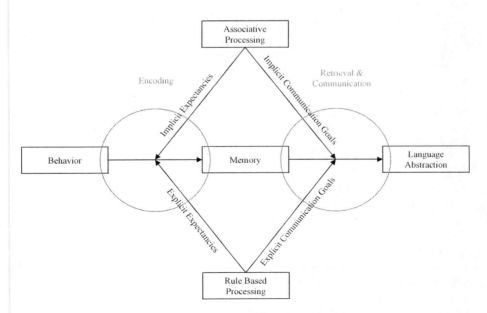

FIGURE 8–2.   Biased language model.

lying the model is that there are two independent routes to language abstraction. That is, processes that influence language abstraction do so during (a) encoding and (b) retrieval (and communication) of information. In addition, the ways in which these processes exert their influence can be divided into (a) associative ones, such as implicit expectancies and associations and implicit communication goals; and (b) rule based ones, such as more explicit expectancies and motives to form an impression and explicit communication goals. So, in fact this is a dual, dual process model in which the two routes to language abstraction (e.g., encoding versus retrieval) and the two ways in which these processes may operate (e.g., associative versus rule based) are orthogonal.

First, during encoding, expectancies, or other relevant associations, may influence language abstraction. For instance, stereotypical associations may affect the way behavioral information is encoded into memory as was demonstrated with the effect of stereotypes on STIs (e.g., Wigboldus et al. 2003). However, also rule based processing may play a role during encoding, for instance when one has a certain impression formation goal or explicit expectancy that is activated before the to-be-encoded behavioral information is perceived (see Wenneker et al., 2005).

Second, during the retrieval and communication of information, rule based processes may be carried out under the influence of explicit communication goals. Whether the goal is to please a recipient (Rubini & Sigall, 2002) or to portray an actor in a favorable or unfavorable way (Douglas & Sutton, 2003), rule based processing may affect the language used. At the same time, more implicit communication goals and other hidden motives may operate during retrieval and communication via associative processing. Recent research has demonstrated that goals can be activated implicitly (e.g., Chartrand & Bargh, 1996). In our model, for example, implicitly activating the goal to portray oneself as likeable probably will result in relatively abstract positive descriptions of others. Communication goal effects thus may be carried out with (explicit) and without (implicit) intention.

During the retrieval and communication phase, expectancies and associations about an actor may be of less influence compared to their influence during the encoding phase. Indeed, Wenneker et al. (2005) found no evidence for LEB or LIB effects when the category label or group membership of the actor was revealed to communicators after the encoding of the information but before the communication. Similarly, Wigboldus et al. (2003) found no effects of stereotypes on STI activation when the category labels were activated after the behavioral information was presented. However, expectancies and associations may exert an effect during retrieval and communication to the extent that they control what information gets activated from memory (and what information does not). For instance, Wigboldus et al. (2005), found no LEB effect when communicators described information about an in-group member to an in-group recipient. One explanation for this finding is that in this intragroup context, stereotypical associations did not get activated in memory. For instance, when a male communicator talks to a male recipient about behavior performed by a male actor, gender stereotypes may not become accessible at all. As a result a LEB based on gender stereotypes will be absent under these conditions. Also in this way, the associative processing mode may play a role during retrieval and communication. Future research could shed a light on if, and if so when and to what extent, effects of associative based processing are of influence during the retrieval and communication stage. Importantly, in our model, both rule based and associative processing may influence biased language use at both encoding and retrieval and communication.

When exploring the biased language model (BLM), the question arises to what extent the two routes to language abstraction represent more automatic or more controlled processes. In respect to this, we should take into account the four horseman of automaticity, namely awareness, intention, efficiency, and control (Bargh, 1994). Effects due to biased encoding mostly seem to be unintentional, unconscious, and effortless, but controllable. After all, they can easily be overruled by communication goals (Douglas & Sutton, 2003). As a result, we like to argue that these encoding effects are always in position to automatically influence language use, when we do not have the cognitive capacity to control them. Also, resisting by trying to inhibit these automatic encoding effects will consume cognitive capacity. Because the language people use is influenced by much more than subtle biased encoding, its effects can be easily overwhelmed, but that does not mean that the way the information was originally encoding has disappeared. Under the right circumstances, biased encoding will reemerge to exert its own influence.

Second, more explicit communication goals, such as the ones investigated by Douglas and Sutton (2003; Douglas et al., in press), are, at least to some extent, controllable and seem to operate intentionally, and consciously. In other words, they influence language use strategically. Explicit communication goals may exert a strong influence on language use and seem to operate under all conditions. In principle, the available cognitive capacity should influence effects due to explicit communication goals to the extent that they are driven by rule based processing (for which motivation and sufficient cognitive capacity is required). However, constructing a message while taking into account a communication goal is something people do all the time, from the moment they start learning to speak. Therefore, communication goals may become automated and as a result become highly efficient. For instance, taking into account the perspective of a recipient when uttering a message is something speakers do all the time. People would not be able to communicate as easily as they do if this process was not highly efficient. These automated communication goals that may be activated spontaneously by cues in the environment when communicating thus may affect language use in a more implicit way, consuming not much cognitive capacity.

With respect to the intentionality of communication goal effects, it is important to note that it is generally assumed that people are unaware of their biased language use (see Maass, 1999) and research performed so far gives strong indications that support this notion (e.g., Franco & Maass, 1996, 1999; von Hippel et al., 1997). Douglas and Sutton (2003) pointed out that when people have a certain explicit communication goal, this does not necessarily imply that they are aware that attaining that goal is facilitated by adjusting the level of linguistic abstraction of their language. Although it seems somewhat counterintuitive, strategic language use can be "unintentional" (see Maass, 1999), because linguistic abstraction is used as a tool of which people are unaware. Explicit communication goal effects thus can be seen as intentional in the sense that they are strategic, but unintentional in the sense that people are (mostly) unaware of the tool they use to reach their goal. One can refer to this as "goal-dependent automaticity" (see Bargh, 1994). That is, people are aware of their goals (e.g., what they are talking about), but they are not aware of the influence of these goals on their word choice.

CONCLUSION

To summarize, the basic idea behind the BLM is that behavioral information is stored into memory, and later on retrieved from memory for communication. Processes that influence language abstraction do so during (a) encoding and (b) retrieval and communication of information. During encoding, activated expectancies, or more general, relevant associations, influence at which level of abstraction the information is stored into memory. However, also more rule based processes may play a role during encoding, for instance when one has an explicit impression formation goal. During the retrieval and communication of information, rule based processes will be of influence (e.g., explicit communication goals), however, associative based processes may operate as well (e.g., implicit communication goals). Future research may reveal to what extent rule based and associative processing affect biased language use during both encoding and retrieval and communication. With this, more insight will be gained into the processes underlying biased language use.

Of course, biased language use by communicators is only the starting point of stereotype transmission and maintenance. As yet, relatively little attention has been paid to the impact of biased language use on recipients (e.g., Maass et al., 1989; Wigboldus et al., 2000, 2006). Future theorizing and research may also focus on the effects of encoding and communication goals in recipients of linguistically biased information. After all, recipients also may have their own expectancies about the information they receive and goals of what they want to do with this information. Only when taking recipients into account as well will we be able to draw the full picture of stereotype transmission and maintenance through biased language use.

ACKNOWLEDGMENTS

Both authors contributed equally to this chapter. Parts of the research discussed in this chapter were supported by the Netherlands Organization for Scientific Research (Grants PPS 98-031, and 425-21-008).

REFERENCES

Barclay, J. R., John, D. B., Franks, J. J., McCarrell, N. S., & Nitsch, K. (1974). Comprehension and semantic flexibility. *Journal of Verbal Learning and Verbal Behavior, 13*, 471–481.

Bargh, J. A. (1994). The four horsemen of automaticity: Awareness, intention, efficiency, and control in social cognition. In J. R. S. Wyer & T. K. Srull (Eds.), *Handbook of social cognition*. Hillsdale, NJ: Erlbaum.

Baron, R. A., & Byrne, D. (2003). *Social Psychology* (10th ed.). Boston: Allyn and Bacon.

Chaiken, S., & Trope, Y. (1999). *Dual-process theories in social psychology*. New York: Guilford.

Chartrand, T. L., & Bargh, J. A. (1996). Automatic activation of impression formation and memorization goals: Nonconscious goal priming reproduces effects of explicit task instructions. *Journal of Personality and Social Psychology, 71*, 464–478.

Correll, J., Park, B., Judd, C. M., & Wittenbrink, B. (2002). The police officer's dilemma: Using ethnicity to disambiguate potentially threatening individuals. *Journal of Personality and Social Psychology, 83*, 1314–1329.

Dijksterhuis, A., & Van Knippenberg, A. (1995). Timing of schema activation and memory; Inhibited access to inconsistent information. *European Journal of Social Psychology, 12*, 383–390.

Dijksterhuis, A. J., & Van Knippenberg, A. (1996). The knife that cuts both ways: Facilitated and inhibited access to traits as a result of stereotype activation. *Journal of Experimental Social Psychology, 32*, 271–288.

Douglas, K. M., & McGarty, C. (2001). Identifiability and self-presentation: Computer-mediated communication and intergroup interaction. *British Journal of Social Psychology, 40*, 399–416.

Douglas, K. M., & McGarty, C. (2002). Internet identifiability and beyond: A model of the effects of identifiability on communicative behavior. *Group Dynamics: Theory, Research, and Practice, 6*, 17–26.

Douglas, K. M., & Sutton, R. M. (2003). Effects of communication goals and expectancies on language abstraction. *Journal of Personality and Social Psychology, 84*, 682–696.

Douglas, K. M., Sutton, R. M., & McGarty, C. (in press) Strategic language use in interpersonal and intergoup communication. In Y. Kashima, K. Fiedler, & P. Freytag (Eds.), *Stereotype dynamics: Language-based approaches to stereotype formation, maintenance, and transformation*. Lawrence Erlbaum.

Fiedler, K., Bluemke, M., Friese, M., & Hofmann, W. (2003). On the different uses of linguistic abstractness: From LIB to LEB and beyond. *European Journal of Social Psychology, 33*, 441–453.

Franco, F. M., & Maass, A. (1996). Implicit versus explicit strategies of out-group discrimination: The role of intentional control in biased language use and reward allocation. *Journal of Language and Social Psychology, 15*, 335–359.

Franco, F. M., & Maass, A. (1999). Intentional control over prejudice: When the choice of the measure matters. *European Journal of Social Psychology, 29*, 469–477.

Gilbert, D. T. (2002). Inferential correction. In T. Gilovich, D. Griffin & D. Kahneman (Eds.), *Heuristics and biases: The psychology of intuitive judgment* (pp. 167–184). Cambridge: University Press.

Hastie, R., & Kumar, P. A. (1979). Person memory: Personality traits as organizing principles in memory for behaviors. *Journal of Personality and Social Psychology, 37*, 25–38.

Howard, J. W., & Rothbart, M. (1980). Social categorization and memory for in-group and out-group behavior. *Journal of Personality and Social Psychology, 38*, 301–310.

Maass, A. (1999). Linguistic intergroup bias: Stereotype perpetuation through language. In M. P. Zanna (Ed.), *Advances in experimental social psychology, Vol. 31* (pp. 79–121). San Diego, CA: Academic Press.

Maass, A., Ceccarelli, R., & Rudin, S. (1996). Linguistic intergroup bias: Evidence for in-group-protective motivation. *Journal of Personality and Social Psychology, 71*, 512–526.

Maass, A., Milesi, A., Zabbini, S., & Stahlberg, D. (1995). Linguistic intergroup bias: Differential expectancies or in-group protection? *Journal of Personality and Social Psychology, 68*, 116–126.

Maass, A., Salvi, D., Arcuri, L., & Semin, G. R. (1989). Language use in intergroup contexts: The linguistic intergroup bias. *Journal of Personality and Social Psychology, 57*, 981–993.

McKoon, G., & Ratcliff, R. (1986). Inferences about predictable events. *Journal of Experimental Psychology: Learning, Memory, and Cognition, 12*, 82–91.

Moscovici, S., & Personnaz, B. (1980). Studies in social influence: V. Minority influence and conversion behavior in a perceptual task. *Journal of Experimental Social Psychology, 16*, 270–282.

Moscovici, S., & Personnaz, B. (1991). Studies in social influence: VI. Is Lenin orange or red? Imagery and social influence. *European Journal of Social Psychology, 21*, 101–118.

Roese, N. J., & Sherman, J. W. (in press). Expectancy. In A. W. Kruglanski & E. T. Higgins (Eds.), *Social psychology: Handbook of basic principles* (Vol. 2). New York, NY: Guilford Press.

Rothbart, M., Evans, M., & Fulero, S. (1979). Recall for confirming events: Memory processes and the maintenance of social stereotypes. *Journal of Experimental Social Psychology, 15*, 343–355.

Rubini, M., & Sigall, H. (2002). Taking the edge off of disagreement: Linguistic abstractness and self-presentation to a heterogeneous audience. *European Journal of Social Psychology, 32*, 343–351.

Ruscher, J. B. (2001). *Prejudiced communication: A social psychological perspective.* New York: Guilford Press.

Samuel, A. G. (1981). Phonemic restoration: Insights from a new methodology. *Journal of Experimental Psychology: General, 110*, 474–494.

Semin, G. R. (2000). Agenda 2000—Communication: Language as an implementational device for cognition. *European Journal of Social Psychology, 30*, 595–612.

Semin, G. R., & Fiedler, K. (1988). The cognitive functions of linguistic categories in describing persons: Social cognition and language. *Journal of Personality and Social Psychology, 54*, 558–568.

Semin, G. R., & Fiedler, K. (1991). The linguistic category model: Its bases, application and range. In W. Stroebe & M. Hewstone (Eds.), *European review of social psychology* (Vol. 2, pp. 1–30). Chichester, England: Wiley.

Semin, G. R., & Fiedler, K. (1992). The inferential properties of interpersonal verbs. In G. R. Semin & K. Fiedler (Eds.), *Language, interaction and social cognition* (pp. 58–78). Thousand Oaks, CA: Sage Publications.

Semin, G. R., Gil de Montes, L., & Valencia, J. F. (2003). Communication constraints on the linguistic intergroup bias. *Journal of Experimental Social Psychology, 39*, 142–148.

Schmid, J., & Fiedler, K. (1996). Language and implicit attributions in the Nuremberg trials. *Human Communication Research, 22*, 371–398.

Schmid, J., & Fiedler, K. (1998). The backbone of closing speeches: The impact of prosecution versus defense language on judicial attributions. *Journal of Applied Social Psychology, 28,* 1140–1172.

Schmid, J., Fiedler, K., Englich, B., Ehrenberger, T., & Semin, G. R. (1996). Taking sides with the defendant: Grammatical choice and the influence of implicit attributions in prosecution and defense speeches. *International Journal of Psycholinguistics, 12,* 127–148.

Smith, E. R., & DeCoster, J. (2000). Dual-process models in social and cognitive psychology: Conceptual integration and links to underlying memory systems. *Personality and Social Psychology Review, 4,* 108–131.

Snyder, M., & Uranowitz, S. W. (1978). Reconstructing the past: Some cognitive consequences of person perception. *Journal of Personality and Social Psychology, 36,* 941–950.

Stangor, C., & McMillan, D. (1992). Memory for expectancy-congruent and expectancy-incongruent information: A review of the social and social developmental literatures. *Psychological Bulletin, 111,* 42–61.

Stewart, T. L., Weeks, M., & Lupfer, M. B. (2003). Spontaneous stereotyping: A matter of prejudice? *Social Cognition, 21,* 263–298.

Tajfel, H., & Turner, J. C. (1979). An integrative theory of intergroup conflict. In S. Worchel & W. G. Austin (Eds.), *The social psychology of intergroup relations* (pp. 33–47). Monterey, CA: Brooks/Cole.

Tajfel, H., & Turner, J. C. (1986). The social identity theory of intergroup behavior. In S. Worchel, & W. G. Austin (Eds.), *Psychology of intergroup relations* (pp. 7–24).

Tulving, E., & Thomson, D. M. (1973). Encoding specificity and retrieval processes in episodic memory. *Psychological Review, 80,* 359–380.

Uleman, J. S., Hon, A., Roman, R. J., & Moskowitz, G. B. (1996). Online evidence for spontaneous trait inferences at encoding. *Personality and Social Psychology Bulletin, 22,* 377–394.

Uleman, J. S., Newman, L. S., & Moskowitz, G. B. (1996). People as flexible interpreters: Evidence and issues from spontaneous trait inference. In M. P. Zanna (Ed.), *Advances in experimental social psychology* (Vol. 28, pp. 211–279). San Diego, CA: Academic Press.

Van Knippenberg, A., & Dijksterhuis, A. (1996). A posteriori stereotype activation: The preservation of stereotypes through memory distortion. *Social Cognition, 14,* 21–53.

von Hippel, W., Sekaquaptewa, D., & Vargas, P. (1995). On the role of encoding processes in stereotype maintenance. In M. P. Zanna (Ed.), *Advances in experimental social psychology* (Vol. 27, pp. 177–254). San Diego, CA: Academic Press.

von Hippel, W., Sekaquaptewa, D., & Vargas, P. (1997). The linguistic intergroup bias as an implicit indicator of prejudice. *Journal of Experimental Social Psychology, 33,* 490–509.

Webster, D. M., Kruglanski, A. W., & Pattison, D. A. (1997). Motivated language use in intergroup contexts: Need-for-closure effects on the linguistic intergroup bias. *Journal of Personality and Social Psychology, 72,* 1122–1131.

Wenneker, C. P. J., Wigboldus, D. H. J., & Spears, R. (2005). Biased language use in stereotype maintenance: The role of encoding and goals. *Journal of Personality and Social Psychology, 89,* 504–516.

Wigboldus D. H. J., & Douglas, K. (2007). Language, stereotypes, and intergroup relations. In K. Fiedler (Ed.), *Social Communication* (pp. 79–106). New York: Psychology Press.

Wigboldus, D. H. J., Dijksterhuis, A., & Van Knippenberg, A. (2003). When stereotypes get in the way: Stereotypes obstruct stereotype-inconsistent trait inferences. *Journal of Personality and Social Psychology, 84,* 470–484.

Wigboldus, D. H. J., Semin, G. R., & Spears, R. (2000). How do we communicate stereotypes? Linguistic bases and inferential consequences. *Journal of Personality and Social Psychology, 78,* 5–18.

Wigboldus, D. H. J., Semin, G. R., & Spears, R. (2006). Communicating expectancies about others. *European Journal of Social Psychology, 36,* 815–824.

Wigboldus, D. H. J., Sherman, J. W., Franzese, H. L., & van Knippenberg, A. (2004). Capacity and comprehension: Spontaneous stereotyping under cognitive load. *Social Cognition, 22,* 292–309.

Wigboldus, D. H. J., Spears, R., & Semin, G. R. (2005). When Do We Communicate Stereotypes? Influence of the Social Context on the Linguistic Expectancy Bias. *Group Processes and Intergroup Relations, 8,* 215–230.

Chapter 9

Strategic Language Use in Interpersonal and Intergroup Communication

Karen M. Douglas and Robbie M. Sutton
University of Kent at Canterbury, United Kingdom

Craig McGarty
The Australian National University

Language is the primary means by which we share information about others. When we describe individuals' and group members' actions and characteristics, we pass on our beliefs about those people to others, and by doing so our beliefs survive over time. Language is indeed a powerful tool for the transmission of beliefs about individuals and groups. Through language, the mass media influence consumers' views (e.g., Ruscher, 2001; van Dijk, 1987; Williams & Giles, 1998), parents shape their childrens' beliefs and stereotypes (Epstein & Komorita, 1966; Fagot, Leinbach, & O'Boyle, 1992), peers influence each others' opinions and preferences (Nesdale, 2001; Weinreich, Luk, & Bond, 1996), and teachers pass on their own values and beliefs to their students (Ruscher, 2001; Stephan & Stephan, 1984).

However, we argue in this chapter that when communicators describe others' actions and traits, they not only pass on their private beliefs but also relay information that is influenced by motives and goals present at the time of communication. What communicators say and how they say it is sensitive to the context in which the communication takes place. The information transmitted can be more heavily influenced by context and motives than by communicators' original beliefs, so that communicators often transmit information to others that is divorced from their private beliefs in intriguing ways. To illustrate our point, how often have you later reread an e-mail or letter you wrote and been surprised by its content? Of course, we could point to changing attitudes as one way of explaining discrepancies between what we said in the past and what we think or would say now, but one other way of explaining those differences is in terms of the powerful yet subtle effects of context. Drawing on our research program to date we argue in this chapter that, without necessarily being aware, communicators' descriptive language use is strongly influenced by contextual and motivational factors. Specifically, communicators are able to use language strategically to present themselves favorably to an audience and achieve specific communication goals.

LANGUAGE AND BELIEF TRANSMISSION

The importance of language in the expression of beliefs and stereotypes has long been acknowledged in social psychology (e.g., Allport, 1954; Katz & Braly, 1933; Lippmann, 1922). Many researchers have argued for the importance of language in the maintenance of racial stereotypes in particular (e.g., Hogg & Abrams, 1990; Maass & Arcuri, 1996; Moscovici, 1981; Stangor & Schaller, 1996; van Dijk, 1987). However, until fairly recently, research on stereotyping and language focused little on the interpersonal functions of language in the processes of transmitting beliefs and stereotypes. Specifically, the role of language as a *tool* for the transmission and maintenance of beliefs has only received recent attention in social psychology (e.g., Lyons & Kashima, 2003; Maass & Arcuri, 1996; Ruscher, 2001; van Dijk, 1987). However, the development of the *linguistic category model* (Semin & Fiedler, 1988, 1991) has led to a wealth of research into the specific linguistic mechanisms underlying the communication of interpersonal beliefs and stereotypes.

The linguistic category model or *LCM* (Semin & Fiedler, 1988, 1991, 1992; see also Semin, 2000; Wigboldus & Douglas, 2007, for a recent review) proposes that social cognition and language influence each other directly. First, language may influence social cognitive processes, so that language influences the cognitive inferences that people make. On the other hand, social cognitive processes also impact upon language use. According to Semin (2000), people use the language "tools" that best meet their socio-cognitive needs. The LCM proposes that there are four such tools, or levels of abstraction, that people can use to describe the actions and traits of others. These tools are (a) *descriptive action verbs* (DAVs, e.g., "Lisa *slaps* Helen"), (b) *interpretative action verbs* (IAVs, e.g., "Lisa *hurts* Helen"), (c) *state verbs* (SVs, e.g., "Lisa *dislikes* Helen") and (d) *adjectives* (ADJs, e.g., "Lisa is *aggressive*") and represent increasing levels of abstraction in descriptive language. As we move from concrete to abstract descriptions of an event, it is possible to infer more information about the actor him- or herself and expect that this information will be consistent across occasions. That is, abstract language implies greater temporal and cross-situational stability (see Maass, Salvi, Arcuri, & Semin, 1989; Semin & Fiedler, 1988, 1991, 1992; Semin & Marsman, 1994; Semin & de Poot, 1997). Put more simply, abstract language enables people to transmit more belief-consistent or expectancy-consistent information about others than does concrete language. When stereotypes correspond with a communicator's expectations, language abstraction also enables people to transmit stereotype-consistent information.

People's use of language abstraction to express their beliefs, expectancies and stereotypes has been explored in some detail in work on the *linguistic intergroup bias* (*LIB*) and *linguistic expectancy biases* (*LEB*). The LIB (Maass et al., 1989) refers to the tendency of people to describe desirable in-group behaviors and undesirable out-group behaviors at higher levels of language abstraction than desirable out-group behaviors and undesirable in-group behaviors. This robust linguistic bias implies that desirable behavior is characteristic of in-groups and in-group members; whereas undesirable behavior is typical of out-groups and out-group members (e.g., Arcuri, Maass, & Portelli, 1993; Cole & Leets, 1998; Maass, 1999; Maass & Arcuri, 1992, 1996; Maass, Milesi, Zabbini, & Stahlberg, 1995; Ng & Chan, 1996; Rubini & Semin, 1994; Werkman, Wigboldus, & Semin, 1999). More generally however, people choose more abstract descriptions for behaviors that are expectancy consistent, and more concrete language for behaviors that are expectancy inconsistent. This general bias has been referred to as the LEB (Wigboldus et al., 2000).

The importance of the LIB and the LEB in the transmission of beliefs and stereotypes becomes evident when examining the cognitive inferences made by recipients of concrete or abstract descriptions. Maass and colleagues (e.g., Maass et al., 1989; Maass, 1999) proposed that, while socio-cognitive biases and stereotypes influence the language that people choose to describe behavioral events, ultimately this process contributes to the transmission and maintenance of those beliefs. The interplay between language and cognition also implies that a describer's language should affect a recipient's inferences about the person being described. When a person therefore describes this behavior onwards, his or her language will have been affected by the language of the original describer. Indeed, research supports this assertion (Wigboldus et al., 2000). However, research suggests that people are unable to exert control over this aspect of their language. So, although language abstraction enables the effective sharing of information about individuals and group members, it does not appear to allow the strategic presentation of this information. Or does it? In the next section, we outline research on the explicit/implicit nature of language abstraction and explicit factors that influence language abstraction, and then move on to discuss our research program to date.

INTENTIONAL CONTROL OVER
LANGUAGE ABSTRACTION

Research suggests that people typically transmit their beliefs through language abstraction without explicit intent (Franco & Maass, 1996, 1999; Schnake & Ruscher, 1998; von Hippel, Sekaquaptewa, & Vargas, 1997). Specifically, individuals are able to censor or alter their responses to explicit or outward measures of stereotyping such as the Modern Racism Scale (McConahay, Hardee, & Batts, 1981), but appear unable to censor or alter the LIB. That is, when people have biased expectancies about groups, the effect of these expectancies on their linguistic choices appears to be "difficult to inhibit" (Franco & Maass, 1996, p. 339). von Hippel and colleagues (1997) also found that the LIB was correlated with implicit but not explicit measures of prejudice. These findings support the view that the LIB and the more general LEB are most likely implicit phenomena by which individuals transmit biased expectancies without intending to do so. In other words, people may be unaware that much of the time, they are saying "what's on their mind".

However, theories of pragmatics and social psychological theories give us some grounds to suspect that language abstraction could be more than a medium whereby people transmit their beliefs without intent, and that concrete/abstract language use could be sensitive to the communication context and the motivations of the communicator. First, speech-act theory (Austin, 1962; Searle, 1975) posits that language is *performative*. That is, in speaking, communicators achieve particular communicative intentions. These *illocutionary* acts are interpreted by recipients who are generally able to infer the communicator's original intentions. This line of thought suggests that language can be used indirectly by communicators to have a desired effect on recipients. Further, according to Higgins' (1981) notion of the "communication game," communication is a purposeful social activity that communicators use to achieve goals, which may include advocacy, derogation, ingratiation, politeness, and the construction of social consensus. What people say does not simply express privately held beliefs but is often tailored to suit communicators' goals and motives. Other social psychological writings also present communication as a flexible, purposive activity (e.g., Edwards & Potter, 1993; Giles & Coupland, 1991; Gil de Montes, Semin, & Valencia, 2003; Jost & Kruglanski, 2002; Semin, Gil de Montes, & Valencia, 2003). Once said, assertions or implications that depart from communicators' original beliefs can influence the beliefs of recipients and even of communicators themselves, such is the case for the "saying is believing" effect (Higgins, 1999; Higgins & Rholes, 1978; Lau, Chiu, & Lee, 2001). In this sense, communication results in the creation of information and not simply its transmission.

Recent research provides some support for the notion that people do not necessarily always use language abstraction in a manner that reflects "what's on their mind" because other *intrapersonal* factors influence the abstractness of their language. As such, the information people transmit to others may not always be their own privately held beliefs. For example, Maass, Ceccarelli, and Rudin (1996) showed that the linguistic intergroup bias is augmented under conditions of high *threat* to in-group members from out-group members. Further, Webster, Kruglanski, and Pattison (1997) demonstrated that people who were higher in cognitive *need-for-closure*, showing a general preference for certainty, preferred more abstract descriptions. These findings are important because they suggest that language abstraction is sensitive to influences that arguably lead to a motivational state in the communicator. For example, one could argue that the participants in Maass et al.'s (1996) research were motivated to protect their in-group from threat. It is likely that such motivations, whether the communicator is aware of them or not, influence how communicators express their beliefs. The information they ultimately communicate may therefore not exactly match their private beliefs.

Further, recent research increasingly suggests that *interpersonal* motivations also affect language abstraction. For example, Schmid, Fiedler, Englich, Ehrenberger, and Semin (1996; see also Schmid & Fiedler, 1996, 1998) demonstrated that prosecution lawyers typically use abstract language to describe defendants' actions, implying dispositionality and personal responsibility; whereas defence lawyers use more concrete language, implying that situational factors were the cause, therefore deflecting the blame from the defendant. Presumably motivated by the desire to gain an acquittal or conviction, lawyers alter their language abstraction to suit their goal. Also, Semin and colleagues (2003) found that biased language use (e.g., positive behaviors of a partner and negative behaviors of an opponent being described more abstractly, and negative partner and positive opponent behaviors being described more concretely) occurred only when the communication had a clear purpose, but not when it did not. Also, Gil de Montes et al. (2003) found that people communicated more abstractly about a target liked by their communicative partner when the communicative context was cooperative and the behavior was positive and when the context was competitive and the behavior was negative. Again, this research suggests that language abstraction may be sensitive to factors related to the situation in which communication takes place (see also Rubini & Sigall, 2002).

Our overall research program to date has explored this issue in greater depth. Specifically, we were first interested in the effects of *communicative context* on people's expression of their beliefs through language abstraction, and here we attempted to identify variables that mediate the relationships between identifiability and language abstraction in a computer-mediated communication setting. Second, we investigated the effects of explicit *communication goals* on language abstraction. Our overall aim was to demonstrate that language abstraction is more than a tool whereby people transmit their beliefs to others. We aimed to demonstrate that language abstraction enables communicators to tailor their language, whether they are aware or not, to present themselves positively to others, or to manipulate the beliefs of others about the individuals and groups being described. As such, we argue that language abstraction can be viewed as a powerful tool for both the transmission of beliefs and the creation of new beliefs. Finally, in this chapter, we outline new research where we have investigated the extent to which recipients are able to infer bias on the part of the describer based on language abstraction, and the extent to which describers are able to inhibit the expression of their biased beliefs. Here, we specifically address the potential implications of strategic language use.

IDENTIFIABILITY AND LANGUAGE ABSTRACTION

As previously mentioned, research has suggested that intrapersonal factors such as feelings of threat (e.g., Maass et al., 1996) and need-for-closure (Webster et al., 1997) influence communicators' use of language abstraction such that they do not always use language abstraction in such a way that is consistent with their overall expectancies. This being the case, it is reasonable to predict that intrapersonal or intrapsychic factors such as these may interact with the context in which the communication takes place, to influence people's descriptive language choices. For example, communicators may feel that their in-group is being threatened when communicating in the presence of out-group members, especially when the out-group members are powerful. In these situations, communicators might be motivated to describe others' actions differently, so as to avoid punishment or derogation. Also, it is possible in a situation where the in-group is present, that people will feel motivated to uphold the norms of the in-group when they describe the actions or traits of others. Under these conditions, descriptions of others' behaviors may be more likely to cohere with the shared opinions and expectations of the in-group. In other words, awareness of contextual features such as the presence of an audience and the nature of that audience, and awareness of the potential consequences of communicating information in a certain way, may influence the choices communicators make in their descriptive language. This issue was explored in the first series of studies we describe here. In particular, we examined the effects of being *identifiable* (or anonymous) to in-group and out-group audiences, on language abstraction.

The social identity model of deindividuation effects (SIDE; Reicher, Spears, & Postmes, 1995) makes predictions about how group members will behave in the presence of others. Of particular relevance to our research, SIDE theorists argue that in the presence of others, there may be *strategic* effects that are related to the enactment of group identity. These effects relate to how deindividuated behavior might be influenced by social category, context and particularly audience characteristics related to situations where the *self* is anonymous or identifiable to *others* (Reicher et al., 1995; Reicher, Levine, & Gordijn, 1998; Spears & Lea, 1994).

We investigated the effects of identifiability on descriptive language use in a computer-mediated communication (CMC) paradigm. In this situation, people are typically able to choose to make themselves either anonymous or identifiable to others. As such, it is a medium where communication is likely to be influenced by intrapersonal concerns about threat, and the desire to uphold communicative as well as groups norms (see also Barreto & Ellemers, 2000, 2002; Noel, Wann, & Branscombe, 1995). In particular, when describing the behavior of others, communicators are likely to have different concerns depending on to whom they are talking and whether or not their comments can be linked to them personally. CMC was also an ideal medium to examine these issues because it was possible to examine archival examples of descriptive language on bulletin boards, and also to set up experimental situations where participants are led to believe that they are anonymous or identifiable to in-group or out-group audiences. Of particular interest here was the language communicators use to describe the behaviors and characteristics of *outgroup* targets. We chose this because much of the "flaming" or hostile communication present on the Internet is directed toward out-groups, and a great deal of negative communication over the Internet is directed at racial/cultural minority groups (Douglas, forthcoming; Douglas, McGarty, Bliuc, & Lala, 2005; Gerstenfeld, Grant, & Chiang, 2003). CMC is therefore a rich context to witness the expression of strong opinions about groups and to examine how identifiability influences the expression of these opinions.

In our first study, we examined a naturalistic setting mixed with anonymous and identifiable communicators from a vast selection of in-groups and out-groups. In this archival study, samples of hostile communication from Internet-based newsgroups were analyzed. These were messages posted by anonymous or identifiable communicators about anonymous or identifiable out-groups and out-group members. In typical newsgroup environments, communicators are either identifiable (by name and e-mail address/geographical location) or anonymous (usually only a nickname supplied) to both in-group and out-group members. We called identifiability by name and e-mail address or geographical location *Internet identifiability*, because it is the most common way in which people can be identifiable when they communicate on the Internet although they are not physically identifiable in this medium.

Our findings revealed that communicators' language abstraction was indeed sensitive to identifiability. Specifically, there was an interaction between source and target identifiability. In the specific case of anonymous out-group targets, communicators used significantly higher levels of language abstraction in their descriptions when they themselves were identifiable than when they were anonymous. No other comparisons were significant. Therefore, communicators were more likely to describe anonymous out-group targets using more expectancy-consistent language when they themselves were identifiable to their "mixed" in-group and out-group audience. Thus, we had preliminary evidence for our hypothesis that language abstraction is sensitive to communicative context; in this case, personal identifiability.

In the remainder of this research program, we sought to (a) replicate this effect under controlled conditions, and (b) establish what mediates the effect. If indeed communicators' language is influenced by intrapersonal motivations under conditions of identifiability to an audience, then the effect of identifiability on language abstraction ought to be mediated by variables such as feelings of accountability, the desire to express one's identity, or a desire to be evaluated positively by the in-group (e.g., Noel et al., 1995).

In the second and third studies (see Douglas & McGarty, 2001), we tested these ideas in turn. In the laboratory, anonymous or identifiable participants were asked to write a response to a message that had been posted on the Web by a member of a White-power group. In doing so, half of the participants were asked to supply their name and country of residence (identifiable) and half were asked to type that they were anonymous. Participants were informed that their responses would be posted on a mailing list comprised of people who are opposed to White-power groups (e.g., an in-group audience). In these two studies, we established that the effect of identifiability on language abstraction described in the archival study (we termed this the *identifiability effect*) occurred due to the presence of in-group members in the audience. The effect was not present in the case of the out-group-only audience. Therefore, we ruled out the desire to present an in-group normative view to resist the out-group as an explanation for the identifiability effect (e.g., Spears & Lea, 1994). Instead, it seemed likely that communicators used more stereotypical descriptions of the out-group target out of some kind of motivation related to the presence of the in-group audience.

As previously mentioned, people who are identifiable to other in-group members may act in a more group-normative manner for strategic reasons such as a desire to be positively evaluated by the in-group (e.g., Noel et al., 1995) or because they do not identify strongly with the group (e.g., Barreto & Ellemers, 2000, 2002). Further, participants who are identifiable may feel under more pressure to adhere to the norms of the group because they are accountable to the group for what they say (e.g., Reicher et al., 1995; Spears & Lea, 1994). Whether or not such factors come into play when descriptions of out-groups are identifiable to an in-group audience, however, remained to be tested. The common feature of these explanations is that they posit strategic or self-presentational motivations for communicators to use more abstract language.

Indeed, our subsequent data support the position that language abstraction is related to strategic concerns. We demonstrated that a communicators' identifiability teamed with low commitment to the issue of racism mediated the identifiability effect (see Douglas & McGarty, 2001, Study 3; see also McGarty, Taylor, & Douglas, 2000). In the studies presented in Douglas and McGarty (2002), we demonstrated that the effect of identifiability on language abstraction was mediated by responses to an item relating to compliance ("My response to the message reflected what I thought the people reading the message would like to read"). The more communicators denied that they were complying with what they thought others would like to read, the higher levels of language abstraction they chose to describe the out-group target. In two subsequent studies also outlined in Douglas and McGarty (2002), we demonstrated that identifiability arouses feelings of sensitivity to the communicative context (e.g., feeling accountable, feeling that writing a message would enable them to enact their in-group identity) but that these did not mediate the effect of identifiability on language abstraction. So, while it was difficult to establish one single mediating variable, it was clear from our results that language abstraction was sensitive to identifiability because identifiability influenced the way communicators were motivated to describe the actions of the out-group target to others.

Of course, the best way to examine if a mediating variable influences a dependent variable is to manipulate the variable in question (Sigall & Mills, 1998). So, to examine if communicative motivations do indeed influence language abstraction, and that communicators can use language abstraction to achieve communicative objectives, it was important to manipulate communicative goals directly. We did this in our next series of experiments, which we will describe here (see also Douglas & Sutton, 2003).

COMMUNICATION GOALS

In summary, participants in some studies appeared unable to control their language abstraction, which is determined by intrapersonal factors such as biased expectancies and need for cognitive closure (Franco & Maass, 1996, 1999; von Hippel et al., 1997; Webster et al., 1997). However, participants in studies of interpersonal processes appeared able to use language abstraction flexibly depending on the communicative motives aroused by the communicative context (e.g., Douglas & McGarty, 2001, 2002; see also Schmid & Fiedler, 1996, 1998; Schmid et al., 1996; Semin et al., 2003). This apparent paradox raises important questions about the regulation and function of language abstraction. Is language abstraction under implicit or explicit control, or both? Are describers able to dissociate their language abstraction from their internal representation of events? Is language abstraction a medium by which information is transmitted, a tool by which it is created, or both?

We advocate the view that when describers have biased expectancies, they are generally unable to inhibit the effects of those expectancies on their language abstraction (Franco & Maass, 1996, 1999). In such cases, biased language abstraction is best seen as a medium of belief transmission without explicit awareness. However, when describers intend to achieve certain communication goals independently of their private beliefs about described actions and persons, we propose that their language abstraction responds appropriately. For example, when communicators wish to present an in-group normative opinion about another group, their language abstraction may facilitate their goal independently of the strength of their own private beliefs. Writing a highly abstract description of the out-group transmits the impression that the communicator has a highly stereotypical view of the out-group, even though this may not be the case. Similarly, if communicators wish to aggrandize or derogate individuals, language abstraction may give them a means to do so independently of whether they like or dislike the actors. In such cases, language abstraction is best characterized as a tool for the purposive creation of beliefs.

To explain this idea in more detail, we note that being unable to inhibit a behavior does not logically mean the same thing as being unable to perform the same behavior when it facilitates a goal (see also Higgins, 1997). Thus, it is consistent to assert that linguistic biases are difficult to suppress, but they are also aroused by communication goals. Also, we do not propose that describers are explicitly aware that their language abstraction varies with their communicative goals. Given communicators' documented inability to inhibit the linguistic expression of cognitive biases, we think it unlikely that they consciously control variations in language abstraction (see Franco & Maass, 1996; von Hippel et al., 1997).

This proposed dissociation between inhibiting and recruiting linguistic biases is psychologically plausible. More than recruiting linguistic bias, inhibiting bias is hindered by describers' biased expectancies. When describers have formed a highly dispositional representation of an individual's behavior, the corresponding biases inherent in abstract descriptions are likely to be difficult for them to detect and therefore to censor. Compared to explicit ideological statements such as those in the Modern Racism Scale, the abstraction of descriptions of individuals' actions is probably more difficult for communicators to consciously relate to social desirability and group-based biases. Therefore, communicators who might want to inhibit bias can rely neither on their own ability to detect bias in descriptions, nor differences in the apparent social desirability of their descriptions. We discuss the concept of inhibition in more depth later in this chapter.

However, when communicators consciously set out to produce language that may be biased, they can generate and select descriptions according to how well they fit their goal, rather than how free from bias they subjectively appear. For example, a communicator who wants to aggrandize a person who performs a positive behavior will, with all else being equal, find that an abstract description (e.g., Barbara is friendly) better fits this communication goal than a concrete description (e.g., Barbara is smiling), given that abstract descriptions tend to imply more temporal stability and convey more information about actors (Semin & Fiedler, 1988).

Coming back to the research we have described so far, we have some evidence for the importance of communication goals but results are not conclusive. In Douglas and McGarty's (2001, 2002) studies, participants' private views of the out-group may have become harsher in the presence of an in-group audience. Such interpersonal effects on private views are theoretically important in their own right (cf. Jost & Kruglanski, 2002; Zajonc, 1960). However, if these shifts in views were sufficient to account for language abstraction effects, expectancies would remain the proximal cause of language abstraction. The degree to which language abstraction can be used flexibly would be constrained by how much describers' expectancies are subject to intrapersonal revision in a given communicative context. In contrast, our current view entails the expression of beliefs that describers have not necessarily privately adopted.

Research to this point had not yet isolated the effects of goals on messages, or disentangled these from the effects of expectancies and other intrapersonal factors such as liking. In the next set of studies we will outline, this was our major aim. To elicit communication goals, we explicitly instructed our participants to describe behaviors in different ways, orthogonally to their expectancies. For example, reconsider our characters Lisa and Helen. Lisa sees Helen slapping another person. Based on the linguistic expectancy bias, we would expect Helen to describe Lisa's behavior in a way that is consistent with her beliefs about Lisa, which may be positive or negative (e.g., Maass et al., 1995; Wigboldus et al., 2000). However, we proposed that communication goals would have a *unique* effect on language abstraction. If Helen wants to describe the act charitably and avoid attributing temporal stability or dispositionality, she can use concrete language. Likewise, Helen can use more abstract language to attribute full responsibility to Lisa for her actions. We predicted that the opposite would occur for positive behaviors. If Helen wishes to describe them charitably, she will use abstract language, but if intends to describe them harshly, she will use concrete language.

In the first of our series of studies, participants were asked to view a series of cartoons depicting a person performing either a positive or negative behavior, and make a forced-choice description from four linguistic category model alternatives (see also Franco & Maass, 1996; Maass et al., 1989; Maass et al., 1995; Maass et al., 1996; Werkman et al., 1999). Participants were asked to imagine the person as either someone they like, such as their best friend, or someone they dislike, such as their worst enemy. Positive behaviors should be expected of best friends but not of worst enemies, and negative behaviors should be expected of worst enemies but not of best friends (see Karpinski & von Hippel, 1996; Maass et al., 1995). We therefore predicted that language abstraction would be high when expectancy was high (positive behaviors of friends and negative behaviors of enemies) and low when expectancy was low (negative behaviors of friends and positive behaviors of enemies).

In addition to expectancy, participants were given an explicit, communication goal for each scene. In each case, participants were asked to select either *favorable* or *unfavorable* descriptions from the four alternatives. If communication goals have a unique influence on language abstraction, independent of expectancies, then the levels of abstraction of descriptions chosen for positive behaviors should be high given a favorable goal but low given an unfavorable goal. Conversely, the level of abstraction chosen for negative behaviors should be high for an unfavorable goal and low for a favorable goal. Further, we examined whether communication goals could *obviate or reverse* the LEB if they are incompatible with expectancies. That is, when communication goals compete with expectancies such as when participants are asked to describe a friend's positive behavior unfavourably, we examined whether the strength of any effect of communication goal would be enough to eliminate or reverse the LEB. If describers with low expectancies can, when suitably motivated, select language that is at least as abstract as other describers with high expectancies, this would underscore the ability for language abstraction to respond to communication goals independently of expectancies.

The results supported our hypotheses. They supported previous findings that descriptions are strongly influenced by intrapersonal factors such as their prior expectancies about events (e.g., Maass et al., 1995; Wigboldus et al., 2000). More relevant to our unique hypotheses however, results showed that the explicit goals to select a favorable or unfavorable description strongly affected the abstraction of the chosen alternative. Several aspects of the results also suggest that, as we predicted, the effects of explicit communication goals can be orthogonal to those of expectancy. In particular, goals obviated and even reversed the LEB when the two biases were placed in conflict. For example, when asked to describe the positive actions of friends unfavourably, participants used significantly more concrete language than when asked to describe the same actions favourably. Likewise for enemies, positive behaviors attracted more abstract descriptions under instructions to describe these actions favourably than unfavourably. This goes against the general notion that positive behaviors of friends should be described abstractly, whereas the same behavior performed by an enemy should be described concretely. The communication goals given to participants overrode this general linguistic tendency. This finding was replicated in a number of other studies. First, it was possible that the best friend/worst enemy distinction may be problematic because individuals are likely to be motivated to aggrandize friends, and thus choose favorable descriptions, and derogate enemies and thus choose unfavorable descriptions, in much the same way as group members are often motivated to favor their in-groups and to derogate their out-groups in order to maintain positive collective self-esteem (e.g., Branscombe & Wann, 1994; Jetten, Spears, & Manstead, 1997; Reynolds, Turner, & Haslam, 2000). The net effect of this may have been an accentuation of the apparent effect of expectancies, for which the friend/enemy manipulation was intended as a proxy, at the expense of the apparent effect of communication goals. We eliminated this possibility by using a "pure" manipulation of expectancies where participants were informed that the actor often or rarely behaves in the manner depicted. The results were the same as in the previous study. In our third study, we replicated the effect in a free-response paradigm, and also in a situation where we asked participants to specifically write their responses in such a way as to influence a potential recipient. We also demonstrated, in a final study, that this effect was not simply an artifact of the valence inherent in the descriptions. Overall, these studies provide evidence that communication goals have a strong effect on language abstraction, that is independent of communicators' prior expectancies.

SUMMARY OF OUR FINDINGS

Previous research has shown that language abstraction is influenced by expectancies (e.g., Maass et al., 1995; Wigboldus et al., 2000), intrapersonal factors such as affective reactions (e.g., Maass et al., 1996), and cognitive need for closure (Webster et al., 1997) and interpersonal factors related to social roles and context (Gil de Montes et al., 2003; Rubini & Sigall, 2002; Schmid & Fiedler, 1996, 1998; Schmid et al., 1996; Semin et al., 2003). Other research, including our own highlights, the importance of aspects of the interpersonal relation between describers and recipients, such as identifiability, and indicates that intrapersonal factors such as accountability can mediate the effects of context on language abstraction (Douglas & McGarty, 2001, 2002). Our more recent research shows that communication goals to shape messages and cause recipients to form certain beliefs can affect language abstraction independently of describers' own expectancies (Douglas & Sutton, 2003). In turn, this suggests that lawyers, political spokespeople, and similarly motivated describers can recruit language abstraction to propagate ideas that they do not privately share.

Our findings complement current thinking about the importance of context in shaping communication. In particular, Semin (2000) argues that interpersonal context is "critical in shaping the structure of a message" (p. 606). Semin further argues that people use language as a "resource to structure the representation of reality in a particular way in order to shape and influence the cognitive processes of the *recipient* of a message" (p. 601). Also, Edwards and Potter (1993; see also Edwards & Potter, 1999; Fiedler & Schmid, 1999; and Schmid & Fiedler, 1999, for an interesting debate about discursive approaches to language and the linguistic category model) argue that language is "an arena for social action, with constructive and pragmatic relationships to world and thought" (p. 38). Our data show that language abstraction can be precisely such a tool for social action and construction of reality insofar as it allows describers, motivated by contextual and interpersonal factors, to convey often novel ideas to recipients about behaviors and protagonists.

This strategic use of language abstraction is much more sophisticated and subtle than the explicit, deceitful assertion of beliefs that describers do not have but wish their recipients to form. Rather, participants in our studies used levels of language abstraction in which the target belief, for example, that White-power groups are racist, or more generally that an observed behavior is characteristic of an actor, was merely implicit. Our participants were not simply telling untruths, but literally "structuring the representation of reality" to fit the demands of the context or their specific communication goal (Semin, 2000, p. 601). Previous research on language abstraction shows that it is a channel through which communicators may betray their biases (e.g., Franco & Maass, 1996; von Hippel et al., 1997). Our program of research demonstrates that it is also a subtle and important channel available to communicators who intend to convey particular impressions of others, for whatever reason. Further, language abstraction is a tool that communicators may not realize they are using.

However, the efficacy of explicit goals such as misleading one's audience in Douglas and Sutton's (2003) studies is important in showing that language abstraction is not an entirely implicit phenomenon. The explicit instructions used in the studies described also allows us to be confident that participants were indeed setting out to tailor their messages. However, as noted by Bargh (1996; Bargh, Gollwitzer, Lee-Chai, Barndollar, & Troetschel, 2001), not all goals are conscious. We think it likely that in everyday communication, in which multiple objectives often need to be met, individuals form implicit communication goals to, for example, be polite, or to make an actor look good. These kinds of implicit goals are likely to affect language abstraction as much as the explicit goals featured in the present studies. Indeed, such processes may have been at work in our earlier research (Douglas & McGarty, 2001, 2002). Although we found some evidence that the effect of context on language abstraction was mediated by explicit self-presentational concerns, it is likely that context aroused some implicit goals which have the same effect. With regard to the creative function of language abstraction, the most important feature of our findings overall is the ability of communication objectives, whether implicit or explicit, to cause messages to differ from private expectancies.

Our studies show that language abstraction, responding to interpersonal factors, can convey new information to recipients (cf. Semin & Fiedler, 1988; Wigboldus et al., 2000). However, it remains to be seen whether these messages may actually influence the describers themselves (cf. the classic counter-attitudinal advocacy study of Bem & McConnell, 1972, and Higgins & Rholes', 1978 "saying is believing effect"). In this regard, there may be a distinction between *preutterance* and *postutterance* effects on describers' beliefs. Specifically, interpersonal factors such as identifiability (Douglas & McGarty, 2001, 2002), and the drive for shared reality (e.g., Lau et al., 2002) may shape the attitudes and beliefs of describers before they generate a message for others, and in this mediated way shape the message itself. In these cases the interpersonal factors, rather than the message itself, can be primarily credited with causing describers to have new, altered, or augmented beliefs. The message fulfils the crucial role of transmitting these beliefs to recipients. This kind of preutterance effect is likely to be the norm in many natural cases of motivated communication. However, at other times, as in Douglas and Sutton (2003), interpersonal factors and communication goals appear to cause describers to voice beliefs to which they are yet to subscribe privately. If describers later come to adopt the beliefs they expressed then the message itself can be said, in a more powerful sense, to cause describers to form those beliefs.

FUTURE DIRECTIONS

Our research to date demonstrates the power of language abstraction as a tool for the attainment of communication and self-presentational goals (e.g., Douglas & McGarty, 2001, 2002; Douglas & Sutton, 2003). In this section, we outline some of our more recent research where we extend and investigate the potential implications of our findings. Two factors we have considered are (a) recipients' ability (or inability) to detect bias on the part of the describer, and (b) describers' ability (or inability) to inhibit linguistic bias.

   1. Detecting linguistic bias.   By documenting the variables that explain variations in language abstraction, the research we have outlined here effectively charts how language abstraction may be somewhat diagnostic of the beliefs, but particularly the goals of the individuals or group members using it. Although language abstraction is a relatively subtle feature of language and its use is somewhat implicit, optimal recipients may be able to exploit this diagnostic capacity, whether or not they are aware of doing so. Indeed, participants are able to recognize some of the corollaries of language abstraction, such as low verifiability, high disputability and temporal endurance (Semin & Fiedler, 1988). It is therefore possible that recipients of descriptions may use language abstraction as a cue to form hypotheses about describers, including their characteristics and goals. If it is the case that participants are able to "read" speakers' intentions and characteristics, then this could be a serious impediment to communicators' ability to transmit their beliefs and achieve their communication goals.

   In some recent research, we investigated this possibility (Douglas & Sutton, 2006). To illustrate our predictions, an abstract description such as "Lisa is *aggressive*" will normally be seen by recipients as more disputable, less verifiable, and as conveying more enduring information about Lisa than a concrete description such as "Lisa *slaps* Helen." Those recipients might well conclude that the abstract describer is less likely to be Lisa's friend, to like Lisa, or to want to portray Lisa favorably, than the concrete describer. In our experiments, participants were asked to view a series of cartoons, each depicting a person performing a positive or negative behavior, and read a description of the behavior. We first tested whether participants would be able to make judgments about describers' personal *relationships* with and likely *attitudes* toward protagonists (Experiment 1). We then tested whether participants' judgments of describers' *communication goals* would be affected by language abstraction (Experiment 2). Overall, our findings revealed that language abstraction influences the inferences that recipients make about describers' relationships, motivations, and attitudes toward their targets. To give an example, when viewing positive behaviors and descriptions, participants rated the describer as more likely to be the protagonist's friend, less likely to be the protagonist's enemy, and less likely to be an unbiased observer, with increasing language abstraction. Also, variations in language abstraction influenced the conclusions that recipients drew about describers, independently of the rated valence of the descriptions (Experiment 3). It could potentially be the case that the more abstract a description is, the more it is likely to be strongly valenced. The degree to which a description carries positive or negative valence is likely to be accessible to conscious awareness, even if language abstraction it not. However, our results suggest that recipients do not rely on perceptions of description valence to make their judgments about describers.

Previous research has shown that language abstraction is influenced by expectancies and motivating factors, supporting the idea that language abstraction is used by describers, either implicitly or explicitly, to achieve communicative objectives (Douglas & McGarty, 2001, 2002; Douglas & Sutton, 2003; Maass et al., 1989; Maass et al., 1995, 1996; Webster et al., 1995; Wigboldus et al., 2000). This research takes this further, demonstrating that recipients are able to use language abstraction as a window to those beliefs, stereotypes and communicative objectives. Although language abstraction enables describers to transmit their expectancies and stereotypes about others' behaviors, there is evidence here to suggest that this may not be without consequences for the describers themselves.

2. Inhibiting linguistic bias. As we mentioned earlier in this chapter, being unable to inhibit a behavior is not the same thing as being able to perform the same behavior to achieve a goal (see Higgins, 1997). We have argued elsewhere that people's ability to inhibit the LIB and LEB is likely to be hindered by biased expectancies more than people's ability to use language abstraction strategically to influence or mislead an audience (Douglas & Sutton, 2003). When describers have formed a highly dispositional representation of a person's behavior, the biases inherent in their corresponding abstract descriptions are likely to be difficult for them to detect and therefore to censor. We therefore cannot assume that because people are able to recruit language abstraction to achieve communication goals, they will be able to inhibit their biased use of language abstraction. We have recently conducted experiments designed to address this issue. Preliminary research shows that people *are* sometimes able to inhibit linguistic bias (Douglas, Sutton, & Wilkin, under review). Participants were shown pictures of behaviors as in previous work outlined here (Douglas & Sutton, 2003; 2006) and a list of concrete and abstract descriptions of those behaviors. Participants' expectancies were manipulated by telling them that the actor behaves in the way depicted either *often* or *rarely* (these methodological features were adapted from Douglas & Sutton, 2003). They were asked either simply to choose a description (control condition), or to disregard the information they were given about the actor and to select an unbiased description (inhibit condition). Results revealed that in the control condition, participants described expected behaviors abstractly and unexpected behaviors concretely, revealing the typical linguistic expectancy bias (Wigboldus et al., 2000). However, in the inhibit condition, the LEB was obviated: expectancy did not affect linguistic choices.

Given that it is possible to inhibit the LEB, it is important to investigate *when* it is possible to do so. Several variables might plausibly affect the inhibition of bias. One such variable is the strength of the expectancies or preexisting beliefs (Johnston, Ward & Hudson, 1997; Wegner, 1992). For example, it might be easier to inhibit expectancies about a distant relative than about your best friend or spouse of whom you have strong opinions. Similarly, people may be able to inhibit the expression of new but not long-standing biases (Wilson, Lindsey, & Schooler, 2000). Also, inhibition may be difficult in contexts where the goal to inhibit bias is in conflict with some other goal, such as protecting the reputation of a friend (Emmons, King, & Sheldon, 1993). Finally, it may be easier to inhibit the LEB when it pertains to individuals rather than groups. Investigating these issues is important because it addresses the perennial issue of the extent to which language can be divorced from private cognition. If language is sometimes a "window" to the mind (Edwards & Potter, 1993), this research will help to show when people are able to draw the curtains. In more practical terms, the research is important because it may provide insight into possible methods of combating the inadvertent transmission and perpetuation of negatively biased perceptions of groups and individuals.

CONCLUSION

Overall, theory and research highlights the importance of language in the process of belief transmission and perpetuation (Epstein & Komorita, 1966; Fagot et al., 1992; Hogg & Abrams, 1990; Lyons & Kashima, 2003; Maass & Arcuri, 1996; Moscovici, 1981; Ruscher, 2001; Stangor & Schaller, 1996; van Dijk, 1987; Weinreich et al., 1996; Williams & Giles, 1998). The work outlined in this chapter adds to this research by again highlighting the importance of language in the transmission of beliefs to others, but also by revealing the importance of communicative context and communication goals in the transmission of those beliefs. The findings of our research program demonstrate that social psychological factors influenced by communication context, as well as explicit communicative intentions, are powerful influences on the language that people use to describe the actions of others.

It is interesting to note that, since writing the original version of this chapter, new research has further explored the complex nature of language abstraction within different communicative settings. Semin, Higgins, Gil de Montes, Estourget, and Valencia (2005) found that language abstraction was influenced by participants' regulatory focus orientation. Specifically, the linguistic signature of promotion focus was found to be typically abstract; whereas the signature of prevention focus was typically concrete. Also, Wenneker, Wigboldus, and Spears (2005) examined the relative contributions of communication goals and encoding processes on biased language use, and found that both processes are important, but the contribution of encoding processes is particularly relevant under conditions of low motivation and lowered cognitive resources. These findings further illustrate the complex nature of the processes influencing language abstraction, and demonstrate that there is a growing interest amongst social psychologists in the processes underlying biased language use.

We should make one point with relation to the role of intentionality in the processes we have described in this chapter. We agree with Franco and Maass (1996, 1999) and others (Schnake & Ruscher, 1998; von Hippel et al., 1997) that people are probably unaware of variations in their language abstraction. However, this does not entail that language abstraction is unresponsive to conscious communication goals. Essentially, we are arguing that although lost to conscious control or awareness, language abstraction is an important weapon in communicators' strategic armoury, allowing them to achieve goals of which they may be consciously aware. Of strategic communicators we might therefore say, "They know what they do, but not entirely how they do it."

By analogy, consider an occasion in which you took some exercise. You formed a conscious intention to exercise, and in order to realize this intention, performed a myriad of actions. You were probably consciously aware and in control of some of these actions, such as changing into suitable clothes and shoes. Other actions did not require this level of conscious control or awareness, such as the precise movement of your arms as you were, say, running. Nonetheless, you were able to assume control and awareness of these actions by paying attention to them. Other actions such as the increasing rapidity of your heart beat were involuntary, but if you stopped and paid attention they would still be available to introspection. Still other actions, such as endocrine responses and the opening of your sweat pores, are subject neither to conscious control nor introspective awareness. The full gamut of these actions— and the point holds whether or not we are prepared to call all of them by that name—were aroused by and performed in the service of your conscious goal to exercise.

Language abstraction is not alone in being a tool at communicators' disposal that is largely a mystery to them. Aspects of body language are similarly rather inscrutable to the communicators who employ them. Likewise, language users typically adhere to rules of grammar that they are unable to articulate. We should not be surprised by this. Much human communication occurs synchronously or "online" and therefore presents communicators with deadlines that conscious, deliberative processes would not be able to meet. As well as being intolerably slow, a speaker who was fully aware of all aspects of his or her communication may find him- or herself hamstrung by undue self-consciousness and moral anxiety about using manipulative tools.

Likewise, we might ask ourselves what use would be the tools of strategic communication if their use were always obvious to recipients. Excessive critical awareness of all aspects of communication may lead recipients to be unduly suspicious of and resistant to the statements of others. It may also hinder some of the incidental benefits of communication such as the promotion of interpersonal attraction. For example, communicators who unconsciously mimic each others' body language grow to like each other (Chartrand & Bargh, 1999). Finally, were people able to fully monitor all aspects of each others' communication it is likely, or at least possible, that every last aspect of their communication would become subject to normative injunctions that would inhibit communicators' ability to signal controversial views, dislike or dissent.

In light of these considerations, we propose that for a given purpose, it is seldom optimal for speakers or recipients to be fully aware of all linguistic and paralinguistic features of their communication. Some degree of unawareness, and of uncritical decoding of symbols is intrinsic to communication. The limits of time and the speed of human cognitive processing impose a natural constraint on the extent to which communicators may have concurrent awareness of what they are doing. In the case of features of language such as abstraction, further constraints are imposed on communicators' awareness by their lack of theoretical expertise. On the other hand, some degree of awareness may be necessary in order for communicators to be able to critically evaluate messages being sent and received. We await the development of an "optimal awareness theory" that tells us what level of awareness of a given feature of communication optimally promotes a given objective.

Pending such a theory, we may speculate on the importance of variations in awareness for the stereotype-communicating role of language abstraction. Crucially, because of ignorance of language abstraction, it is not a criterion of normative appraisal. People cannot be sanctioned for using language abstraction in a stereotype-consistent way. This lack of awareness is optimal for the transmission of stereotypes that may normally be subject to normative constraint. Although individuals are unaware of language abstraction, they may under helpful conditions (e.g., when there are no time limits and they are reading written messages) be able to glean something of each others' attitudes from it (Douglas & Sutton, 2006). Thus under some circumstances, people may be able to implicitly signal their beliefs to each other in order to create or reinforce the sense that representations of individuals and groups are socially shared (cf. Lyons & Kashima, 2003). In short, unawareness of the medium makes it suitable for the transmission of a stereotype itself and for the implicit communication that it is socially shared.

Clearly, further research is needed in order to establish the precise speech production processes whereby communication goals, and indeed expectancies, come to cause variations in language abstraction. However, our findings to date support a complex and contextual view of the determinants and functions of language abstraction. Language abstraction is indeed a tool with which motivated communicators can fashion new realities for their recipients.

ACKNOWLEDGMENTS

The authors acknowledge the Economic and Social Research Council (RES-000-22-0559) for its support in producing parts of the research outlined in this chapter.

REFERENCES

Allport, G. (1954). *The nature of prejudice.* Reading, MA: Addison-Wesley.
Arcuri, L., Maass, A., & Portelli, G. (1993). Linguistic intergroup bias and implicit attributions. *British Journal of Social Psychology, 32,* 277–285.
Austin, J. L. (1962). *How to do things with words.* Oxford: Oxford University Press.
Bargh, J. A. (1996). Automaticity in social psychology. In E. T. Higgins & A. W. Kruglanski (Eds.), *Social Psychology: Handbook of Basic Principles.* (pp. 169–183). New York: Guilford Press.
Bargh, J. A., Gollwitzer, P. M., Lee-Chai, A., Barndollar, K., & Troetschel, R. (2001). The automated will: Nonconscious activation and pursuit of behavioral goals. *Journal of Personality and Social Psychology, 81,* 1014–1027.
Barreto, M., & Ellemers, N. (2000). You can't always do what you want: Social identity and self-presentational determinants of the choice to work for a low-status group. *Personality and Social Psychology Bulletin, 26,* 891–906.
Barreto, M., & Ellemers, N. (2002). The impact of anonymity and group identification on progroup behavior in Computer-Mediated Groups. *Small Group Research, 33,* 590–610.
Branscombe, N. R., & Wann, D. L. (1994). Collective self-esteem consequences of outgroup derogation when a valued social identity is on trial. *European Journal of Social Psychology, 24,* 641–657.
Cole, T., & Leets, L. (1998). Linguistic masking devices and intergroup behavior: Further evidence of an intergroup linguistic bias. *Journal of Language and Social Psychology, 17,* 348–371.
Douglas, K. M., & McGarty, C. (2001). Identifiability and self-presentation: Computer-mediated communication and intergroup interaction. *British Journal of Social Psychology, 40,* 399–416.
Douglas, K. M., & McGarty, C. (2002). Internet identifiability and beyond: A model of the effects of identifiability on communicative behavior. *Group Dynamics, 6,* 17–26.
Douglas, K. M., McGarty, C., Bliuc, A. M., & Lala, G. (2005). Understanding cyberhate: Social competition and social creativity in online White supremacist groups. *Social Science Computer Review, 23,* 68–76.
Douglas, K. M., & Sutton, R. M. (2003). Effects of communication goals and expectancies on language abstraction. *Journal of Personality and Social Psychology, 84,* 682–696.
Douglas, K. M., & Sutton, R. M. (in press). When what you say about others says something about you: Language abstraction and inferences about describers' attitudes and goals. *Journal of Experimental Social Psychology.*

Douglas, K. M., Sutton, R. M., & Wilkin, K. (under review). *Could you mind your language? On the (in)ability to inhibit linguistic bias.* University of Kent.

Edwards, D., & Potter, J. (1993). Language and causation: A discursive action model of description and attribution. *Psychological Review, 100,* 23–41.

Edwards, D., & Potter, J. (1999). Language and causal attribution. A rejoinder to Schmid and Fiedler. *Theory and Psychology, 9,* 823–836.

Emmons, R. A., King, L. A., & Sheldon, K. (1993). Goal conflict and the self-regulation of action. In D. M. Wegner, & J. W. Pennebaker, J. W. (Eds.), *Handbook of mental control. Century psychology series,* (pp. 528–551). Upper Saddle River, NJ: Prentice-Hall.

Epstein, R., & Komorita, S. S. (1966). Prejudice among Negro children as related to parental ethnocentrism. *Journal of Personality and Social Psychology, 4,* 643–647.

Fagot, B. I., Leinbach, M. D., & O'Boyle, C. (1992). Gender labelling, gender stereotyping, and parenting behaviors. *Developmental Psychology, 28,* 225–230.

Fiedler, K., & Schmid, J. (1999). Implicit attributions and biases. An answer to Edwards and Potter's rejoinder. *Theory and Psychology, 9,* 837–845.

Fiedler, K., & Semin, G. R. (1988). On the causal information conveyed by different interpersonal verbs: The role of implicit sentence context. *Social Cognition, 6,* 21–39.

Franco, F. M., & Maass, A. (1996). Implicit versus explicit strategies of out-group discrimination: The role of intentional control in biased language use and reward allocation. *Journal of Language and Social Psychology, 15,* 335–359.

Franco, F. M., & Maass, A. (1999). Intentional control over prejudice: When the choice of the measure matters. *European Journal of Social Psychology, 29,* 469–477.

Gerstenfeld, P. B., Grant, D. R., & Chiang, C. P. (2003). Hate online: A content analysis of extremist internet sites. *Analyses of Social Issues and Public Policy, 3,* 29–44.

Gil de Montes, L. G., Semin, G. R., & Valencia, J. F. (2003). Communication patterns in interdependent relationships. *Journal of Language and Social Psychology, 22,* 259–281.

Giles, H., & Coupland, N. (1991). *Language: Contexts and consequences.* Milton Keynes UK, Open University Press.

Higgins, E. T. (1981). The 'communication game': Implications for social cognition and persuasion. In E. T. Higgins, M. P. Zanna & C. P. Herman (Eds.), *Social cognition: The Ontario Symposium, Vol. 1* (pp. 343–392). Hillsdale NJ: Erlbaum.

Higgins, E. T. (1997). Beyond pleasure and pain. *American Psychologist, 52,* 1280–1300.

Higgins, E. T. (1999). "Saying is believing" effects: When sharing reality about something biases knowledge and evaluations. In L. L. Thompson, J. M. Levine, & D. M. Messick (Eds.), *Shared cognition in organizations: The management of knowledge* (pp. 33–48). Mahwah, NJ: Erlbaum.

Higgins, E. T., & Rholes, W. S. (1978). "Saying is believing": Effects of message modification on memory and liking for the person described. *Journal of Experimental Social Psychology, 14,* 363–378.

Hogg, M. A., & Abrams, D. (1990). *Social identifications: A social psychology of intergroup relations and group processes.* New York: Routledge.

Jetten, J. A., Spears, R., & Manstead, A. S. R. (1997). Distinctiveness threat and prototypicality: Combined effects on intergroup discrimination and collective self-esteem. *European Journal of Social Psychology, 27,* 635–657.

Johnston, L., Ward, T., & Hudson, S. M. (1997). Deviant sexual thoughts: Mental control and the treatment of sexual offenders. *Journal of Sex Research, 34,* 121–130.

Jost, J. T., & Kruglanski, A. W. (2002). The estrangement of social constructionism and experimental social psychology: History of the rift and prospects for reconciliation. *Personality and Social Psychology Review, 6,* 168–187.

Karpinski, A., & von Hippel, W. (1996). The role of the linguistic intergroup bias in expectancy maintenance. *Social Cognition, 14,* 141–163.

Katz, D., & Braly, K. (1933). Racial stereotypes in one hundred college students. *Journal of Abnormal and Social Psychology, 28,* 280–290.

Lau, I. Y. M., Chiu, C., & Lee, S. (2001). Communication and shared reality: Implications for the psychological foundations of culture. *Social Cognition, 19,* 350–371.

Lippmann, W. (1922). *Public opinion.* New York: Harcourt Brace.

Lyons, A., & Kashima, Y. (2003). How are stereotype maintained through communication? The influence of stereotype sharedness. *Journal of Personality and Social Psychology, 85,* 989–1005.

Maass, A. (1999). Linguistic intergroup bias: Stereotype perpetuation through language. *Advances in Experimental Social Psychology, 31,* 79–121.

Maass, A., & Arcuri, L. (1992). The role of language in the persistence of stereotypes. In G. R. Semin & K. Fiedler (Eds.), *Language, interaction and social cognition.* London: Sage.

Maass, A., & Arcuri, L. (1996). Language and stereotyping. In C. N. Macrae, C. Stangor & M. Hewstone (Eds.), *Stereotypes and stereotyping.* (pp. 193–226). New York: The Guilford Press.

Maass, A., Ceccarelli, R., & Rudin, S. (1996). Linguistic intergroup bias: Evidence for an in-group-protective motivation. *Journal of Personality and Social Psychology, 71,* 512–526.

Maass, A., Milesi, A., Zabbini, S., & Stahlberg, D. (1995). Linguistic intergroup bias: Differential expectancies or in-group protection? *Journal of Personality and Social Psychology, 68,* 116–126.

Maass, A., Salvi, D., Arcuri, A., & Semin, G. (1989). Language use in intergroup contexts: The linguistic intergroup bias. *Journal of Personality and Social Psychology, 57,* 981–993.

McConahay, J., Hardee, B., & Batts, V. (1981). Has racism declined in America? It depends on who is asking and what is asked. *Journal of Conflict Resolution, 25,* 563–579.

McGarty, C., Taylor, N., & Douglas, K. M. (2000). Between commitment and compliance: Obligation and the strategic dimension of SIDE. In T. Postmes, R. Spears, M. Lea & S. D. Reicher (Eds.), *SIDE issues centre stage: Recent developments in studies of deindividuation in groups.* (pp. 143–150). Amsterdam: Royal Netherlands Academy of Arts and Sciences.

Moscovici, S. (1981). On social representations. In J. Forgas (Ed.), *Social cognition* (pp. 181–209). London: Academic Press.

Nesdale, D. (2001). Language and the development of children's ethnic prejudice. *Journal of Language and Social Psychology, 20,* 90–110.

Ng, S. H., & Chan, K. K. (1996). Biases in the description of various age groups: A linguistic category model analysis. *Bulletin of the Hong Kong Psychological Society, 36,* 5–20.

Noel, J. G., Wann, D. L., & Branscombe, N. R. (1995). Peripheral in-group membership status and public negativity toward out-groups. *Journal of Personality and Social Psychology, 68,* 127–137.

Reicher, S., Levine, R. M., & Gordijn, E. (1998). More on deindividuation, power relations between groups and the expression of social identity: Three studies on the effects of visibility to the in-group. *British Journal of Social Psychology, 37,* 15–40.

Reicher, S., Spears, R., & Postmes, T. (1995). A social identity model of deindividuation phenomena. *European Review of Social Psychology, 6,* 161–197.

Reynolds, K. J., Turner, J. C., & Haslam, S. A. (2000). When are we better than them and they worse than us? A closer look at social discrimination in positive and negative domains. *Journal of Personality and Social Psychology, 78,* 64–80.

Rubini, M., & Semin, G. R. (1994). Language use in the context of congruent and incongruent in-group behaviors. *British Journal of Social Psychology, 33,* 355–362.

Rubini, M., & Sigall, H. (2002). Taking the edge off of disagreement: Linguistic abstractness and self-presentation to a heterogeneous audience. *European Journal of Social Psychology, 32,* 343–351.

Ruscher, J. B. (2001). *Prejudiced communication: A social psychological perspective.* New York: Guilford Press.

Schmid, J., & Fiedler, K. (1996). Language and implicit attributions in the Nuremberg trials. *Human Communication Research, 22,* 371–398.

Schmid, J., & Fiedler, K. (1998). The backbone of closing speeches: The impact of prosecution versus defense language on judicial attributions. *Journal of Applied Social Psychology, 28,* 1140–1172.

Schmid, J., & Fiedler, K. (1999). A parsimonious theory can account for complex phenomena. A discursive analysis of Edwards and Potter's critique of non-discursive language research. *Theory and Psychology, 9,* 807–822.

Schmid, J., Fiedler, K., Englich, B., Ehrenberger, T., & Semin, G. R. (1996). Taking sides with the defendant: Grammatical choice and the influence of implicit attributions in prosecution and defense speeches. *International Journal of Psycholinguistics, 12,* 127–148.

Schnake, S. B., & Ruscher, J. B. (1998). Modern racism as a predictor of the linguistic intergroup bias. *Journal of Language and Social Psychology, 17,* 484–491.

Searle, J. R. (1975). Indirect speech acts. In J. P. Cole & J. L. Morgan (Eds.), *Syntax and Semantics: Speech Acts.* (pp. 59–82). Academic Press.

Semin, G. R. (2000). Agenda 2000—Communication: Language as an implementational device for cognition. *European Journal of Social Psychology, 30,* 595–612.

Semin G. R., & de Poot C. J. (1997). You might regret it if you don't notice how a question is worded! *Journal of Personality and Social Psychology, 73,* 472–480.

Semin, G. R., Gil de Montes, L., & Valencia, J. F. (2003). Communication constraints on the linguistic intergroup bias. *Journal of Experimental Social Psychology, 39,* 142–148.

Semin, G. R., & Fiedler, K. (1988). The cognitive functions of linguistic categories in describing persons: Social cognition and language. *Journal of Personality and Social Psychology, 54,* 558–568.

Semin, G. R., & Fiedler, K. (1991). The linguistic category model, its bases, applications and range. *European Review of Social Psychology, 2,* 1–30.

Semin, G. R., & Fiedler, K. (1992). The inferential properties of interpersonal verbs. In G. R. Semin & K. Fiedler (Eds.), *Language, interaction and social cognition,* (pp. 58–78). London: Sage Publications.

Semin, G. R., Higgins, T., Gil de Montes, L., Estourget, Y., & Valencia, J. F. (2005). Linguistic signatures of regulatory focus: How abstraction fits promotion more than prevention. *Journal of Personality and Social Psychology, 89,* 36–45.

Semin, G. R., & Marsman, J. G. (1994). On the "multiple inference inviting properties" of interpersonal verbs: Event instigation, dispositional inferences, and implicit causality. *Journal of Personality and Social Psychology, 67,* 836–849.

Sigall, H., & Mills, J. (1998). Measures of independent variables and mediators are useful in social psychology experiments: But are they necessary? *Personality and Social Psychology Review, 2,* 218–226.

Spears, R., & Lea, M. (1994). Panacea or panopticon? The hidden power in computer-mediated communication. *Communication Research, 21,* 427–459.

Stangor, C., & Schaller, M. (1996). Stereotypes as individual and collective representations. In C. N. Macrae, C. Stangor, & M. Hewstone (Eds.), *Stereotypes and stereotyping* (pp. 3–37). New York: The Guilford Press.

Stephan, W. G., & Stephan, C. W. (1984). The role of ignorance in intergroup relations. In N. Miller & M. B. Brewer (Eds.), *Groups in contact: The psychology of desegregation* (pp. 229–257). Orlando, FL: Academic Press.

van Dijk, T. A. (1987). *Communicating racism. Ethnic prejudice in thought and talk.* Thousand Oaks, CA: Sage Publications.
von Hippel, W., Sekaquaptewa, D., & Vargas, P. (1997). The linguistic intergroup bias as an implicit indicator of prejudice. *Journal of Experimental Social Psychology, 33,* 490–509.
Webster, D. M., Kruglanski, A. W., & Pattison, D. A. (1997). Motivated language use in intergroup contexts: Need-for closure effects on the linguistic intergroup bias. *Journal of Personality and Social Psychology, 72,* 1122–1131.
Wegner, D. M. (1992). You can't always think what you want: Problems in the suppression of unwanted thoughts. In M. P. Zanna (Ed.), *Advances in Experimental Social Psychology, 25,* (pp. 193–225). San Diego, CA: Academic Press.
Weinreich, P., Luk, C. L., & Bond, M. H. (1996). Ethnic stereotyping and identification in a multicultural context: "Acculturation", self-esteem and identity diffusion in Hong Kong Chinese university students. *Psychology and Developing Societies, 8,* 107–169.
Wenneker, C. P. J., Wigboldus, D. H. J., & Spears, R. (2005). Biased language use in stereotype maintenance: The role of encoding and goals. *Journal of Personality and Social Psychology, 89,* 504–516.
Werkman, W. M., Wigboldus, D . H. J., & Semin, G. R. (1999). Children's communication of the linguistic intergroup bias and its impact upon cognitive inferences. *European Journal of Social Psychology, 29,* 95–104.
Wigboldus, D. H. J., & Douglas, K. M. (2007). Language, expectancies and intergroup relations. In K. Fiedler (Ed.), *Social Communication* (pp. 79–106). New York: Psychology Press.
Wigboldus, D. H. J., Semin, G. R., & Spears, R. (2000). How do we communicate stereotypes? Linguistic bases and inferential consequences. *Journal of Personality and Social Psychology, 78,* 5–18.
Williams, A., & Giles, H. (1998). Communication of ageism. In M. L. Hecht (Ed.), *Communicating prejudice* (pp. 136–160). Thousand Oaks, CA: Sage Publications.
Wilson, T. D., Lindsey, S., & Schooler, T. Y. (2000). A model of dual attitudes. *Psychological Review, 107,* 101–126.
Zajonc, R. B. (1960). The process of cognitive tuning in communication. *Journal of Abnormal and Social Psychology, 61,* 159–167.

Chapter 10

Sender-Receiver Constellations as a Moderator of Linguistic Abstraction Biases

Peter Freytag
University of Heidelberg, Germany

The term communication refers to the transmission of information from a sender to a receiver. According to philosophers of language, successful communication observes certain rules that have been summarized by the cooperativeness principle (Grice, 1975). The joint application of these rules makes sure that the content of a message is true, relevant, informative, and readily understood by its receiver. Notably, the latter aspect implies that a sender has to determine prior to sending a message whether a receiver has the background knowledge necessary to make sense of its content. The outcome of this process, in turn, depends on the perceived common ground; that is, on a sender's subjective representation of relevant background knowledge shared with a recipient (Schwarz, 1996).

In the context of stereotyping, the information transmitted in a message refers to the members of some target group, with both the sender and the receiver either belonging or not belonging to the target group. As people tend to be more familiar with in-groups than with out-groups, the perceived common ground in stereotype-related communication should vary as a function of the group affiliations of senders, targets, and receivers. Moreover, as members of mutually exclusive groups tend to hold diverging beliefs about the behavior of in-group and out-group members, senders may feel entitled to assume a broader common ground when communicating to in-group members. To account for variation in the stereotype-related messages sent by different senders to different receivers, then, we need to know who is talking to whom about which target group. Accordingly, approaches to the contribution of communication to stereotyping may be expected to provide a framework linking different constellations of senders, targets, and receivers to different patterns of language use.

As Krauss and Fussel (1996) have argued in their analysis of the field, however, social psychological research on communication is rather specialized, with different approaches examining different parts of the communication triad almost in isolation. For instance, some research has examined how senders tailor messages to receivers (e.g., Higgins, 1981, 1992), how receivers make sense of messages (e.g., Schwarz, 1994, 1996), how senders and receivers jointly establish shared knowledge (e.g., Clark & Brennan, 1991; Clark & Schober, 1992), or how sender and receiver characteristics affect qualitative (e.g., Maass, Salvi, Arcuri, & Semin, 1989; Maass, 1999) and quantitative (e.g., Kashima, 2000; Lyons & Kashima, 2003) features of messages, respectively.

From a strategic point of view, the field's fragmentation seems to reflect an attempt to exert control over aspects of communication that are irrelevant to one's research question. If you were interested in audience effects, for instance, wouldn't it be reasonable to vary relevant characteristics of a message's receiver while controlling those of senders and targets? And if you were interested in the effects of target-group affiliation on language use, wouldn't it be reasonable to vary the group affiliation of a message's target while controlling that of its sender and receiver? Of course, it would. Moreover, communication is a complex matter— and effect sizes are often weak. Under these conditions, not to control for extraneous factors that would otherwise claim their share of explained variance may result in a Type II error as long as one is preoccupied with the conventional .05 level of statistical, not practical, significance.

From an epistemological point of view, the field's fragmentation is unfortunate, though. For one thing, the relative contribution of the microlevel processes identified by different approaches to macrolevel phenomena such as stereotyping has to remain underdetermined when there is no framework linking the diverse processes to each other. Moreover, fragmentation inhibits knowledge transfer and synergy effects by mismatching constructs, procedures, and measures. Most importantly, however, fragmentation can pose serious threats to the external and internal validity of research findings when one of the constituents of the communication triad is fixed in the set up of one's experimental paradigm. Threats to external validity revolve around the question, "Will my effects retain in constellations involving a sender/a target/a receiver other than the one I have used?" And threats to internal validity revolve around the question, "Will my causal paths retain in constellations involving a sender/a target/a receiver other than the one I have used?"

What may be an advantage when judged against criteria of experimental control may thus turn out to be a disadvantage when judged against criteria

of scientific progress. On the one hand, fixing constituents of the communication triad threatens external validity by leaving the range of constellations
unspecified across which a pattern of language use will or will not replicate.
On the other hand, fixing constituents also threatens internal validity by con-
cealing potential variation in the causal paths along which different constellations affect language use. Finally, fixing constituents may counteract the integration of approaches targeting the same phenomena at the macrolevel but
examining different processes (and using different sender-receiver constellations) at the microlevel.

OVERVIEW

The goal of the present report is to introduce a simple heuristic for the generation of informed guesses about the degree to which the validity of communication effects is threatened when one element of the communication
triad is fixed. This heuristic consists in examining how different constellations among a message's sender, target, and receiver might affect the independent, mediational, and dependent variables identified by a given approach. Mainly for illustrational purposes, the present report focuses on
research on the impact of linguistic abstraction on stereotype maintenance
(cf. Maass, 1999). A brief introduction to the pioneering work on linguistic
abstraction will serve to highlight that research has been concerned mainly
with sender characteristics to the neglect of receiver characteristics; thereby
focusing attention on intrapersonal determinants of language use originating
in senders rather than on interpersonal determinants originating in the dynamic interplay of a message's sender, target, and receiver. Against this background, a simple taxonomy of *sender-receiver constellations* will be introduced,
putting forward the idea that moderator variables (e.g., stereotype salience),
mediator variables (e.g., communication goals) and—as a consequence—
dependent variables (e.g., abstraction bias strength) should vary with the
group affiliations of senders, targets, and receivers. A literature review capturing modern classics as well as recent findings will serve to substantiate
this position. Finally, to illustrate that an examination of the full communication triad can also contribute to the solution of the knowledge transfer and
relative contribution problems, respectively, promising routes toward an integration of research on linguistic abstraction with research on the reproduction of stereotype-related information (cf. Kashima, 2000) will be outlined. Conclusions will be presented in the form of a provisional mediational
model of biased language use in intergroup contexts that distinguishes between (largely implicit) intrapersonal processes and (largely explicit) interpersonal processes.

BRIEF INTRODUCTION TO RESEARCH ON THE IMPACT OF LINGUISTIC ABSTRACTION ON STEREOTYPING

The Linguistic Category Model

The empirical investigation of processes involving communication depends on tools that help extract observable features of communication. One of the most powerful tools currently available has been derived from the *linguistic category model* (LCM) proposed by Semin and Fiedler (1988, 1991, 1992). Starting from the observation that the same behavior can be described more or less abstractly, these authors proposed the distinction of at least four different levels of linguistic abstraction—each bearing specific attributional implications. At the most concrete level, descriptive action verbs (DAV) provide neutral descriptions of a behavior (e.g., to push someone). Interpretative action verbs (IAV) go beyond mere description by implying intentions underlying the behavior observed (e.g., to hurt someone). State verbs (SV) go beyond individual actions by referring to more enduring states (e.g., to hate someone). Adjectives (ADJ), finally, refer to stable characteristics of persons (e.g., to be hostile).

As to the effects of abstractness on the impressions formed by receivers, Semin and Fiedler (1988) found increased abstractness to be related to (a) increases in the perceived temporal stability of the behavioral tendency implied; (b) increases in the informativeness about the person described; and (c) decreases in the informativeness about the situation. In brief, more abstract messages point to more enduring qualities of people. To assess the attributional implications of a message, researchers only have to identify its individual propositions (e.g., those of the subject-verb-object type) and to code each unit for its level of linguistic abstraction (e.g., coding DAVs = 1, IAVs = 2, SVs = 3, and ADJs = 4). The mean level of abstraction of propositions describing episodes that differ in theoretically meaningful ways (e.g., valence: positive vs. negative; stereotype-consistency: consistent vs. inconsistent) then serves as the main dependent variable.

The Linguistic Intergroup Bias (LIB)

The category system introduced in the LCM (Semin & Fiedler, 1988) has since been applied successfully to various domains, such as actor-observer differences in attribution (e.g., Semin & Fiedler, 1989; Fiedler, Semin, & Koppetsch, 1991), the attributional implications of media coverage (e.g., Schmid, 1999), or the structure of closing speeches in court-room settings (e.g., Schmid & Fiedler, 1996, 1998). The most successful application of the LCM, however, has been established in the domain of intergroup processes. Specifically, Maass et al. (1989) suggested that group members might exploit the differential implications of abstract versus concrete descriptions as a subtle mechanism that helps portray the in-group in a positive light. As abstract descriptions imply stable characteristics, these authors argued, group members might create a positive impression of the in-group by describing positive in-group/negative out-group behavior more abstractly than negative in-group/positive out-group behavior. In between, the hypothesized target group × behavior valence interaction has become well known as the *linguistic intergroup bias* (LIB), and it has been demonstrated in a host of both laboratory studies and field studies (for a review, see Maass, 1999).

As to the underlying mechanisms, Maass et al. (1989) discussed two pathways based on in-group-protective motivation and differential expectancies, respectively. Following the *in-group protection* explanation, group members strive to achieve a positive social identity and describe behavioral episodes in a way that highlights the positivity of in-group members relative to that of out-group members. In line with this perspective, the LIB has been shown to be stronger under conditions that foster social identification such as intergroup conflict and derogation by out-group members (e.g., Franco & Maass, 1996; Maass, Ceccarelli, & Rudin, 1996). On the other hand, following the *differential expectancies* explanation, most people simply expect in-group members rather than out-group members to show positive behavior. As abstract descriptions imply similar behavior on future occasions, the argument goes on, expected (unexpected) behavior should be communicated more abstractly (concretely) in order to convey information about the temporal stability of the underlying behavioral tendencies.

Obviously, the two explanations arrive at diverging predictions only when positive behavior is atypical of the in-group and negative behavior is atypical of the out-group. In fact, Maass, Milesi, Zabbini and Stahlberg, (1995) demonstrated that expectations override in-group-protective motives when mutually acknowledged stereotypes make positive in-group and negative out-group behavior appear atypical in a specific domain. Accordingly, Maass (1999) suggested resolving the issue of primacy by regarding differential expectancies as a sufficient condition and in-group protection as a moderator that determines the strength of the LIB.

The Linguistic Expectancy Bias (LEB)

The idea that the LIB may be driven primarily by the expectations held by the sender of a message received further support by a line of research conducted by Wigboldus, Spears, and Semin (2000). These authors asked participants to describe a target person performing behaviors typical of its in-group (SC behavior) versus typical of its out-group (stereotype-inconsistent behavior) in their own words. Using intergroup settings based on gender and nationality groups, respectively, descriptions of SC behavior were found to be more abstract than descriptions of stereotype-inconsistent (SI) behavior. Moreover, receivers of these free descriptions made stronger dispositional inferences for SC behavior. Finally, mediational analyses confirmed that linguistic abstraction mediated the effects of SC on dispositional inferences.

The latter finding received much attention because the effects of linguistic abstraction on dispositional inferences by receivers of a message had not been demonstrated so far in research on the LIB. As illustrated in Fig. 10–1, the status of the pioneering work about the impact of linguistic abstraction on stereotype maintenance can be summarized as follows: First, work on the LCM has demonstrated that linguistic abstraction is associated with dispositional inferences such that receivers infer more stable characteristics from more abstract descriptions. Second, work on the LIB has demonstrated that linguistic abstraction is associated with stereotypical expectations such that senders describe SC behavior more abstractly. Finally, work on the LEB has demonstrated that the effects of SC on the level of linguistic abstraction chosen by senders extend to the level of dispositional inferences drawn by receivers; thereby lending support to the idea that linguistic abstraction indeed promotes stereotype maintenance.

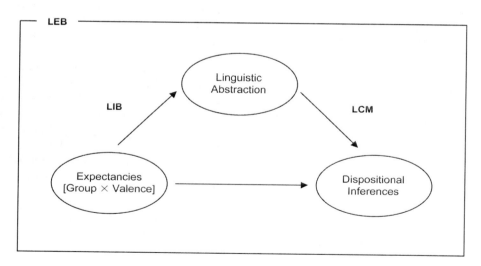

FIGURE 10–1. Mediator model of the impact of stereotypical expectancies of senders on (a) the linguistic abstraction of their descriptions of stereotype-related behavior and on (b) the corresponding dispositional inferences drawn by receivers of these descriptions. The antecedents of abstraction have been examined in research on the linguistic intergroup bias (LIB), the link between abstraction and dispositional inference has been examined in research on the linguistic category model (LCM), and the full mediational model has been examined in research on the linguistic expectancy bias (LEB).

A TAXONOMY OF SENDER-RECEIVER CONSTELLATIONS

It should be obvious from the preceding section that the pioneering research on the LIB/LEB has paid much more attention to the role of senders than to the role of receivers. The bottom line seems to read that senders raise and lower the level of abstraction in their descriptions of other people's behavior to the extent that doing so serves *their* in-group-protective motivation and to the extent that a behavior fits *their* stereotypical expectations. Yet, the observation that the pioneering work does not mention any effects of receiver characteristics on abstraction bias strength may simply reflect that receiver characteristics had been fixed in the set up of the basic experimental paradigm. And in fact, summarizing the first decade of research on the LIB, Maass (1999, p. 106) noted "that most studies were conducted in rather artificial situations in which the participant either selected or produced descriptions of hypothetical scenes without knowing the recipient of the 'message'."

At a first glance, the notion of "the unknown receiver" implies that the artificiality of communicative contexts in previous research on the LIB is an issue of external validity, that is, of the degree to which the basic finding will generalize to everyday communication. As I have argued at the outset, however, fixing a constituent of the communication triad also poses a threat to internal validity to the extent that moderator variables and/or mediator variables are confounded with the variable fixed. In the case of fixed receiver characteristics, two related questions come to mind instantly. First, we may ask whether the LIB/LEB pattern might vary with receiver characteristics. At least the literatures on both common-ground construction and audience effects would suggest that the answer might be "yes." For instance, would we expect an LIB of comparable strength when a jobless, neo-fascist sender applying for a position is confronted with a pro-immigration versus an anti-immigration employer asking for the applicant's beliefs about the immigrant population? Presumably not. Polemic though the example may be, a motivation to reveal versus to conceal one's beliefs—driven by the different sender-receiver constellations—may be an intuitively plausible and potent moderator of abstraction bias strength. For the moment, however, it shall suffice to note that the same information about the same target might be communicated differently in different sender-receiver constellations.

Second, we may ask whether there might have been significant commonalities in the subjective representations that senders had formed of their receivers in early research on the LIB—commonalities that could help explain the impressive stability of the LIB pattern. To the extent that the procedures used in these studies could be shown to be conducive to forming specific representations of receivers (and similarly specific communication goals), the stability of the LIB pattern would have more to say about the stability of the basic experimental setting than about the pervasiveness of subtle forces biasing communication toward SC. Taken together, these questions cast some doubt on the veridicality of the (sender-focused) intrapersonal accounts of linguistic abstraction biases derived from the pioneering work. Therefore, an examination of the way in which different constellations among a message's sender, target, and receiver might affect abstraction biases seems worthwhile.

Table 10–1 provides a taxonomy of sender-receiver constellations for communicative contexts involving behavioral descriptions of the members of two mutually exclusive groups. Taking the perspective of a sender affiliated with one of the groups, the taxonomy features 12 constellations that result from the orthogonal variation of target affiliation (in-group vs. out-group), receiver affiliation (unaffiliated vs. in-group vs. out-group), and receiver status (equal vs. superior). Regarding the effects of constellation on language use, the taxonomy addresses effects on stereotype salience, communication goals, and abstraction bias strength. In principle, both stereotype salience and communication goals could be conceived of as mediator variables that vary with constellation and that affect the strength of linguistic abstraction biases. Functionally, it is more appropriate to conceive of stereotype salience as a moderator variable determining whether or not target affiliation will affect the level of linguistic abstraction at which stereotype-related target behavior is described (cf. Baron & Kenny, 1986, for the treatment of context variables yielding an all-or-none

TABLE 10–1.
Category Salience, Communication Goal, and Abstraction Bias
in Descriptions of Stereotype-Related Behavior as a Function
of Target Affiliation, Receiver Affiliation, and Receiver Status

	Receiver Affiliation					
	Uninvolved		*In-Group*		*Out-Group*	
	Receiver Status		*Receiver Status*		*Receiver Status*	
Target Affiliation	*Equal*	*Superior*	*Equal*	*Superior*	*Equal*	*Superior*
In-group						
Category salience	Yes	Yes	No	No	Yes	Yes
Communication goal	Convey	Convey	Share	Share	Argue	Play to
Abstraction bias	++	++	±	±	++	−
Out-group						
Category salience	Yes	Yes	Yes	Yes	Yes	Yes
Communication goal	Convey	Convey	Share	Share	Argue	Play to
Abstraction bias	++	++	+	+	++	−

Note: A positive (negative) sign in abstraction bias rows means that behaviors consistent (inconsistent) with a stereotype are described at a higher level of linguistic abstraction (yielding in-group-serving patterns of language use to the extent that behavior valence is confounded with stereotype consistency).

pattern for a given effect). Of course, given the complexity of communication, the set of variables taken into account here cannot be exhaustive. As we shall see, however, it is sufficient to account for most of the findings accumulated over the past 15 years or so and to derive several hypotheses that have not been tested yet. Before addressing these issues in detail, a look at the underpinnings of the different constellations is in place.

Uninvolved Receivers

Let us start with the sender-receiver constellation referred to in the left column, in which the receiver is neither involved in the intergroup context to which the communication refers nor known to have taken sides with the in-group or the out-group (in the latter cases, the center or the right column, respectively, of Table 10–1 would apply). For such a constellation to qualify as an arena for linguistic abstraction biases, the characteristics of in-group and out-group members have to be established as the topic of the communication, of course. In laboratory settings, this may be accomplished by written instructions and/or by within-participant manipulations of target affiliation (cf. Fischhoff, Slovic, & Lichtenstein, 1979)—and in everyday communication, this may be accomplished by agreement (cf. Clark & Brennan, 1991). Once the relevant categorization into in-group and out-group has been made salient, however, a sender's communication goal will consist in *conveying* his or her opinion about the characteristics of in-group *and* out-group members, respectively, to the receiver. Consequently, a pronounced in-group-serving abstraction bias should emerge, irrespective of the target's group affiliation.

In-Group Receivers

A completely different picture arises in the center column of Table 10–1, in which the receiver is a member of the in-group. Granting that there is consensus within the in-group regarding the typical attributes of in-group and out-group members, the communication goal of senders in this constellation consists in *sharing* new information with the receiver. Under these conditions, target affiliation can be assumed to moderate the strength of abstraction biases, because the target's category membership should be much more salient for out-group targets than for in-group targets. Just as fish will be least to recognize the ocean, in-group members will be least to recognize the category membership of an in-group member in intragroup communication unless the behavior referred to has occurred in an explicit intergroup situation. Therefore, *no* abstraction bias should occur when an in-group member talks to a fellow in-group member about yet another in-group member. This prediction can be derived from the principles of structural fit and normative fit proposed by self-categorization theory (Turner, Hogg, Oakes, Reicher, & Whetherell, 1987). Finally, an in-group-serving abstraction bias of at least moderate strength can be expected when in-group members talk to each other about out-group members (see the bottom row of the in-group receiver column), because the target's group membership should always be salient in this case.

Out-Group Receivers

Turning to the right column of Table 10–1, in which the receiver is a member of the out-group, it becomes evident why receiver status should be taken into account, too. As can be seen from a column-wise comparison of equal status and superior status receivers, receiver status moderates both communication goals and abstraction bias, although the relevant social categorization should be salient in either setting. Specifically, a pronounced in-group-serving abstraction bias, based on the communication goal to *argue* against the out-group's perspective, can be expected when the receiver is of equal status. However, *no* abstraction bias or even a *reversal* of the common LIB/LEB pattern may emerge when the receiver is of superior status. This assumption is based on the idea that a sender confronted with a superior status recipient, who is known not to share the sender's perspective on the intergroup setting, may be tempted to conceal his or her privately held beliefs—and instead *play to* the receiver.

Taken together, the taxonomy provided in Table 10–1 allows for the generation of several directional predictions. First, regarding stereotype salience, the taxonomy suggests that a target affiliation × receiver-affiliation interaction should emerge in studies using between-participant manipulations of these variables. Second, regarding communication goals, the taxonomy suggests that a main effect of receiver affiliation should emerge, and that this main effect should be qualified by a receiver affiliation × receiver-status interaction, driven by equal status receiver versus superior-status-receiver participants in the out-group receiver conditions of studies using between-participant manipulations of receiver status and receiver affiliation. Finally, regarding abstraction bias strength, the taxonomy predicts a main effect of receiver affiliation, with the strongest biases emerging for unaffiliated receivers, intermediate biases emerging for in-group receivers, and the weakest biases emerging for out-group receivers. Importantly, this main effect should be qualified by a three-way interaction involving target affiliation, receiver affiliation, and receiver status. None of these predictions have been targeted by previous research on LIB/LEB, thereby highlighting the potential of the taxonomy for the derivation of new research questions that deserve to be tested.

OF UNKNOWN RECEIVERS
AND PURPOSEFUL SENDERS

The Unknown Receiver

How do these predictions articulate with previous research on linguistic abstraction in intergroup contexts? Starting with the pioneering work, it should be obvious that the ease with which the in-group-serving LIB pattern replicated across a wide range of intergroup contexts (cf. Maass, 1999) is at variance with the effects of sender-receiver constellations anticipated in the preceding section—covering in-group-serving, indifferent, and out-group-serving patterns of language use. This discrepancy can be resolved in two ways. On the one hand, one could argue on purely theoretical grounds that participants in the pioneering studies may have formed similar representations of their receivers simply because receiver characteristics had not been manipulated. After all, when the description of receiver characteristics had been invariant, so too should have been their representation, except for error variance. On the other hand, one could argue that participants in the pioneering studies may have formed similar representations of their receivers simply because the experimental setting was conducive to forming quite specific representations. Much in line with the latter argument, a review of the pertinent literature reveals that senders in most key publications on the LIB at least knew that the receiver of their message would be knowledgeable regarding the relevant stereotypes—at times, they even have been entitled to assume that they would communicate to an in-group receiver.

To substantiate these claims, consider the references listed in Table 10–2. As indicated in the right column, several studies provided participants with cues to the prior knowledge of the receiver. In essence, there were three types of receivers: expert experimenters, expert organizations, and expert participants.[1] In the case of *expert experimenters*, the experimenter not only served as

---

[1]The term "expert" is used here to signal that a receiver is familiar with both the content of a stereotype and the application of a stereotype in the processing of information about a target person belonging to a stereotyped group. Thus, I would like to suggest that the distinction between novices and experts used in studies on domain-specific knowledge (such as the speed and accuracy with which lay persons as opposed to professionals can encode complex configurations on a chess board) can be extended to the distinction between persons that have versus that have not grown up in an environment in which certain beliefs about the members of certain groups are consensually held. For instance, West Germans and East Germans tend to think that East Germans are less efficient than West Germans. Thus, German participants should describe efficiency-related behavior of a German target person differently depending of the target person's regional affiliation; whereas most readers of this volume would presumably be unaffected by the information that a target person comes from one or the other part of Germany. Against this background, non-German senders and receivers may well be considered novices regarding their knowledge about the stereotypical properties of different kinds of Germans.

TABLE 10–2.

Overview of Studies on Linguistic Abstraction Using Receivers Knowledgeable of the Stereotypes Governing the Intergroup Context Addressed in the Communication.

Reference	Intergroup Context	Design	Receiver
Arcuri, Maass, & Portell (1993)	Diverse	W	*Expert experimenter* providing scenarios relevant to the intergroup contexts
Franco & Maass (1996)	Fans of rival basketball teams	W	*Expert organization* running a project on basketball fans
Maass et al. (1989)	Inhabitants of rival neighborhoods	W	*Expert experimenter* providing scenarios relevant to the intergroup context
Maass et al. (1995), Experiment 1	Northern *vs.* Southern Italians	W	*Expert experimenter* studying representations of northern vs. southern Italians
Maass et al. (1996), Experiment 1	Hunters *vs.* Environmentalists	W	*Expert organization* running nation-wide research project on environmental protection
Maass et al. (1996), Experiment 2	Northern *vs.* Southern Italians	W	*Expert experimenter* running a national research project on Italian emigrants
Schnake & Ruscher (1998)	European *vs.* African Americans	W	*Expert participants* sharing cultural race stereotypes
Wigboldus et al. (2000), Experiment 1	Men *vs.* Women	W	*Expert participants* sharing cultural gender stereotypes
Wigboldus et al. (2000), Experiment 2	Dutch *vs.* Flemish	B	*Expert participants* sharing national stereotypes
Wigboldus et al. (2005), Experiment 2	UvA students *vs.* VU students	B	*Expert participants* sharing local university stereotypes

Note. W = within-participant; B = between-participant. *UvA* = Universiteit van Amsterdam; *VU* = Vrije Universiteit. All senders belonged to one of the target groups.

the receiver of a message, but also selected behaviors pertinent to the intergroup context under consideration; thereby communicating indirectly to participants that the receiver knew which kinds of behavior would be consistent versus inconsistent with a stereotype. The same is true for *expert organizations* as receivers. Moreover, in these two cases, each of the corresponding studies used within-participants manipulations of SC *and* target group, thereby communicating to participants that the receiver also knew which out-groups would be particularly meaningful to participants. Finally, in the case of *expert participants*, senders knew that the receiver would be "another participant." In the case of nationality groups, for instance, this means that participants knew that the receiver would be another member of their national in-group.

To give an example, in a study on the national stereotypes of the Dutch versus the Flemish (Wigboldus et al., 2000, Exp. 2), Dutch students from Amsterdam were recruited on campus and tested in groups. Before participants reproduced a story about an in-group protagonist or an out-group protagonist about which they had just read, they learned that their reproduction would later be read by "another participant." Based on the Grice's (1975) cooperativeness principle, most participants may have assumed that the "other participant" referred to in the instructions would be another Dutch student from Amsterdam—that is, a person similar to themselves in age, status, and nationality (see Schwarz, 1994, for similar effects of indirect communication in social psychological experimentation). Note that such a receiver would not only be knowledgeable of the relevant national stereotypes, but also would be likely to share the sender's attitudes toward the group to which the target person belonged. Moreover, a sender anticipating to communicate to such a receiver may not realize at all that national group affiliation is to be taken into account in describing the target's behavior, but instead process the information provided about a target's behavior in terms of its fit with the stereotype of the protagonist's age group (e.g., young people), gender group (e.g., men), or profession group (e.g., psychology students). In line with these considerations, no abstraction bias occurred for Dutch participants communicating to Dutch participants about the behavior of a Dutch protagonist.

Interestingly, the same research group (Wigboldus, Spears, & Semin, 2005, Exp. 2) recently tested the prediction that biases in linguistic abstraction may be limited to contexts that render the relevant social categorization into in-group and out-group salient. In this set of studies, no abstraction bias occurred when students of the University of Amsterdam communicated to students of the University of Amsterdam about the behavior of yet another student of the University of Amsterdam. Narrow though this setting may seem, a moderate abstraction bias was observed for the same participant population, when the target and/or the receiver was affiliated with the rival Free University of Amsterdam. In the latter case, abstraction bias even generalized to the behavioral descriptions of in-group members. Granting that students of a University A who communicate to students from a University B do not perceive the receivers as being of superior status, the latter finding lends indirect support to the predictions derived above for equal-status out-group receivers. Unfortunately— and even though Wigboldus et al. (2005) based their research on the *hypothesis* that abstraction bias would be restricted to sender-receiver constellations that render target affiliation salient—no measure of category salience (or social identification) has been administered in their studies. Thus, the ultimate proof of the veridicality of the salience hypothesis is still missing. At least, however, these data support the idea that category salience—as determined by sender-receiver constellations *plus* target affiliations—constitutes another *necessary condition* of abstraction bias.

In sum, it seems fair to state that the pioneering work on the LIB has been limited to the examination of sender characteristics in communicative settings involving mostly unaffiliated receivers knowledgeable of the relevant stereotypes. According to our taxonomy of sender-receiver constellations, however, such communicative contexts should be particularly conducive to bringing about the LIB/LEB pattern of linguistic abstraction (see the left column of Table 10–1). Thus, the ease with which the basic effect has been replicated for a wide range of intergroup contexts in the first decade of research on linguistic abstraction might rather overestimate the importance of stereotypical expectancies and in-group-protective motivation.

In a related fashion, our taxonomy of sender-receiver constellations also suggests that linguistic abstraction may vary as a function of both independent variables originating from sources other than sender characteristics and communicative contexts involving receiver characteristics other than cues to prior knowledge. Importantly, an LIB/LEB varying in strength should emerge when the same sender describes the same behavior of the same target person to different receivers, because different sender-receiver constellations should activate different communication goals. So far, this idea has been based on the silent assumption that senders can *actually* vary the level of linguistic abstraction at which they describe a person's behavior in a way that supports their current communication goals. Interestingly, several research teams have recently started to examine whether the pragmatic function of communication has a direct effect on linguistic abstraction.

The Purposeful Sender

Although the communication of stereotype-related information was not the primary concern of these studies, their findings do speak to the usefulness and plausibility of the predictions derived above from the taxonomy of sender-receiver constellations. As a useful starting point, remember that Maass (1999) suggested regarding stereotypical expectancies as a sufficient condition of the LIB and in-group-protective motivation as a moderator of LIB strength. This perspective rested on the assumption that the strength of the LIB—determined primarily by the strength of senders' expectancies—is subject to variation with the strength of in-group-protective motivation. Thus, the same sender should manifest an LIB of variable strength depending on the presence and absence of factors raising in-group-protective motivation. Apparently, then, the pioneering work on the LIB had already opened the door for factors originating from sources outside the sender—in this case, from threats to social identity. Note, however, that such an impact of motivation does not refer the effects of explicit communication goals, but instead refers to some kind of implicit amplification of preexisting tendencies in language use.

Such an interpretation of the effects of in-group-protective motivation was in line with previous work on the status of the LIB as an implicit measure of prejudice (e.g., Franco & Maass, 1996; Karpinski & von Hippel, 1996; Schnake & Ruscher, 1998). Notably, von Hippel, Sekaquaptewa, and Vargas (1997) found the LIB to be stronger for high-prejudice senders than for low-prejudice senders. Moreover, LIB strength was related to implicit measures of prejudice only, but not to explicit measures of prejudice. Thus, there was strong evidence for the existence of an *implicit component* to linguistic abstraction that is reflected primarily in interindividual differences in bias strength. All else being equal, then, both prejudiced and nonprejudiced senders will exhibit stronger abstraction bias under conditions fostering in-group identification, but abstraction bias will be stronger for prejudiced people under all conditions— hence the correlation with implicit measures. Despite these convincing findings, recent work by several research groups suggests that there may be an *explicit component* to linguistic abstraction, too. Although these lines of research started from different considerations, their findings nicely fit an interpretation of the LIB/LEB as a phenomenon affected by the explicit goals of senders that derive, in turn, from the current sender-receiver constellation. In view of the heterogeneity of these approaches, their link to the present analysis shall be established separately.

Communication goals.   The most direct approach to the impact of explicit communication goals on linguistic abstraction has been taken by Douglas and Sutton (2003). In a series of experiments, these authors asked participants to describe positive (negative) as well as expected (unexpected) behaviors of a target person. In addition, participants were instructed to describe the behavior in a way that would *create* specific impressions of the target person. Instructions referred either to the favorableness or to the expectedness conveyed by a description. As predicted, descriptions were more abstract for positive (negative) behavior when instructions called for favorable (unfavorable) descriptions. Likewise, descriptions were more abstract for expected (unexpected) behavior when instructions called for descriptions that matched (mismatched) senders' privately held expectations for a target person. As anticipated above for scenarios involving a sender confronted with an out-group receiver of superior status, then, Douglas and Sutton found abstraction biases that mismatched senders' privately held beliefs.[2]

These findings demonstrate that people do have the language use competence necessary to portray the same behavior in a way that emphasizes the latent positivity (negativity) of a person as well as the expectedness (unexpectedness) of behaviors. The latter finding is particularly instructive, because it demonstrates that people can produce descriptions that convey expectedness for behavioral episodes they consider unexpected—depending solely on the *communication goals* induced by the experimental instructions. Moreover, these findings imply that participants in previous research on abstraction biases presumably wanted to portray in-group rather than out-group members in a positive light. Douglas and Sutton (2003) argue that the processes underlying their results do not stem from a conscious decision to use linguistic abstraction to meet one's ends, though. Rather, they assume that communicative goals affect the level of abstraction in speech production without senders being aware of the precise mechanisms by which their speech acts create a desired impression in receivers (see also Douglas, Sutton, & McGarty, this volume; Douglas & McGarty, 2001; Douglas & Sutton, 2003).

Communication purpose. In a similar fashion, Semin, Gil de Montes, and Valencia (2003) argued that people might vary their description of valence-laden behavior when messages serve a specific *communication purpose*. Participants were asked to describe positive and negative behavior of a target person known to be liked (disliked) by another participant with whom participants would cooperate (compete) at a later stage of the experiment. Whereas participants' behavioral description were allegedly passed on to the future interaction partner in the experimental conditions of these experiments, participants in the control conditions were informed that their descriptions served no communication purpose, but were only intended to help them form an impression of the target person. As expected, positive behavior was described more abstractly than negative behavior for target persons liked (disliked) by future partners (opponents), whereas the reverse pattern emerged for target persons disliked (liked) by future partners (opponents). No systematic variation in linguistic abstraction was found in the control conditions. The latter finding implies that behavioral descriptions in previous research on abstraction biases presumably served a communicative purpose. More importantly, however, the interaction between liking and type of future interaction implies that peo-

---

[2]Note in passing that communication based on the explicit goal to conceal one's privately held beliefs does not fall within the scope of the cooperativeness principle (Grice, 1975) because the cooperative construction of common ground is no longer the ultimate purpose of such communication.

ple are capable of adjusting their level of linguistic abstraction in a way that fits their current sender-receiver constellation (see also Gil de Montes, Semin, & Valencia, 2003).

Communication tasks.   Finally, yet another approach to explicit processes in the emergence of abstraction biases has been taken by Fiedler, Bluemke, Friese, and Hofmann (2003). These authors question the assumption that abstract language primarily serves to signal expectedness, arguing that the use abstract descriptions can serve a variety of additional purposes, depending on the requirements of senders' *communication tasks*. When communicating to a receiver who is not knowledgeable about a stereotype, for instance, senders may interpret their task as that of conveying an unambiguous impression of the target group (e.g., by providing predominantly abstract descriptions). Similarly, when communicating to a receiver who does not share one's beliefs, senders may interpret their task as that of revising seemingly inaccurate beliefs (e.g., by providing highly abstract descriptions of target features that disconfirm the recipient's prior beliefs). To put these ideas to a test, Fiedler et al. (2003) asked participants to describe positive and negative behaviors that were typical or atypical of out-group members to an uninvolved receiver. The receiver either had or did not have extensive first-hand experience with the out-group and held either positive or negative beliefs about it. As expected, participants tended to portray out-group members in a negative way. Notably, however, the strength of this abstraction bias was moderated by both the receiver's prior beliefs and the receiver's prior knowledge. Specifically, abstraction bias was stronger when the receiver had no first-hand experience (requiring teaching) and when the receiver did not share participants negative beliefs about the out-group (requiring counter-arguing).[3]

Taken together, the different lines of research on the impact pragmatic concerns on linguistic abstraction have shown that people do have the language-use competence necessary to *actually* vary the level of linguistic abstraction at

------

[3]Fiedler et al. (2003) also invoke two novel constructs in explaining their findings: *target expectedness* (e.g., the fit between sender expectations and target behavior) and *receiver expectedness* (e.g., the fit between receiver expectations and target behavior). In any intergroup setting involving stereotypical expectations shared among in-group members, target expectedness and receiver expectedness will converge in intragroup communication and they will diverge in intergroup communication. If senders confronted with receiver expectations that diverge from privately held target expectations simply stick to the latter, data will show the *common* abstraction bias pattern when expectedness is defined based on *target expectedness,* whereas data will show a *reversed* abstraction bias pattern when expectedness is defined based on *receiver expectedness.* Fiedler et al. (2003) claim that their data show that the common abstraction bias pattern reverses into an *ANTI-LEB* when a sender is confronted with the task of revising receivers' beliefs. In the context of the present discussion, however, the ANTI-LEB pattern may be more appropriately classified as an instance of "normal" abstraction bias when communicating to an equal status receiver in a sender-receiver constellation rendering the relevant stereotype salient (cf. Table 10–1 above).

which a behavior is described. The level of linguistic abstraction chosen has been shown to be determined by the current communication goals across a wide range of experimental procedures such as *blatant instruction* (Douglas & Sutton, 2003), *type of future interaction* (Semin et al., 2003), and *task requirements* implied by receiver characteristics (Fiedler et al., 2003). Combined with the idea that the communicative settings used in early work on the LIB/LEB may have given rise to rather specific communication goals, the observation that communication goals do have a direct effect on linguistic abstraction lends further support to the heuristic potential of the taxonomy of sender-receiver constellations proposed in this chapter. Specifically, the systematic examination of the full communication triad advanced here might be capable of (a) providing a more comprehensive explanation on the basic LIB/LEB pattern obtained in the pioneering work; while (b) assimilating the recent trend toward pragmatic concerns; and (c) offering informed guesses about the causal paths along which expectancies and pragmatic concerns might affect language use. Importantly, future research on biases in linguistic abstraction in intergroup settings may want to examine the effects of sender-receiver constellations on communication goals in attempt to quantify the relative contribution of *intrapersonal factors* (such stereotypical expectancies and in-group-protective motives) as opposed to *interpersonal factors* (such as communication goals arising from the interplay of target affiliation, receiver affiliation, and receiver status).

BEYOND LINGUISTIC ABSTRACTION

So far, I have been concerned primarily with issues of internal and external validity. As I have argued at the outset, however, the fragmentation of social psychological research on communication is not only problematic with respect to the validity of the individual approaches, but also with respect to their theoretical integration. Again, the LIB/LEB literature provides a case in point, because there is a neighboring approach that shares with it an interest in the macrolevel phenomenon of communication-based processes in stereotype maintenance, but that differs from it in the micro-level processes examined. In fact, the two approaches do not only converge in the *explanandum* but also in the *explanans* in that both invoke the SC of a target person's behavior as the major explanatory construct. Despite this promising conceptual overlap, there are as yet substantial mismatches in the procedures used, in the role assigned to receiver characteristics, and in the dependent measures assessed. As we shall see, however, the theoretical integration of the LIB/LEB literature with its conceptual neighbor might again be facilitated by a systematic examination of the impact of sender-receiver constellations—in this case, by emphasizing the role of sender's subjective representation of relevant background knowledge shared with a receiver.

In the pioneering work on this approach, Kashima (2000) applied Bartlett's (1932) serial reproduction paradigm to the domain of stereotype maintenance. A story comprising SC and SI episodes was presented to participants who served as the first link of a five-link communication chain. Participants were asked to read the story carefully and, after some delay, to reproduce the story in their own words. Typed copies of the reproduced stories were then presented to new groups of participants until the original story had been reproduced five times. In line with research on the memory advantage of SI information (cf. Stangor & McMillan, 1992), a higher proportion of SI rather than SC episodes was reproduced in step one, but a stable and reliable reproduction bias in favor of SC episodes was observed after no more than three reproductions of the original story.

This finding implies that the proliferation of stereotype-relevant information in natural communication networks might contribute to stereotype maintenance by the selective transmission of information that fits stereotypical expectancies. Moreover, subsequent research has shown that the magnitude of this bias depends on both the stereotypical expectancies held by senders and the sender-receiver constellation in the communication chain. Specifically, Lyons and Kashima (2003) found no reproduction bias when the members of a communication chain held opposing beliefs about the stereotyped group and when senders assumed that the receivers of their message would not endorse the stereotype. As in the abstraction bias literature, then, the research on reproduction bias has shown that communication can contribute to stereotype maintenance, and that the magnitude of the respective biases depends strongly on the stereotypical beliefs held by senders and on the sender-receiver constellation in which the communication takes place.

From an epistemological point of view, however, the co-existence of theoretical approaches overlapping in both the independent variables considered and the phenomena to be explained is problematic (cf. Platt, 1964). For one thing, methodological folk wisdom has it that the same variance (in stereotype maintenance) can only be explained once. Thus, the significance of the findings obtained by the different approaches remains underdetermined unless their contribution to stereotype maintenance is disentangled in research assessing the effects of either type of biased language use simultaneously. Interestingly, a first data point relevant to the issue has been presented recently by Karasawa (2005). As in previous studies on reproduction bias, participants reproduced a carefully composed story comprising SC and SI episodes, and the content of the reproduced stories was coded for both the linguistic abstraction of SC and SI episodes and the reproduction likelihood of SC and SI episodes. The results showed that the two biases coexist. That is, Karasawa found that SC behaviors were communicated more abstractly and reproduced more frequently than SI behaviors. Unfortunately, the correlation between the magnitude of abstraction bias and that of reproduction bias was not reported.

Therefore, we cannot yet tell whether this alignment of two biases in a single set of data means that the two go hand in hand.

The missing piece of information could be easily distilled, though, not only from Karasawa's (2005) data but also from the data obtained in previous research on the serial reproduction paradigm (e.g., McIntyre, Lyons & Clark, 2004; Kashima, 2000; Lyons & Kashima, 2003). Given the alignment observed for the two indices of communication bias, a positive—but probably less than perfect correlation—may be expected to emerge. This follows from the fact that the two indices of communication bias are conceptually independent. That is, a reproduced story can comprise equal proportions of SC and SI episodes and yet contribute to stereotype maintenance by way of the linguistic abstraction at which SC and SI episodes are being described. Conversely, reproductions of SC and SI episodes may be characterized by equal levels of linguistic abstraction and yet contribute to stereotype maintenance by way of the relative proportion of SC and SI episodes included. Assessing the relative contribution of the different processes thus seems worthwhile in its own right.

Apart from competitive tests of the significance of qualitative (e.g., mean abstraction) and quantitative (e.g., mean reproduction) features of stereotype-relevant messages, the two approaches might also inform each other with respect to their lacunae. On the one hand, previous research on reproduction bias has paid little attention to the impressions formed by receivers of a (reproduced) message. In this regard, an inclusion of the dispositional inference measures applied in studies on the LEB would be a first step (e.g., "To what extent was the behavior described caused by the person/by the situation?", "How much does the episode described reveal about the person/about the situation?"). On the other hand, previous research on abstraction bias has paid little attention to senders' beliefs about stereotype sharedness. Senders in most studies either knew that the receiver would be knowledgeable regarding stereotype content or they knew that the receiver would be an in-group member. Of course, some recent research also addressed the issue of receiver affiliation (e.g., Douglas & McGarty, 2001; Wigboldus et al., 2005), but the crucial question of senders' assumptions regarding stereotype sharedness was neither addressed by experimental manipulations (cf. McIntyre, Lyons, & Clark, 2004; Lyons & Kashima, 2003) nor by measures of senders' subjective representation of receiver characteristics (cf. Higgins, 1981, 1992).

CONCLUSION

I have argued that the epistemological value of previous research about the effects of linguistic abstraction on stereotype maintenance is limited by both its conceptualization of communicative contexts and its assessment of the significance of linguistic abstraction. As to the conceptualization of communicative contexts, researchers have been concerned with the impact of sender characteristics to the neglect of receiver characteristics, most of the time providing senders with strong cues to receivers' prior knowledge and affiliation (cf. Table 10–2). However, a simple taxonomy of sender-receiver constellations revealed that the magnitude of abstraction biases could be expected to vary with context (cf. Table 10–1). Thus, research on the processes affecting linguistic abstraction in a given communication setting may benefit from distinguishing between an (implicit) intrapersonal component (reflecting senders' expectancies) and an (explicit) interpersonal component (reflecting senders' goals in a given sender-receiver constellation). As to the significance of linguistic abstraction to stereotype maintenance, finally, research has been concerned with qualitative aspects of messages (e.g., mean abstraction) to the neglect of quantitative aspects (e.g., mean reproduction). In this regard, research may benefit from integration with recent work on the impact of stereotype-consistency and stereotype-sharedness in the serial reproduction of messages.

Fig. 10–2 summarizes the implications of the present analysis in the form of a provisional mediational model of biased communication that distinguishes an intrapersonal component from an interpersonal component. The *intrapersonal component* is assumed to reflect senders' stereotypical expectancies, whereas the *interpersonal component* is assumed to reflect senders' communication goals. Moreover, variation in the interpersonal component is assumed to reflect the implications of sender-receiver constellations, whereas variation in the intrapersonal component is assumed to reflect inter-individual differences in strength of stereotypical associations that could be assessed by indirect measures of associative strength (e.g., Fazio, 1995, 2001; von Hippel et al., 1997) *prior* to experimental sessions.

Going beyond previous models on the impact of linguistic abstraction, the model also includes reproduction bias as an additional mediational variable ultimately affecting receivers' impressions. Regarding the relative contribution of the different biases to stereotype maintenance, reproduction bias can be assumed to be the more potent factor, because describing an episode of SI behavior at a lower level of abstraction can only minimize the episode's impact on stereotype change, whereas dropping it altogether from a (reproduced) message can eliminate its impact on stereotype change effectively. Finally, we should keep in mind that the decision to include an episode in a reproduced story might be quite deliberate—at least compared to the decision to describe it at a higher or a lower level of linguistic abstraction. Thus, reproduction decisions should be more susceptible to forces operating on the explicit component of biased language use. Conversely, abstraction decisions should be more susceptible to forces operating on the implicit component. Of course, this is not to say that participants will be more likely to mention factors belonging

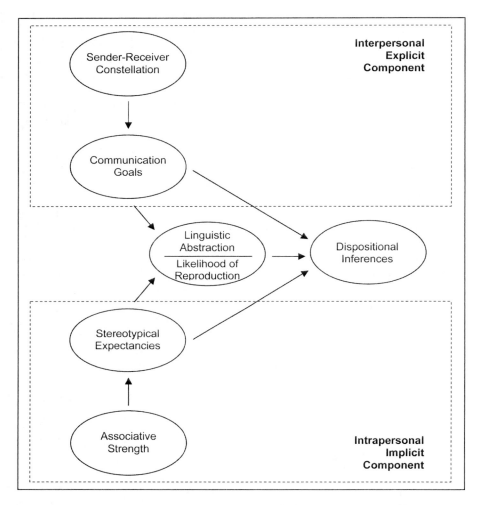

FIGURE 10–2.   Provisional model of the joint impact of stereotypical expectancies and communication goals on the linguistic abstraction of descriptions of stereotype-related behavior and on the corresponding dispositional inferences. Expectancies are assumed to be determined by intrapersonal factors that originate in sender characteristics and exert their impact through implicit processes, whereas communication goals are assumed to be determined by interpersonal factors that originate in sender-receiver constellations and exert their impact through explicit processes.

to the one or the other pathway depicted in Fig. 10–2 when interviewed about their communication strategies. However, the hypothesized differential explicitness of the processes affecting the different indices of biased language use may help to disentangle them empirically in future research.

REFERENCES

Arcuri, L., Maass, A., & Portelli, G. (1993). Linguistic intergroup bias and implicit attributions. *British Journal of Social Psychology, 32,* 277–285.

Baron, R. M., & Kenny, D. A. (1986). The moderator-mediator variable distinction in social psychological research: Conceptual, strategic, and statistical considerations. *Journal of Personality & Social Psychology, 51,* 1173–1182.

Bartlett, F. C. (1932). *Remembering: A study in experimental and social psychology.* Cambridge: Cambridge University Press.

Clark, H. H., & Brennan, S. E. (1991). Grounding in communication. In L. B. Resnick, J. M. Levine, & S. D. Teasley (Eds.), *Perspectives on socially shared cognition* (pp. 127–149). Washington: American Psychological Association.

Clark, H. H., & Schober, M. F. (1992). Asking questions and influencing answers. In J. M. Tanur (Ed.), *Questions about questions: Inquiries into the cognitive bases of surveys* (pp. 15–48). New York: Russell Sage Foundation.

Douglas, K. M., Sutton, R. M., & McGarty, C. (2000). Strategic language use in interpersonal and intergroup communication. In Y. Kashima, V. Fiedler, & D. Freytas (eds.). *Stereotype Dynamics: Language-based approaches to the formation, maintenance, and transformation of stereotypes* (pp. 191–217). Mahwah, NJ: Lawrence Earlbaum.

Douglas, K. M., & McGarty, C. (2001). Identifiability and self-presentation: Computer-mediated communication and intergroup interaction. *British Journal of Social Psychology, 40,* 399–416.

Douglas, K. M., & Sutton, R. M. (2003). Effects of communication goals and expectancies on language abstraction. *Journal of Personality & Social Psychology, 84,* 682–696.

Fazio, R. H. (1995). Attitudes as object-evaluation associations: Determinants, consequences, and correlates of attitude accessibility. In R. E. Petty & J. A. Krosnick (Eds.), *Attitude strength: Antecedents and consequences* (pp. 247–282). Mahwah: Erlbaum.

Fazio, R. H. (2001). On the automatic activation of associated evaluations: An overview. *Cognition & Emotion, 15,* 115–141.

Fiedler, K., Bluemke, M., Friese, M., & Hofmann, W. (2003). On the different uses of linguistic abstractness: From LIB to LEB and beyond. *European Journal of Social Psychology, 33,* 441–453.

Fiedler, K. Semin, G. R., & Koppetsch, C. (1991). Language use and attributional biases in close personal relationships. *Personality and Social Psychology Bulletin, 17,* 147–155.

Fischhoff, B., Slovic, P., & Lichtenstein, S. (1979). Subjective sensitivity analysis. *Organizational Behavior & Human Performance, 23,* 339–359.

Franco, F. M., & Maass, A. (1996). Implicit versus explicit strategies of out-group discrimination. The role of intentional control in biased language use and reward allocation. *Journal of Language and Social Psychology, 15,* 335–359.

Gil de Montes, L., Semin, G. R., & Valencia, J. F. (2003). Communication patterns in interdependent relationships. *Journal of Language and Social Psychology, 22,* 259–281.

Grice, H. P. (1975). Logic and conversation. In P. Cole & J. L. Morgan (Eds.), *Syntax and Sematics 3: Speech acts,* (pp. 41–58). New York: Academic Press.

Higgins, E. T. (1981). The 'communication game': Implications for social cognition and persuasion. In E. T. Higgins, C. P. Herman, & M. P. Zanna (Eds.), *Social cognition: The Ontario symposium* (pp. 343–392). Hillsdale: Erlbaum.

Higgins, T. E. (1992). Achieving "shared reality" in the communication game: A social action that creates meaning. *Journal of Language and Social Psychology, 11,* 107–131.

Karasawa, M. (2005). *The linguistic intergroup bias in the context of message transmission.* Paper presented at the 14th General Meeting of the European Association of Experimental Social Psychology at the University of Wuerzburg, Germany.

Karpinski, A., & von Hippel, W. (1996). The role of the linguistic intergroup bias in expectancy maintenance. *Social Cognition, 14*, 141–163.

Kashima, Y. (2000). Maintaining cultural stereotypes in the serial reproduction of narratives. *Personality and Social Psychology Bulletin, 26*, 594–604.

Krauss, R. M., & Fussel, S. R. (1996). Social psychological models of interpersonal communication. In E. T. Higgins & A. W. Kruglanski (Eds.), *Social psychology: Handbook of basic principles* (pp. 655–701). New York: Guilford Press.

Lyons, A., & Kashima, Y. (2003). How are stereotypes maintained through communication? The influence of stereotype sharedness. *Journal of Personality & Social Psychology, 85*, 989–1005.

Maass, A. (1999). Linguistic intergroup bias: Stereotype perpetuation through language. In M. P. Zanna (Ed.), *Advances in experimental social psychology, Vol. 31* (pp. 79–121). San Diego: Academic Press.

Maass, A., Ceccarelli, R., & Rudin, S. (1996). Linguistic intergroup bias: evidence for in-group-protective motivation. *Journal of Personality & Social Psychology, 71*, 512–526.

Maass, A., Milesi, A., Zabbini, S., & Stahlberg, D. (1995). Linguistic intergroup bias: Differential expectancies or in-group protection? *Journal of Personality and Social Psychology, 68*, 116–126.

Maass, A., Salvi, D., Arcuri, L., & Semin, G. R. (1989). Language use in intergroup contexts: The linguistic intergroup bias. *Journal of Personality & Social Psychology, 57*, 981–993.

McIntyre, A., Lyons, A., & Clark, A. (2004). The microgenesis of culture: Serial reproduction as an experimental simulation of cultural dynamics. In M. Schaller & C. S. Crandall (Eds.), *Psychological foundations of culture* (pp. 227–258). Mahwah: Erlbaum.

Platt, J. R. (1964). Strong inference. *Science, 146*, 347–353.

Schmid, J. (1999). Pinning down attributions: the linguistic category model applied to wrestling reports. *European Journal of Social Psychology, 29*, 895–907.

Schmid, J., & Fiedler, K. (1996). Language and implicit attributions in the Nuremberg trials: Analyzing prosecutors' and defense attorneys' closing speeches. *Human Communication Research, 22*, 371–398.

Schmid, J., & Fiedler, K. (1998). The backbone of closing speeches: The impact of prosecution versus defense language on judicial attributions. *Journal of Applied Social Psychology, 28*, 1140–1172.

Schnake, S. B., & Ruscher, J. B. (1998). Modern racism as a predictor of the linguistic intergroup bias. *Journal of Language and Social Psychology, 17*, 484–491.

Schwarz, N. (1994). Judgment in a social context: Biases, shortcomings, and the logic of conversation. In M. P. Zanna (Ed.), *Advances in Experimental Social Psychology, Vol. 26* (pp. 123–162). San Diego: Academic Press.

Schwarz, N. (1996). *Cognition and communication: Judgmental biases, methods, and the logic of conversation* (pp. 1–31). New Jersey: Erlbaum.

Semin, G. R., & Fiedler, K. (1988). The cognitive functions of linguistic categories in describing persons: Social cognition and language. *Journal of Personality & Social Psychology, 54*, 558–568.

Semin, G. R., & Fiedler, K. (1989). Relocating attributional phenomena within the language-cognition interface: The case of actor-observer perspectives. *European Journal of Social Psychology, 19*, 491–508.

Semin, G. R., & Fiedler, K. (1991). The linguistic category model, its bases, applications, and range. *European Review of Social Psychology, 2*, 1–30.

Semin, G. R., & Fiedler, K. (1992). The inferential properties of interpersonal verbs. In G. R. Semin & K. Fiedler (Eds.), *Language, interaction, and social cognition* (pp. 58–78). Newbury Park: Sage.

Semin, G. R., Gil de Montes, L., & Valencia J. F. (2003). Communication constraints on the linguistic intergroup bias. *Journal of Experimental Social Psychology, 39,* 142–148.

Stangor, C., & McMillan, D. (1992). Memory for expectancy-congruent and expectancy-incongruent information: A review of the social and social developmental literatures. *Psychological Bulletin, 111,* 42–61.

Turner, J. C., Hogg, M. A., Oakes, P. J., Reicher, S. D., & Whetherell, M. S. (1987). *Rediscovering the social group: A self-categorization theory.* Oxford: Basil Blackwell.

von Hippel, W., Sekaquaptewa, D., & Vargas, P. (1997). The linguistic intergroup bias as an implicit indicator of prejudice. *Journal of Experimental Social Psychology, 33,* 490–509.

Wigboldus, D. H. J., Semin, G. R., & Spears, R. (2000). How do we communicate stereotypes? Linguistic bases and inferential consequences. *Journal of Personality & Social Psychology, 78,* 5–18.

Wigboldus, D. H. J., Spears, R., & Semin, G. R. (2005). When do we communicate stereotypes? Influence of the social context on the linguistic expectancy bias. *Group Processes & Intergroup Relations, 8,* 215–230.

Part 4

STEREOTYPE SHAREDNESS
AND DISTINCTIVENESS

Retention and Transmission of Socially Shared Beliefs: The Role of Linguistic Abstraction in Stereotypic Communication

Minoru Karasawa
Nagoya University, Japan

Sayaka Suga
Kobe University, Japan

The social cognition approach to the study of stereotypes has mainly focused on psychological processes operating within individual perceivers (Hamilton & Sherman, 1994; Stangor & Lange, 1994); however, there is a growing recognition in recent studies that stereotypes are collectively shared by members of a group or a community (e.g., Gardner, 1994; McIntyre, Lyons, Clark, & Kashima, 2004; Schaller & Conway, 2001; Stangor & Schaller, 1996; Wigboldus, Spears, & Semin, 1999; see also the distinction between "personal" and "cultural" stereotypes by Ashmore, Del Boca, & Wohlers, 1986). Yet despite its intuitive appeal, a concept such as "collectively shared representation" easily faces obstacles at both the theoretical and empirical levels. Social psychology has a traditional proclivity to avoid the assumption of mental states in collectives (e.g., the "group mind") mainly because of the difficulty in its operationalization.

As a counter view against such skepticism, we discuss in this chapter the possibility of empirically approaching the collectively shared aspects of stereotypic beliefs. In particular, we will emphasize that understanding why and how communication works is a key to clarifying some critical aspects of shared cognition. This approach should be a reasonable choice because the high consensus in stereotype contents is typically formed through communication processes taking place both at interpersonal (e.g., through parents and peers) and at macro levels (e.g., mass media, arts and literature, and religious texts; e.g., Maass, 1999; Mullen, Rozell, & Johnson, 1996; Norenzayan & Atran, 2004; Ruscher, 2001; van Dijk, 1987). Incorporating the theoretical and empirical perspectives of communication studies will provide a useful framework for the understanding of how stereotypes are shaped and maintained as shared representations and, in turn, influence communication among people.

In the following sections, we will first lay out a theoretical framework to understand how communication is achieved, drawing on a linguistic theory of pragmatics. From this perspective, we then discuss potential roles of stereotypes in communication. The importance of linguistic analyses in examining the shared aspects of stereotypes will be emphasized. Finally, we will report evidence from our own experimental research that demonstrated the relationship between language and stereotypic information processing. As a whole, our analysis will demonstrate the usefulness of the pragmatic approach for the study of stereotypes as collectively shared representations.

THE PRAGMATICS APPROACH TO SOCIAL STEREOTYPES

Stereotypic Communication and Social Inferences

Researchers of stereotyping have long been interested in the role of stereotypes in social *inferences*. Substantial research has revealed the details of inductive processes in which concrete behavioral information associated with different members are synthesized into abstract representations of group traits (e.g., Mackie, Hamilton, Susskind, & Rosselli, 1996). Likewise, the details of deduction have also been thoroughly investigated. We have now rich knowledge concerning how abstract and categorical trait expectations guide interpretations of concrete behavioral episodes (e.g., Hamilton & Sherman, 1994). One chief assumption in the study of these stereotype effects, particularly in those employing the "information processing" approach, has pertained to the notion of "cognitive misery" (e.g., Fiske & Taylor, 1991). That is, preexisting expectancies such as stereotypes are thought to help perceivers save their cognitive efforts and make efficient information processing.

A limitation of this perspective, however, becomes visible when we turn to viewing the consensual nature of stereotypes. Specifically, people at times send messages that contain stereotypic characterizations of a group so that the receiver can draw inferences about an unspoken meaning embedded in the message (Oakes, Haslam, & Turner, 1994). Consider the following conversation between two persons, A and B:

(1)   A: "Ken works 80 hours a week!"
(2)   B: "Well, he is Japanese."

One may claim that Person B's reference to categorical information (i.e., "Japanese") reflects cognitive misery relying on information reduction. From a different viewpoint, however, Person B can be seen as demanding even greater cognitive effort on Person A than making an explicit statement such as "He is hardworking." Person A needs to fill the gap between what was told and what was meant by B's utterance because Ken's nationality logically has nothing to do with either the number of working hours or the trait. From a pragmatic perspective, these communicators can be seen as helping each other to draw spontaneous inferences about the untold parts of the message. Indeed, communicators may try to *reduce* the amount of explicitly transmitted information on the one hand, but they also create *additional* meanings out of the message on the other.

For an attempt to understand how meanings are constructed through communication, a linguistic theory of pragmatics named Relevance Theory (Sperber & Wilson, 1986) provides a useful framework. In this theory, Sperber and Wilson proposed that communication is a process through which the sender of a message helps the recipient construct reality of the situation (i.e., "cognitive environment" in their own terms). They furthermore emphasized that the sender's concern for the recipient's cognitive environment is reflected in their effort to maximize the cognitive utility of the message (i.e., "relevance"; see also Grice, 1975). In this theory, relevance is defined as a trade-off between two crucial factors: (a) the size of "contextual effects" and (b) the cognitive effort invested by the recipient. Contextual effects refer to the extent to which the recipient can acquire new meanings by inference from a given set of information. The contextual effect will certainly be enhanced in proportion to the sheer quantity of nonredundant information transmitted, but the amount would also incur cognitive burden on the side of the recipient. Thus, the message sender needs to consider the optimal amount of information that is actually transmitted, as well as the size of an information gap that could be filled by the recipient's inferences. Going back to our example of the conversation between Persons A and B, Ken's nationality was brought up because it was expected to be of an optimal conciseness and potential for inferences.

It should be evident from the above description that Relevance Theory presupposes the role of *common grounds* in knowledge and meaning between the communicators. Before this theory was proposed, the traditional framework in communication studies used to be a linear sequence model of (a) encoding the sender's mental representation into signals, (b) transmitting the signals through a medium, and (c) decoding the signals back into the receiver's representation.[1] Instead, Sperber and Wilson (1986) emphasized that communicators trust their communication partner for their ability to draw inferences from their common

---

[1]Not surprisingly, this sequential model has been a predominant framework in the information processing approach to stereotyping that mainly focused on intraindividual processes.

background with respect to what was actually *not* mentioned in the message (see also Clark, Schreuder, & Buttrick, 1983; Fussel & Krauss, 1989).

Stereotypes as Common Ground

Drawing on the pragmatic perspective presented above, we may argue that social stereotypes generally render a high level of relevance when they are contained in a communicated message, due to the expected cognitive efficiency *and* contextual effects. For one thing, stereotypes summarize characteristics of different members of a group in succinct and abstract trait terms. Stereotypic depiction of a group is thus expected to ease the recipient's cognitive load as one special kind of "social schemas" (Fiske & Taylor, 1991; Schank & Abelson, 1977). Furthermore, as we pointed out at the outset of this chapter, contents of group stereotypes are typically shared by members of a community or a culture. The high level of consensuality may serve as a useful common ground for communicators. Comments referring to category membership or stereotypic traits will induce inferences in the hearer so that he or she can comprehend the implicated meaning. Indeed, the emergent nature of meaning construction as a cultural act is pointed out not only in association with social stereotypes, but with categorical knowledge in general (Bruner, 1990).

The preference for stereotype-based communication has been demonstrated in studies that compared the impact of stereotype-consistent (SC) and stereotype-inconsistent (SI) information exchanged among people. For instance, a series of studies conducted by Ruscher and her colleagues investigated contents of dyadic conversations in laboratories (Ruscher, 1998). In one of their studies, Ruscher, E. Y. Hammer, and E. D. Hammer (1996) presented pairs of participants with a number of descriptions of a target person who belonged to a stereotyped group (e.g., "alcoholics"). Some of the stimulus sentences describing characteristics of the person confirmed the group stereotype (i.e., SC), whereas other descriptions were designed to violate stereotypic expectations (i.e., SI). The participants were then allowed to engage in dyadic conversations. Content analyses revealed that the participant pairs made comments referring to a greater number of SC than SI characteristics and spent a longer time talking about the former. Subsequent studies also revealed that the bias toward SC conversations was facilitated by the pairs' awareness that the stimulus information was shared with the partner (Ruscher & Duval, 1998). From a related and yet different perspective, Kashima (2000) also compared the roles of SC and SI information in communication. Instead of studying bidirectional dyadic conversations, he examined how SC and SI information would be serially passed on to a chain of other people (i.e., the "serial reproduction" method). Results showed that SC information was more likely to survive the serial transmission, and this tendency has been replicated in a number of studies (e.g., Lyons & Kashima, 2003; McIntyre et al., 2004).

Results from these studies have demonstrated that descriptions of a group member containing both SC and SI characteristics tend to be distorted toward SC representations through communication. One possible interpretation for these findings is that, with everything else being equal, SC information renders a greater relevance to the communication partner. Cases disproving stereotypes are likely to require the recipient an extra effort to resolve the contradiction or ambiguity, whereas stereotype-confirming cases would help the recipient process information smoothly. Because of the higher level of comprehensibleness, inferences can be more easily generated based on SC information, such as explanations of why the target person engaged in a certain behavior (e.g., McGarty, Yzerbyt, & Spears, 2002). Consequently, the recipient may achieve a new understanding about the depiction of the target with lesser cognitive effort.[2]

Relevance and Linguistic Forms

The relevance of stereotype-based communication can be manifested not only in the composition of produced communication (e.g., the number of SC vs. SI utterances), but also in the lexical format of the message as well. In particular, stereotypic beliefs are known to be reflected in lexical choices when behavior of a group member is described. When we describe someone's behavior, and that behavior is consistent with a prior expectancy about the person, we tend to use predicates that allow generalizations from the specific observation to other situations or occasions. In contrast, when the observed behavior is inconsistent with an expectation, we tend to describe it in concrete terms— typically, descriptive verbs that do not allow simple generalizations about the dispositions of the actor (i.e., the Linguistic Expectancy Bias, which will be explained in detail shortly).

In the linguistic analysis concerning represented dispositions of the actor, currently, the most frequently used framework in the social psychological literature is the Linguistic Category Model (LCM) developed by Semin and

---

[2]Arguably, summary information has a potential danger of misleading the recipient to exaggerated views of the target person. Also, we should admit the possibility that SI information may at times more useful for achieving a new understanding of the target (e.g., disconfirmation of the stereotypic expectation). Relevance Theory does not allow us to derive specific hypotheses to predict under what circumstances either SC or SI can be more relevant. Other theories and research are therefore necessary to provide such specific predictions and explanation. Discussing those possibilities, however, goes beyond the scope of this chapter. All we propose here is that SC information can be generally more relevant than SI, with effects of all other potential factors held constant.

Fiedler (1988). According to this model, the category of predicates that provide the least information about dispositional characteristics of the actor (i.e., low in the level of abstraction) is Descriptive Action Verbs (DAVs). It is difficult to draw dispositional inferences and make generalizations based on verbs such as "run," "hit," and "speak." However, if we use a verb at a next level of abstraction (i.e., Interpretive Action Verb, or IAV) in saying "He *yelled* at someone," instead of saying "He *spoke* to someone" (e.g., DAV), then the former statement implies some inferences concerning dispositional characteristics of the actor. A typical example of such inferences is positive or negative evaluation of the character. Furthermore, if we refer to an internal state of the actor using State Verbs (SV) (e.g., "He *disliked* the person"), then stronger dispositional inferences and generalizations would be implicated. Finally, the LCM maintains that Adjectives (ADJ) (e.g., *aggressive, extrovert,* and *helpful*) are at the highest level of abstractness in expressing the dispositions. A number of studies have provided evidence that dispositional inferences about the actor are certainly facilitated to the extent that the actor's behavior is described in predicates with higher level of abstractness (Semin & Fiedler, 1988; Wigboldus, Semin, & Spears, 2000; see also Maass, Karasawa, Politi, & Suga, 2006, study 5).

The LCM has been adopted in studies of how people represent acts of individuals and groups. One well-known and fairly robust finding from these studies is the Linguistic Expectancy Bias (LEB; Maass, Milesi, Zabbini, & Stahlberg, 1995). An observed behavior consistent with prior expectations tends to be described in more abstract terms, whereas unexpected behavior is more likely to be described in less abstract (or more concrete) words. For instance, when someone who is expected to be an extrovert had fun at a party, his behavior consistent with the extroversion expectancy may be characterized in more abstract terms such as "He was *sociable* at the party" (i.e., ADJ) or "He *enjoyed* the party" (SV). In contrast, if the actor was expected be an introvert, the same behavior may be described in more concrete terms, such as "He *talked* with many people at the party" (DAV). Furthermore, a special form of LEB called the Linguistic Intergroup Bias (LIB) is often observed in intergroup contexts (Maass, 1999; Maass, Salvi, Arcuri, & Semin, 1989). Desirable behavior by a member of one's own group (i.e., the in-group) tends to be depicted in relatively abstract dispositional terms, whereas the same desirable behavior is described in more concrete terms when the actor belongs to an out-group. The reverse takes place when the behavior is undesirable. This bias is assumed to take place because positive expectations are typically associated more strongly with the in-group than with the out-group.

Whether the expectancy involves evaluative connotations associated with group membership (i.e., LIB) or general stereotypic expectations, the LEB can be seen as stemming from the difference in informativeness concerning dispositional characteristics of the target. Abstract predicates such as trait adjectives are concise and allow a wide variety of generalizations, and thus provide more information about stable characteristics of the target across different situations. Indeed, empirical findings by Semin and Fiedler (1988) indicate that people are intuitively aware of such differences. Restating in the terminology of Relevance Theory, a description with more abstract terms may improve the cognitive environment of someone who hears or reads it. The recipient of the information will be able to construct a reality concerning dispositional characteristics of the target with relatively little cognitive effort. Because of the ease in incorporating the information, the description may even strengthen prior expectations.

The above discussion may apply to situations in which verbally described behavioral events are *consistent* with prior expectations. On the contrary, when expectation-inconsistent events are described, the high information potential of trait words may demand a great amount of cognitive effort and hinder efficient communication; that is, the recipient will need to resolve the contradiction between a prior expectation and the observed cases, by either disconfirming the prior expectation or integrating the unexpected events. For example, one should find a great difficulty in understanding the following statement:

(3)   Jim is introvert, and he is sociable.

Suppose we have a prior expectation that Jim is introvert. This trait expectation, as well as the new information represented by the latter adjective *sociable*, would respectively induce a number of inferences. Consequently, it will be difficult to resolve the contradiction and establish a coherent cognitive environment. In contrast, the following statement appears easier to understand:

(4)   Jim is introvert, and he goes to the party.

In this case, because of the concreteness of the behavioral episode (e.g., going to the party), we are allowed to make interpretations and withhold a generalization. For instance, we could understand the instance as an exception, or we may provide an explanation that there must be something special either in the party or in Jim to go to this particular party in this particular occasion. In other words, the contextual effect can be more easily established in Example (4) than in Example (3).

Audience Design: Effects of Communicative Contexts

The foregoing discussion suggests that the Linguistic Expectancy Bias can be a reflection of high relevance of abstract trait terms in representing expectancy-consistent cases. On the other hand, in describing inconsistent cases, a high relevance of concrete verbs may be responsible for the bias. This explanation resting on a pragmatic viewpoint leads us to a testable hypothesis concerning the effect of communicative contexts. That is, if the LEB is caused by a pragmatic reason, then the bias can be enlarged under a communicative goal.

Past studies have demonstrated that in a communicative setting, people show their pragmatic concern for the message recipient when they produce a message; that is, communicators adjust the contents of their message in accordance with the recipient's knowledge, attitudes, goals, and so forth (e.g., Fussell & Krauss, 1989; Krauss & Fussell, 1996; Higgins, 1992). This phenomenon, called "audience design," should be likewise observed involving stereotypic expectations. Considering the high consensus among people, it is plausible that communicators are more willing to transmit stereotype-consistent rather than stereotype-inconsistent information.

Furthermore, a study by Wigboldus, Spears, and Semin (2005) has demonstrated that the pragmatic nature of stereotype-related communication affects even the linguistic abstraction of the message. These researchers systematically varied the in-group versus out-group membership in the three-way relationship among the sender, receiver, and target. The results indicated a straight LEB (abstract expressions for SC and concrete for SI) between the sender and receiver, but only when the receiver belonged to the sender's in-group and the target was an out-group member. When the target was an in-group member, a reverse was true in that SI information was transmitted in more abstract terms than SC. Because the out-group is generally perceived to comprise more SC instances than is the in-group (i.e., the out-group homogeneity effect; Park & Rothbart, 1982), and probably because the message sender expected that this perception was shared with the in-group receiver, the sender modified the message so that the SI information fit the receiver's representation of the in-group target; however, such adjustment due to a common ground can be expected only for the in-group receiver. Indeed, the communication directed toward an out-group receiver showed an ordinary LEB regardless of the target's group identity.

To summarize, consequences of stereotypes, particularly linguistic effects such as the LEB, should not be regarded as a mere result of cognitive tendencies in individual perceivers. Rather, there is a possibility that the linguistic bias stems from mutual and communicative acts between the communication sender and the receiver. In other words, the LEB can be regarded as one form of audience design. In the following section, we will draw on some of our own studies that examined this possibility.

COMMUNICATION CONTEXTS AND LIGUISTIC BIAS

Studying Linguistic Biases

The experimental paradigm employed in our research program had one distinct feature markedly different from previous studies of the LEB. Participants in our studies were presented with written information including expectancy-consistent and expectancy-inconsistent attributes of the target. The predicates of the stimulus sentences were held at a constantly low level of abstraction, typically Descriptive Action Verbs. Our primary interest was in how the given behavioral information would be transformed into different levels of abstraction when it is transmitted through intended communication.

In contrast, the abstractness of target information in previous studies of the LEB was not necessarily under the investigator's control. For instance, in their original work on the LEB, Maass et al. (1989) presented participants with cartoons depicting various behaviors of protagonists (e.g., helping someone, littering wastes). Participants were then asked to choose one phrase from out of four that they thought best fit the target cartoon. The predicates of those four alternatives were derived from the different abstraction levels in the LCM. The study by Maass et al. (1989) hence examined how ambiguous behavioral information is verbally constructed into a certain abstraction level, which was clearly different from our research purposes.

A number of subsequent studies extended the Maass et al. (1989) paradigm, but the transformation or distortion in reproductions has not been their primary research interest. These studies, therefore, typically did not place systematic linguistic constraints on the stimulus information (e.g., Fiedler, Blumke, & Friese, 2003; Karpinski & von Hippel, 1996; Ruscher & Duval, 1998; Semin, Gil de Montes, & Valencia, 2003; von Hippel, Sekaquaptewa, & Vargas, 1997; Webster, Kruglanski, & Pattison, 1997). In still other studies, participants were not even given any concrete behavioral information, but the LEB was nonetheless observed. For example, Wigboldus et al. (2000) asked participants to think of different groups (e.g., men vs. women, in-group vs. out-group members) and to report their behavioral characteristics that were either stereotypic or counter-stereotypic of the target group. When the participants activated particular exemplars (either concrete instances or an abstract and summated representation of typical features-"prototype") on their own, the linguistic expressions took the form of LEB.

Our study aimed to go one step further to investigate how unambiguously concrete behavioral information is transformed when it is expressed in a linguistic representation. Even when behavioral episodes are presented in extremely concrete terms of DAVs, the information is likely to be encoded, retained in memory, and interpreted for reconstruction in more abstract terms, and the extent of such modulation should be a function of the strength of prior expectancies for actor's enduring dispositions. We therefore predicted that stereotype-consistent (SC) information would be reproduced in more abstract predicates than stereotype-inconsistent (SI) information. Furthermore, we predicted that the abstraction for SC cases would be facilitated to the extent to which the perceiver was aware that the linguistic characterization was communicated to others. Previous studies using the serial reproduction method have demonstrated that SC information tends to be regarded as more

informative for the audience and thus more prevalently used in message transmission (e.g., Kashima, 2000; Lyons & Kashima, 2003). We predicted that the
expected relevance would be reflected not only in the quantity of SC information contained in the message, but also in its level of abstraction. Support
for this prediction comes from findings by Semin et al. (2003). They demonstrated that the LEB was observed especially when the participants expected
their message to be transmitted to another participant. The experimental setting in Semin et al. (2003) was different from the present study in that they
used a cartoon rather than verbal stimuli, and thus did not place any direct
control over the linguistic abstractness of the stimulus. Also, the target of the
description was the intended receiver him- or herself in that study. Despite
these differences, we expected that a similar underlying process (e.g., communicative consideration for the message recipient, namely, audience design)
would result in an enhanced LEB in our experiment as well.

Stereotype-Based Linguistic Expectancy Bias

In our first study, we aimed to establish that the LEB can be observed in the
Japanese linguistic system with regard to group stereotypes (Suga & Karasawa,
2006). In a preliminary investigation, we had discovered that Japanese college
students held fairly clear stereotypes about international students from Asia,
especially for students from the People's Republic of China. Trait characteristics such as *hardworking, poor, frugal,* and *family oriented* were judged to be stereotypic of Chinese students, while Japanese students were seen as relatively *lazy,
wealthy, spoiled,* and *gregarious.* In association to these stereotypic traits, we further identified behavioral descriptions that were judged by another group of
pilot respondents to be stereotypic of Chinese students, but at the same time
counter-stereotypic of Japanese students, as well as descriptions that were
judged to be typical of the Japanese, but atypical of the Chinese. A list of these
stimulus sentences is given in Table 11-1. Note again that Descriptive Action
Verbs were used in all of these sentences.

In the main experiment, participants read the 10 behavioral sentences
listed in Table 11-1 that were purportedly describing a college student. One
half of the participants were told that the stimulus sentences described a student from the Kansai area (e.g., Western part of Japan, where the experimental site was located), implying that he was Japanese. The remaining participants were told that the stimulus individual was a student from China who is
currently studying in Japan. In other words, the participants were randomly assigned to either the in-group (e.g., Japanese) or the out-group (e.g., Chinese)
target condition. Before starting to read the stimulus sentence, participants
were also informed that they were going to be asked later to recall and write
down what they were about to read. One half of the participants were told

TABLE 11–1.
Stimulus Descriptions in the Stereotype Study

Japanese-Consistent Behaviors	Chinese-Consistent Behaviors
• *took* a back seat in the classroom	• *got up* at 7:00 A.M.
• *photocopied* a friend's lecture notes	• *went* to school on foot
• *bought* clothes for 10,000 yen	• *arrived* at school 5 minutes before the class
• *watched* a TV comedy show	• *wore* 5-year old clothes
• *went* to *karaoke*	• *wrote* a letter to his family

All sentences were written in DAVs. (From Suga, S., & Karasawa, M., 2006, *Jinbutsu no zokusei hyougen ni mirareru shakaiteki sutereotaipu no eikyou.* [Effects of social stereotypes on language use in the description of person dispositions.]. *Japanese Journal of Social Psychology, 22,* 180–188) Copyright 2006 by the Japanese Society of Social Psychology. Translated by permission.

that this reproduction would be made for a communication purpose; that is, they were informed that their reproductions would be transmitted to another participant so that she or he could use the information as a basis for their judgments about the stimulus person (i.e., the communicative goal condition). In actuality, the reproduced information was not transmitted to any other individual, but the psychological reality created for participants in this condition can be seen as comparable to the ones used in the serial reproduction procedure (e.g., Kashima, 2000). The other half of the participants were told that later in the experiment they were going to be asked questions about their impressions of the target individual and that their reproductions would be used as a basis for their judgments (e.g., the individual goal condition). After these instructions, participants in both conditions read the stimulus descriptions carefully. In accordance with the prior instruction, they were then asked to write down what they could recall from the original stimulus information so that the reproduced message would be useful either for the other participant or for themselves, depending on the experimental condition.

We conducted content analyses on the reproductions regarding two aspects. First, in order to assess the overall stereotypicality of each participant's reproduction, we counted the number of SC and SI characterizations of the target. These included an accurate recall of the stimulus item (e.g., "arrived at school five minutes early") as well as inferences (e.g., "motivated to study") as long as the descriptions were attributable to the original descriptions. As illustrated in Fig. 11–1, the description of an out-group target included a significantly greater number of SC reproductions than SI, whereas an in-group member was described by evenly distributed SC and SI characteristics. The out-group target was hence represented in a more stereotypic manner than the in-group target.

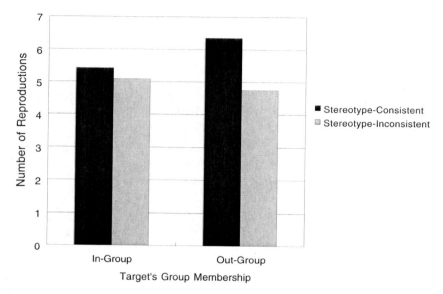

FIGURE 11–1.   The number of stereotype-relevant reproductions.

The second index in the content analysis was the level of abstraction.[3] On the basis of the LCM, we measured the level of abstraction up to which each stimulus information was abstracted, by giving abstraction values of 1, 2, 3, and 4 to DAV, IAV, SV, and ADJ, respectively. These values weighted on the predi-

---

[3]Because of a number of peculiar characteristics of the Japanese language, we needed to modify the original LCM (Semin & Fiedler, 1988). Particularly notable are the highly distinct features of Japanese adjectives. In the Japanese language, adjectives are divided into two subclasses. The first subclass is adjectives ending with *-i*, and they are equivalent to adjectives in Western languages. The second type is called "nominal adjectives," ending with *-da*. More important, both types of adjectives inflect to qualify verbs, transforming into what is equivalent to adverbs in Western languages. For example, one may say "Kanojo wa kashikoku suru" (meaning "She behaves wisely") or "Kare wa shinsetsu-ni suru" (meaning "He behaves kindly"). Note that the authentic adjective *kashikoi* is inflecting into *kashikoku*, and the nominal adjective *shinsetsu-da* into *shinsetsu-ni*. Grammatically, the verb *suru* ("do") is the predicate of these sentences. In the traditional use of the LCM in the Western languages, sentences with adverbs would normally be treated as a verb sentence because the verb in the predicate position would still carry some meaning. In Japanese sentences such as this, however, the informative value of the verb, *suru*, is extremely minimal because it is a semantically vacuum "do" which is nominally given in the predicate position without any clarification of the act. Thus, we concluded that we should focus on the inflected adjective when we apply the LCM to a Japanese sentence of this kind, rather than coding the meaningless predicate *suru* as a verb. Interestingly, even if we allow this lenience to Japanese adjectives in our coding, Japanese still seem to be generally reluctant to adopt adjectives to represent a dispositional characteristic of a person. Instead, they show a greater preference for using verbs, compared to people using Western languages. This greater inclination for verbs among Japanese can be observed not only in their spontaneous verbal descriptions of a person, but also in memory biases (Maas et al., 2006).

cates were summed for each participant and then divided by the number of predicates so that the average level of abstraction was computed. Not surprisingly, it was revealed that even a single behavioral episode was often reproduced at multiple levels of abstraction. For instance, a stimulus sentence, "He *went* to Karaoke with his friends," could be transformed into "He is *sociable* (ADJ), because he *likes* (SV) Karaoke." This case was coded as ADJ (=4) to represent the highest level of abstraction that this episode resulted in. The abstraction score was computed for each participant separately for the reproduced SC and SI items. The mean abstraction levels in each condition are illustrated in Fig. 11–2. As for reproductions of the out-group target behavior, significantly more abstract words were used for SC than for SI. On the other hand, no difference in abstractness was found between SC and SI for the in-group target. In other words, the LEB was observed only for the out-group target in this experiment.

The results of this experiment established that the LEB does take place even in the reproduction of given information which was originally presented in highly concrete terms (i.e., DAVs); however, the predicted effect of the communication goal was not statistically significant. One possible explanation for this is that the experimental reality of the communication goal was not sufficiently salient. Considering the fact that participants came to the experimental sessions individually, the awareness of the existence of a potential receiver may have been generally low, even if they were told that their reproduction was going to be transmitted to another person.

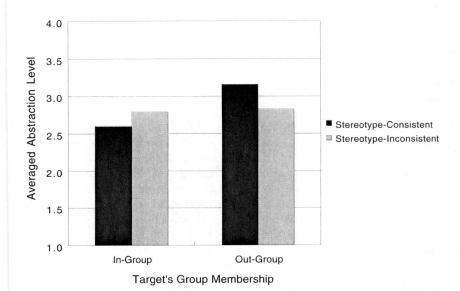

FIGURE 11–2.   Mean abstraction levels of stereotype-consistent and stereotype-inconsistent information.

In order to enhance the presence of the receiver in the communication goal condition, we conducted a second experiment (Suga & Karasawa, 2005). This time, the participants were invited to the experiment in groups with sizes ranging from 6 to 9, instead of individually. The rest of the experimental manipulations and materials were identical to the first study, except one modification. In the communication goal condition, participants were told that their reproduction will be passed on to one of the other participants concurrently at present in the same experimental room. Compared to the previous experiment, the visibility of the potential receiver was expected to increase the salience of the communicative goal.

Indeed, the effect of the communication goal was evident in this experiment. As for the number of reproductions, a 3-way interaction between the target membership (in- vs. out-group), the reproduction goal (individual vs. communicative), and the type of reproduction (SC vs. SI) reached statistical significance. As in the previous study, a greater number of SC items were reproduced than SI items when the target was an out-group (i.e., Chinese) member, but more importantly, this was the case only when the reproduction was intended to be transmitted to another participant. The difference between SC and SI was nonsignificant even under the out-group target condition when the explicit communicative goal was removed (i.e., the individual goal condition). On the other hand, results from the in-group target condition again showed no difference between SC and SI reproductions, regardless of the reproduction goal. Results for abstraction levels showed an identical pattern. The LEB was found only for the out-group target with a higher level of abstraction for SC than for SI items, but the difference between the two kinds of information was visibly larger in the communicative goal condition. The LEB was hence enhanced under the condition where an explicit goal of message transmission was installed.

The results from our study hence demonstrated that a communicative goal facilitates linguistic abstraction of behavioral information about an out-group member. It should be emphasized again that our data presents a special form of the LEB in that the effect was observed in linguistic distortions, with the original information experimentally controlled at a low level of abstraction. This is in contrast with previous studies that examined verbalization of ambiguous representations, such as an interpretation of cartoons or vignettes, or stereotypic representations retrieved from long-term memory.

Another nonobvious and consistent finding was that the LEB, as well as the predominance of SC over SI in reproductions, was observed only for the out-group target. This result suggests that stereotypic expectations among the present participants were stronger for the out-group than for the in-group. This may be due to a potential difference in information values that the categories *Japanese* and *Chinese* would render for our Japanese participants; that is, in-group membership is generally less informative when it is a default category because of its excessive inclusiveness (Haslam, Oakes, Turner, & McGarty, 1996).

For example, no American citizen living in the United States would refer to another American citizen living in next door as "my American neighbor" because the nationality is taken for granted. It is only when a nondefault, minority category is brought up that the categorization becomes meaningful (e.g., "my Chinese neighbor," or "the guy from Scandinavia"). Likewise, in our in-group condition with a between-participant design, there was no explicit indication that the protagonist was a Japanese person because it would have been redundant otherwise. We instead indicated the region in Japan where he was supposedly from. In contrast, the Chinese identity in the out-group condition must have been of substantial informational value, and any common ground expectation among the Japanese participants should have exerted influence on their information processing. Consequently, stereotypes about the Chinese may have produced a greater impact on the communication contents.

It is also worth noting that the out-group target used in this experiment was associated with expectations for *positive* traits such as hardworking, frugal, and family oriented, at least in contrast to the relatively negative trait expectations for the in-group Japanese students (e.g., spoiled and lazy). This can be an interesting addition to the literature of intergroup cognition. In the past research of intergroup relations, an overwhelming majority of the studies has defined the contexts with a positive in-group and a negative out-group (Tajfel, 1981; Sedikides, Schopler, & Insko, 1998; but see Fiske, Cuddy, Glick, & Xu, 2002; Brewer, 1999). This is also true to the study of Linguistic Intergroup Bias (e.g., Maass et al., 1989). The present finding that the LEB can be observed for positive characteristics of an our-group member presents another piece of evidence for the independence of the linguistic bias from the valence associated with group identity (Maass et al., 1995).

Effects of the Audience Size

Drawing on the characterization of the LEB as a subclass of audience design, we argue that the nature of the audience can be an important determinant of the effect. Specifically, the magnitude of message modification may depend on the size of the assumed audience. Compared to a situation with a small number of receivers, a communication sender who expects a large number of receivers would face a greater demand on the message relevance for more people. To achieve this communication goal, the sender is more likely to tailor the message so that the transmitted information shares a common ground with a large number of people. This will make the communication more consistent with prior expectations shared by the potential audience. This was the main hypothesis that we tested in our next study.

Another purpose of the study reported below is to extend the domain of the LEB. Viewing the LEB as a special case of audience design, we propose that the domain of the bias should not be confined to transmission of stereotype-relevant information. Instead, a similar effect can be observed involving other types of expectancies. One interesting way of testing this possibility is to look at message transmission concerning consumer products. In daily contexts, the exchange of information regarding commodities is an ordinary and yet engaging activity. The relevance of the information for the communication partner should be an important matter for communicators to take into account under such contexts. It is conceivable that different kinds of symbolic social significance are attached to the images of consumer products, such as the association between social classes and statuses on one hand, and product categories, manufacturer brands, and so forth on the other (e.g., inner-city teenagers and rap music, soccer moms on MPVs, and geeks with scientific calculators). The fact that such associations render particular meanings in our social life illustrates that those symbols are collectively shared by members of a cultural community. Such sharedness should have a profound impact on the pragmatic concerns among communicators.

In our third experiment, we presented personal computers as the target because they are a familiar category of products for college students (i.e., the participants of the study) and often appear in their daily conversations. We prepared, on the basis of a pilot testing, a list of five positive and five negative aspects of a PC. As listed in Table 11–2, the stimulus descriptions were constructed in such a way that the usage of trait adjectives was avoided. Instead, DAVs and IAVs were used as the predicate of each sentence. (Unlike in the case of person descriptions, it turned out to be extremely difficult to develop descriptions of machinery in DAVs alone.) Participants were randomly assigned to one of the three experimental conditions. Two experimental conditions, called the "individual goal condition" and "single audience condition," were essentially identical to the ones established in our previous studies. Participants were asked to reproduce the original information and were told that the reproduction was going

TABLE 11–2.
Stimulus Descriptions in the Computer Study

Positive Features
    It *came* out with a 10-year warranty.
    The audio speakers *received* a noise reduction treatment through a digital amplifier.
    It *improved* in its processing speed compared to the previous model.
    The user's manual *helped* me when I became confused with unknown functions.
    It *allowed* an immediate access to e-mailing software by pushing a single button.
Negative Features
    It *took* a long time to boot.
    The wireless mouse *failed* to function from a certain direction.
    It *came* out with an older version of operation system.
    It occasionally *went* into freeze.
    It *allowed* only 2 hours of motion picture recording.

to be used as a basis for judgments about the target product to be made either by him- or herself, or by another participant. An additional, third condition was called the "multiple audience condition," in which the reproduction was purportedly to be transmitted to a group of 15 participants. The experimenter explained that the receiver group was going to use the transmitted information to make a group decision concerning their evaluation of the target.

As in our previous studies on stereotypes, we first analyzed the number of positive and negative comments mentioned in the reproductions. The results revealed a trend for positivity bias, with a significantly greater number of positive features ($M = 3.70$) than negative features ($M = 3.36$) included in the reproductions.[4] The positivity bias was unpredicted, but not surprising. Because descriptions of PCs are typically framed in positive terms in places like product catalogues, participants might have been led to focus more on positive features. The baseline tendency of positivity bias was also manifested in the linguistic abstraction, but in a more intricate manner. Here, too, the main effect for valence (positive vs. negative reproductions) was significant, with positive attributes described in predicates at a higher level of abstraction ($M = 1.45$) than negative ones ($M = 1.37$); however, this was qualified by a significant interaction between the valence and the size of the audience. As Fig. 11–3 illustrates, the positivity bias in abstraction level was enlarged when participants anticipated that their reproductions would be transmitted to multiple receivers. The difference between the positive and negative items reached statistical significance in the multiple audience condition, but not in the other two conditions. In view that the positivity bias was a general baseline expectation about the quality of this PC, we can define its positive attributes as *expectation-consistent* and its negative attributes as *expectation-inconsistent*. Drawing on this assumption, the present results can be interpreted to present a special form of the LEB, with more abstract predicates used for expectation-consistent features and less abstract predicates for inconsistent features.

As we repeated in this chapter, predicates with a higher level of linguistic abstraction are assumed to render a greater relevance for the audience, with a greater potential for expanding their cognitive environment (e.g., the ease to understand the message with lesser cognitive effort; see Sperber & Wilson,

---

[4]An additional independent variable was manipulated in this experiment. We considered the possibility of stereotypic expectation associated with a personal computer may influence linguistic abstraction. Half of the participants were told that the computer was manufactured by NEC, a well-known Japanese company, whereas the other half were told that the manufacturer was a fictitious Vietnamese company named "Mekong Star"; however, this manipulation of manufacturer brand did not produce any significant effects on the dependent variables, and thus will not be discussed in the following sections. In other words, the positivity bias was found to be a common baseline tendency, regardless of the brand names. One possible reason for this is that the strong positivity bias may have simply overridden potential stereotypic brand effects. Alternatively, Asian manufacturers such as Vietnamese companies may no longer render a negative association with their products because of the recent industrial development in this region.

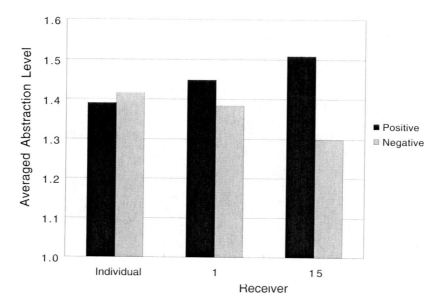

FIGURE 11–3.   Mean abstraction levels of positive versus negative information.

1986). Participants in the transmission goal conditions used more dispositional (i.e., abstract) terms, probably because they judged that these words were more informative for other participants to represent the overall characteristics of the PC. For instance, by modifying original descriptions such as "This new model *improved* in its processing speed" into more dispositional terms that allow generalizations (e.g., "fast, better than the old model"), they might have well expected that these expressions would be informative for the audience as a basis for comprehending stable characteristics of the target. In contrast, preserving concrete terms in reproducing negative aspects (e.g., "came out with an older version of operating system") rather than abstracting the information (e.g., "the old operating system was disappointing") might prevent generalizations.[5]

Particularly important for this discussion is the finding that this particular form of LEB was facilitated as the size of the anticipated audience was enlarged from none (e.g., the individual goal condition) through one receiver (e.g., single-audience) and up to 15 receivers (e.g., multiple-audience). In sending communication to a greater number of receivers, the communicators presumably faced a greater demand to compose a message that commonly fits

---

[5]We assumed from the overall tendency that providing a positive evaluation was conceived as a default among the participants in this particular context. Our interpretation that transmitting positive evaluations would facilitate relatively effortless communication holds only under this assumption. Admittedly, however, giving negative evaluations can rather be an expected behavior in other occasions. Further examinations under such various expectations are needed.

the beliefs and expectations of different receivers. Languages at higher levels of abstraction are plausible candidates to satisfy this demand. The abstraction level hence appears to correspond to the perceived size of a common ground assumed in the audience. In this case, the perception that expectations for positive features of this PC were shared among a large number of other participants seems to have served as a basis for word choices.

CONCLUSION

In this chapter, we discussed the possibility of empirically approaching socially shared beliefs such as group stereotypes. We maintained that the examination of communicative contexts can serve this attempt because sharedness is likely reflected in communicators concern for the cognitive environment of their communication partner; that is, communicators attempt to maximize the relevance of their messages so that the recipients can achieve a good understanding of the intended meaning of the messages through inferences with minimal cognitive effort (Sperber & Wilson, 1986). Congruent with this argument, our empirical data demonstrated that communicators' considerations on relevance were embodied in the Linguistic Expectancy Bias with regard to the level of abstractness; that is, behavioral descriptions of a stimulus person were modulated when they were reproduced so that stereotypic preconceptions of the target (and possibly, of their group as a whole) were maintained or bolstered. More dispositional and abstract terms (e.g., adjectives and state verbs) were used to represent expectancy-consistent characteristics, whereas less abstract words (e.g., interpretive and descriptive action verbs) were used to represent attributes betraying the expectancy. The bias was especially visible when the goal of reproduction was to transmit information to another participant.

Interestingly, our results also indicated that the LEB under the communicative goal can be facilitated in proportion to the size of the assumed audience. Here too, consideration on the relevance for the audience seems to have played an important role. In order to produce a message that can be commonly understood by a greater number of receivers, the communicator presumably relied on what was expected to be shared by that audience. Admittedly, a caveat is necessary because the effect of audience size was not found in the LEB involving a group stereotype (i.e., that for Chinese students), but was found only in the positivity bias for a consumer product. Further research is necessary to validate the existence of the audience size effect in stereotype-based LEB.

As demonstrated above, collaborations between linguistic theories, such as Relevance Theory, and analytical methods developed by social psychologists, such as LCM (Semin & Fiedler, 1988), can make significant contributions to the study of shared aspects of social cognition. Mutual consideration among communicators is easily manifested in their language use when transmitting messages. Our analyses primarily focused on the transmission of reproduced information, but the same idea can be applied to other communicative contexts. Also, the analyses of shared cognition should not be limited to the study of stereotypes, but may rather cover a wide variety of research issues (Smith & Semin, 2004). The pragmatics approach is expected to provide both conceptually and empirically useful tools for the study of socially shared cognition.

ACKNOWLEDGMENTS

We thank Masami Sato for his assistance in data collection. The preparation of this manuscript was supported by Grant-in-Aid for Scientific Research by Japan Society for the Promotion of Science (#15330134).

REFERENCES

Ashmore, R. D., Del Boca, F. K., & Wohlers, A. J. (1986). Gender stereotypes. In R. D. Ashmore & F. K. Del Boca (Eds.), *The social psychology of female-male relations* (pp. 69–119). New York: Academic Press.

Brewer, M. B. (1999). The psychology of prejudice: Ingroup love or outgroup hate? *Journal of Social Issues, 55*, 429–444.

Bruner, J. S. (1990). *Acts of meaning.* Cambridge, MA: Harvard University Press.

Clark, H. H., Schreuder, R., & Buttrick, S. (1983). Common ground and the understanding of demonstrative reference. *Journal of Verbal Learning & Verbal Behavior, 22*, 245–258.

Fiedler, K., Blumke, M., & Friese, M. (2003). On the different uses of linguistic abstractness: From LIB to LEB and beyond. *European Journal of Social Psychology, 33*, 441–453.

Fiske, S. T., Cuddy, A. J. C., Glick, P., & Xu, J. (2002). A model of (often mixed) stereotype content: Competence and warmth respectively follow from perceived status and competition. *Journal of Personality and Social Psychology, 82*, 878–902.

Fiske, S. T., & Taylor, S. E. (1991). *Social cognition* (2nd ed.). New York: McGraw-Hill.

Fussell, S. R., & Krauss, R. M. (1989). The effects of intended audience on message production and comprehension: Reference in a common ground framework. *Journal of Experimental Social Psychology, 25*, 203–219.

Gardner, R. C. (1994). Stereotypes as consensual beliefs. In M. P. Zanna & J. M. Olson (Eds.), *The psychology of prejudice: The Ontario symposium* (Vol. 7, pp. 1–31). Hillsdale, NJ: Lawrence Erlbaum.

Grice, H. P. (1975). Logic and conversation. In P. Cole & J. Morgan. (Eds.), *Syntax and semantics 3: Speech acts* (pp. 41–58). New York: Academic Press.

Hamilton, D. L., & Sherman, S. J. (1994). Stereotypes. In R. S. Wyer, Jr. & T. K. Srull (Eds.), *Handbook of social cognition,* (2nd ed., Vol. 2, pp. 1–68). Hillsdale, NJ: Lawrence Erlbaum Associates.

Haslam, S. A., Oakes, P. J., Turner, J. C., & McGarty, C. (1996). Social identity, self-categorization, and the perceived homogeneity of ingroups and outgroups: The interaction between social motivation and cognition. In R. M. Sorrentino & E. T. Higgins (Eds.), *Handbook of motivation and cognition* (Vol. 3, pp. 182–222). New York: Guilford

Higgins, E. T. (1992). Achieving hared reality in the communication game: A social action that creates meaning. *Journal of Language and Social Psychology, 11*, 107–131.

Karpinski, A. T., & von Hippel, W. (1996). The role of the Linguistic Intergroup Bias in expectancy maintenance. *Social Cognition, 14,* 141–163.

Kashima, Y. (2000). Maintaining cultural stereotypes in the serial reproduction of narratives. *Personality and Social Psychology Bulletin, 26,* 594–604.

Krauss, R. M., & Fussell, S. R. (1996). Social psychological models of interpersonal communication. In E. T. Higgins & A. Kruglanski (Eds.), *Social psychology: A handbook of basic principles* (pp. 655–701). New York: Guilford Press.

Lyons, A., & Kashima, Y. (2003). How are stereotypes maintained through communication? The influence of stereotype sharedness. *Journal of Personality and Social Psychology, 85,* 989–1005.

Maass, A. (1999). Linguistic intergroup bias: Stereotype-perpetuation through language. In M. P. Zanna (Ed.), *Advances in experimental social psychology* (Vol. 31, pp. 79–121). San Diego CA: Academic Press.

Maass, A., Karasawa, M., Politi, F., & Suga, S. (2006). Do verbs and adjectives play different roles in different cultures? A cross-linguistic analysis of person representation. *Journal of Personality and Social Psychology, 90,* 734–750.

Maass, A., Milesi, A., Zabbini, S., & Stahlberg, D. (1995). Linguistic intergroup bias: Differential expectancies or in-group protection? *Journal of Personality and Social Psychology, 68,* 116–126.

Maass, A., Salvi, D., Arcuri, L., & Semin, G. (1989). Language use in intergroup contexts: The linguistic intergroup bias. *Journal of Personality and Social Psychology, 57,* 981–993.

Mackie, D. M., Hamilton, D., Susskind, J., & Rosselli, F. (1996). Social psychological foundations of stereotype formation. In C. N. Macrae, C. Stangor, & M. Hewstone (Eds.), *Stereotypes and Stereotyping* (pp. 41–78). New York: Guilford Press.

McGarty, C., Yzerbyt, V. Y., & Spears, R. (2002). *Stereotypes as explanations: The formation of meaningful beliefs about social groups.* Cambridge, UK: Cambridge University Press.

McIntyre, A. M., Lyons, A., Clark, E. A., & Kashima, Y. (2004). The microgenesis of culture: Serial reproduction as experimental simulation of cultural dynamics. In M. Schaller & C. Crandall (Eds.), *The psychological foundations of culture* (pp. 227–258). Mahwah, NJ: Lawrence Erlbaum Associates.

Mullen, B., Rozell, D., & Johnson, C. (1996). The phenomenology of being in a group: Complexity approaches to operationalizing cognitive representations. In J. Nye & A. Brower (Eds.), *What social about social cognition?* (pp. 205–229). Thousand Oaks, CA: Sage.

Norenzayan, A., & Atran, S. (2004). Cognitive and emotional processes in the cultural transmission of natural and nonnatural beliefs. In M. Schaller & C. Crandall (Eds.), *The psychological foundations of culture* (pp. 149–169). Hillsdale, NJ: Lawrence Erlbaum Associates.

Oakes, P., Haslam, S. A., & Turner, J. C. (1994). *Stereotyping and social reality.* Oxford: Blackwell.

Park, B., & Rothbart, M. (1982). Perception of out-group homogeneity and levels of social categorization: Memory for the subordinate attributes of in-group and out-group members. *Journal of Personality and Social Psychology, 42,* 1051–1068.

Ruscher, J. B. (1998). Prejudice and stereotyping in everyday communication. In M. P. Zanna (Ed.), *Advances in experimental social psychology* (Vol. 30, pp. 241–307). San Diego, CA: Academic Press.

Ruscher, J. B. (2001). *Prejudiced communication: A social psychological perspective.* New York: Guilford Press.

Ruscher, J. B., & Duval, L. L. (1998). Multiple communications with unique target information transmit less stereotypical impressions. *Journal of Personality and Social Psychology, 74,* 329–344.

Ruscher, J. B., Hammer, E. Y., & Hammer, E. D. (1996). Forming shared impressions through conversation: An adaptation of the continuum model. *Personality and Social Psychology Bulletin, 22,* 705–720.

Schaller, M., & Conway, L. G., III. (2001). From cognition to culture: The origins of stereotypes that really matter. In G. B. Moscowitz (Ed.), *Cognitive social psychology: The Princeton symposium on the legacy and future of social cognition* (pp. 163–176). Mahwah, NJ: Erlbaum.

Schank, R. C., & Abelson, R. P. (1977). *Scripts, plans, goals, and understanding: An inquiry into human knowledge structures.* Hillsdale, NJ: Lawrence Erlbaum

Sedikides, C., Schopler, J., & Insko, C. A. (1998). *Intergroup cognition and intergroup behavior.* Mahwah, NJ: Erlbaum .

Semin, G. R., & Fiedler, K. (1988). The cognitive functions of linguistic categories in describing persons: Social cognition and language. *Journal of Personality and Social Psychology, 54,* 558–568.

Semin, G. R., Gil de Montes, L., & Valencia, J. F. (2003). Communication constraints on the Linguistic Intergroup Bias. *Journal of Experimental Social Psychology, 39,* 142–148.

Smith, E. R., & Semin, G. R. (2004). Socially situated cognition: Cognition in its social context. In M. P. Zanna (Ed.), *Advances in experimental social psychology* (Vol. 36, pp. 53–117). San Diego CA: Elsevier Academic Press.

Sperber, D., & Wilson, D. (1986). *Relevance: Communication and cognition.* Cambridge, Mass: Harvard University Press.

Stangor, C., & Lange, J. E. (1994). Mental representations of social groups: Advances in understanding stereotypes and stereotyping. In M. P. Zanna (Ed), *Advances in experimental social psychology* (Vol. 26, pp. 357–416). San Diego, CA: Academic Press.

Stangor, C., & Schaller, M. (1996). Stereotypes as individual and collective representations. In C. N. Macrae, C. Stangor, & M. Hewstone (Eds.), *Stereotypes and Stereotyping* (pp. 3–37). New York: Guilford Press.

Suga, S., & Karasawa, M. (2005, April). *Effects of stereotypic expectations on impression formation: Communication of social stereotypes.* Paper presented at the 6th Biennial Conference of the Asian Association of Social Psychology. Wellington, New Zealand.

Suga, S., & Karasawa, M. (2006). *Jinbutsu no zokusei hyougen ni mirareru shakaiteki sutereotaipu no eikyou* [Effects of social stereotypes on language use in the description of person dispositions]. *Japanese Journal of Social Psychology, 22,* 180–188 (in Japanese with an English abstract).

Tajfel, H. (1981). *Human groups and social categories.* Cambridge, UK: Cambridge University Press.

van Dijk, T. A. (1987). *Communicating racism: Ethnic prejudice in thought and talk.* Newbury Park, CA: Sage.

von Hippel, W., Sekaquaptewa, D., & Vargas, P. (1997). The Linguistic Intergroup Bias as an implicit indicator of prejudice. *Journal of Experimental Social Psychology, 33,* 490–509.

Webster, D. M., Kruglanski, A. W., & Pattison, D. A. (1997). Motivated language-use in intergroup contexts: Need for closure effects on the linguistic intergroup bias. *Journal of Personality and Social Psychology, 72,* 1122–1131.

Wigboldus, D. J., Semin, G. R., & Spears, R. (2000). How do we communicate stereotypes? Linguistic bases and inferential consequences. *Journal of Personality and Social Psychology, 78,* 5–18.

Wigboldus, D., Spears, R., & Semin, G. (1999). Categorization, content and the context of communicative behavior. In N. Ellemers, R. Spears, & B. Doosje (Eds.), *Social Identity* (pp. 147–163). Oxford: Blackwell.

Wigboldus, D. H. J., Spears, R., & Semin, G. R. (2005). When do we communicate stereotypes? Influence of the social context on the linguistic expectancy bias. *Group Processes and Interpersonal Relations, 8,* 215–230.

Chapter 12

The Consensualization
of Stereotypes in Small Groups

Olivier Klein
Université Libre de Bruxelles, Belgium

Scott Tindale
Loyola University of Chicago

Markus Brauer
Université Blaise Pascal, France

During the months leading to the genocide of the Tutsi population in Rwanda, between April and June 1994, one of the strategies carried out by the Extremist Hutu government involved relying on one of the national radio channels (The *Radio des Milles Collines*), to instigate negative stereotypes of the Tutsis in order to justify their later destruction. Propaganda typically described Tutsis as "cockroaches," "snakes," or as secret agents of the Rwandese Patriotic Front (RPF), made of exiled Tutsis, which attempted to conquer the country. Given that most Rwandese citizens own a radio, this medium enabled the government to reach the whole population. Several analysts and observers (Braeckman, 1994; Dallaire & Beardsley, 2003; Franche, 2004; Hatzfeld, 2000) suggested that this strategy instigated in the Hutu population a shared sense of the necessity to destroy the out-group and of the legitimacy of such a project. If this factor alone does not explain the genocide, it appears to have played a significant role in its occurrence.

This example illustrates how intragroup social influence can lead to the formation and diffusion of shared stereotypes that eventually contributed to one of the most gruesome instances of collective mobilization in the 20th century. Although the Rwandese example is extreme and does not reflect the ordinary effects of stereotype consensus, it shows that the emergence of such consensus is an intriguing phenomenon that can have profound, even if usually more benign, consequences on intra- and intergroup processes (Stangor & Schaller, 1996).

Obviously, the expansion of negative stereotypes of the Tutsis in the early 1990s was to a great extent the outcome of intergroup phenomena and more specifically, of the Civil War with the RPF. Social psychology has extensively studied the influence of the intergroup context on stereotypes and stereotyping (see e.g., Alexander, Brewer, & Hermann, 1999; Alexander, Brewer, & Livingston, 2005; Haslam, Turner, Oakes, McGarty, & Reynolds, 1998; Oakes, Haslam, & Turner, 1994; Poppe, 2001). Nevertheless, to be shared within a group, the interpretations of these phenomena, and the stereotypes underlying these interpretations, had to be disseminated and communicated. This "intragroup dimension" has received much less research attention. The processes through which stereotype consensus unfolds within small groups and affects intra-group dynamics, will precisely be the focus of this chapter.

To address this issue, we shall first consider a conceptual issue: Should we define stereotypes as consensual? Then, we shall reflect on several strategies available for examining the emergence of stereotype consensus, and its inevitable counterpart, stereotype communication, within groups. We will subsequently focus one such strategy, experimental research with small groups or dyads, and suggest that insights from the small-group literature can be meaningfully applied to the issue of stereotype consensus. In the body of this chapter, we will then review some of the literature on stereotype communication and consensus in this light.

SHOULD STEREOTYPES BE DEFINED AS CONSENSUAL?

Until the late 1960s, the scientific curiosity for stereotypes was mainly confounded with an interest for consensus: Stereotypes were defined and measured as consensual beliefs, in line with Katz and Braly's seminal paper on ethnic stereotypes among college undergraduates (Katz & Braly, 1933). This early interest for the consensus issue seems to have faded from most of the literature on social stereotypes that flourished since the 1970s (Haslam, Turner, Oakes, McGarty, & Reynolds, 1998). Such a state of affairs can be attributed in part to John Brigham's influential review (Brigham, 1971): Brigham regretted the emphasis generations of social psychologists since Katz and Braly had placed on consensus as a defining feature of stereotypes. This emphasis, he claimed, derived from the assumption that consensus necessary reflects the use of unreliable sources of information (e.g., hearsay) regarding group characteristics. However, as this assumption was itself untested, such a preoccupation for consensus was unwarranted in his view. Brigham's article contributed to the redirection of stereotype research toward a consideration of the motivational and cognitive factors involved in stereotyping. Rather than studying stereotypes, treated as consensual beliefs, researchers now turned their attention to the stereotyping process, considered at the level of the individual perceiver. This redirection involved a double movement: from the group to the individual on the one hand, and from content to process on the other.

At a conceptual level, this movement also implied that consensus was viewed as an unnecessary feature of stereotypes: If stereotypes are defined at an individual level, the very nature of these mental representations cannot be contingent on social sharedness alone. Yet, several authors rejected such an emphasis on individual cognitive processes. Haslam (1997; Haslam, Turner, Oakes, McGarty et al., 1998), for example, argued that stereotypes are of little scientific interest if they are not shared. Indeed, it is their sharedness that makes their supposed large-scale social effects tangible. In a different vein, Gardner (1993) proposed that some of the processes involved in stereotyping may be restricted to shared stereotypes. In this view, leaving the consensus issue aside raises the danger of overgeneralization. It was therefore important to reconsider the issue of stereotype consensus. Following this guideline, several recent contributions have addressed stereotype consensus both as a dependent (Haslam, Oakes, Reynolds, & Turner, 1999; Haslam, Turner, Oakes, Reynolds et al., 1998) and as an independent variable (Sechrist & Stangor, 2001; Stangor, Sechrist, & Jost, 2001).

Although we applaud this renewed interest for the consensus issue, we believe the introductcion of consensus into the definition of stereotypes is not necessary an adequate move. First, it demands to select arbitrary criteria regarding the level of consensus that needs to be achieved for a representation to be considered as a proper stereotype. Even the most frequently endorsed traits are rarely chosen by more than 50% of participants in studies using the traditional checklist procedure (Devine & Elliot, 1995; for an exception, see: Haslam, Oakes, Reynolds, & Turner, (1999).

But, in our opinion, the main problem raised by considering consensus as a necessary feature of stereotypes resides in the limitation it places on our ability to address significant social psychological phenomena. Ironically, the very process of stereotype consensualization (e.g., how a stereotype can become consensual within a group) cannot be addressed if stereotypes are considered as consensual by definition. Yet, the issue of how people's individual experiences merge to form a sense of shared reality is one of the most fascinating questions faced by social psychology (Hardin & Higgins, 1996). In comparison with the massive amount of research devoted to the individual cognitive and motivational underpinnings of stereotypes, the question of how they become socially shared has been largely neglected. For these reasons, we shall not consider consensus as a necessary feature of stereotypes.

Note also that in this chapter, we will use the terms *stereotype sharedness* and *consensus* interchangeably. More specifically, these terms will refer to the degree to which a given trait is viewed as descriptive of a target group within another "perceiving" group. It is also important to distinguish "real" from "perceived" consensus: Members of a group may all believe that a stereotype is shared without endorsing it (Devine, 1989; Gordijn, Koomen, & Stapel, 2001). Conversely (and probably more rarely), they may all share a stereotype without knowing that it is shared.

The process through which individuals who initially had distinct beliefs about a target group come to endorse a consensual view of this group through within-group communication is known as stereotype consensualization (Haslam et al., 1998a,b). Such a process is predicated on group members' discovering and acknowledging their respective views. Hence, it also tends to lead group members to develop a shared sense of what constitutes consensual beliefs as well (e.g., perceived consensus).

INFORMATION SHAREDNESS AND CONSENSUS

Why is stereotype consensus an issue worthy of scientific interest? The most obvious reason is simply that the large-scale social effects of stereotypes derive mainly from their being shared (Klein & Snyder, 2003; Stangor & Schaller, 1996), as exemplified in the Rwandese example. The second reason involves mere scientific curiosity: Members of a social group are likely to differ in terms of the information they possess about a given out-group. They may have been in contact with different examplars or may have encountered members of this group in different contexts (e.g., as neighbors, coworkers, tourists). As a consequence, they may have been exposed to different information about the characteristics of this group; or they may be more or less familiar with this group. Whereas some of this information may be shared and known by all group members, other pieces of information may be possessed by only a few. Given this variety of experiences, the existence of some form of consensus about the characteristics of important in-groups and out-groups is not a trivial issue. Then, how do group members come to share a common view of a target group?

This question resembles one that has been the focus of small-group research (for a recent review, see: Baron & Kerr, 2003) for decades: How do members of small groups elaborate consensual decisions in spite of their variety of experiences, knowledge, and expertise? In line with its use in the group decision-making literature (Stasser & Titus, 1987), the word "sampling" can be used to refer to how information about a target group is distributed within a small group. Using this terminology, the above question becomes, "How does sampling of information affect the emergence of consensus about the characteristics of a social group?"

HOW CAN WE STUDY STEREOTYPE CONSENSUALIZATION?

Several strategies are available for studying the processes through which stereotypes become consensual. One such strategy involves considering how the mass media portrays social groups and how these media influence recipients (for a review, see Ruscher, 2001). This strategy is based on the assumption that the actual distribution of information within a social group determines the emergence of a shared representation. Given that information provided by the mass media are most widely distributed, it is also likely to be most influential in determining the content of emerging shared representations.

A second fruitful strategy involves considering how children acquire stereotypes. This strategy is premised on the assumption that acquiring the shared representation of relevant out-groups is part of the infant's socialization process (Aboud, 1989; Bennett & Sani, 2004; Hirschfeld, 1996).

Whereas both of these strategies are extremely valuable, they present methodological drawbacks that limit investigators' ability to address the actual processes involved in consensualization. First, researchers are usually dependent on the choice of information sources of influence (e.g., parents, television, etc.) choose to communicate. Like all forms of communication, this information is often strategically oriented as a function of the audience (McCann & Higgins, 1992). The factors prompting influence sources to select specific types of information about social groups in their messages are therefore likely to be neglected.

This dynamic interaction between source and target is extremely difficult to address in the context of developmental and media studies especially in view of the widespread use of correlational designs in such studies. Although experimental manipulations would be methodologically possible, inoculating stereotypes through the media or to children obviously presents ethical problems that may offset the methodological advantages of such a choice. Moreover, in such studies, the communicated information is usually already part of the audience's or child's knowledge which places barriers on our ability to study the initial processes involved in the consensualisation of representations that were not previously shared or known to be shared.

At a theoretical level, another limitation of these approaches lies in the fact that sharing information about a social group does not necessarily lead to stereotype consensus. It only does so if the shared information is collectively interpreted as forming the basis of a meaningful representation of the outgroup (Hardin & Higgins, 1996; Haslam, 1997). For example, if a popular television show mentioned every day that members of group B love football, this information could form the basis of very different stereotypes as a function of whether this information is interpreted as reflecting "laziness," "patriotism," or "team-spirit." It is only through within-group communication (e.g., consensualization) that raw information can form the basis of shared stereotypes. Hence, media studies cannot in and by themselves inform us on the emergence of consensual stereotypes. The construal of information about groups by audiences, and the processes through which these audiences reach a common interpretation, need to be subjected to an investigation as well. Even when individuals share information about a social group, they may fail to discuss this information and to reach a common understanding of this information.

Besides media and developmental studies, another avenue for studying the consensualization of stereotypes involves distributing information about members of a social group to a small group[1] and examining how they develop a shared representation of this group. The advantage of this strategy is that it lends itself more easily to experimental control and therefore enables researchers to address more precisely the processes hypothesized to be involved in stereotype consensualization. For example, researchers can influence group members' communicational goals, the extent to which the information they possess is shared, and the content of this information, and they can establish more easily the causal direction of the observed effects. Second, and most importantly, working with small groups enables investigators to treat groups as units of analysis, a useful asset when studying consensualization, precisely because it is a group-level phenomenon.

In the following section, we investigate how small-group research has treated the emergence of consensus within groups, or dyads, as a function of the distribution of information about the discussion issue. In order to do so, we shall not only present research directly involved with stereotypes, but also theoretical frameworks considering other types of decisions or representations as we believe that this research can be meaningfully applied to stereotypes. We shall consider how these perspectives may help us understand the development of new shared stereotypes among group members who did, initially, possess different information about the target group.

Once they have been "consensualized," how do these new stereotypes influence communication about the target group? We will tackle this topic in section 3 of this chapter. As we shall see, stereotype consistent (SC) information tends to have a communicational advantage, which contributes to the maintenance of stereotypes. This may lead to a "vicious circle," with stereotype self-perpetuating through interpersonal communication.

In the last section of this chapter, we will consider some of the factors that may detract group members from communicating SC information and lead them to communicate and agree on stereotype inconsistent (IC) information. We shall argue that stereotype communication does not only serve to maintain stereotypes, but also to change them.

---

[1] In this chapter, a dyad will be considered as a small group.

HOW STEREOTYPES BECOME CONSENSUAL
THROUGH COMMUNICATION

Groups as Information Processors and "Social Sharedness"

Although small groups form for many reasons and have many purposes (Mc-Grath, 1984), one of the key aspects of group interaction is information processing (Hinsz, Tindale, & Vollrath, 1997). Whether groups serve mainly a social or task-oriented function, information processing remains a vital component of the dynamics of group interaction. Hinsz et al. (1997) defined group-level information processing as "the degree to which information, ideas, or cognitive processes are shared, and are being shared, among the group members . . ." (p. 43). Such "sharedness" and/or sharing of information can relate to the task, the group, group members' interaction patterns within the group, or the general context in which the group exists. Whether information is shared prior to or during the group process can affect all aspects of information processing, including what information is attended to, how it is encoded, stored, retrieved, and integrated with other information.

Tindale and Kameda (2000; see also, Kameda, Tindale, & Davis, 2003) expanded on the Hinsz et al. (1997) definition of group information processing, focusing on the idea of "social sharedness." In essence, Tindale and Kameda argued that things that are shared to a greater degree among the members of a group tend to have more influence on group processes and outcomes than things shared to a lesser degree. The set of "things" that can be shared is still somewhat "fuzzy," but research has explored a number of the elements of the set to date. Shared preferences have received the greatest amount of research attention in the small-group literature, partially due to their ease of measurement and their prominence in early theories of group decision making (Davis, 1973; Kameda et al., 2003). A large body of research has shown that the largest preference faction within a group (e.g., the majority or plurality position) tends to become the final group response (Davis, 1982). For continuous-response dimensions, the median position or positions than minimizes the overall distance from initial member preferences tend to be chosen (Davis, 1996; Kameda et al., 2003).

Although majorities/pluralities tend to define the final group response, there are a number of situations where minority positions do prevail (Laughlin, 1980; Laughlin & Ellis, 1986; Tindale, Smith, Steiner, Filkins, & Sheffey, 1996). Laughlin and his associates have consistently demonstrated that minorities favoring "correct" alternatives on tasks where the "correctness" of the alternative can be "demonstrated" during group discussion can often win out over incorrect majorities. Laughlin and Ellis (1986) argued that one of the key aspects of this process concerned the shared background knowledge members had about the task. If all members of the group shared knowledge about how "correctness" would be defined for a given task, even if they could not themselves discover the correct answer, they would recognize it if one or more of the other group members proposed it as an alternative. Thus, for highly demonstrable tasks, it only takes one or two members of a group to prefer the correct alternative in order for the group to eventually reach consensus and choose it.

When discussions concern individual and groups' psychological traits, the material that serves to elaborate stereotypes, this criterion of demonstrability is usually not fulfilled. A stereotype is indeed a multifaceted representation that includes descriptive information relevant to central tendancy ("Group B is on average more x than group A") as well as to variability ("All members of Group B are "x"). It also includes explanatory information about the underlying source of these surface features (McGarty, Yzerbyt, & Spears, 2002). Contrary to the situations studied by Laughlin, in the context of a small group, it is often impossible for a minority to convincingly "demonstrate" that any of these criteria is successfully fulfilled and therefore that a stereotype espoused by the majority is incorrect.

Tindale et al. (1996) extended Laughlin and Ellis' perspective to group decision making generally through the concept of a "shared-task representation." Shared-task representations are task-relevant cognitions or cognitive processes that are shared among most or all of the group members. Task relevant means that the cognitions or processes have implications for (e.g., favor) a particular response alternative. Whenever a group shares a particular task representation, alternatives consistent with the representation are easier to defend and thus more likely to end up as the group's collective choice. Evidence for the effects of shared-task representations has come from focusing on asymmetries in the social influence processes of interacting groups. Both majorities and minorities favoring alternatives consistent with a shared task representation tend to be more influential than equal-sized factions favoring alternatives inconsistent with the representation. In many cases, research has shown that minorities favoring the alternative in line with the shared representation win out over majorities favoring other alternatives (Tindale, 1993; Tindale et al., 1996).

A number of different types of shared-task representations have been studied. For example, Tindale, Sheffey and Scott (1993) showed that a shared "loss oriented" frame for Tversky and Kahneman's (1981) "Asian Disease" problem led groups to choose the risky alternative even when a majority of members originally favored the less risky or certain alternative. McCoun and Kerr (1988) have shown that the shared-processing objective given to mock criminal juries (e.g., vote guilty only if you have no reasonable doubts about the defendant's guilt) leads factions favoring "not guilty" to be more influential than equal-sized factions favoring guilty. Smith, Dykema-Engblade, Walker, Niven, and Mc-Gough (2000) found that couching arguments against the death penalty in shared religious beliefs was far more influential in changing group members' attitudes that were similar, nonreligious arguments. Finally, Tindale (1993) found that for problems where cognitive heuristics used to estimate probabilities were highly shared, members using the heuristics were more influential than members who responded in more normatively correct ways.

There are many situations where a shared stereotype could function as a shared task representation. For example, if a personnel committee was attempting to choose among applicants for an entrepreneurial leadership position, shared gender stereotypes could influence the group to use more masculine characteristics as selection criteria, thus potentially favoring male candidates. There is also some evidence that shared stereotypes could affect jury decisions. Bodenhausen and Wyer (1985) found that mock jurors were more likely to judge a defendant guilty if the crime matched stereotypes associated with his or her ethnicity.

Evidence for the social sharedess effect is prevalent at the information level as well. Probably the best example stems from the seminal work by Stasser and Titus (1985; 1987). Stasser and Titus attempted to assess how well groups would process information that we distributed across group members using a "hidden-profile" paradigm. This paradigm gives certain pieces of information to all group members, while giving other pieces of information to only one of the members. For example, in a three-person group trying to decide which of two job candidates to hire (A or B), each group member may know the same two positive pieces of information about candidate B. In addition, they may each know one different positive piece of information about candidate A. Thus, each member would tend to prefer B, because he or she has more positive information about B than about A. However, if members discuss all of the information they possess, they will discover that there are three pieces of positive information about A and only two pieces of positive information about B. Using this paradigm, Stasser and Titus found that groups mainly discuss shared information and more often than not reach consensus on a nonoptimal choice. The basic findings that groups tend to discuss shared as opposed to unshared information and that shared information plays a larger role in determining the final group outcome have now been replicated numerous times (see Wittenbaum & Stasser, 1996 for a review).

Stasser and Titus (1985; 1987) showed that a rather simple probabilistic model (information-sampling model) did a fairly good job of describing the data from their experiments. The model is based on a binomial probability distribution and simply predicts that the likelihood of a given piece of information being brought up in discussion is a function of the likelihood of any given member being able to recall the piece of information and the number of members who have the information at their disposal. Thus, pieces of information that are shared by all of the group members have a sampling advantage for being brought up over information that is only available to one member. In the hidden-profile paradigm, often groups reach consensus on the nonoptimal choice alternative before much of the unshared information has a chance to come out. Thus, this model argues that the dominance of shared information is a natural process of basic group dynamics.

Klein, Jacobs, Gemoets, Licata, and Lambert (2003: Study 1) applied Stasser's paradigm to the consensualisation of social stereotypes. Information about three groups, A, B, and C, was designed so that there was more information supporting group A's sociability and B's competence than the reverse. Thus, prevalent information suggested that group A was more sociable and less competent than group B. This information was, however, distributed among three members of a discussion group differently. In the "representative" condition, information representative of the prevalent information was shared and information contradicting these differences was unshared. As a result, participants had individually more information supporting the view that A is more sociable but less competent than B. In the "unrepresentative" condition, information unrepresentative of the prevalent information was shared. As a consequence, each member of the discussion group had more information that reflected the opposite of the "accurate" preponderance of the evidence, so that group A would have been seen to be more competent and less sociable than group B. In the "all-shared" condition, all participants received all the information about the three target groups. Note, however, that all the information was collectively available in all conditions. Participants' impressions of the groups was measured before and after a 10-minute discussion in which group members had to collectively decide which target group was most competent and sociable. Consistent with Stasser's perspective, group members were more likely to communicate shared than unshared information. The discussion also had an effect on participants' emerging impressions of the target group. They were indeed less consistent with the stereotype in the unrepresentative condition than in the other conditions: In this condition, the discussion of unshared information, which was inconsistent with the stereotype of the target groups, led to less stereotypical impressions than in the two other conditions. Importantly, in all conditions, the discussion led to a greater certainty in the validity of the stereotypes and to a greater consensus in the perception of the three groups (as indicated by a lower variance in judgments within the discussion group) compared to prediscussion judgments. Thus, in line with classic social-influence research (Asch, 1956; Moscovici, 1976), intragroup consensus seemed to lead to greater certainty. Hence, this study demonstrates that the *distribution* of information about a target group across communicators strongly affects the emerging consensual representation of the target group, even if all members have access to the same information collectively. However, the very discussion of this information increases consensus indicating that consensus is driven not only by information sharedness but by a collective interpretation of this information.

Using a different paradigm, Gigone and Hastie (1993, 1996) demonstrated a similar trend in group information processing, which they refer to as the "common knowledge effect." Their theoretical and empirical framework revolved around Brunswik's (1956) "lens model" of judgment. Gigone and Hastie had three-person groups estimate the grade that different students would receive in a college course based on six different information cues (e.g., entrance exam score, high school GPA, other workload, etc.). Each group member first made an estimate based on the information he or she had been given, and then the group discussed and reached consensus on an estimate for the group. Different experimental conditions altered the number of members of the group who received each cue: either one, two, or all three. A series of regression analyses generally showed that information became more important for the group estimate to the degree it was shared by a greater number of members. It also was more likely to be discussed if it was shared to a greater degree. However, the information-sharing effect was mediated by individual member preferences; when individual member preferences were entered into the regression equation, all of the information effects became nonsignificant.

Based on the above research, it appears that shared stereotypes could affect group decision making through different routes. First, information (e.g., trait attributes) associated with a stereotype that is shared among all group members may be more likely to come up during a discussion than information uniquely known by only one member. Thus, the discussion could be dominated by SC information when all members share the stereotype. In addition, each member's judgment or choice preference could be influenced by the stereotype and subsequently guide the group as a whole to a SC choice. In this way, even stereotypes that are not considered "socially acceptable" and, thus, would not be openly discussed, could still influence group decisions.

A number of other factors have also been shown to affect the likelihood of shared information dominating group discussions. Larson, Foster-Fishman, and Keys (1994) showed that shared information is particularly likely to come out early as opposed to later in group discussions. They demonstrated that the temporal difference can be explained in terms of a modification of the information-sampling model by Stasser and Titus (1985) by assuming sampling without replacement. Thus, once much of the shared information has been brought up, most of the new information that is left is unshared. The processing goals or performance norms assigned to groups can also influence how much shared versus unshared information is discussed. Stasser and Stewart (1992) showed that shared information is especially likely to dominate if group members feel that they are making a decision as opposed to solving a problem. It seems that defining the situation as a solvable problem or emphasizing accuracy makes thorough information processing a higher priority: thus more information (including unshared information) gets discussed. There is also evidence that assigned roles or known member expertise can attenuate the dominance of shared over unshared information (Stasser, Stewart, & Wittenbaum, 1995). Groups where each member is assigned to be the "expert" on a particular decision alternative discussed more of the unshared information on each alternative. It is conceivable that such a situation, the "accuracy norm" is made salient: In view of their assigned expertise, group members probably feel that they have an obligation to be as accurate as possible. However, it seems that role or expertise assignments must be public, or "shared" among the group members, in order for it to improve information sharing.

Much of the work on the shared information bias or common-knowledge effect has dealt with structural or task-oriented aspects of the group and its environment. However, recent work has shown that other more self-relevant processes may also be at play. Wittenbaum, Hubbell, and Zuckerman (1999) have argued and shown that group members are motivated to present mainly shared information and are more impressed with other members who do the same. They found that dyads discussing shared information evaluated themselves and their partners more positively (in terms of competence) than did dyads discussing unshared information. Wittenbaum et al. explain these findings in terms of common ground and mutual validation or enhancement. Providing information that others know tends to lead to nods of approval and agreement, whereas presenting unshared information may lead to skepticism. Also, when someone else brings up information as important that others also feel is important, it provides common ground for the discussion. The bias toward providing shared information seems to be stronger for lower- rather than higher-status members (Wittenbaum, 1998), which fits with the notion that providing shared information helps to enhance one's standing in the group.

Another, quite distinct perspective that may explain the prevalence of shared information in small-group discussion is the self-categorization theory (Turner et al., 1987). According to this framework, individuals endorse group norms to the extent that they define themselves as members of this group. As a function of the social context, however, different categories may be salient, and lead people to choose different self-categorizations. Group members may therefore adhere to different norms. The actual content of these norms follows the principle of metacontrast: People are likely to choose norms that best differentiate their ingroup from salient outgroups. In this perspective, consensus is predicated on social validation. People will consider a specific view as correct to the extent that it is socially validated by other individuals sharing the same group membership (Turner, 1991).

However, group norms are not necessarily given and uncontroversial. Individual group members may disagree as to what constitutes an appropriate group norm. In such cases, self-categorization theory argues that group members will strive to *consensualize* these norms, e.g., to reach an agreement as to what constitutes the group's norms. When individual group members share a common self-categorization, interpersonal, within-group, communication will serve this function. Hence, for shared information to become the basis of group consensus, it needs first to be articulated with the group identity and integrated in the group's "frame of reference."

In this view, stereotypes are considered as group norms that are inherently variable depending on the evolution of the social context. When group members share a common self-category, they will try to develop a shared representation of the group (Haslam, Turner, Oakes, Reynolds, Eggins, Nolan and et al., 1998). Theoretically, the prevalence of shared information in small-discussion groups may then be explained by the fact that shared information can more easily facilitate the emergence of a consensus than unshared information. In line with this assumption, when groups are driven by a consensus goal, they indeed tend to value shared information more, which leads them to elaborate a consensus on the basis of such information (Postmes, Spears, & Cihangir, 2001).

STEREOTYPE CONSENSUALIZATION AND COMMUNICATION

In his influential chapter, Tajfel (1981) argued that understanding stereotype sharedness demanded the consideration of the means through which stereotypes were diffused within groups and communities. One of the primary insights we can extract from our review so far is that information sharedness has a powerful influence on the emergence of stereotype consensus. Based on the different perspectives we have highlighted, it seems that shared information is more likely to influence initial preferences as well as consensual representations and decisions, although this influence may be moderated by several factors.

According to several of the perspectives we have highlighted (Wittenbaum's mutual enhancement perspective, the social identity perspective, and even Stasser's probabilistic model of information pooling), the influence of sharedness on group consensus seems to be predicated using a process of social validation that takes place through group discussion and/or interaction. In other words, group members need to communicate about the target group and *consensualize* their interpretation.

In communicational terms, the consensualization process can be described in terms of "grounding" (Clark, 1996; Clark & Brennan, 1991; Krauss & Fussell, 1996). Common ground refers to a set of assumptions that are (a) shared, (b) known to be shared, (c) that are known to be shared and known to be shared by a group of individual discussants. These assumptions can concern different aspects of the communication process such as the information that has already been exchanged, the purpose of the conversation, background, information about the discussants' characteristic, but also general information (such as social stereotypes) known to be shared by members of a given group. This latter set of information is called "generalized" common ground and encompasses cultural knowledge. By contrast, contextual common ground refers to the set of information that is mutually shared by discussants. It evolves as the conversation(s) between discussants unfold.

Consensualizing stereotypes involves integrating them in this common ground, or *grounding* them. Grounding is a two-way process by which one person presents new information resulting in the other person's acceptance through either verbal or nonverbal means. To achieve this goal, several exchanges may be needed. Consider the following example:

A—Bobby made strozzapretti al pesto yesterday [Presentation]
B—Strozza what?
A—Strozzapretti. A kind of pasta
B—O, I see! (*acceptance*)

The interpretation of new information involves establishing logical, or pseudological, links with other information already shared by discussants. These links can take several forms, such as inclusion (e.g., "strozzapretti are a kind of pasta"), comparison (e.g., "it is like penne"), transformation (e.g., "that's what you get if you turn a macaroni on itself"), etc. Information may be easier to ground when it is consistent with other assumptions already shared by discussants. Indeed, inconsistent information may need to be reinterpreted, accounted for, to be properly grounded. It is therefore likely that this grounding process unfolds more smoothly when members of small groups communicate shared information, as this information is easier to integrate by an audience already familiar with it. In this respect, "mutual enhancement" and "social validation" can be viewed as manifestations of successful grounding: By mutually enhancing each others' expression of shared information, members of small groups acknowledge that this information has been successfully grounded. Thereby, the shared information will be easily grounded and form the basis of a consensual stereotype.

As this analysis highlights, the process of stereotype consensualization within small groups is necessarily based on the existence of communication channels through which group members may share the information they have about other group members. The actual content of the emerging stereotype will be dependent on the nature of the information group members choose to communicate through these channels. Understanding the emergence of stereotype consensus not only demands to know what each group member believes about a given group but what makes him or her choose to communicate this information and to whom.

HOW STEREOTYPES ARE MAINTAINED
THROUGH COMMUNICATION

Once new stereotypes have been consensualized, they can be maintained only if they are regularly or continuously communicated in the context of interpersonal exchanges (Kashima, Klein, & Clark, in press). This can be done by either talking about the group as a whole or describing individual group members in line with the stereotype (Schaller & Conway, 2001; Schaller, Conway, & Tanchuk, 2002). This reproduction of stereotypes through communication is the topic of this section. Although this "reconsensualization" can involve many communication channels, in this section, as in the rest of the chapter, we will focus on interpersonal, face-to-face communication.

Stereotype Communication: The Evidence

Regardless of the paradigm being used, most of the literature concurs in suggesting that SC information has a communicational advantage: Although features of the communicational context may moderate this trend, when communicators have the choice to either communicate SC or SI information about an individual, they tend to opt for the former (for a recent review, see Kashima et al., 2005). For example, this has been observed in the serial-reproduction paradigm (for a review, see: McIntyre, Lyons, Clark, & Kashima, 2004) in which individuals tell a story involving a character who performs both SC and SI behaviors to a second individual, who tells it to a third, etc. It has also been found to occur among dyads discussing an unknown target face to face (see Ruscher, 1998 for a review) as well as in small groups conversing about an entire group (Harasty, 1997).

Grounding Stereotypes

Which factors may promote the communication of stereotype-consistent information in such interpersonal exchanges? Technically, a stereotype can only be maintained if it is continuously or regularly "regrounded" in communication. This grounding process can unfold more or less smoothly depending on various factors. For example, intimate speakers may experience less difficulty grounding each others' utterances because their common ground is more extensive.

   Based on our description of the grounding process, effectively communicating information that is consistent with the common ground (e.g., that can be easily inferred from already shared assumptions) should require fewer resources (e.g., in terms of communication time, number of utterances, or length of utterances) than communicating information that is either inconsistent or irrelevant with respect to the common ground. Inconsistent or irrelevant information runs a greater risk of generating controversy or of being "misunderstood" by the audience, as it is harder to reconcile with existing assumptions. This may in part explain why communicators tend to preferentially communicate information that is consistent with existing stereotypes when they have the opportunity to do so.

   Support for this assumption was found in a study by Ruscher and Duval (1998, Study 1). In this study, participants received information about a target person described as an alcoholic, discussed their impression of this target for three minutes, and then jointly described the target to an imaginary mutual friend. In the shared condition, both communicators had the same set of SC and SI information about the target, whereas in the unique condition, the information about the target was distributed so that the communicators had different sets of SC and SI information. In their joint description, participants in the unique condition spent more time communicating SI, but not SC, information than dyads in the shared condition. This finding can be interpreted in terms of differential groundability of SC and SI information. When SI information was shared between the participants (shared condition), they could ground it as easily as SC information; however, when SI information was not shared (unique condition), it took them longer to ground SI information than SC information.

Communicating information that is consistent with the common ground does not only convey an informational value. Kashima et al. (2005) argue that it also serves to indicate one's "connection" with the audience. Claiming common ground is a way to enhance politeness (Brown & Levinson, 1987). Indeed, Clark (cited by Kashima et al., 2005) found that stereotype-consistent information was more likely to be communicated to the extent that it was viewed as consistent with the common ground. This observation echoes the finding by Wittenbaum and her colleagues (cf. above) showing that communication of shared information in small group is "mutually enhanced" through verbal and nonverbal means. For example, a member of a personnel committee might mention that a particular candidate's young age might make her or him less suitable for an important leadership position. This would fit with stereotypes of leaders as more mature and experienced and might receive virtually automatic agreement from the other group members (Lord & Maher, 1990). Thus, even if age in this particular circumstance was irrelevant, the person making the point would be perceived as insightful and the others would feel that their perceptions on that issue were validated. Group members who communicate such information receive feedback indicating that they are perceived as more competent. This enhancement can also be considered as a politeness strategy that serves to enhance group members' face.

Direct evidence for the influence of grounding in the communication of stereotypes comes from a study by Klein and Lyons (2005). In this study, participants read a description of an (imaginary) group of Pacific islanders, the Jamayans. The purpose of this task was to lead participants to form a stereotype about this group. After this task, participants were asked to discuss their view of this group with another participant who was also present in the laboratory. Then, they had to read a story involving a character, Jai. Participants in the discussion condition wrote their story either for their discussion partner or for an unknown person. In this story, Jai performed several behaviors, some of which were consistent with the stereotype of Jamayans and some were not. Judges then counted the number of SC and SI behaviors that were included in the story. Results indicated that participants were more likely to communicate SC behaviors, and less likely to communicate SI behaviors when they narrated their story to the audience with whom they had previously discussed rather than an unknown participant. It is likely that the discussion served to make the stereotypes part of the discussants' contextual common ground. In other words, it instigated not only sharedness, but *a sense of sharedness*, and a common interpretation of Jamayans' traits and characteristics. SC Information about Jay narrated in the story could then easily be grounded in this mutually shared stereotype. Further evidence in support of this interpretation comes from a control condition, in which participants did not discuss with their partner but merely individually listed their thoughts about Jamayans. In this condition, participants were less likely to use SC information and more likely to use SI information in their story to their "partner" (e.g., another participant in the laboratory) than when they had previously discussed with this person.

A preliminary conclusion: The vicious circle of stereotype communication

We have reviewed two types of evidence so far. First, we have reported findings suggesting that when group members discuss the information they possess about an unknown group, they tend to develop an interpretation of this group that is primarily influenced by shared information, even when unshared information is more "accurate." This is due in part to the preferential communication of shared information. Second, we have found that, when stereotypes are part of the "generalized common ground" of a group, information consistent with these stereotypes tends to be preferentially communicated as well.

Taken together, these findings suggest that stereotypes may tend to "self-reproduce": To the extent that information consistent with a stereotype is shared, or even perceived as such, it may be communicated more easily and facilitate the emergence of this very stereotype within the group. The existence of this stereotype seems to facilitate the communication of SC information, and thereby reinforces the stereotype which in turn drives an SC bias in communication, etc. Hence, all the conditions seem to be set for the emergence of a vicious circle in which stereotypes reproduce themselves effortlessly. In the next section, we shall suggest that this vision of stereotypes as self-perpetuating hydra may be a bit too pessimistic: in several important contexts and situations, this cycle can be broken or even vanish completely.

HOW STEREOTYPES CAN CHANGE THROUGH COMMUNICATION

There are several reasons why stereotypes may fail to "self-perpetutate". One reason, that we shall hardly discuss here, involves what has been loosely defined as "the social context" in the social-identity literature (Tajfel & Turner, 1986; Turner, Hogg, Oakes, Reicher, & Wetherell, 1987). As we mentioned, stereotypes may only maintain themselves to the extent that they provide the basis for a common interpretation of the target group and of its relation to the out-group. If, due to the evolution of the intergroup context, this stereotype cannot meaningfully account for the out-group's behavior, group members may seek to consensualize a new, or modified stereotype. The vast literature on minority influence (for a review, see: Wood, Lundgren, Ouellette, & Busceme, 1994) suggests that if this stereotype offers a more meaningful interpretational framework, such attempts may prove successful, even if their sources constitute a minority. However, for changes in the intergroup context to influence the content of shared stereotypes, these new and more meaningful stereotypes need to be communicated within the group. In other words, the inadequacy of current stereotypes to the social context is not sufficient to change these stereotypes. Such an inadequacy needs to be rhetorically constructed as such and effectively communicated within the group. Some group members need to articulate these new stereotypes and influence other group members into adhering to these new stereotypes. This often will be the function of group leaders: For example, Klein and Licata (2003) have shown how, in the late 1950s, the Congolese nationalist leader Patrice Lumumba developed new stereotypes of Belgians and Congolese in order to mobilize his audiences into supporting his project of independence for the Congo.

Second, although "biases" promoting the communication of shared or stereotype-consistent information are well documented, there are some situations in which such biases can be attenuated, thereby breaking the "vicious circle" of stereotype maintenance. Sometimes, people will strive to communicate unshared, or IC information. We shall examine two lines of evidence supporting this claim: one is based on the application of Grice's maxims to stereotype communication and the other on Burnstein and Vinokur's persuasive arguments perspective.

Grice's Maxim of Quantity and the Communication of IC Information

According to Grice's theory of conversational implicature, communicators are expected to obey the "cooperative principle": "Make your contribution such as is required, at the stage at which it occurs, by the accepted purpose or direction of the talk in which you are engaged." (p. 308). It is only by making this assumption that audiences can understand the meaning of an utterance. Consider for example the following exchange:

> A—Do you like Francis?
> B—He is stingy.

A can construe B's answer as meaning, "No, I don't like him" only to the extent that B is viewed as a cooperative conversational partner e.g., by assuming that B's statement indeed constitutes an answer to A's question and that B shares A's evaluation of "stinginess" as an undesirable characteristic.

Grice has suggested that communicators were expected to obey a variety of specific communicational rules subsumed under this general principle. One of these rules is the "maxim of quantity," which is stated by Grice (1975) as follows: "(i) Make your contribution as informative as is required for the purpose of the exchange and (ii) Do not make your contribution more informative than is required" (p. 308). To illustrate the use of this maxim, let us remain in the domain of Italian cuisine and consider the following exchange:

> A: What's in these raviolis?
> B: Ricotta. It is an Italian cheese.

B's answer reflects the assumption that A is ignorant of ricotta. Giving an informative answer therefore demands to specify the food category to which it belongs. If B's assumption is correct, he may therefore be considered to observe the maxim of quantity. By contrast, if B's assumption is incorrect and if A knows what ricotta is, B's utterance would convey more than what is needed and would fail to respect the maxim of quantity. Failing to specify what ricotta is might also be considered a violation of the maxim of quantity if A expects more than a simple label for what he is consuming. This analysis illustrates the two violations of the maxim of quantity: reiterating what is already part of the mutual knowledge and failing to communicate novel (and relevant) information.

Based on this communicational rule, we would hence expect communicators to focus more on information that is novel to the audience rather than on information already espoused by the audience. More specifically, assuming that the audience is aware of the group membership of a target, communicators may be expected to communicate IC information when they wish to be particularly informative to their audience.

Hence, information that cannot be directly derived from the common ground can have the comparative advantage of being more informative than information that is inconsistent with it because it is more likely to violate existing assumptions or to add new assumptions to the existing common ground. How does this apply to the stereotyping domain?

In line with this analysis, Clark (cited by Kashima et al., 2005) found that, when communicating about an individual target, communicators rated IC information as more informative than SC information. There is also evidence that speakers who are motivated to develop an accurate representation of a particular target tend to devote more communication time to IC information (Ruscher, Hammer, & Hammer, 1996). By contrast, when their purpose is to develop a shared impression of the target, speakers devote relatively more time to stereotype-consistent information probably because it is more easily "groundable."

Second, to the extent that common ground allows speakers to easily infer assumptions from presented information, it may also be useful resource when they are under communicational pressure e.g., when they may only communicate a limited number of utterances (e.g., because they have limited time, or use a poor code such as SMS or morse). In such conditions, speakers may abstain from communication information that is already part of the common ground and focus on information that is inconsistent with it because it is more informative.

If this is the case, shared stereotypes may constitute a useful resource for communicating information under situations of communicational pressure. For example, when describing a target belonging to a given social category, pressured speakers may preferentially communicate information that is inconsistent with the stereotype associated with this social category in an effort to be particularly informative. Klein, Demoulin, Licata, and Lambert (in press) precisely tested this prediction. They handed participants a description of a hypothetical target categorized as an engineer. This description included 14 traits that were consistent with the stereotype of engineers (e.g., intelligent, rational, etc.) and traits that were inconsistent with this stereotype (e.g., warm, sensitive). Participants were asked to use five of these traits to describe the target to an audience. It was explicitly stated that they should pick these five traits to try to ensure that the audience have the richest possible view of the target. The crucial manipulation concerned the audience, who was either described as being aware that the target was an engineer or unaware of it. Consistent with the "maxim of quantity" hypothesis, when the audience was unaware of this information, participants were more likely to communicate SC traits, and by the same token less likely to communicate SI traits, than when the target was aware of it. Thus, participants seemed particularly likely to communicate SI information if it had a relative informational value compared to SC information, e.g., when the audience was aware of the target's group membership and could therefore access the stereotype.

Although these studies suggest that people may communicate IC information in an effort to follow the maxim of quantity, they do not involve a real interaction within the group. A study by Klein et al.'s (2003: study 2) responds to this drawback by suggesting that stereotypes, when they are in generalized common ground, play an important role in determining informativeness within small-discussion groups. In this study, members of triads received some information that was shared in the whole triad (shared information), and other information that was unique to each participant (unshared information). In the congruent condition, *unshared* information was consistent with the stereotypical differences between the groups A and B, where members of group A were presented as petanque players and group B as "statisticians" (petanque players are viewed as sociable and unintelligent and computer engineers as unsociable but intelligent). In the incongruent condition, the group labels were reversed, so that unshared information was inconsistent with the stereotypical differences between the two groups. Participants then discussed for 10 minutes and were asked to choose which was the most "competent" and the most "sociable" group. If people follow the maxim of quantity, unshared information would have more informational value when it was inconsistent with the existing stereotypes than when it was consistent with them. In line with this reasoning, people were more likely to discuss unshared information if it was *inconsistent* with the labels associated to group A and B than if it was *consistent.* This discussion apparently had an influence on their emerging impressions: Group members perceived the target groups in less stereotypical terms when unshared information was inconsistent than when it was consistent with these labels.

PERSUASIVE ARGUMENTS AND THE COMMUNICATION OF IC INFORMATION

In this section, we shall consider work by Brauer, Judd, and Jacquelin (2001) who conducted two studies designed to examine the conditions under which group discussion does and does not lead to more stereotypic perceptions. In one of their studies, Brauer et al. gave groups of three participant's information about a hypothetical target group. The information took the form of different behaviors that had presumably been performed by members of the target group and that referred either to the dimension of selfishness or violence. Three fourths of these described selfish and violent behaviors. The remainder described behaviors that were inconsistent with this general stereotype e.g., they described altruistic and pacifistic behaviors. Thus, the group was stereotypically described as selfish and violent, but there were numerous IC behaviors. The distribution of the different behaviors across group members was varied, so that the IC information was shared in half of the groups and unshared in the other half of the groups. In the *shared* condition, each group member read three times as many stereotypic than IC behaviors on each of the two trait dimensions used to describe the target group. In the *unshared* condition, one group member saw two thirds of the IC behaviors while the other two group members saw relatively few of them (each of them saw one sixth of the counterstereottypic behaviors). The total numbers of behaviors read by each group member was held constant, so that in the unshared condition, the participant who saw more IC behaviors saw fewer stereotypic ones. The other between-group manipulation varied whether or not there was group discussion. Half of the groups were asked to discuss their impressions about the target group and then filled out dependent measures assessing perceived dispersion, perceived stereotypicality, and liking for the target group. The other half of the groups did not engage in a group discussion and filled out the dependent measures immediately after having read the behaviors.

The relevant means for the perceived stereotypicality ratings are reported in Fig. 12–1. The informal group discussion led to more stereotypical perceptions of the target group, but only when the IC information was shared rather than unshared. Analyses on the liking measure showed that groups in the discussion/shared condition liked the target group significantly less than groups in the other three conditions. The coded group discussions revealed that groups in

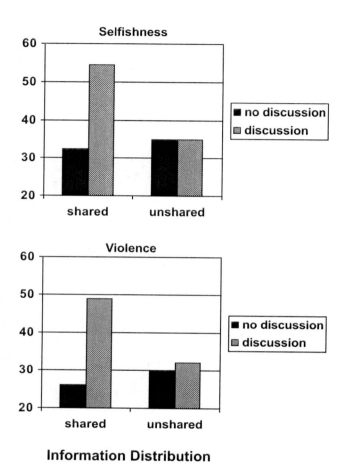

FIGURE 12–1.   Perceived stereotypicality on the selfishness dimension (top panel) and the violence dimension (bottom panel) as a function of discussion condition and information distribution (Study 2 of Brauer, Judd, & Jacquelin, 2001).

the unshared condition discussed sterotypic information less and counterssterotypical information more than groups in the shared condition. To summarize, discussion led to more stereotyping when each of the group members was familiar with the same proportion of stereotypic (three fourths) and countersterotypic (one fourth) information (in the shared condition). However, no polarizing effects of discussion were found when the IC information was concentrated within one group member, and thus group members differed in the proportion of stereotypic to countersterotypic information they were familiar with (in the unshared condition). These results are entirely consistent with Burnstein and Vinokur's (1977) persuasive arguments approach: Group members have a preference for putting forward belief-supporting arguments during the group discussion. In the dispersed condition, all group members are familiar with both stereotypic and IC information. As such, the IC information does not have a great interest value, and group members talk longer about the information that is consistent with their prediscussion attitudes, e.g., the stereotypic information. As a result, their perceptions of the target group polarize during the group discussion. The situation is entirely different in the unshared condition. Given that the IC information is held primarily by one group member, two group members start out with a very stereotypic view of the target group; whereas the third group member starts out with a less stereotypic view. Not surprisingly, the discussion focuses largely on the IC behaviors and the extent to which they should be considered valid and diagnostic evidence. These results nicely illustrate the grounding perspective. When people have the same access to stereotypic and IC information about a group, they prefer to talk about information that is easy to communicate and that supports everybody's beliefs, e.g., stereotypic information. A common ground is already established, and they simply refer to this common ground by discussing stereotypic information. If however, people differ in the extent to which they are familiar with IC information, they have to establish a common ground by talking about the information that is new and controversial, e.g., the IC information. In other words, the IC information has to be scrutinized for its validity, reinterpreted, and accounted for. This process of establishing a common ground leads group members to talk more about IC behaviors, and the group discussion does not lead to more stereotypical perceptions

RELEVANCE AS AN INTEGRATING PRINCIPLE

Sperber and Wilson (1995) reformulated Grice's maxims by suggesting that they are all based on the assumption that communicators follow what they called "the principle of relevance": they try to maximize the effect of their utterances on the audience at the minimal interpretative cost for their audience. Work on the application of the maxim of quantity to stereotype communication can be easily interpreted in this light: When information is limited, and the audience knows the target's social category, speakers tend to focus on the information that maximizes this ratio e.g., IC information. But it has the potential to offer a much broader interpretation of the relative prevalence of SC versus inconsistent information in the communication of social information. For example, the role of group leaders in articulating new stereotypes can be considered in this perspective: New stereotypes should be communicated to the extent that they are perceived relevant in view of the evolution of the social context. When such changes take place, their relevance should become much higher e.g., their effects on the audience should be greater because they have a greater potential to effectively modify the audience's assumptions about the target group. By comparison, in such conditions, their interpretative "cost" reduces as well: IC information, that was hard to reconcile with the "former" social context can suddenly become more easily interpretable. Consider the use by Patrice Lumumba of the stereotype of European colonizers as ruthless exploiters (studied by Klein & Licata, 2003). This stereotype may have become easier to communicate in the late 1950s when other Third-world countries had experienced extremely violent wars of independence or when, after the independence of Congo, the Belgian government encouraged the secession of Katanga, the richest region of Congo and tried to keep military control on it.

The persuasive argument's account can be considered in this light as well: In Brauer et al.'s studies, IC information is communicated to the extent that it can be meaningfully integrated in an alternative view of the target group. This view is all the more effective in Sperber and Wilson's sense, and therefore relevant, to the extent that other group members start out with more extremely stereotypic vision of the target group.

In other words, under conditions in which IC information becomes communicationally relevant and has more potential to change the audience's assumptions at a minimal interpretational cost, it becomes more likely to be communicated.

It is also important to consider an important moderator of the communication of IC information: The effects we have reviewed in this section mainly take place when communicators are primarily motivated by a desire to be informative and accurate. As we have seen, it is also in these conditions that the members of small groups are likely to pool unshared information.

By contrast, when communicators' primary goal is to create a social connection with the audience, we have seen that SC information may be favored because its "effects," with respect to that goal, are probably stronger than the effects of IC information. It is also generally easier to interpret than IC information.

Overall, our analysis suggests that, the relevance of a specific utterance always needs to be considered in relation to a specific goal, e.g., mobilizing the audience, modifying his or her view of a target group, creating a social connection, fostering a consensus, etc. In this perspective, trying to determine which information is communicationally relevant or not may demand to assess costs and effects on a variety of dimensions (e.g., in terms of information processing but also in terms of the quality of the relationship to the audience). This means that it is relevant to draw general rules as to the nature of the moderators that will promote the communication of stereotype-inconsistent information.

CONCLUSION

We opened this chapter with a tragic example illustrating how stereotype consensus can breed terror and violence. Our purpose was to examine how social psychology could contribute to an understanding of both the formation and consequences of such stereotype consensus. To this end, we reviewed some of the evidence bearing on the emergence of stereotype consensus in situations in which information about a target group was unevenly distributed with some information more likely to be shared than others. Most of the findings we have considered highlight that groups tend to "consensualize" their stereotypes based on shared rather than unshared information, even if this unshared information is actually more "accurate." Then, we considered how existing stereotypes may influence the communication of social information in small groups, and the emergence of consensual representations or decisions on the basis of such information. We showed that SC information was much more likely to be communicated and to be integrated in such representations and decisions than inconsistent information. Through this route, social stereotypes can be maintained via a consistent "regrounding" in small groups. Such a conclusion seems to echo the findings of social cognitive work on stereotype formation and application. For example, in an influential chapter, Bargh (1999) described a creature he called a "cognitive monster" who was eternally doomed to perceiving others in terms of automatically activated stereotypes without being able to rely on IC information. Is there a "communicational monster" as well, eternally condemned to maintain the existing stereotypes when communicating about others? At the end of this chapter, we can conclude that this creature may exist but is not human. Just like bacteria, stereotypes need a friendly environment to proliferate. Changes in the social context, and particularly in the texture of intergroup relations, may make them less meaningful in the interpretations of these relations and reduce the likelihood that information consistent with these stereotypes will be communicated. We highlighted a communicational principle, the principle of relevance, which may sometimes promote the communication of IC information. Although the resistances to stereotype change are strong in any group, communicators and minorities who can effectively articulate the evolution of the social context with a convincing view of the target group, ultimately achieve to modify stereotypes.

In sum, within-group communication does promote stereotype consensualization. Once stereotypes have been consensualized, group members may even find it much easier to communicate about SC than inconsistent information. However, it is also through communication only that these very same stereotypes do change.

REFERENCES

Aboud, F. E. (1989). *Children and prejudice.* Oxford, UK: Blackwell.
Alexander, M. G., Brewer, M. B., & Hermann, R. K. (1999). Images and affect: A functional analysis of out-group stereotypes. *Journal of Personality and Social Psychology, 77,* 78–93.
Alexander, M. G., Brewer, M. B., & Livingston, R. W. (2005). Putting Stereotype Content in Context: Image Theory and Interethnic Stereotypes. *Personality and Social Psychology Bulletin, 31,* 781–794.

Asch, S. E. (1956). *Studies of independence and conformity.* Washington: American Psychological Association.

Bargh, J. A. (1999). The cognitive monster: The case against the controllability of automatic stereotype effects. In S. Chaiken (Ed.), *Dual process theories in social psychology* (pp. 361–382). New York: Guilford Press.

Baron, R. S., & Kerr, N. L. (2003). *Group process, group decisions, group action* (2nd ed.). Philadelphia, PA: Open University Press.

Bennett, M., & Sani, F. (2004). *The development of the social self.* Hove, New York: Psychology Press.

Bodenhausen, G. V., & Wyer, R. S. Jr. (1985). Effects of stereotypes on decision making and information processing strategies. *Journal of Personality and Social Psychology, 48,* 267–282.

Braeckman, C. (1994). *Rwanda: Histoire d'un génocide [Rwanda: History of a genocide].* Paris: Fayard.

Brauer, M., Judd, C. M., & Jacquelin, V. (2001). The Communication of Social Stereotypes: The Effects of Group Discussion and Information Distribution on Stereotypic Appraisals. *Journal of Personality and Social Psychology, 81,* 463–475.

Brigham, J. (1971). Ethnic stereotypes and attitudes: A different mode of analysis. *Psychological Bulletin, 76,* 15–38.

Brown, P., & Levinson, S. C. (1987). *Politeness: Some universals in language usage.* Cambridge: Cambridge University Press.

Brunswik, E. (1956). *Perception and the representative design of psychological experiments.* Berkeley: University of California Press.

Burnstein, E. and A. Vinokur (1977). Persuasive argumentation and social comparison as determinants of attitude polarization. *Journal of Experimental Social Psychology, 13,* 315–332.

Clark, H. H. (1996). *Using language.* Cambridge: Cambridge University Press.

Clark, H. H., & Brennan, S. E. (1991). Grounding in communication. In L. Resnick, J. Levine, & S. Teasley (Eds.), *Perspectives on socially shared cognition* (pp. 127–149). Washington, DC: American Psychological Association.

Dallaire, R., & Beardsley, B. (2003). *Shake hands with the devil: The failure of humanity in Rwanda.* Toronto: Random House Canada.

Davis, J. H. (1973). Group decisions and social interactions: A theory of social decision schemes. *Psychological Review, 80,* 97–125.

Davis, J. H. (1982). Social interaction as a combinatorial process in group decision. In H. Brandstatter, J. H. Davis, & G. Stocker-Kreichgauer (Eds.), *Group decision making* (pp. 27–58). London: Academic Press.

Davis, J. H. (1996). Group decision making and quantitative judgments: A consensus model. In E. Witte & J. H. Davis (Eds.), *Understanding group behavior: Consensual action by small groups* (Vol. 1, pp. 35–59). Mahwah, NJ: Lawrence Erlbaum.

Devine, P. G. (1989). Stereotypes and prejudice: Their automatic and controlled components. *Journal of Personality and Social Psychology, 56,* 5–18.

Devine, P. G., & Elliot, A. J. (1995). Are racial stereotypes really fading? The Princeton trilogy revisited. *Personality and Social Psychology Bulletin, 21,* 1139–1150.

Franche, D. (2004). *Généalogie du génocide rwandais [Genealogy of the Rwandan Genocide].* Brussels, Belgium: Tribord.

Gardner, R. C. (1993). Stereotypes as consensual beliefs. In J. M. Olson (Ed.), *The psychology of Prejudice: The Ontario Symposium.* Hillsdale, NJ: Erlbaum.

Gigone, D., & Hastie, R. (1993). The common knowledge effect: Information sharing and group judgment. *Journal of Personality and Social Psychology, 65,* 959–974.

Gigone, D., & Hastie, R. (1996). The impact of information on group judgment: A model and computer simulation. In E. Witte & J. H. Davis (Eds.), *Understanding group behavior: Consensual action by small groups* (Vol. 1, pp. 221–251). Mahwah, NJ: Lawrence Erlbaum.

Gordijn, E. H., Koomen, W., & Stapel, D. A. (2001). Level of prejudice in relation to knowledge of cultural stereotypes. *Journal of Experimental Social Psychology, 37,* 150–157.

Grice, H. P. (1975). Logic and conversation. In P. Cole & J. L. Morgan (Eds), *Syntax and Semantics* (pp. 41–58). San Diego CA: Academic Press.

Harasty, A. S. (1997). The interpersonal nature of social stereotypes: Differential discussion patterns about in-groups and out-groups. *Personality & Social Psychology Bulletin, 23,* 270–284.

Hardin, C. T., & Higgins, E. T. (1996). Shared reality: How Sscial verification makes the subjective objective. In E. T. Higgins (Ed.), *Handbook of motivation and cognition Vol. 3.* New York: Guilford.

Haslam, S. A., Oakes, P. J., Reynolds, K. J., & Turner, J. C. (1999). Social identity salience and the emergence of stereotype consensus. *Personality and Social Psychology Buletin, 25,* 809–818.

Haslam, S. A., Turner, J. C., Oakes, P. J., McGarty, C., & Reynolds, K. J. (1998). The group as a basis for emergent stereotype consensus. In M. Hewstone (Ed.), *European Review of Social Psychology, Vol. 8.* (pp. 203–239). Chichester, UK: John Wiley & Sons.

Haslam, S. A., Turner, J. C., Oakes, P. J., Reynolds, K. J., Eggins, R. A., Nolan, M., et al. (1998). When do stereotypes become really consensual ? Investigating the group-based dynamics of consensualization process. *European Journal of Social Psychology, 28,* 755–776.

Hatzfeld, J. (2000). *Dans le nu de la vie: récits des marais rwandais.* Paris: Seuil.

Hinsz, V. B., Tindale, R. S., & Vollrath, D. A. (1997). The emerging conception of groups as information processors. *Psychological Bulletin, 121,* 43–64.

Hirschfeld, L. A. (1996). *Race in the making: cognition, culture, and the child's construction of human kinds.* Cambridge, Mass.: MIT Press.

Kameda, T., Tindale, R. S., & Davis, J. H. (2003). Cognitions, preferences, and social sharedness: Past, present and future directions in group decision making. In S. L. Schneider & J. Shanteau (Eds.), *Emerging perspectives on judgment and decision research* (pp. 458–485). New York: Cambridge University Press.

Kashima, Y., Klein, O., & Clark, A. E. (in press). Grounding: Sharing Information in Social Interaction. In K. Fiedler (Ed.), *Handbook of social psychology and communication.* Philadelphia: Psychology Press.

Katz, D., & Braly, K. (1933). Racial stereotypes of one hundred college students. *Journal of Abnormal and Social Psychology, 28,* 280–290.

Klein, O., & Licata, L. (2003). When group representations serve social change: The speeches of Patrice Lumumba during the Congolese decolonization. *British Journal of Social Psychology, 42,* 571–593.

Klein, O., & Lyons, A. (2005). [The influence of communicational grounding of stereotypes on the stereotype-consistency bias in communication]. Unpublished raw data: Université Libre de Bruxelles, Belgium.

Klein, O., & Snyder, M. (2003). Stereotypes and Behavioral Confirmation: from interpersonal to intergroup perspectives. In M. P. Zanna (Ed.), *Advances in experimental social psychology* (Vol. 35, 153–234). San Diego: Academic Press.

Klein, O., Demoulin, S., Licata, L., & Lambert, S. (in press). "If you know he is an engineer, I don't need to tell you he is smart": The influence of stereotypes on the communication of social information. *Cahiers de Psychologie Cognitive/Current Psychology of Cognition.*

Klein, O., Jacobs, A., Gemoets, S., Licata, L., & Lambert, S. M. (2003). Hidden profiles and the consensualization of social stereotypes: How information distribution affects stereotype content and sharedness. *European Journal of Social Psychology, 33,* 755–777.

Krauss, R. M., & Fussell, S. R. (1996). Social psychological models of interpersonal communication. In E. T. Higgins (Ed.), *Social psychology: Handbook of basic principles* (pp. 655–701). New York: Guilford Press.

Larson, J. R., Jr., Foster-Fishman, P. G., & Keys, C. B. (1994). Discussion of shared and unshared information in decision-making groups. *Journal of Personality and Social Psychology, 67,* 446–461.

Laughlin, P. R. (1980). Social combination processes of cooperative, problem-solving groups on verbal intellective tasks. In M. Fishbein (Ed.), *Progress in social psychology* (Vol. 1, pp. 127–155). Hillsdale, NJ: Lawrence Erlbaum.

Laughlin, P. R., & Ellis, A. L. (1986). Demonstrability and social combination processes on mathematical intellective tasks. *Journal of Experimental Social Psychology, 22,* 177–189.

Lord, R. G., & Maher, K. J. (1990). Perceptions of leadership and their implications in organizations. In J. S. Carroll (Ed.), *Applied social psychology and organizational settings.* Hillsdale, NJ: Lawrence Erlbaum.

MacCoun, R., & Kerr, N. L. (1988). Asymmetric influence in mock jury deliberations: Juror's bias for leniency. *Journal of Personality and Social Psychology, 54,* 21–33.

McCann, C., & Higgins, T. E. (1992). Personal and contextual factors in communication: A review of the 'communication game.' In G. R. Semin (Ed.), *Language, interaction and social cognition* (pp. 144–172). Thousand Oaks, CA: Sage Publications, Inc.

McGarty, C., Yzerbyt, V., & Spears, R. (2002). *Stereotypes as explanations: the formation of meaningful beliefs about social groups.* London; New York: Cambridge University Press.

McGrath, J. E. (1984). *Groups: Interaction and performance.* Englewood Cliffs, NJ: Prentice Hall.

McIntyre, A., Lyons, A., Clark, A., & Kashima, Y. (2004). The Microgenesis of Culture: Serial Reproduction as an Experimental Simulation of Cultural Dynamics. In C. Crandall (Ed.), *The psychological foundations of culture* (pp. 227–258). Mahwah, NJ: Lawrence Erlbaum Associates.

Moscovici, S. (1976). *Social influence and social change.* London; New York: Academic Press.

Oakes, P., Haslam, S. A.; Turner, J. C. (1994). *Stereotypes and Social Reality.* Oxford: Blackwell.

Poppe, E. (2001). Effects of changes in GNP and perceived group characteristics on national and ethnic stereotypes in central and eastern Europe. *Journal of Applied Social Psychology, 31,* 1689–1708.

Postmes, T., Spears, R., & Cihangir, S. (2001). Quality of decision making and group norms. *Journal of Personality and Social Psychology, 80*(6), 918–930.

Ruscher, J. B. (1998). Prejudice and stereotyping in everyday communication. In M. P. Zanna (Ed.), *Advances in experimental social psychology* (Vol. 30, pp. 241–307). San Diego: Academic Press.

Ruscher, J. B. (2001). *Prejudiced communication: A social psychological perspective. New York:* Guilford Press.

Ruscher, J. B., Hammer, E. Y., & Hammer, E. D. (1996). Forming shared impressions through conversation: An adaptation of the continuum model. *Personality and Social Psychology Bulletin, 22,* 705–720.

Schaller, M., & Conway, L. G. (2001). From cognition to culture: The origins of stereotypes that really matter. In G. Moscowitz (Ed.), *Cognitive social psychology: On the tenure and future of social cognition* (pp. 163–176). Manwah, NJ: Erlbaum.

Schaller, M., Conway, L. G., & Tanchuk, T. L. (2002). Selective pressures on the once and future contents of ethnic stereotypes: Effects of the Communicability of Traits. *Journal of Personality and Social Psychology, 82,* 861–877.

Sechrist, G. B., & Stangor, C. (2001). Perceived consensus influences intergroup behavior and stereotype accessibility. *Journal of Personality and Social Psychology, 80,* 645–654.

Smith, C. M., Dykema-Engblade, A., Walker, A., Niven, T. S., & McGrough, T. (2000). Asymmetrical social influence in freely interacting groups discussing the death penalty: A shared representations interpretation. *Group Processes and Intergroup Relations, 3,* 387–401.

Sperber, D., & Wilson, D. (1995). *Relevance: Communication and Cognition.* Oxford: Blackwell.

Stangor, C., & Schaller, M. (1996). Stereotypes as individual and collective representations. In M. Hewstone (Ed.), *Stereotypes and stereotyping* (pp. 3–40). New York: Guilford.

Stangor, C., Sechrist, G. B., & Jost, J. T. (2001). Changing racial beliefs by providing consensus information. *Personality and Social Psychology Bulletin, 27*(4), 486–496.

Stasser, G., & Stewart, D. (1992). Discovery of hidden profiles by decision-making groups: Solving a problem versus making a judgment. *Journal of Personality and Social Psychology, 63,* 426–434.

Stasser, G., & Titus, W. (1985). Pooling of unshared information in group decision making: Biased information sampling during discussion. *Journal of Personality and Social Psychology, 48,* 1467–1478.

Stasser, G., & Titus, W. (1987). Effects of information load and percentage of shared information on the dissemination of unshared information during group discussion. *Journal of Personality and Social Psychology, 53,* 81–93.

Stasser, G., Stewart, D. D., & Wittenbaum, G. M. (1995). Expert roles and information exchange during discussion: The importance of knowing who knows what. *Journal of Experimental Social Psychology, 31,* 244–265.

Tajfel, H. (1981). Social stereotypes and social groups. In H. Giles (Ed.), *Intergroup Behavior* (pp. 144–167). Oxford, U.K.: Blackwell.

Tajfel, H., & Turner, J. C. (1986). The social identity theory of intergroup behavior. In W. G. Austin (Ed.), *The psychology of intergroup relations* (pp. 7–24). Chicago: Nelson-Hall.

Tindale, R. S. (1993). Decision errors made by individuals and groups. In N. Castellan, Jr., (Ed.), *Individual and group decision making: Current issues* (pp. 109–124). Hillsdale, NJ: Lawrence Erlbaum Associates.

Tindale, R. S., & Kameda, T. (2000). Social sharedness as a unifying theme for information processing in groups. *Group Processes and Intergroup Relations, 3,* 123–140.

Tindale, R. S., Sheffey, S., & Scott, L. A. (1993). Framing and group decision-making: Do cognitive changes parallel preference changes? *Organizational Behavior and Human Decision Processes, 55,* 470–485.

Tindale, R. S., Smith, C. M., Thomas, L. S., Filkins, J., & Sheffey, S. (1996). Shared representations and asymmetric social influence processes in small groups. In E. Witte, & J. H. Davis (Eds.), *Understanding group behavior: Consensual action by small groups* (Vol. 1, pp. 81–103). Mahwah, NJ: Lawrence Erlbaum.

Turner, J. C. (1991). *Social influence.* Pacific Grove, CA.: Brooks/Cole.

Turner, J. C., Hogg, M. A., Oakes, P. J., Reicher, S. D., & Wetherell, M. S. (1987). *Rediscovering the social group: A self-categorization theory.* New York: Basil Blackwell.

Tversky, A., & Kahneman, D. (1981). The framing of decisions and the psychology of choice. *Science, 211,* 453–458.

Wittenbaum, G. M. (1998). Information sampling in decision making groups: The impact of members' task-relevant status. *Small Group Reseearch, 29,* 57–84.

Wittenbaum, G. M., & Stasser, G. (1996). Management of information in small groups. In J. L. Nye & A. M. Brower (Eds.), *What's social about social cognition* (pp. 3–28). Thousand Oaks, CA: Sage.

Wittenbaum, G. M., Hubbell, A. P., & Zuckerman, C. (1999). Mutual enhancement: Toward an understanding of collective preference for shared information. *Journal of Personality and Social Psychology, 77*, 967–978.

Wood, W., Lundgren, S., Ouellette, J. A., & Busceme, S. (1994). Minority influence: A meta-analytic review of social influence processes. *Psychological Bulletin, 115*, 323–345.

Chapter 13

How Communication Practices and Category Norms Lead People to Stereotype Particular People and Groups

Felicia Pratto
University of Connecticut

Peter J. Hegarty
University of Surrey, United Kingdom

Josephine D. Korchmaros
Southwest Institute for Research on Women, Arizona University

SOME ARE MORE EQUAL THAN OTHERS

All animals are equal, but some are more equal than others.

By the end of George Orwell's (1945) novel *Animal Farm*, the farm animals who have overthrown their oppressive human owners find that the egalitarian principles of their revolution are expounded in explicit declarations but not evident in practice. Along with the Communist society that Orwell lampooned, Western democracies and capitalist societies also describe themselves as providing equal rights and opportunities to all, while differentially doling those out to some more than to others. There are many causes of group-based inequality, including stereotyping, personal and institutional discrimination, and the differential psychological consequences of those processes (see Sidanius & Pratto, 1999). This chapter highlights a different contributor to social inequality, namely, asymmetries in the construction of categorical social identities and their uses.

As the epigraph implies, not all identities are constructed to be equal. This is not simply because stereotypes of some groups have more pernicious contents than others, nor is it solely because some groups are more powerful at defining stereotypes than others. In addition, some identities (e.g., race, gender, nationality, and sexual orientation) classify people either into sets who deserve rights, privileges, and power, and sets who do not.

Some of the processes that privilege or de-privilege particular identities are explicit. For example, the law often bars nonadults from control of particular resources and from making decisions for themselves. In all nations, those legally defined as citizens have rights that noncitizens do not. The law must therefore define identity categories such as who can be considered an adult or a citizen to prescribe rights, privileges, or other differential treatment (Collier, Maurer, & Suarez-Navaz, 1995).

Much civil and human rights activism has been aimed at eliminating certain forms of explicit identity-based exclusion. Such activism contests the link between categories and rights or privileges in several ways. One way is to expand the definition of legal categories (e.g., to consider 18- to 21-year-olds to be adults). Another way is to expand the set of categories which are provided a right or privilege (e.g., to allow permanent residents rather than only citizens to vote in elections). Other forms of activism contest the explicit or de facto exclusion of some identities from privileges granted to other identities. This may occur by changing the abstractness or inclusiveness of the category determining treatment. For example, many legal actions combat race and ability discrimination in education, and gender and age discrimination in employment on the grounds that citizens (regardless of race, gender, or age) should be treated equally. Such arguments can proceed by highlighting parallels between categories that are, and that are not, a basis for the denial of rights (e.g., disability due to mental illness is akin to disability due to physical infirmity, and so should be provided comparable accommodations).

The subject of this chapter is the more subtle but equally important implicit processes that privilege or de-privilege particular identities. There is myriad evidence that some people are more psychologically included in social categories in which they and others are logically included. For example, using an implicit association task, Devos and Banaji (2005) showed that many European Americans implicitly include European Americans in the category American much more strongly than they include African Americans or Asian Americans in that category. In many societies, members of out-groups are often assumed to possess fewer of the qualities that define persons as human, whereas members of in-groups are thought to fit the definition of human quite well (e.g., Cortes,

Demoulin, Rodriguez, Rodriguez, & Leyens, 2005). These kinds of implicit asymmetries in category inclusion extend to self-categorization as well. For example, although the United States is often idealized as a mixed salad, in which all kinds of ethnic identities are included as being American, in fact, being patriotic and identifying with the superordinate group American correlate positively with ethnic identification only among dominant ethnic groups (Whites). To the extent that Blacks and Latinos identify with their ethnic groups, they are less patriotic or less identified as Americans (Sidanius, Feshbach, Levin, & Pratto, 1997).

Such asymmetries in social category inclusion contribute to group-based inequality by causing more problems for those implicitly excluded groups than for those implicitly included groups. One hundred years ago, W. E. B. DuBois (1903) wrote that Black Americans needed a double consciousness as both Black and American to survive in the United States. Half a century later, Simone de Beauvoir (1949) described women as the second sex. Most recently, queer theory has articulated a broad-ranging critique of the ways that heterosexuality is confused with the entirety of human experience (e.g., Warner, 1993). Implicit exclusion foists problems of identity and stereotyping on people in particular groups, including women, gays, poor people, and Blacks, more than others (e.g., Crocker & Major, 1989; Maass & Cadinu, 2003; Waldo, 1999). For these reasons, it is necessary to investigate how prejudice operates through processes of categorization that conflate membership in human categories with such privileged identities as Whiteness (e.g., Devos & Banaji, 2005; Dyer, 1997; Fine, Weis, Pruitt, & Burns, 2004), masculinity (Broverman, Broverman, Clarkson, Rosenkrantz, & Vogel, 1970; Eagly & Kite, 1987; Edley & Wetherell, 1995) and heterosexuality (Rose, 2000; Wilkinson & Kitzinger, 1993).

In addition to causing more identity-related and stereotype-related problems for some groups than others, implicit exclusions also promote institutional discrimination. Here again, the explicit processes may differ from implicit ones. Overtly, early liberal theorists (e.g., Mill, 2002; Paine, 1791–92) relied on the conception of the Universal Rights of Man to institutionalize social equality. Yet as early feminists pointed out, the term *man* and the way it was conceived was not universal. In fact, as they founded democracies, early liberal theorists prescribed gender inequalities in inheritance, education, and political participation. The struggle to eliminate legal androcentrism in democracies is not over. Legal standards for what behavior is considered to constitute sexual harassment are based on the viewpoint of the reasonable man rather than of the reasonable woman, despite the fact that women experience sexual harassment at far higher rates than men do (e.g., Rotundo, Nguyen, & Sackett, 2001; see Bem, 1993 for a review of androcentrism in law and other institutional discrimination).

Andocentric expressions such as "reasonable man" are best known for seeming inclusive while in operation implicitly excluding certain groups. Implicit linguistic discrimination that is reflected in ordinary language use and the implicit categories to which words refer also occurs for sexual orientation and ethnic groups. Bars and other establishments that serve primarily gay and lesbian clientele may be shut down as violations of community standards, as if gays and lesbians are not part of the community, whereas establishments that serve primarily heterosexual clientele rarely are (Bricknell, 2000; Warner, 1993). Americans understand the statement, "Americans are prejudiced against Blacks" to make sense, but not the statement, "Americans are prejudiced against Whites." Evidently, then, Americans implicitly presume that Americans are not Black (Leach, Snider, & Iyer, 2002). Thus, a considerable amount of implicit discrimination stems from language use that conflates general category labels with particular groups.

Such biases in language use are hard to notice. Even now when instruction explicitly prohibits androcentric language use (e.g., American Psychological Association, 2005), most American undergraduates, particularly men, do not notice androcentric language and do not find it problematic (Swim, Mallett, & Stangor, 2004; see also Parks & Roberton, 2004). Likewise, because the forms of discrimination discussed above are based on implicit standards, and because they do not explicitly privilege members of privileged groups, they are hard for many to recognize as discrimination.

To account for why these language use biases occur as often as they do and for why they are hard to notice, we now review relevant psychological and psycholinguistic theory and research. In particular, we examine the way that language that appears explicitly inclusive and universal can limit inclusion, and why we often fail to notice the inequalities that result. We first explain the concept of a social category norm. Rather than thinking of categories as logical, we must consider how social categories such as man are represented mentally. When people think of a category label, they call to mind particular exemplars of that category. The most prevalent features of the exemplars that come to mind become mental norms for the category. These mental category norms ensure that the people who might be logical members of a category are never all equally psychological members of the category norm. For example, women are often said to be included in the term *men* when *men* means *human* (e.g., "all men are created equal"), but the term *men* brings to mind representations of males more than representations of females (e.g., Gastil, 1990; Hamilton, 1988, 1991; Martyna, 1978; Ng, 1990).

We then detail how category norms influence stereotyping and stereotype contents by describing how category norms influence explanations for group differences and events. In particular, we examine which group tends to be the focus of explanations and how this focus biases the contents of explanations toward stereotypes of nonnormative groups. Next we examine how category norms create common ground in conversations because people tend to assume that the way that they instantiate a social category will be common with that of their conversational partners. Fourth, we explain how the online cognitive construction of temporary category norms together with Gricean (1975) demands to produce only relevant contributions to conversation leads to the asymmetric marking of racial and gender identities. Finally, we discuss the consequences of implicit exclusions of certain groups from category-based privileges for stereotyping, prejudice, and intergroup relations.

BACKGROUND IN NORM THEORY

To understand how psychological norms are constructed to privilege certain identities rather than others, we have to explain both how implicit norms occur to individuals and what makes these norms consensual within in a community. We argue that privileged identities such as maleness, Whiteness, and heterosexuality become the default for many social categories because they are consensually constructed as the norm for those categories. This consensual construction involves at least three processes. First, people in the same culture are exposed to similar aspects of the social world due to social segregation and exposure to the same mass media (Linville & Fischer, 1993; Miller & Prentice, 1996). This common exposure makes the same or similar exemplars come to mind in different individuals when they think of category labels. Second, people use their own category norms in communicating with others because they generally can expect other people to share their category norms. Third, people communicate by relying on the assumption that their own category norms are shared by others. This presumption of consensuality helps to reinforce those same category norms in speakers' audiences. Through these processes, certain social features, such as Whiteness, become consensually shared category norms, and particular privileges are accorded to people who have those normative features.

Mental norms are described by Kahneman and Miller's (1986) norm theory: Such norms are defined as "temporary patterns of knowledge activation" that are constructed online and provide the comparative background against which reality is understood.[1] In other words, norms come from bringing to mind already-learned aspects of the world. Stimulus norms are evoked in response to objects and events. For example, thinking of going to a restaurant might lead some people to immediately assume they will be given plates and knives and forks, whereas it will lead other people to assume they will be given bowls and chopsticks, depending on which cuisines have been prevalent in their restaurant experiences.

Events lead people to imagine counterfactual alternatives to those events which are in some ways different from those events. For example, one might

---

[1]The reader should note that this definition of *norm* drives from an exemplar theory of memory, and thus differs from other common meanings of *norm*, such as social standard or most common behavior.

wish one could be given chopsticks without changing the cuisine one is eating. Kahneman and Miller (1986) proposed several hypotheses regarding the relative mutability of aspects of events. Mutated (mentally altered) aspects of events were described as being exceptional rather than routine (see also Kahneman & Tversky, 1982), being less ideal rather than more ideal, being less reliable rather than more reliable in their factuality, being effects rather than causes, and as being focal rather than in the background. The subsequent explosion of research on counterfactual thinking has explored and contested these and other hypotheses about event norms (for reviews see Roese, 1997; Roese & Olson, 1995).

Even more pertinent to our concerns, norm theory also states that category norms are evoked by reference to category labels. In contrast to the plethora of research on event norms, Kahneman and Miller's (1986) claims about the construction of category norms have received less research attention. Category norms were said to be constructed as follows. References to a category label lead people to recruit actual and fictional exemplars of the relevant category. The most likely exemplars to be called to mind are those that are most recently used or highly typical members of the category (see Rothbart, Sriram, & Davis-Stitt, 1996; Smith & Zaraté, 1992; Srull, Lichtenstein, & Rothbart, 1985; Zárate & Smith, 1990). The attributes of recruited exemplars are implicitly aggregated to form ranges of normal values for category members. These ranges constitute the category norm. It is important to note that the normativeness of category norms is implicit. That is, unlike prototypic memory representations (e.g., Rosch & Mervis, 1975) in which people can declare what features are central in defining a prototypic category member, category norms form expectancies that are not necessarily conscious. However, Kahneman and Miller (1986) argued that, in parallel with counterfactual event norms, the attributes of category instances that fall outside of normative ranges are experienced as surprising, are available to consciousness, and are perceived as mutable.

There are various kinds of evidence that people within a culture come to share category norms due to similar experience and exposure to the same mass media. Miller, Taylor, and Buck (1991) found that more than 90% of men and women college participants who were asked to think of a typical American voter called to mind a male exemplar. In other words, their participants held an implicit, consensual category norm of maleness for a category (voters) that is not logically defined as male nor statistically described as normatively male (see also Moyer, 1997). When the present authors asked college students to list names of famous people who are members of celebrity categories, they showed considerable consensus on the normative race and gender of such categories. For example, 79% (22 of 28) of the students surveyed named particular Black men most prevalently for the category professional basketball player (Korchmaros & Pratto, 1999). Indirect evidence that norms develop due to exposure to exemplars can be shown when people with different experiences hold different category norms. For example, when asked to nominate American heroes, White

American participants nominated only 7 African Americans, but African American participants nominated 20 (Korchmaros, 2000). Moreover, most (55% or 34 of 62) African American participants nominated at least one African American, but only 23% of European American participants (26 of 112) nominated at least one African American as an American hero (Korchmaros, 2000). Further, older Whites held different category norms than younger Whites for categories in which the exemplars have changed over the decades. For example, 84% (26 of 31) of older Whites had the norm of White male for professional baseball player, whereas only 33% (27 of 81) of younger Whites had the norm of White male for professional baseball player (Korchmaros, 2000). Still, it should be noted that the degree of consensus we measured in these studies across participants' races and ages was quite high.

CATEGORY NORMS AND EXPLANATIONS FOR DIFFERENCES BETWEEN SOCIAL GROUPS

Kahneman and Miller's (1986) theory of category norms has important implications for stereotyping and other forms of group bias. Norm theory holds that features that contrast with category norms will be surprising, and will consequently receive explanatory attention. Thus, when people compare those who have normative features with those who do not, people will tend to focus their explanations on the nonnormative features. Consider such effects with respect to explaining differences between men and women. Logically, one could explain a difference between men and women in terms of how women differ from men, how men differ from women, or how much each gender differs from some other reference point. When asked to explain gender differences in voting behavior, both men and women participants focused their explanations on women's attributes rather than on men's attributes (Miller et al., 1991), as was expected given that the category norm for voters was male. Further, a majority of participants judged that if men and women became more similar, women would be more likely than men to change. In short, groups who are implicitly not normative receive more explanatory attention and their attributes are assumed to be more mutable than normative groups.

  These predictions are derived from a theory of mental representations, not a theory of stigma, stereotyping, prejudice, or discrimination. As such, norm theory does not accord femaleness any special status as being nonnormative, nor does it speak directly to the contents of stereotypes. Indeed, according to norm theory, if the category label leads people to think of mainly women exemplars, then male exemplars should be surprising and the focus of attention and men should be perceived to be more likely to become like women than vice versa. Further, the processes specified by norm theory are not contingent on the contents of existing social stereotypes.

To test these assumptions, Miller et al. (1991) asked participants to explain gender differences within a male-normative category (e.g., college professors) and a female-normative category (e.g., teachers). Participants explained gender differences in rates of going to the doctor. Their results partially support the idea that norms are based on category typicality; explanations of differences among college professors referred to women more than to men as predicted. However, participants focused on men and women equally when explaining gender differences among teachers rather than focusing on men for a female-normative category. Miller et al. (1991) explained their failure to completely reverse the focus of explanations onto men's attributes by appealing to participants' stereotypes about women visiting doctors. But, given that they did not invoke participants' stereotypes about women and voting to explain the results of earlier experiments, their account of their findings is not entirely satisfying.

WHAT MAKES A GROUP NORMATIVE?

A more refined theory of the relation between category norms, category typicality, and stereotypes is needed. In addition to typicality in a particular category, what factors could contribute to a group becoming perceived to be generally normative across categories? Maleness may be a robust norm even though men are not statistically predominant because men are called to mind as exemplars and as typical of many, many social categories (e.g., virtually all but a handful of occupations, famous people, representatives of nations, etc.). Further, female-normed category labels such as *teacher* may activate knowledge about more general categories that are male-normed (e.g., professional or worker). The meaning of category norms in a larger category context than just the category label has not been examined.

Expressions that use specific terms as general (e.g., "man in the street") may render specific groups (e.g., male voters) more typical and mark excluded groups (e.g., female voters) as atypical. Third, social knowledge about categories and groups may also help determine exemplars and/or category normative. For example, people's historical knowledge that voters used to be defined as male may make male exemplars more likely to come to mind and determine the male category norm for voter. Finally, another hypothesis suggested by Miller et al.'s (1991.)Experiment 3 results is that the combination of nonnormative category features (e.g., female gender) with nonnormative events (e.g., going to the doctor) especially leads people to explain group differences in terms of nonnormative identities.

These hypotheses mandate further experimentation to identify those factors which may determine how normative social groups are implicitly presumed to be. Pratto, Hegarty, Lemieux, and Glasford (2005) examined (mostly White college students) Americans' race norms by asking participants to explain differences between Black and White Americans. We explored which kinds of social knowledge impinged on the robust normativity of Whiteness. All four experiments showed that Whiteness is a robust category norm in that race differences were explained more often with respect to attributes of Blacks than to attributes of Whites. However, we also identified several other factors that modified this asymmetry.

In the first experiment, participants explained a race difference in public confidence in the local police reported in a survey. Pretests confirmed that participants generally expected Americans to have confidence in the police, so we expected that the race group said to have less confidence would violate this expectancy and be explained more. Second, we suspected that having majority status would make a group more normative, as we had earlier observed this to be the case with regard to sexual orientation categories (Hegarty & Pratto, 2001). In one condition, the racial composition of the survey was unspecified; in a second condition Blacks were described as being a majority of those surveyed, and in a third Whites were described as the majority. As expected, participants' explanations of the race difference focused on Blacks less when Blacks were a majority group, and less when they were said to have confidence in the police. This suggests that statistical rarity and perceived social deviancy (e.g., behaving differently than people are generally expected to behave) both contribute to nonnormativity. However, the number of references to Whites was unchanged by the experimental manipulations (see Fig. 13–1). That is, neither being the statistical minority nor social deviancy were sufficient to increase the explanatory focus on Whites. As with men in Miller et al.'s (1991) experiments, Whites appeared to be robustly normative to White Americans.

Stereotypic expectancies also influenced the mutability measure in Experiment 1 of Pratto et al. (2005). After they had explained the race difference, participants were told that a new poll had been conducted and had found no race difference. They were then asked whether they believed the first poll (showing a race difference) or the new poll (showing a race similarity). When the first poll had shown that more Whites than Blacks had confidence in the police, three fourths of the participants trusted that poll more. In other words, most participants found it plausible that Whites fit the pretested implicit norm for Americans, and Blacks were different than that. When the first poll showed that more Blacks than Whites had confidence in the police, only 50% of participants trusted this first poll. These results confirm that it was more plausible to participants that Whites are like Americans in their trust of police more than Blacks are. Evidently, category norms influence how people evaluate evidence in ways that maintain the category norm. Further, these results indicate that people do not always assume that nonnormative groups will mutate to become more like normative ones. Rather, when nonnormative groups are different, such difference is fairly plausible. This may be part of the reason that people accept stereotypes of others as being somewhat peculiar and even violating of general social norms.

Mean references to Blacks and Whites

Whites more confident   **Blacks more confident**

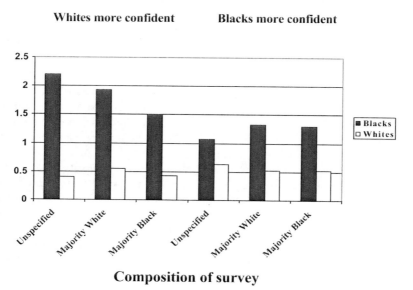

Composition of survey

FIGURE 13–1.   Mean foreground references to Whites and Blacks as a function of majority in sample and which group was more confident in police.

Other experiments by Pratto et al. (2005) confirm that behaving in unexpected ways or being associated with unexpected outcomes also contributes to groups becoming implicitly nonnormative. In other words, event norms and category norms both contribute to determining who becomes the effect to be explained. In Experiment 2, participants explained a race difference in the effectiveness of a drug intervention program. When the program was more effective for White teenagers (and more Black teenagers failed to abstain or relapsed into drug use), Blacks were explained much more frequently than Whites. When the program was said to be more effective for Blacks, participants explained Blacks and Whites at equivalent rates. As in Experiment 1, then, when Blacks upheld a social standard (staying off drugs) they became less nonnormative, but Whites' failure to adhere to a social standard did not focus explanatory attention on them.

Experiment 1 involved a behavior that could be said to be expected of American citizens (e.g., trusting the police), and Experiment 2 involved an undesirable and socially deviant behavior (e.g., drug use). Experiment 3 tested whether desirable behaviors that violate expectations similarly lead a group to become implicitly nonnormative. Participants explained race differences in donating to charity, a behavior that pretests showed that participants perceived to be very low in frequency. When Blacks were said to donate more than Whites, Blacks were explained more. But when Whites were said to donate to charity more often than Blacks, Whites were explained more. This was the first reliable increase in references to Whites in this series of experiments. In Experiment 4, we manipulated participants' expectancies. We stated that a new blood pressure medication had a 60% effectiveness rate in a pilot study. Participants then explained race differences in the effectiveness of the medication. Whereas Blacks were referenced more frequently overall, this was especially the case when the drug was either more or less than 60% effective for Blacks. Collectively, these four studies show that race differences are especially explained by references to attributes of Blacks when Blacks violate a general expectation, whether that violation is biological or volitional, or takes the form of desirable or undesirable behavior.

These experiments show how difficult it is to render a robustly normative group (such as Whites) as the effect to be explained by tampering with feature typicality. However, another line of research shows that typical groups can be made to seem nonnormative by making atypical groups the starting point for generalization processes. By presenting data about nonnormative groups and asking participants to draw inferences and make predictions about normative groups, experimenters can make the features of nonnormative groups function as premises. The features of premise groups provide a backdrop against which the attributes of groups about which conclusions are drawn more accessible for explaining group differences. For example, when people generalize from women voters (the premise group) to men voters (the conclusion group), explanations of gender differences focus on men (Hegarty, 2006). These findings are quite consistent with models of feature-based generalization which presume that the unique features of conclusion categories are more salient than those of premise categories (Sloman, 1993). Likewise, explanations of age and national group differences focus on conclusion groups rather than premise groups, regardless of the general normativity or typicality of the groups in the premise or conclusion positions (Hegarty & Chryssochoou, 2005; Robinson & Hegarty, in press). Moreover, the tendency to focus on conclusion groups is strong and overrides effects of typicality within the category (see Table 13.1). Forming category norms from premise groups can engender ethnocentrism: Hegarty and Chryssochoou (2005) found that the distinctive attributes of participants' own nation reduced both generalization from that nation to others and perceived similarity between others and that nation more when the ingroup was positioned as a conclusion than as a premise. As a result, participants were quicker to generalize a home-grown policy on foreigners than to accept an equally successful policy, developed abroad, for their own nation.

Let us summarize what the experiments on explanations of group differences indicate about social category norms. First, the effects for generally normative groups (e.g., for the populations tested, Whites, heterosexuals, and

TABLE 13.1.
References in Explanations in Experiments on Premise-Based Category Norms

Study	Participant Groups	Target Groups	Premise (A) Conclusion (B)	Conclusion (A) Premise (B)
Hegarty and Chrysochoou (2005)	British Adults	A: British B: French	0.82 2.20	2.32 0.94
Robinson and Hegarty (in press)	Older & Young Adults	A: Older Adults B: Young Adults	0.55 1.10	1.00 0.60
Hegarty (2006) Experiment 1	Females & Males	A: Females B: Males	0.50 1.86	2.43 0.56
Experiment 2	Females & Males	A: Females B: Males	0.31 2.31	2.60 0.80

men) are not symmetric for generally nonnormative groups (e.g., Blacks, gay men and lesbians, and women), except when they are rendered the effect to be explained. The robustness of such normativity can be seen in the failures to reverse the focus of explanation for group differences. Manipulations of category typicality, majority status, and expectedness of behavior fail to completely reverse the focus of explanations of intergroup differences. Atypicality in a category, either in terms of frequent exemplars or being a statistical minority, does not reverse which group gets explained for Whites (versus Blacks; Pratto et al., 2005), men (versus women; Miller et al., 1991), or straight men (versus gay men; Hegarty & Pratto, 2001). When normative groups violate a relevant group stereotype, they are not explained more often (Hegarty & Pratto, 2001; Hegarty & Pratto, 2004). When normative groups violate general expectancies (Miller et al., 1991; Pratto et al., 2005), they are not explained more. To date, with the exception of experiments on premise-based category norms, only two experiments increased rates of referencing normative groups, both under conditions in which Whites could be said to uphold a moral norm: When Whites stayed off drugs more often than Blacks, and when Whites donated to charity more often than Blacks (Pratto et al., 2005). In fact, in one experiment in which participants were instructed to focus their explanations for group differences on the normative group (straight men), they referenced the normative group only marginally more often than the nonnormative group (Hegarty & Pratto, 2001). Taken together, these results suggest that explanations for group differences will rarely focus on normative groups, and that the one circumstance in which explanations do so is when such groups are rendered the effect to be predicted.

Explanations for group differences refer much more frequently to features of nonnormative groups. Indeed, across the three gender experiments, four sexual orientation experiments, and four race experiments described above, participants referred to nonnormative groups over normative groups to explain group differences at a ratio of 2.79 to 1.[2] To explain group differences in terms of attributes of the nonnormative group, stereotypic knowledge may be either drawn upon or invented.

CATEGORY NORMS AND STEREOTYPING

The influence category norms exert on explanations for group differences has implications for stereotyping, stereotype contents, stereotype maintenance and stereotype change. In the United States, stereotypes of Blacks and Whites, and of women and men, are widely known. But in a review of stereotyping research, Fiske (1998) noted that "women have gender, and blacks have race more than men and whites respectively do" (p. 366). What Fiske meant was that women are stereotyped according to gender more often than men are, and Blacks are stereotyped more often according to race than Whites are. Given that people are equally knowledgeable of stereotypes, one must explain why stereotypes are not symmetrically applied. The research on category norms we have just described provides a reason why this occurs.

Hegarty and Pratto (2001) proposed that category norms relate to stereotyping in a two-stage process. First, category norms highlight nonnormative features as people construct explanations for difference. When those norms make nonnormative social identities salient, stereotypes of such groups may become accessible. Second, stereotypes and other kinds of social knowledge can be used to construct explanations. Often, this implies that stereotypes become explanations, consistent with the view that they are lay social theories (e.g., Hilton & von Hippel, 1996). For example, when our participants have explained why gays and lesbians recall playing more with feminine and masculine toys, respectively, than their straight same-gender counterparts did, they often rely on the inversion stereotype that gay men are like women and lesbians are like men (Kite & Deaux, 1987; see Hegarty & Pratto, 2001; Hegarty & Pratto, 2004). We have also observed social knowledge or beliefs about Blacks in participants' explanations for race differences. For example, some participants attributed Black mistrust of police on racial profiling and high crime rates in Black neighborhoods, or Black charitable donation as due to Blacks' understanding poverty. By virtue of being the effect to be explained, nonnormative groups are far more likely to be stereotyped than normative groups.

---

[2]This excludes the explicit instruction condition of Hegarty and Pratto (2001) in which participants were explicitly instructed to focus on attributes of straight men in their explanations. The three gender experiments showed the highest ratio, 3.79, but only one was balanced with respect to stereotypic content. Lower, but still high ratios were found for sexual orientation, 2.86, and for race, 1.97, and all such experiments included manipulations to reduce category normativity.

Hence, understanding category norms is essential in understanding which groups are likely to be stereotyped and why stereotypes are not applied symmetrically to all groups. Category norms also imply that, because they are used more often, stereotypes of nonnormative groups will become well-learned and more accessible than stereotypes of normative groups.

However, people do not simply recapitulate stereotypes when explaining group differences. For example, if gays and lesbians reported playing more gender-stereotypic activities than straight people, participants presumed that they were overcompensating for feelings of gender-inferiority or that their recollections were false (Hegarty & Pratto, 2001; Hegarty & Pratto, 2004). Such explanations take stereotypes into account, but instead of using the evidence of group differences provided to refute stereotypes, such explanations could be considered a work around that leaves the stereotype of the nonnormative group apparently valid (see also Yzerbyt, Rocher, & Schadron, 1997). Explaining counterstereotypic group differences in terms of the norm violations, then, may serve to maintain stereotypes rather than to change stereotypes. Future research should test this possibility using other groups and other stereotype contents.

Research on participants' explanations for group differences also tells us something important about the likely contents of stereotypes of different groups. Recall that nonnormative groups were especially likely to be explained when they were said to have behaved in such a way or even had experienced an outcome that violated a moral standard, behavioral norm, or expectancy. Because these events to be explained are nonnormal, if these explanations become stereotypes, then stereotypes of nonnormative groups are likely to focus on attributes that make them appear peculiar, deviant, and strange. Although we have yet to test this hypothesis directly, we note that attributes such as hysterical, immoral, sexually deviant, exotic, superstitious, infirm, inscrutable, abnormal, untrustworthy, weird, and quirky have been much more often applied to Asians, women, gays and lesbians, and Blacks than to Whites, men, and straight people.

COMMUNICATION PRAGMATICS

Thus far, we have discussed category norms and their relation to group stereotyping. We believe that category norms also influence the extent to which individuals are explicitly identified as having social category features. The phenomenon of marking also shows asymmetries in which features are assumed to be normal in particular contexts of categories. For example, the term *male nurse* suggests that people assume that most nurses are women, and the term *Black doctor* shows that most people assume that doctors are White. Indeed, we have shown that the discomfort that a gay man might feel in a straight bar is attributed to his being gay, but the discomfort a straight man might feel in a gay bar is attributed to the bar's catering to gay clientele, not to the straight man's sexual orientation (Hegarty, Pratto, & Lemieux, 2004).

Norm theory might suggest that people designate nonnormative features simply because they are surprising to the speaker. However, there is still another reason why asymmetric marking occurs. Over and above the intrapsychic processes described above, when people talk, they do so against a background of shared assumptions called "common ground" (e.g., Clark, 1985). We argue that category norms are often presumed to be part of common ground. In other words, a person who calls to mind White men when asked to think about golfers may also assume that others will instantiate the category similarly. Because of mass media, the person may also be right.

CONSIDERING CATEGORY NORMS AND GRICEAN NORMS TOGETHER

Cognitive processes such as those described by norm theory and Gricean communication norms may together explain when people mark other's social identities. A series of studies by Pratto, Korchmaros, and Hegarty (2007) examined designation of race and gender of individuals and provided support for this idea. We first conducted pilot studies to determine the category norms of occupations from popular entertainment (e.g., professional basketball player and fashion model) and to identify stimulus persons for use in experiments. The stimulus persons were equally well-known but had race or gender features that were either typical or atypical of the categories.

The first experiment examined when people do and do not designate race and gender features. Undergraduate college students were given names of typical and atypical celebrities and asked to write down what makes celebrities either typical or not typical of their occupational categories. Coders noted whether participants' free responses included explicit designations of race and gender. Had participants relied only on Grice's (1975) maxim of relation, which is to address the topic at hand, they would have designated typical features when asked what makes a celebrity typical, and atypical features when asked what makes a celebrity not typical. However, participants only mentioned race or gender in the latter of these two situations. This finding is inconsistent with Grice's (1975) maxim of relation, but supports our supposition that normative race and gender identities are implicit, and, thus, unlikely to receive mental attention or verbal designation. However, these results are consistent with Grice's (1975) maxim of quantity, which implies that people should state no more than is necessary in a given context. If participants assumed that their category norms were shared, then their failure to mention typical identities when prompted to do so would be in compliance with this maxim. It is as if people think, "Why mention that Whiteness makes Cindy Crawford a typical supermodel? Surely it goes without saying that fashion models are White."

The second experiment examined when people designate race and gender features during interpersonal spoken communication with a peer. Pairs of un- acquainted same-sex undergraduate college students played an experimenter- controlled game in which one participant—the clue-giver—gave clues as to a celebrity's identity to another participant, the guesser, who guessed who it was in the shortest amount of time and using as few clues as possible. We ex- amined whether race and gender were mentioned as clues and the effec- tiveness and efficiency of communication. A secondary purpose of this ex- periment was to determine whether preventing clue-givers from designating atypical features makes communication less efficient in terms of time and number of clues used to identify the celebrity; some clue-givers could use any clues they wanted, some could not mention race, and a third group could not mention gender.

As norm theory might predict, clue-givers who were allowed to provide any clues that they wanted designated atypical race and gender features more of- ten than typical race and gender features. These results are also consistent with Grice's maxim of quantity; clue-givers were explicitly designating identity on those trials where they could not presume that guessers' category norms would give them the right information about the target celebrity's race and gender.

Another finding indicates support for the unique role of conversation prag- matics over and above category norms in determining when race and gender were designated. Clue-givers designated race and gender features when the guessers seemed to have the wrong race or gender identity in mind. Clue- givers designated race or gender in their clues most often when the guessers' first guesses did not match the race or gender of the target celebrity. This find- ing shows how attunement during communication and Gricean communica- tion norms, rather than the salience of the nonnormative feature, determined designation of race and gender features.

Further, results indicated that communication was less efficient for atypical but not typical celebrities when participants were not allowed to designate race or gender features as clues. When participants were not allowed to use race or gender features as clues, they had to use more clues and more time before the guesser identified atypical celebrities as compared to typical celebrities. By inference, designating atypical race and gender features extends common ground to make communication more efficient, but designating typical race and gender features does not. These results also support a hypothesis derived from Grice's (1975) maxim of quantity in that providing information that may be unknown or incorrectly presumed increases communication efficiency while stating information that is already known decreases efficiency without increasing effectiveness.

In a third experiment, we tested whether people designate atypical race and gender identities merely because they judge that information important to know in its own right, or because they judge it to be useful to communica- tion and the development of common ground. Participants were given one of three goals and then described typical or atypical celebrities. In the information condition, participants described what information was important to know about each celebrity. In the common ground condition, participants were to provide information about a celebrity that would enable someone else to guess who it was. In the no common ground condition, participants were to provide information that would seem to be informative, but not actually enable someone else to guess the celebrity's identity. Participants designated atypical race or gender more than typical race or gender only in the common ground condition, despite the fact that more features were described in the no common ground condition. These results show that the goal to communicate or extend common ground is crucial in the higher rates of designating atypical race and gender features. Thus, both category norms and communication pragmatics determine the asymmetric marking of atypical race and gender features.

These results may have important implications for the communication of category norms and stereotyping. First, because people know that common ground does not need to be stated, designating atypical features and acceptance of that designation as ordinary confirms that the norm is shared by others. Evidence from others that they share one's own sense of what is nonnormative may increase the sense one has of what is not normal. As with explanations for group differences, failure to designate typical features may nonetheless leave norms un-noticed and unconsidered. Second, to the extent that labeling an individual by his or her race or gender is a form of verbal categorization, such individuals are more likely to be stereotyped than people whose race or gender is not designated (Fiske & Neuberg, 1990). On the other hand, people may sometimes designate the race or gender of an accomplished individual to point out that person's counterstereotypicality or even that the person is breaking a category norm (e.g., first woman astronaut). Whether this serves to disrupt stereotypes or simply to exempt the person in question from stereotyping is not generally clear.

CATEGORY NORMS, STEREOTYPING, AND OTHER FORMS OF DISCRIMINATION

Finally, we also argue that category norms play a role in group-based discrimination and in whether people detect the unfairness of such discrimination or not. For example, when the qualifications of Black and White men and women are compared against a norm that includes members of all race and gender groups, the effects of stereotypes are more evident than when individuals are compared only against members of their own gender or ethnic group (Biernat & Kobrynowitz, 1997). Limiting the implicit comparison points increases the influence of stereotypes. Conversely, men and women prefer to compare their own task performance with that of same-sex peers, leading them to overlook gender discrimination. This leads them to erroneously perceive that unfair systems are egalitarian (Major & Testa, 1989, see also Major, 1989). However, others compare a woman who fails at a male-typed task to men rather than to other women. This comparison makes such a woman exemplary and representative of her gender, no doubt confirming stereotypes of women, while leaving implicit the fact that male-based norms are standard (McGill, 1993). Thus, category norms serve to hide the implicit privileges of comparison standards that are biased in that they are derived from normative groups.

Moreover, pointing out features that contrast with attributes that are mutually understood to be normal may well stigmatize particular persons or groups. Indeed, people with both typical and atypical race features find the explicit designation of their identities to be aversive, and avoid social situations where such designations might occur (Tropp, Stout, Boatswain, Wright, & Pettigrew, 2006). Such designations call into question whether individuals belong to valued social categories, or even whether they are first and foremost, or even completely, human (Goffman, 1963).

CONCLUSION

We have argued that category norms become shared through common experience and through communication. In turn, category norms tell us why particular groups and members of particular groups are more likely to be stereotyped than are members of other groups, why stereotypes of such groups are overpracticed compared with stereotypes of other groups, why providing counterstereotypic information about group differences is unlikely to get rid of stereotypes, and possibly why stereotypes of nonnormative groups include peculiar, deviant, and strange contents. Moreover, we have shown that category norms function implicitly on communication processes regarding groups and individuals. Last, category norms set implicit standards of comparison that favor normative groups but which often go undetected. The systematic nature of group-based discrimination and stereotyping is due, then, in part, to shared category norms.

REFERENCES

American Psychological Association. (2005). *Publication Manual.* Washington, DC: APA.
Bem, S. L. (1993). *The lenses of gender.* New Haven: Yale University Press.
Biernat, M., & Kobrynowicz, D. (1997). Gender- and race-based standards of competence: Lower minimum standards but higher ability standards for devalued groups. *Journal of Personality and Social Psychology, 72,* 544–557.
Bricknell, C. (2000). Heroes and invaders: Gay and lesbian pride parades and the public/private distinction in New Zealand media accounts. *Gender, Place, and Culture, 7,* 163–178.

Broverman, I. K., Broverman, D. M., Clarkson, F. E., Rosenkrantz, P. S., & Vogel, S. R. (1970). Sex-role stereotypes and clinical judgments of mental health. *Journal of Consulting and Clinical Psychology, 34,* 1–7.

Clark, H. H. (1985). Language use and language users. In G. Lindzey & E. Aronson (Eds.), *Handbook of social psychology* (pp. 179–231). NY: Random House.

Collier, J., Maurer, B., & Suarez-Navaz, L. (1995). Sanctioned identities: Legal constructions of modern personhood. *Identities, 2,* 1–27.

Cortes, B., Demoulin, S., Rodriguez, R. T, Rodriguez, A., & Leyens, J. P., (2005). Infrahumanization or familiarity? Attribution of uniquely human emotions to the self, the in-group, and the out-group. *Personality and Social Psychology Bulletin, 31,* 243–253.

Crocker, J., & Major, B. (1989). Social stigma and self-esteem: The self-protective properties of stigma. *Psychological Review, 96,* 608–630.

de Beauvoir, S. (1949). *The second sex.* New York: Random House.

Devos, T., & Banaji, M. (2005). American = White? *Journal of Personality and Social Psychology, 88,* 447–466.

DuBois, W. E. B. (1903). *Souls of black folks.* Chicago: Ac McClurg & Co.

Dyer, R. (1997). *White.* London: Routledge.

Eagly, A. H., & Kite, M. E. (1987). Are stereotypes of nationalities applied equally to both men and women? *Journal of Personality and Social Psychology, 53,* 457–462.

Edley, N., & Wetherell, M. (1995). *Men in perspective: Practice, power, and identity.* London: Prentice Hall.

Fine, M., Weis, L., Pruitt, L. P., & Burns, A. (Eds.) (2004). *Off White.* New York and London: Routledge.

Fiske, S. T. (1998). Stereotyping, prejudice, and discrimination. In D. T. Gilbert, S. T. Fiske, & G. Lindzey (Eds.), *Handbook of social psychology* (pp. 357–411). Boston: McGraw-Hill.

Fiske, S. T., & Neuberg, S. L. (1990). A continuum model of impression formation: From category-based to individuating processes as a function of information, motivation, and attention. In M. P. Zanna (Ed.), *Advances in experimental social psychology,* (Vol. 23, pp. 1–108). San Diego, CA: Academic Press.

Gastil, J. (1990). Generic pronouns and sexist language: The oxymoronic character of masculine generics. *Sex Roles, 23,* 629–643.

Goffman, E. (1963). *Stigma: Notes on the management of spoiled identity.* NY: Simon & Schuster.

Grice, H. P. (1975). Logic and conversation. In P. Cole & J. L. Morgan (Eds.), *Syntax and semantics 3: Speech acts* (pp. 41–48). NY: Academic Press.

Hamilton, M. C. (1988). Using masculine generics: Does generic *He* increase male bias in the user's imagery. *Sex Roles, 19,* 785–799.

Hamilton, M. C. (1991). Masculine bias in the attribution of personhood: People = male, male = people. *Psychology of Women Quarterly, 15,* 393–402.

Hegarty, P. (2006). *Undoing androcentrism: Explaining 'the effect to be predicted.'* Sex Roles, 55, 861–867.

Hegarty, P., & Chryssochoou, X. (2005). Why 'our' policies set the standard more than 'theirs': Category norms and generalization between European Union countries. *Social Cognition, 23,* 507–544.

Hegarty, P., & Pratto, F. (2001). The effects of category norms and stereotypes on explanations for inter-group differences. *Journal of Personality and Social Psychology, 80,* 723–735.

Hegarty, P., & Pratto, F. (2004). The differences that norms make: Empiricism, social constructionism and the interpretation of group differences. *Sex Roles: A Journal of Research, 50,* 445–453.

Hegarty, P., Pratto, F., & Lemieux, A. F. (2004). Heterosexist ambivalence and heterocentric norms: Drinking in intergroup discomfort. *Group Processes and Intergroup Relations, 7,* 119–130.

Hilton, J. L., & von Hippel, W. (1996). Stereotypes. *Annual review of psychology, 47*, 237–271.

Kahneman, D., & Miller, D. T. (1986). Norm theory: Comparing reality to its alternatives. *Psychological Review, 93*, 136–153.

Kahneman, D., & Tversky, A. (1982). The simulation heuristic. In D. Kahneman, P. Slovic, & A. Tversky (Eds.), *Judgment under uncertainty: Heuristics and biases* (pp. 201–208). Cambridge: Cambridge University Press.

Kite, M. E., & Deaux, K. (1987). Gender belief systems: Homosexuality and the implicit inversion theory. *Psychology of Women Quarterly, 11*, 83–96.

Korchmaros, J. D. (2000). [The influence of exposure on category norms]. Unpublished raw data.

Korchmaros, J. D., & Pratto, F. (1999). [Category norms of occupational and social categories]. Unpublished raw data.

Leach, C. W., Snider, N., & Iyer, A. (2002). "Poisoning the consciences of the fortunate:" The experience of relative advantage and support for social equality. In I. Walker (Ed.), *Relative deprivation: Specification, development and integration* (pp. 136–163). New York: Cambridge University Press.

Linville, P. W., & Fischer, G. W. (1993). Exemplar and abstraction models of perceived group variability and stereotypicality. *Social Cognition, 11*, 92–125.

Maass, A., & Cadinu, M. (2003). Stereotype threat: When minority members underperform. *European Review of Social Psychology, 14*, 243–275.

Major, B. (1989). Gender differences in comparisons and entitlement: Implications for comparable worth. *Journal of Social Issues, 45*, 99–115.

Major, B., & Testa, M. (1989). Social comparison processes and judgments of entitlement and satisfaction. *Journal of Experimental Social Psychology, 25*, 101–120.

Martyna, W. (1978). What does 'he' mean? Use of the generic masculine. *Journal of Communication, 28*, 131–138.

McGill, A. L. (1993). Selection of a causal background: Role of expectation versus feature mutability. *Journal of Personality and Social Psychology, 64*, 701–707.

Mill, J. S. (2002). *The basic writings of John Stuart Mill: On liberty, the subjection of women and utilitarianism.* NY: Modern Library.

Miller, D. T., & Prentice, D. A. (1996). The construction of norms and standards. In E. T. Higgins & A. W. Kruglanski (Eds.), *Social Psychology: Handbook of basic principles.* NY: Guilford (pp. 799–829).

Miller, D. T., Taylor, B., & Buck, M. L. (1991). Gender gaps: Who needs to be explained? *Journal of Personality and Social Psychology, 61*, 5–12.

Moyer, R. (1997). Covering gender on memory's front page: Men's prominence and women's prospects. *Sex Roles, 37*, 595–618.

Ng, S. H. (1990). Androcentric coding of man and his in memory by language users. *Journal of Experimental Social Psychology, 26*, 455–464.

Orwell, G. (1945). *Animal Farm.* Florida: Harcourt, Inc.

Paine, T. (1791–1792). *Rights of Man.* Retrieved October 4, 2005, from http://odur .let.rug.nl/~usa/D/1776–1800/paine/ROM/rofm04.htm

Parks, J. B., & Roberton, M. A. (2004). Attitudes toward women mediate the gender effect on attitudes toward sexist language. *Psychology of Women Quarterly, 28*, 233–239.

Pratto, F., Hegarty, P., Lemieux, A., & Glasford, D. (2005). *Why Whites are (perceived to be) normal.* Unpublished manuscript, University of Connecticut.

Pratto, F., Korchmaros, J., & Hegarty, P. (2007). When race and gender go without saying. *Social Cognition, 25*, (pp. 241–247).

Robinson, E., & Hegarty, P. (in press). Premise-based category norms and the explanation of age differences. *New Review of Social Psychology.*

Roese, N. J. (1997). Counterfactual thinking. *Psychological Bulletin, 121*, 133–148.

Roese, N. J., & Olson, J. (Eds.) (1995). *What might have been: The social psychology of counterfactual thinking.* (pp. 57–79). Hillsdale, NJ: Lawrence Erlbaum.

Rosch, E., & Mervis, G. (1975). Family resemblances: Studies in the internal structure of categories. *Cognitive Psychology, 7,* 573–605.

Rose, S. (2000). Heterosexism and the study of women's romantic and friend relationships. *Journal of Social Issues, 56,* 315–328.

Rothbart, M., Sriram, N., & Davis-Stitt, C. (1996). The retrieval of typical and atypical category members. *Journal of Experimental Social Psychology, 32,* 309–336.

Rotundo, M., Nguyen, D. H., & Sackett, P. R. (2001). A meta-analytic review of gender differences in perceptions of sexual harassment. *Journal of Applied Psychology, 86,* 914–922.

Sidanius, J., Feshbach, S., Levin, S., & Pratto, F. (1997). The interface between ethnic and national attachment: Ethnic pluralism or ethnic dominance? *Public Opinion Quarterly, 61,* 102–133.

Sidanius, J., & Pratto, F. (1999). *Social dominance: A theory of hierarchy and oppression.* NY: Cambridge.

Sloman, S. A. (1993). Feature-based induction. *Cognitive Psychology, 25,* 231–280.

Smith, E. E., & Zárate, M. A. (1992). Exemplar-based model of social judgment. *Psychological Review, 99,* 3–21.

Srull, T. K., Lichtenstein, M., & Rothbart, M. (1985). Associative storage and retrieval processes in person memory. *Journal of Experimental Psychology: Learning, Memory and Cognition, 11,* 316–345.

Swim, J. K., Mallett, R., & Stangor, C. (2004). Understanding subtle sexism: Detection and use of sexist language. *Sex Roles, 51,* 117–128.

Tropp, L. R. Stout, A. M., Boatswain, A., Wright, S. C., & Pettigrew, T. F. (2006). Trust and acceptance in response to references to group membership: Minority and majority perspectives on cross-group interactions. *Journal of Applied Social Psychology, 36,* 769–794.

Waldo, C. (1999). Working in a majority context; A structural model of heterosexism as minority stress in the workplace. *Journal of Counseling Psychology, 46,* 218–232.

Warner, M. (Ed.). (1993). *Fear of a queer planet.* St. Paul: University of Minnesota Press.

Wilkinson, S., & Kitzinger, C. C. (1993). *Heterosexuality: A feminism and psychology reader.* London: Sage.

Yzerbyt, V., Rocher, S., & Schadron, G. (1997). Stereotypes as explanations: A subjective essentialistic view of group perception. In R. Spears, P. J. Oakes, N. Ellemers, & S. A. Haslam (Eds.), *The social psychology of stereotyping and group life* (pp. 20–50). Cambridge, England: Blackwell.

Zárate, M., & Smith, E. E. (1990). Person categorization and stereotyping. *Social Cognition, 8,* 161–185.

Part 5

IDENTITY, SELF-REGULATION, AND STEREOTYPING

Kernel of Truth or Motivated Stereotype?: Interpreting and Responding to Negative Generalizations About Your Group

Matthew J. Hornsey
University of Queensland, Australia

When—and to what extent—should we be upset by those who stereotype? Ever since the early theorizing on stereotyping (e.g., Allport, 1954; Lippman, 1922), there has been a growing acknowledgment that stereotyping is natural, inevitable, and perhaps even functional. The world is a complex place, and it is unreasonable to expect that people could hold all that complexity in their minds when thinking about social categories. If we did not simplify or chunk the social world, it is quite possible that we would feel overwhelmed and disoriented by the constant stream of information, as we struggled to navigate our way through all the buzzing, teeming complexity. So we rely instead on sketchy stereotypes, which might not be totally accurate or nuanced, but at least will give us a basic blueprint to understand and predict the world we live in.

These already simplified images then become more simplified when we face the linguistic constraints associated with *communicating* our attitude. We only have a limited number of words to utilize, and we only have limited capacity to string these words together in ways that reflect our thoughts and feelings. No wonder, then, that when we hear people talk about social groups, we sometimes cringe because the attitudes seem crude, simplified, and overly generalized. But this perspective on stereotyping is a relatively forgiving perspective, because it paints a picture of humans as small and limited, trying to get by in a world of near-infinite complexity. Stereotyping might never be desirable or optimal, but it is hard to feel anger and judgment towards people who hold stereotypes because of genuine cognitive constraints. Furthermore, it is possible to argue that many of these crude generalizations at least approximate reality, in the sense that some stereotypes carry with them a kernel of truth (Lee, Jussim, & McCauley, 1995). If this is the case, stereotypes might occasionally carry with them important and diagnostic information.

It is much easier to feel anger and to be judgmental when you suspect that stereotypes are motivated. Some stereotypes are outcomes of the fact that humans have a talent for preserving and prosecuting their interests at the expense of others. Rather than using stereotypes as a roadmap to understand the world, there are cases where stereotypes are used in an active way to preserve power differences, to protect the status quo, to make people feel better about themselves, or to demoralize those who threaten them (Chen & Tyler, 2001; Jost & Banaji, 1994; Pratto, Sidanius, Stallworth, & Malle, 1994; Sidanius, 1993). For example, men might be motivated to nurture a stereotype of women as unambitious, overly emotional, and liable to crack under pressure, not because their experience tells them that this is true, but because it helps legitimize the fact that men have disproportionate representation in company boardrooms. Slave owners might have been motivated to believe that Africans are intellectually and morally inferior because this helped legitimize the illegitimate power they held. We judge people who hold stereotypes such as these because we see their behavior as being an overt expression of prejudice, a destructive type of cunning. Even when the content of stereotypes might be ostensibly positive (e.g., women are pure and delicate; Blacks have great rhythm), we can feel anger if we sense that these stereotypes are coded ways of reinforcing institutional power or distracting attention from more status-relevant qualities (e.g., Glick & Fiske, 2001). In short, the assumed motives behind a stereotype might be more predictive of people's emotional response than the valence of the stereotype itself.

Let us consider, now, a situation in which somebody makes the following statement: "Australians tend to be relatively uncultured." This statement fulfills most of the criteria for a stereotype: It is a simplified but widely shared generalization about a social group. But, as an Australian, how negatively should I feel about this speaker? Below, I argue that the most powerful predictor of how people feel about comments such as these is the assumed motives behind the comments. Are the comments a simplified reflection of the speaker's experience or are they manufactured attitudes designed to prosecute another agenda? Is criticism intended to provoke debate and to be a catalyst for positive change, or is it, in the words of U.S. editor M. L. Mencken, "prejudice made plausible"? I go on to discuss the heuristics that people use to make such decisions, the intuitive rules of thumb that people use to judge what is going on in the hearts and minds of those who make generalizations about others. As we shall see, whether people label a criticism as an honest attitude or as a cruel stereotype depends largely on an interplay between identity issues and the way people use language to frame their message. Before reviewing the evidence surrounding this argument, however, it is worth pausing to reflect on why such a research question is important.

THE PROS AND CONS OF MAKING NEGATIVE GENERALIZATIONS ABOUT A GROUP

I have met people who hold the view that we should avoid making generalizations about any group, particularly when the expressed attitudes are negative. In reality, however, it is sometimes functional for groups to be criticized. If aspects of a group's culture are suboptimal, destructive, or abusive, pointing these qualities out provides a signpost for reform and positive change. So if Australians are, in fact, less cultured than they could be (in other words, if the stereotype contains a kernel of truth), then pointing this out might play a useful function in the long run because it can suggest ways that Australia could become a better place. Indeed, a lack of criticism, or an overemphasis on harmony, can lead to suboptimal and unimaginative decision making (Hornsey, 2006; Janis, 1982; Nemeth, 1985; Postmes, Spears, & Cihangir, 2001). Finally, there are times when people might feel a moral imperative to criticize a group. For example, if a nation is violating international standards of human rights, or environmental responsibility, or military conduct, many people expect that grievances be aired and that pressures be brought to bear against these countries. The process of activism and protest is largely a process of controlled, strategic, and constructive criticism of groups.

Having said that, negative generalizations about a group are not always constructive, but rather can reflect a mean and abusive agenda. Sometimes people criticize groups out of spite or revenge, or they do it to perpetuate prejudices, stir up hatred, score points, or legitimize the disproportionate power and status of their own group (a motivated stereotype). If people perceive destructive motives behind the criticisms, such comments might lead to anger, denial, and an inflammation of tensions. In short, depending on the assumed motives behind the comments, criticisms can either be catalysts for reform, or the exact opposite. But if people have destructive motives for their comments, they are unlikely to admit it; instead, people have to make educated guesses about speakers' motives. The question then becomes, "Under what circumstances are people likely to attribute constructive as opposed to destructive motives to a negative generalization about their group?"

GROUP MEMBERSHIP AND ASSUMPTIONS ABOUT MOTIVE

One piece of information people might rely on when making assumptions about motive is the group membership of the speaker. There is now a convergence of evidence that group membership is a heuristic that helps tell us who can be trusted and who cannot. This argument is most often attributed to Brewer (1981), who argued that "as a consequence of shifting from the personal to the social group level of identity, the individual can adopt a sort of 'depersonalized trust' based on category membership alone. Within categories the probability of reciprocity is assumed, a priori, to be high, while between categories it is presumed to be low" (1981, p. 356). Consistent with this, research on the Prisoner's Dilemma consistently shows that people cooperate more readily with in-group than with out-group members (Brewer & Kramer, 1986; Kramer & Brewer, 1984; Van Vugt & de Cremer, 1999). Yamagishi and Kiyonari (2000) went on to argue that it is the assumption of reciprocity among in-group members—rather than in-group membership, per se—that drives this effect, but regardless of the underlying mechanism, the conclusion is the same: We look out for in-group members and we expect that they will look out for us (see also Tanis & Postmes, 2005). This general conclusion is reinforced by research on leadership. In cases where a group has a leader that is aligned to a subgroup or faction, there tends to be an understanding among group members that the leader will favor or "look out for" the subgroup to which they are aligned (e.g., Duck & Fielding, 2003; Jetten, Duck, Terry, & O'Brien, 2002; Platow, Hoar, Reid, Harley, & Morrison, 1997).

When it comes to out-groups, it seems that the reverse is true; that we view their actions and motives through a lens of suspicion and mistrust (Worchel, 1979). Research on the minimal group paradigm—in which participants are categorized into groups on the basis of random or trivial criteria and asked to allocate points to members of each group—shows that people expect out-groups to discriminate against them (Vivian & Berkowitz, 1992) and that their own acts of discrimination partly represent a preemptive strike against the discrimination they anticipate from others (Locksley, Ortiz, & Hepburn, 1980; Vivian & Berkowitz, 1993). Parallel research on small group processes suggests that group members expect out-groups to have a competitive mindset, and that their own lack of cooperativeness in intergroup contexts reflects a defensive withdrawal from the expected aggression of the out-group (Insko, Schopler, Hoyle, Dardis, & Graetz, 1990).

Although much of this research has been conducted on minimal or ad hoc groups, there is ample evidence from more real-world contexts that leads to the same conclusion. For example, on the basis of interviews conducted during the Cold War, Bronfenbrenner (1961) postulated that protagonists in intergroup conflicts frequently have identical assumptions about their enemy ("mirror images"). One of these assumption is that *they* cannot be trusted, meaning that neutral or even conciliatory messages can be interpreted as covert messages of hostility. This suspicion of out-group motives can obviously place severe impediments in the way of the process of conflict resolution. As an example of this, Maoz, Ward, Katz, and Ross (2002) presented Jews and Arabs with a peace proposal and told them that the proposal was put forward either by Israeli or by Palestinian authorities. When participants were led to believe that the proposal had been designed by their own side, they perceived the plan to be relatively balanced and fair. When the plan was attributed to the "enemy," however, they viewed the plan to be heavily stacked against them. A similar finding emerged in the context of Muslim-Christian conflict in Indonesia (Ariyanto, Hornsey, & Gallois, in press). Muslim and Christian participants read a neutral article describing high-level, inter-religious conflict. When the article was attributed to a Christian newspaper, Muslims (but not Christians) perceived the article to be biased against Muslims. In contrast, when the same article was attributed to a Muslim newspaper, participants perceived the article to be biased against Christians. In short, participants seemed to be operating from the assumption that the out-group would be working to prosecute their own interests, and this biased assumption taints how they perceive messages.

NEGATIVE GENERALIZATIONS ABOUT GROUPS AND THE INTERGROUP SENSITIVITY EFFECT

The research reviewed above helps frame some clear predictions regarding how negative generalizations about a group might be received. If Australians hear a speaker say "Australians tend to be relatively uncultured," they might be taking into account two quite distinct factors. On one hand, they would presumably reflect on their own experience of Australia and Australians before making a response. In addition, however, I argue that the recipient would be very aware of the group membership of the speaker. If the comments were made by another Australian, then the recipient of the message might attribute the message to relatively constructive motives. Working from the assumption that in-group members typically work in the best interests of their own group, the receiver might interpret the comments as a well-meaning attempt to shine light on shortcomings within the group, with an eye to improving it in the future. The receiver might feel threatened by the message, and they still might judge the comment as being inaccurate depending on experience, but it is unlikely that the receiver will feel overt hostility toward the speaker or their comments because they have judged their motives to be relatively pure.

In contrast, the very same comments from a non-Australian might be perceived through a different attributional lens. If we are to accept that people are prone to read messages from out-group members as hostile and competitive, then it seems reasonable to expect that people might find a reason to dismiss the comments as part of an ongoing contest for intergroup supremacy. Rather than reflecting a genuine attitude, then, the criticism might be seen as a motivated stereotype. The result would be heightened levels of emotional negativity toward the comments and the speaker, and a general reluctance to accept any kernel of truth within the comments.

The paradigm used for testing this question is very simple. Participants receive what they believe is an extract from an interview with somebody who makes a number of criticisms of the participants' in-group. For example, Australians might be criticized for being anti-Asian, racist toward Aborigines, and uncultured. Maths-science participants might be criticized as being arrogant, conformist, and as having a weak sense of social conscience. The comments are then attributed either to an in-group member or to an out-group member. Finally, participants record what they think and feel about the speaker and their comments. This type of experiment has been conducted a number of times in recent years, and a range of conclusions can now be drawn from them.

1. Out-group criticisms arouse more defensiveness than in-group criticisms. The most newsworthy conclusion of these studies is that group membership has a profound effect on how people respond to criticism. When criticisms are attributed to an in-group member, people are more likely to agree with the comments and feel less negativity toward both the speaker and their comments, than if the very same comments are made by an outsider. In other words, when deciding whether to accept or reject group criticism, people do not just focus on the message but the *source* of the message. Criticisms that can seem reasonable and uncontroversial in the mouth of an insider can be rejected as being offensive and untrue when spoken by an outsider. This basic phenomenon has been dubbed the *intergroup sensitivity effect*.

2. The intergroup sensitivity effect is both large and robust. The tendency for in-group critics to arouse less defensiveness than out-group critics is not specific to any particular population or sociohistorical circumstance. It has been observed in relation to criticisms of Australia (Hornsey, Oppes, & Svensson, 2002; Hornsey & Imani, 2004; Hornsey, Trembath, & Gunthorpe, 2004), schools (O'Dwyer, Berkowitz, & Alfeld-Johnson, 2002), university students (Elder, Sutton, & Douglas, 2005; Hornsey et al., 2002), maths-science students (Hornsey et al., 2002), social science students (Hornsey, de Bruijn, Creed, Allen, Ariyanto, & Svensson, 2005), Queenslanders (members of a state in Australia; Hornsey et al., 2005), allied health professionals (Hornsey, Grice, Jetten, Paulsen, & Callan, in press), and Muslims (Ariyanto, Hornsey, & Gallois, 2006). It has been demonstrated in samples from Australia (e.g., Hornsey & Imani, 2004), Indonesia (Ariyanto et al., 2006), the United Kingdom (Elder et al., 2005), and the United States (O'Dwyer et al., 2002). Finally, it is not a weak or subtle effect. Typically, the effect of group membership has a double-digit effect size, and on occasions, the effect of group membership is enormous. For example, when maths-science students were criticized by other maths-science students, the median agreement score was 5 on a 7-point scale. When the same comments were made by a social-science student, the median agreement rating was 2 (Hornsey et al., 2002, Exp. 2). Similarly, when faced with criticisms of Australia, Hornsey and Imani (2004, Exp. 1) showed that median ratings of agreement ranged from 5 when the comments were made by another Australian, to 1.5 when the comments were made by a non-Australian. In short, depending on who is making the comments, responses to criticisms can range from cautious acceptance to outright denial.

3. The effects of group membership do not apply to praise.   On three occasions (Hornsey et al., 2002, Exp. 1a and Exp. 1b; Hornsey & Imani, 2004, Exp. 1), the experimental design allowed for comparisons to be made between how people respond to negative and positive generalizations about their group. These studies showed quite conclusively that the relative generosity extended to in-group speakers did not apply when speakers praised the group. In other words, the intergroup sensitivity effect was specific to criticisms. This is important because it suggests that the intergroup sensitivity effect is not simply another demonstration of the already established tendency for in-group members to be more persuasive than out-group members (Mackie, Worth, & Asuncion, 1990; Turner, 1991). Rather, there seems to be something specific about criticisms that opens up an intergroup bias.

4. The intergroup sensitivity effect is mediated by attributions of motive.   Earlier, I have argued that attributions of motive can be pivotal in predicting how people think and feel in response to critical generalizations made about the group. Consistent with this, there is now ample evidence that attributions of motive underpin the intergroup sensitivity effect. When participants rate how constructive the comments were intended to be, attributions of constructiveness are typically much stronger when in-group members make the comments than when out-group members make the comments. Furthermore, this intergroup bias in attribution of motive fully mediates the intergroup sensitivity effect (Hornsey & Imani, 2004; Hornsey et al., 2004). The importance of attributions is brought into focus also by experimental studies in which participants are given reason to doubt the motives of the in-group critic. As might be predicted by the attributional account, the relative tolerance toward in-group critics is eliminated when participants have reason to doubt the ongoing commitment of the critic to the group, either because they are a low identifier (Hornsey et al., 2004) or because they are a newcomer to the group (Hornsey, Grice et al., in press). In other words, in the absence of any other information, participants assume that in-group critics are committed to the group and are making their comments with the best interests of the group at heart. If this assumption is called into question, however, then in-group critics arouse just as much defensiveness as outsiders.

OVERCOMING THE INTERGROUP
SENSITIVITY EFFECT: WHAT DOES NOT WORK

Although there are many situations in which it is functional and important that people be suspicious of the underlying motives behind the rhetoric of outsiders, one wonders what hope there is for the outsider whose motives are pure. As argued above, there are times when it is not only acceptable for outsiders to criticize a group culture, it might be morally imperative; however, research on the intergroup sensitivity effect shows that outsiders will face an uphill battle to initiate change. Indeed, rather than promoting change, it is possible that criticisms from outsiders will inhibit change as the group withdraws into a state of denial about problems that it might otherwise be prepared to acknowledge. What, then, can outsiders do if they have a genuine commitment to promote positive change in a group or culture to which they do not belong?

Research designed to answer this question throws up some surprises. Some conditions which one might expect to overcome defensiveness—both on the basis of literature on persuasion and on the basis of intuition—do not seem to work. For example, it could be that the mere process of generalizing might be generating some of the negativity observed in the face of criticism. Consistent with this possibility, Mae and Carlston (2005) found that speakers who made generalizations about other groups—even positive generalizations—were seen as relatively unlikable. Indeed, it is possible that out-group members might be downgraded particularly strongly on this basis. If an Australian were to say "Australians tend to be relatively uncultured," other Australians would assume that this person is aware of the great variability that exists within the country. We tend to have a relatively nuanced appreciation of the variability that exists within our groups, partly because we have more experience with members of our in-groups (Linville, Fischer, & Salovey, 1989), and partly because we know at least one exemplar of the group (ourselves) very well (Park, Judd, & Ryan, 1991). In contrast, people have a tendency to homogenize out-groups (Ostrom & Sedikides, 1992), and people are intuitively aware of this phenomenon (Judd, Park, Yzerbyt, Gordijn, & Muller, 2005). Thus, it could be that when we receive criticism from outsiders, part of our discomfort stems from our assumption that the outsider is overgeneralizing their comments. This potentially adds another stratum of threat to the situation because not only are the comments a criticism of the group, but they are also an implied criticism of you as an individual. So even if we see some kernel of truth to the comments, it could be that we feel the need to protest "But we're not *all* like that!"

If this were the case, it could be that critics could defuse negativity about their comments merely by qualifying them. By acknowledging that the comments are relevant only for some members of the group, it might alleviate some of the defensiveness people feel. To test this, Hornsey, Robson, Smith, Esposo, and Sutton (2006) showed Australians criticisms of Australia as being racist toward Aborigines and intolerant of Asians, comments which were attributed either to another Australian or to a foreigner. In some conditions the comments were unqualified. In other conditions the speakers added qualifying language. For example, they prefaced the criticisms with the words "Some Australians . . .," and at the end of their statement they added the rider "Of course, not all Australians are like that, but many are." The results showed that, although the manipulation was internalized by participants (they believed the speaker was intending their comments to apply to a smaller percentage of Australians when they qualified) the qualifying language did not help at all to reduce defensiveness. Regardless of whether they qualified their criticism or not, out-group critics aroused much stronger defensiveness than in-group critics.

Another possible option for out-group members might be to work to prove they have sufficient experience with the group to justify their criticisms. One handicap that outsiders typically face is that they do not have the level of expertise that insiders have about the group and its culture. As a result, it is remarkably easy to dismiss criticism from outsiders as grounded in ignorance, secondhand insight, or prejudice. But what if out-group members could demonstrate that they have a level of experience with the group that is comparable to that of in-group members? If perceptions of epistemic authority underpin responses to negative generalizations about a group, out-group members need only equip themselves with the relevant expertise to overcome the intergroup sensitivity effect.

Hornsey and Imani (2004) investigated this by having Australians read criticisms of their country stemming either from another Australian or from somebody from overseas. Across three experiments, Hornsey and Imani incorporated conditions in which the out-group critic could be considered to have extraordinary levels of expertise with Australia. In Experiment 1, one of the out-group critics had spent all their life in Australia, but had recently left and taken out citizenship overseas. In Experiment 2, one of the out-group critics had been born overseas but had spent several years living and working in Australia. In Experiment 3, one of the out-group critics had been born overseas but had moved to Australia as an infant; despite living all their lives in Australia they were citizens of another country and still self-categorized as a citizen of that country. The key finding was that in all of these experiments, the experienced outsider aroused just as much defensiveness as an outsider who had never set foot in Australia. Regardless of their levels of experience, outsiders aroused more defensiveness than insiders, an effect mediated by attributions of constructiveness. In short, knowing what you were talking about appeared to be no defense against the heightened level of defensiveness faced by outsiders.

Another intuitive method of overcoming defensiveness is to seek safety in numbers. One outsider who criticizes a group can be easily discounted, but several outsiders who independently come to the same conclusion might be more persuasive. Indeed, research on persuasion and social influence has consistently shown that influence is greater the larger the number of change-agents (Latane, 1981), although the relationship between group size and influence begins to plateau when the group reaches about three or four (e.g., Rosenberg, 1961; Stang, 1976). If outsiders can overcome defensiveness by demonstrating that their views are shared by many, this would suggest that intergroup criticisms are better delivered by committees or groups of concerned individuals rather than by lone critics.

To test this, Esposo and Hornsey (2006) had people read criticisms of Australia stemming from either Australians or non-Australians. Furthermore, the criticisms were either delivered by individuals, by three independent individuals who happened to have similar comments about Australia, or by three people in a committee who were asked to formulate their perceptions of Australia and Australians. When the criticisms were read by non-Australians (i.e., by international students), the classic social impact finding emerged; participants were more likely to agree with the comments and expressed less negativity toward the comments when they came from groups of three than when they came from an individual. However, when the participants were Australians, the size of the source had no effect at all. Non-Australians aroused more defensiveness than Australians, and it did not matter whether the criticisms were delivered by individuals or by multiple sources. When it came to criticism, size did not matter.

The results summarized above suggest that it is difficult to translate findings from traditional persuasion studies into the arena of group criticism. The notions that (a) experienced (or credible) people are more persuasive and (b) groups are more persuasive than individuals comprise two of the most reliable findings in the literature on persuasion, and yet neither variables proved to be useful in predicting responses to negative generalizations about ingroups. Perhaps this is not surprising, given that much of the persuasion literature is based on issues that are mostly neutral and lack a great deal of ego-involvement (e.g., judgments of line lengths, or attitudes toward recycling, legalization of marijuana, sex education, bicycle paths). These issues are qualitatively distinct from group directed criticisms, in which an important aspect of one's social self is being directly challenged and downgraded. Whereas the former type of persuasion might be more likely to activate cold, cognitive considerations about the integrity of the message, criticisms are more likely to involve "hot," emotional processing wrapped in issues of trust. As such, qualitatively different solutions need to be found to the question, "How can we get a critical message across?"

USING LANGUAGE TO OVERCOME
THE INTERGROUP SENSITIVITY EFFECT

If we are to take seriously the notion that the intergroup sensitivity effect is grounded in attributions of motive, then strategies to overcome defensiveness would need to directly address this attributional bias. In short, outsiders would need to demonstrate that they care about the group that they are criticizing, and that they are making the comments with the best interests of the group at heart. This could be why previous attempts to erase the intergroup sensitivity effect had failed. Demonstrating experience with the group or demonstrating that one's views are shared by many do not respond to the central issue of trust that appears to underpin the effect. But how can outsiders convince a skeptical audience that they care about the group at the same time as they are criticizing it?

One possibility is that outsiders could tailor their rhetoric so as to make a bid for insider status. This might be particularly useful for people who lie on the cusp of being an in-group or out-group member. For example, the in-group/out-group status of many immigrants is not clear. An Asian Australian is an out-group member in terms of ethnicity to Anglo-Australians, and might also have dual citizenship, meaning that their national identity is ambiguous. For these people, whether they are regarded as an in-group or an out-group member might depend largely on how they frame their language. Consider, for example, the difference between an Asian Australian saying "Australians, *they* have a problem with Asians" and "Australians, *we* have a problem with Asians". In the former case, the critic is locating him- or herself as an out-group member, peering in on the group and casting judgment. In the latter case the critic is self-categorizing as an in-group member, suggesting ongoing commitment and loyalty to the group. Note that the two sentences are identical in terms of the content of the criticism, but the simple change in the use of pronouns results in a very different statement in terms of signifying the underlying thoughts and emotions of the speaker.

To examine this strategy, Hornsey et al. (2004, Exp. 2) showed Anglo-Australians what they believed was an extract from an interview, in which the speaker criticized Australians for having anti-Asian attitudes. The group membership of the speaker was manipulated such that they were either unambiguously in-group (an Anglo-Australian) or their in-group status was more ambiguous (an Asian Australian). In some conditions, the speaker used inclusive, identity-embracing language (e.g., *we, our*), whereas in the other conditions, the speaker used exclusive, identity-distancing language (e.g., *they, their*). Results showed that, in terms of predicting how participants felt about the speaker and the speaker's comments, the language used was far more important than the group membership of the speaker, per se. When Asian Australians made a bid for insider status by using inclusive language, they were received in just as open-minded fashion as if they had been an Anglo-Australian. Furthermore, path analysis suggested a causal pattern that is consistent with the assumed role of trust and attributions. Those who used inclusive language were seen to be more attached to their Australian identity, which led to more constructive attributions of motive, which in turn led to lower levels of negativity toward the speaker and their comments.

It should be noted, however, that this strategy is really only available to out-groups that share a coherent, well-defined identity at the superordinate level. In the case of Asian Australians and Anglo-Australians, there is a tight, meaningful fit between these groups and their shared superordinate identity (Australia). But this is not always going to be the case. It is difficult to see, for example, what superordinate identity Americans and Iraqis share, or homosexuals and heterosexuals. In this case, attempts to locate oneself at a shared superordinate level would require one to invoke notions of humanity, which might be too abstract to imply true in-group membership. Thus, thought needs to be given to generating other strategies that out-group members can use to dispel the perception that they have sinister motives.

One alternative way for out-group critics to minimize distrust with regard to their motives might be to include praise along with the criticism; praise might send out the message that the outsider *does* care, and that they *are* trying to be constructive. One potential problem with "buttering up," however, is that the strategy might be seen by a skeptical in-group audience as a transparent attempt to win favor. Furthermore, it could be that people cognitively focus on the more threatening, negative feedback and do not process the positive feedback as carefully.

To test whether praise can help buffer the negative effects of criticism, Hornsey et al. (2006) had Australians read negative comments about Australia, stemming either from another Australian or from a foreigner. In some conditions, the criticisms were made in the absence of praise, whereas in the other conditions, they contextualized their criticisms with praise; that Australians were well educated, friendly, warm, and could see the funny side to things. Overall, the results showed that critics who praised were seen to be much more likable than those who did not, and participants were somewhat more likely to agree with the criticisms when they were attached to praise. It should be noted that the positive effects of praise applied equally to in-group and out-group members, and that the size of the effect of praise was considerably weaker than the size of the effect of group membership. Furthermore, praise did not have an effect on ratings of how negatively participants felt about the comments. However, the general conclusion that can be drawn from the data is that praise helps. Furthermore, the positive effects of praise were driven by attributions of motive, just as the model predicts. People who used praise were seen to have more constructive motives for their criticisms than those who did not, and it was this that resulted in increased acceptance of the criticisms.

Another rhetorical strategy that outsiders might use to defuse suspicion about motive is to acknowledge the failings of their own group as well as the target group. If the critic acknowledges their own group's shortcomings (e.g., "we *also* are racist"), it might help ease the in-group members' suspicions that the comments are made in an attempt to establish intergroup supremacy, and so the members of the criticized group might be less likely to attribute the comments to competitive motives. To test this, Hornsey et al. (2006) again exposed Australians to criticism of their country. These criticisms stemmed from either (a) another Australian, (b) a foreigner who did not mention their own country, or (c) a foreigner who acknowledged that their own group shared some of the failings they had accused Australians of possessing. Consistent with expectations, an intergroup sensitivity effect emerged, such that the foreign critic aroused more defensiveness than the Australian; however, this intergroup sensitivity effect was erased when the foreigner acknowledged problems within the foreigner's own country. Again, attributions of constructiveness were central in driving this effect; specifically, the outsider who used acknowledgement received a more generous response because they were seen to be motivated by more constructive reasons than the critic who did not acknowledge.

As always, caution should be exercised when generalizing these results across cultures. Research suggesting that the intergroup sensitivity effect is driven by attributions about the motives of the critic has been conducted exclusively in individualist cultures; however, there is reason to believe that this attributional explanation—which prioritizes the motives and conscience of the individual agent—might not be applicable to Japan, for example, where attributions of responsibility tend to be more socially negotiated (Hamilton & Hagiwara, 1992). A priority for future research is to examine whether the rhetorical strategies described above—rooted as they are in changing attributions of intent—are universally effective or culturally specific.

COMMUNICATING DEFENSIVENESS: THE RECEIVER'S RHETORICAL STRATEGIES

The research described above has given us some insight into how critics can strategically tailor their rhetoric to reduce defensiveness in the face of negative generalizations about a group. To fully understand the psychology of group criticism, however, one must not focus exclusively on the messengers' strategic behaviors; it is also important to think about the strategic rhetoric of the *recipients* of group criticism. To date, most research has focused on examining how people think and feel after receiving criticism of their groups, but it is also important to focus on what people say and do. One reason for this is that we are social and strategic creatures, who learn from an early age to manage our impression of ourselves in order to maximize social advantage (Baumeister, 1982). On occasions, we might find ourselves suppressing attitudes that we feel will alienate ourselves from important others (Reicher & Levine, 1994), or we might even articulate attitudes that are totally inconsistent with our attitudes simply to get along, to get ahead, or to be liked (Asch, 1951; Deutsch & Gerard, 1955). So even if it is true that people *feel* more defensive in the face of out-group critics relative to in-group critics, this is not to say that people will *express* more defensiveness in the face of out-group critics relative to in-group critics.

Intuitively, one can imagine situations in which the disconnection between what one thinks and what one says in response to criticism might be particularly dramatic. For example, if a coach of a football team criticizes the members of the team, it could be that the members would experience resentment or anger. But it is unlikely that they would express that resentment or anger, because they are aware that the coach has power over them and their futures.

The implication is that powerful individuals need not win over genuine support for their criticisms in order to extract behavioral concessions.

Brander and Hornsey (2006) found circumstantial evidence of this process in relation to the war in Iraq. In the weeks leading up to the declaration of war in Iraq, they showed Australians what they believed was an extract from an interview with somebody who criticized Australians for not being supportive enough of the war effort. In some conditions, the criticisms were made by an Australian, and in some conditions they were made by a U.S. citizen. They found that when the criticisms stemmed from a U.S. citizen, participants felt more negatively about the war after receiving the criticism than before, a result that might be expected on the basis of the intergroup sensitivity effect; however, they also expressed less of a desire to protest against the war after being criticized by a U.S. citizen than before the criticism. In other words, after receiving criticism from a US citizen, Australians rebelled in their minds but conformed to the out-group's expectations in terms of behavioral intentions. Although the specific mechanisms underpinning this effect were not established, it is reasonable to assume that Australians felt reluctant to defy the criticism behaviorally because they are aware that the out-group in this case has a great deal of military and economic power over the in-group.

There are other situations where one might expect the opposite effect; that is, people might feel the need to present themselves as being more defensive in the face of criticism than they feel in reality. Imagine, for example, that you are in a committee meeting, and a colleague of yours makes negative comments about the culture of the workplace. In response to the criticism, the boss calls on everyone else to say what they think, and it is your turn to speak. What do you say? In this case, your response is likely to be guided not just by whether you think the critic is right or not, but also by what you think is the most strategically advantageous thing for you to say in front of the important in-group audience (Jetten, Hornsey, & Adarves-Yorno, 2006; Noel, Wann, & Branscombe, 1995). You might be tempted to publicly express negativity toward the critic even if privately you are thinking "They're right; I'm glad they said that."

To examine this, Hornsey, Frederiks, Smith, and Ford (in press) showed participants criticism of their group from either in-group or out-group speakers. Participants were either given standard reassurances about confidentiality and anonymity (the private condition), or they were told that their responses would be made visible to a group of Australians (the public condition). In the private condition, a standard intergroup sensitivity emerged. However, when participants felt their responses would be made public, expressions of defensiveness toward the in-group critic were heightened, to the point that the intergroup sensitivity effect disappeared. A subsequent study showed that this tendency emerged only when the in-group audience was relatively high status, providing further evidence that the effect is a result of strategic considerations. In short, people are reluctant to endorse criticisms when their responses are visible to important in-group members. This might help explain why in organizations, management are frequently not informed of suboptimal aspects of the organization's culture and practices (Morrison & Milliken, 2000). It might also help explain why people express somewhat more criticisms of out-groups than of in-groups, even when they acknowledge that the former type of criticism is relatively nonnormative (Sutton, Elder, & Douglas, 2006).

In short, the results suggest that when it comes to group criticism, people's public and private views can shear apart. Listening to what people say in response to criticism might give one a misleading or incomplete guide as to what people are really thinking. There are two worlds—the internal one and the one that is projected through language to the world—and to understand the psychology of group criticism one needs to carefully disentangle the two.

A QUICK NOTE ON THE ROLE OF NORMS AND RULES

In Fig. 14–1, I summarize the attributional and strategic considerations associated with predicting responses to group criticism. Readers will note, however, that a third set of considerations have been included in the model, a set of considerations that surround the rules or norms associated with the timing and delivery of criticism. This path of inquiry is still in its infancy, although Sutton and colleagues (2006) have made good progress recently in marking this territory (see chapter in this volume).

Life is replete with common wisdoms and aphorisms about the "correct" timing and delivery of criticism, and violations of these rules are likely to arouse negativity independent of the attributional and strategic considerations summarized earlier (Hornsey, 2005). One of these rules is to "never air your dirty laundry," or in other words, to keep criticism of your group "in-house." Consistent with this notion, it has been shown that making critical comments directly to an outgroup audience is seen to be less appropriate, and in some cases has been shown to arouse more negativity, than when comments are made to an in-group audience (Ariyanto et al., 2006; Hornsey et al., 2005; Elder et al., 2005).

Another rule that is often invoked is that people should hold off criticizing their group in times of extreme intergroup conflict, such as in times of war. For some, the "united we stand" mantra or "criticism is irresponsible right now" rule is a sensible precaution against emboldening the enemy and endangering the fortunes of one's own group members. For others, it is a way of stifling debate and entrenching the power of the presiding leadership hierarchy. Regardless, there is some evidence that violations of the rule do have consequences. Ariyanto and Hornsey (2006), for example, exposed Muslims to negative generalizations about their religion (that they are fanatical and intolerant). They read these comments either after having read a newspaper article on football, or a newspaper article describing intense inter-religious conflict. After having primed the intergroup conflict, negativity toward the in-group critic increased, to the point that they aroused as much defensiveness as an

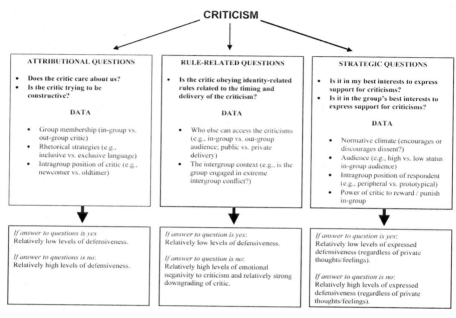

CRITICISM

ATTRIBUTIONAL QUESTIONS	RULE-RELATED QUESTIONS	STRATEGIC QUESTIONS
• **Does the critic care about us?** • **Is the critic trying to be constructive?**	• **Is the critic obeying identity-related rules related to the timing and delivery of the criticism?**	• **Is it in my best interests to express support for criticisms?** • **Is it in the group's best interests to express support for criticisms?**
DATA	**DATA**	**DATA**
• Group membership (in-group vs. out-group critic) • Rhetorical strategies (e.g., inclusive vs. exclusive language) • Intragroup position of critic (e.g., newcomer vs. oldtimer)	• Who else can access the criticisms (e.g., in-group vs. out-group audience; public vs. private delivery) • The intergroup context (e.g., is the group engaged in extreme intergroup conflict?)	• Normative climate (encourages or discourages dissent?) • Audience (e.g., high vs. low status in-group audience) • Intragroup position of respondent (e.g., peripheral vs. prototypical) • Power of critic to reward / punish in-group
If answer to questions is yes Relatively low levels of defensiveness. *If answer to questions is no:* Relatively high levels of defensiveness.	*If answer to question is yes:* Relatively low levels of defensiveness. *If answer to question is no:* Relatively high levels of emotional negativity to criticism and relatively strong downgrading of critic.	*If answer to question is yes:* Relatively low levels of expressed defensiveness (regardless of private thoughts/feelings). *If answer to question is no:* Relatively high levels of expressed defensiveness (regardless of private thoughts/feelings).

FIGURE 14–1.   A model predicting responses to group-directed criticism.

out-group critic. It should be noted that, in each of the cases mentioned above, the rule violation had effects on emotional responses to the critic and their comments, but did not have an effect on the extent to which people agreed with the comments. In short, it appears that people were able to disentangle their emotional response to the rule violation from their objective recognition of whether or not the comments carried with them a kernel of truth.

Elsewhere in this volume, Sutton and colleagues argued convincingly for the existence of another rule: One should not criticize groups other than your own. They cited direct evidence for this notion, in that participants acknowledge that criticizing other groups is less appropriate than criticizing one's own group (Sutton et al., 2006, Study 3). Consistent with this, it has also been found that bystanders exhibit an intergroup sensitivity effect; British participants felt more negativity about a Canadian, for example, who criticized Australia than an Australian who made the same comments (Sutton et al., 2006, Study 1).

This research raises some interesting questions with regard to the mechanisms underpinning the intergroup sensitivity effect. For example, why should we assume that the intergroup sensitivity effect is about identity issues when bystanders display a similar pattern of responses to in-group members? Is it possible that people—regardless of group membership—are simply punishing violation of a communication rule? In other words, when outsiders criticize our groups, do we feel defensive per se (in the sense of wanting to protect a valued group identity), or do we merely feel offended by the nonnormative nature of the communication?

I should state up front that I have no data that speak directly to this question, but it is important to note that the two perspectives are not mutually exclusive. It is quite possible that intergroup criticism results in strong defensive reactions, and that recognition of this psychological process over time has crystallized into a "rule" designed to maintain intergroup harmony. If this were true, it might mean that both in-group members and third parties might exhibit an intergroup sensitivity effect, but for different reasons. Whereas third parties might feel negatively toward intergroup criticism because it is a violation of important rules designed to maintain intergroup harmony, for in-group members, the same response might be tinged with the kind of emotion and heat associated with a truly defensive response to an attack on a valued social identity. It is not possible to disentangle the two responses without digging deeper into the way these messages are processed, such as by examining whether critical messages are processed through central or peripheral routes, or by incorporating affective responses more systematically into the analysis. This is a priority for future research.

It should also be noted that research has uncovered a number of moderators of the intergroup sensitivity effect; for example, the effect disappears if the in-group critic is seen to be a weak identifier (Hornsey et al., 2004), or if the out-group critic uses language to suggest they have no ulterior motives (Hornsey, Robson et al., 2006). It is possible that there are a cluster of microrules that can be invoked to explain all of the effects that have been uncovered to date, but for now, the data seem consistent with the notion that people are scouring for information about motives, a process that is partly motivated by issues of trust wrapped up in the intergroup dynamic. It is interesting that, even for bystanders, this process seems to be at play; when British participants reported higher negativity toward foreigners as opposed to Australians criticizing Australia, this intergroup sensitivity effect was mediated by attributions of constructiveness (Sutton et al., 2006). In the absence of a great deal of firsthand information about the target of criticism, it perhaps makes sense that bystanders will also by skeptical about the motives for criticism. Research on persuasion has shown that if comments are seen to be made with vested interest, or merely to please an internal audience, the message is somewhat discounted (Eagly, Wood, & Chaiken, 1978). By the same token, when bystanders witness an intergroup criticism, it is reasonable for them to ask the same question that might preoccupy in-group members: "Why would they say that?" If they suspect ulterior (or destructive) motives, then bystanders might show a degree of resistance toward the comments. Although this experience might intellectually be identical to what in-group members go through, it remains to be seen whether the experience is equivalent in terms of the emotions and defenses engaged. Again, a greater focus on affect is imperative in future research before deeper questions can be answered about the subjective experience of receiving negative generalizations about one's group.

CONCLUSION

Considerable attention has been paid to investigating why people stereotype. In some cases, stereotypes might be internalized because people believe that they are diagnostic of real-world characteristics, or in other words, that the stereotype carries a kernel of truth. For others, it could be that people are motivated to believe a stereotype is true, despite a lack of genuine evidence, because it helps prosecute an intergroup agenda. Of course, it is vitally important to come to grips with the question of what inspires people to express stereotypical attitudes, and to investigate the extent to which stereotyping has sinister or non-sinister motives. But it is also worth keeping in mind that, when it comes to predicting how people will respond to a negative generalization about a group, the processes that *really* led to the formation of the attitude are less important than people's *assumptions* about what led to the formation of the attitude. For the receiver, perception is reality.

In this chapter, I have reviewed evidence suggesting that perceptions of what motivated a negative generalization about a group have powerful consequences, both in terms of how people feel about the speaker and in terms of the extent to which people lend credence to the message. In some cases, perceptions of motive appear to be out of the speaker's control, rooted as they are in superficial characteristics such as the group membership of the speaker. But it is not the case that out-group critics are doomed to face resistance. Through the strategic use of rhetoric and language, outsiders can go some of the way to breaking down the suspicion that is brought to bear when they make negative generalizations about a group. This process highlights one of the key themes of this book: that stereotypes do not just reside "under the skull," but emerge, take shape, and are interpreted through a dynamic process of communication and negotiation.

ACKNOWLEDGMENTS

Much of the research presented in this paper was supported by an Australian Research Council-Discovery grant.

REFERENCES

Allport, G. W. (1954). *The nature of prejudice*. Reading, MA: Addison-Wesley.
Ariyanto, A., & Hornsey, M. J. (2006). *Ingroup criticism in the context of intergroup conflict*. Manuscript submitted for publication.

Ariyanto, A., Hornsey, M. J., & Gallois, C. (in press). Group allegiances and perceptions of media bias: Taking into account both the perceiver and the source. *Group Processes & Intergroup Relations.*

Ariyanto, A., Hornsey, M. J., & Gallois, C. (2006). Group-directed criticism in Indonesia: Role of message source and audience. *Asian Journal of Social Psychology, 9,* 96–102.

Asch, S. E. (1951). Effects of group pressure upon the modification and distortion of judgements. In H. Guetzkow (Ed.), *Groups, leadership and men* (pp. 177–190). Pittsburg, PA: Carnegie Press.

Baumeister, R. R. (1982). A self-presentational view of social phenomena. *Psychological Bulletin, 91,* 3–26.

Brander, T., & Hornsey, M. J. (2006). Intergroup sensitivity effect and the war in Iraq: A case of attitudes and intentions diverging. *Australian Journal of Psychology, 58,* 166–172.

Brewer, M. B. (1981). Ethnocentrism and its role in interpersonal trust. In M. B. Brewer & B. E. Collins (Eds.), *Scientific inquiry and the social sciences* (pp. 345–360). San Francisco, CA: Jossey-Bass.

Brewer, M. B., & Kramer, R. M. (1986). Choice behavior in social dilemmas: Effects of social identity, group size, and decision framing. *Journal of Personality and Social Psychology, 50,* 543–549.

Bronfenbrenner, U. (1961). The mirror-image in Soviet-American relations. *Journal of Social Issues, 3,* 45–56.

Chen, E. S., & Tyler, T. R. (2001). Cloaking power: Legitimizing myths and the psychology of the advantaged. In A. Y. Lee-Chai & J. A. Bargh (Eds.), *The use and abuse of power: Multiple perspectives on the causes of corruption* (pp. 241–261). Philadelphia, PA: Psychology Press.

Deutsch, M., & Gerard, H. (1955). A study of normative and informational social influences upon individual judgment. *Journal of Abnormal and Social Psychology, 51,* 629–636.

Duck, J. M., & Fielding, K. S. (2003). Leaders and their treatment of subgroups: Implications for evaluations of the leader and the superordinate group. *European Journal of Social Psychology, 33,* 387–401.

Eagly, A. H., Wood, W., & Chaiken, S. (1978). Causal inferences about communicators and their effect on opinion change. *Journal of Personality and Social Psychology, 36,* 424–435.

Elder, T. J., Sutton, R. M., & Douglas, K. M. (2005). Keeping it to ourselves: Effects of audience size and composition on reactions to criticism of the in-group. *Group Processes & Intergroup Relations, 8,* 231–244.

Esposo, S., & Hornsey, M. J. (2006). *Social influence in the context of group-directed criticism: Are three critics more persuasive than one?* Manuscript in preparation.

Glick, P., & Fiske, S. T. (2001). An ambivalent alliance: Hostile and benevolent sexism as complementary justifications for gender inequality. *American Psychologist, 56,* 109–118.

Hamilton, V. L., & Hagiwara, S. (1992). Roles, responsibility, and accounts across cultures. *International Journal of Psychology, 27,* 157–179.

Hornsey, M. J. (2006). In-group critics and their influence on groups. In T. Postmes & J. Jetten (Eds.), *Individuality and the group: Advances in social identity* (pp. 74–91). London, UK: Sage.

Hornsey, M. J. (2005). Why being right is not enough: Predicting defensiveness in the face of group criticism. In W. Stroebe & M. Hewstone (Eds.), *European Review of Social Psychology* (Vol. 16, pp. 301–334). Hove, E. Sussex, England: Psychology Press.

Hornsey, M. J., de Bruijn, P., Creed, J., Allen, J., Ariyanto, A., & Svensson, A. (2005). Keeping it in-house: How audience affects responses to group criticism. *European Journal of Social Psychology, 35,* 291–312.

Hornsey, M. J., Frederiks, E., Smith, J., & Ford, L. (in press). Strategic defensiveness: Public and private responses to group criticism. *British Journal of Social Psychology.*

Hornsey, M. J., Grice, T., Jetten, J., Paulsen, N., & Callan, V. (in press). Group directed criticisms and recommendations for change: Why newcomers arouse more resistance than old-timers. *Personality and Social Psychology Bulletin.*

Hornsey, M. J., & Imani, A. (2004). Criticizing groups from the inside and the outside: An identity perspective on the intergroup sensitivity effect. *Personality and Social Psychology Bulletin, 30,* 365–383.

Hornsey, M. J., Oppes, T., & Svensson, A. (2002). "It's ok if we say it, but you can't": Responses to intergroup and intragroup criticism. *European Journal of Social Psychology, 32,* 293–307.

Hornsey, M. J., Robson, E., Smith, J., Esposo, S., & Sutton, R. (2006). *Testing the effectiveness of rhetorical strategies designed to overcome defensiveness in the face of group criticism.* Manuscript submitted for publication.

Hornsey, M. J., Trembath, M., & Gunthorpe, S. (2004). 'You can criticize because you care': Identity attachment, constructiveness, and the intergroup sensitivity effect. *European Journal of Social Psychology, 34,* 499–518.

Insko, C. A., Schopler, J., Hoyle, R. H., Dardis, G. J., & Graetz, K. A. (1990). Individual-group discontinuity as a function of fear and greed. *Journal of Personality and Social Psychology, 58,* 68–79.

Janis, I. L. (1982). *Groupthink: Psychological studies of policy decisions and fiascoes.* Boston: Houghton Mifflin.

Jetten, J., Duck, J., Terry, D. J., & O'Brien, A. (2002). Being attuned to intergroup differences in mergers: The role of aligned leaders and low-status groups. *Personality and Social Psychology Bulletin, 28,* 1194–1201.

Jetten, J., Hornsey, M. J., & Adarves-Yorno, I. (2006). When group members admit to being conformist: The role of relative intragroup status in conformity self-reports. *Personality and Social Psychology Bulletin, 32,* 162–173.

Jost, J. T., & Banaji, M. R. (1994). The role of stereotyping in system-justification and the production of false consciousness. *British Journal of Social Psychology, 33,* 1–27.

Judd, C. M., Park, B., Yzerbyt, V., Gordijn, E. H., & Muller, D. (2005). Attributions of intergroup bias and out-group homogeneity to in-group and out-group others. *European Journal of Social Psychology, 35,* 677–704.

Kramer, R. M., & Brewer, M. B. (1984). Effects of group identity on resource use in a simulated commons dilemma. *Journal of Personality and Social Psychology, 46,* 1044–1057.

Latane, B. (1981). The psychology of social impact. *American Psychologist, 36,* 343–356.

Lee, Y., Jussim, I., & McCauley (Eds.) (1995). *Stereotype accuracy.* Washington, DC: American Psychological Association.

Linville, P. W., Fischer, F. W., & Salovey, P. (1989). Perceived distributions of characteristics of in-group and out-group members: Empirical evidence and a computer simulation. *Journal of Personality and Social Psychology, 42,* 193–211.

Lippman, W. (1922). *Public opinion.* New York: Harcourt Brace.

Locksley, A., Ortiz, V., & Hepburn, C. (1980). Social categorization and discriminatory behavior: Extinguishing the minimal intergroup discrimination effect. *Journal of Personality and Social Psychology, 39,* 773–783.

Mackie, D. M., Worth, L. T., & Asuncion, A. G. (1990). Processing of persuasive in-group messages. *Journal of Personality and Social Psychology, 58,* 812–822.

Mae, L., & Carlston, D. E. (2005). Hoist on your own petard: When prejudiced remarks are recognized and backfire on speakers. *Journal of Experimental Social Psychology, 41,* 240–255.

Maoz, I., Ward, A., Katz, M., & Ross, L. (2002). Reactive devaluation of an "Israeli" vs. "Palestinian" peace proposal. *Journal of Conflict Resolution, 46,* 515–546.

Morrison, E. W., & Milliken, F. J. (2000). Organizational silence: A barrier to change and development in a pluralistic world. *Academy of Management Review, 25*, 706–725.

Nemeth, C. J. (1985). Dissent, group process and creativity: The contribution of minority influence. In J. E. Lawler (Ed.), *Advances in group processes* (pp. 57–75). Greenwich, CT: JAI Press.

Noel, J. G., Wann, D. L., & Branscombe, N. R. (1995). Peripheral in-group membership status and public negativity toward out-groups. *Journal of Personality and Social Psychology, 68*, 127–137.

O'Dwyer, A., Berkowitz, N. H., & Alfeld-Johnson, D. (2002). Group and person attributions in response to criticism of the in-group. *British Journal of Social Psychology, 41*, 563–588.

Ostrom, T. M., & Sedikides, C. (1992). Out-group homogeneity effects in natural and minimal groups. *Psychological Bulletin, 112*, 536–552.

Park, B., Judd, C. M., & Ryan, C. S. (1991). Social categorization and the representation of variability information. In W. Stroebe & M. Hewstone (Eds.), *European review of social psychology, Vol. 2*. Chichester, UK: Wiley.

Platow, M. J., Hoar, S., Reid, S., Harley, K., & Morrison, D. (1997). Endorsement of distributively fair and unfair leaders in interpersonal and intergroup situations. *European Journal of Social Psychology, 27*, 465–494.

Postmes, T., Spears, R., & Cihangir, S. (2001). Quality of decision making and group norms. *Journal of Personality and Social Psychology, 80*, 918–930.

Pratto, F. Sidanius, J., Stallworth, L. M., & Malle, B. F. (1994). Social dominance orientation: A personality variable predicting social and political attitudes. *Journal of Personality and Social Psychology, 67*, 741–763.

Reicher, S., & Levine, M. (1994). Deindividuation, power relations between groups and the expression of social identity: The effects of visibility to the out-group. *British Journal of Social Psychology, 33*, 145–163.

Rosenberg, L. (1961). Group size, prior experience, and conformity. *Journal of Abnormal and Social Psychology, 63*, 436–437.

Sidanius, J. (1993). The psychology of group conflict and the dynamics of oppression: A social dominance perspective. In S. Iyengar & W. J. McGuire (Eds.), *Explorations in political psychology* (pp. 183–219). Durham, NC: Duke University Press.

Stang, D. J. (1976). Group size effects on conformity. *Journal of Social Psychology, 98*, 175–181.

Sutton, R. M., Elder, T. J., & Douglas, K. M. (2006). Reactions to internal and external criticism of out-groups: Social convention in the intergroup sensitivity effect. *Personality and Social Psychology Bulletin, 32*, 563–575.

Tanis, M., & Postmes, T. (2005). A social identity approach to trust: Interpersonal perception, group membership and trusting behaviour. *European Journal of Social Psychology, 35*, 413–424.

Turner, J. C. (1991). *Social influence*. Buckingham, UK: Open University Press.

Van Vugt, M., & de Cremer, D. (1999). Leadership in social dilemmas: The effects of group identification on collective actions to provide public goods. *Journal of Personality and Social Psychology, 76*, 587–599.

Vivian, J. E., & Berkowitz, N. H. (1992). Anticipated bias from an out-group: An attributional analysis. *European Journal of Social Psychology, 22*, 415–424.

Vivian, J. E., & Berkowitz, N. H. (1993). Anticipated out-group evaluations and intergroup bias. *European Journal of Social Psychology, 23*, 513–524.

Worchel, S. (1979). Trust and distrust. In W. G. Austin & S. Worchel (Eds.), *The social psychology of intergroup relations* (pp. 174–187). Monterey, CA: Brooks/Cole.

Yamagishi, T., & Kiyonari, T. (2000). The group as the container of generalized reciprocity. *Social Psychology Quarterly, 63*, 116–132.

Chapter 15

Social Identity and Social Convention in Responses to Criticisms of Groups

Robbie M. Sutton, Karen M. Douglas,
and Tracey J. Elder
University of Kent at Canterbury, United Kingdom

Mark Tarrant
Keele University, United Kingdom

One of the authors of this chapter recalls attending an unusual high school lesson when growing up in New Zealand. The lesson was part of a course in liberal studies, and its specific objective was to examine the sexist, unsavory attitudes underlying many curses or swear words. The teacher began the lesson by waiting at the blackboard, chalk in hand, for the pupils to generate the most vituperative swear words they could think of. For what felt like an eternity, silence reigned. After some cajoling, the pupils eventually volunteered *ass* and other words of its ilk—scarcely the strong stuff required to make the teacher's point. Although the pupils did warm up a bit, ultimately the teacher was forced to provide most of the examples herself. For their parts, the pupils were generally too uncomfortable even to titter, struck dumb by the norm that such words do not comprise the intercourse of the classroom. Lest the reader gain the wrong impression of these students, we should offer an assurance that they liberally and enthusiastically employed these same words in other settings.

Social psychologists who are interested in prejudice and related problems, such as the communication of stereotypes, face an analogous difficulty. Increasingly, social norms appear to militate against the overt expression of prejudice (Crandall & Eshleman, 2003). It is difficult to get experimental research participants to own up to their prejudices, and to rely upon them to do so is to risk consigning one's hypotheses to the oblivion of floor effects. Ironically, this problem is likely to be especially severe in the very domains that arguably are most in need of study—for example, where destructive prejudices against disadvantaged minorities persist despite being widely abhorred. Here then seems to be a case in which a sociological phenomenon, namely the prevalence of restrictive social norms, obstructs empirical inquiry into social psychological phenomena such as prejudice and the communication of stereotypes. A theoretical puzzle accompanies this empirical conundrum: stereotypes and prejudices flourish, despite restrictive social sanctions, the best efforts of policymakers, and in many cases the egalitarian motives of the very people who perpetuate them (Monteith, 1993). To a large extent, the recent history of social psychological research on prejudice has been one of responding to these challenges (e.g., Devine, 1989; Maass, 1999; McConahay, Hardee, & Batts, 1981).

In this chapter, we follow others in attempting to respond to these challenges by applying the conceptual tools of social psychology to the norms themselves (cf., Crandall & Eshleman, 2003). Although the prevalence of social norms that restrict the overt communication of stereotypes and prejudice is at least in part the domain of sociologists and historians, their impact on communicators' behavior is psychologically mediated. In order for social norms to be effective, communicators must acquire some knowledge of those social norms, whether tacit or otherwise (Rutland, Cameron, Milne, & McGeorge, 2005). In order for speakers to learn the norms and to be motivated to adhere to them, norm violations ought to be accompanied with some regularity by adverse social consequences such as disapproval and conflict, which in turn requires that recipients have learned these norms and are willing and able to enforce them (cf. Mae & Carlston, 2005). Speakers then need to build these norms into their self-regulatory processes (Crandall, Eshleman, & O'Brien, 2002; Monteith, 1993). This is rich turf for social psychologists, covering various aspects of social cognition, motivation, and persuasion.

Further, the empirical tools of experimental social psychology are extremely well suited to identifying when social norms serve to prevent stereotype communication from occurring and when they do not. A very important boundary condition has been suggested by recent research on how social identity concerns may affect people's reactions to criticisms of their groups. Specifically, people respond with less hostility and stronger agreement when criticisms are voiced by fellow in-group members than when precisely the same criticisms are voiced by outsiders (Ariyanto, Hornsey, & Gallois, in press; Elder, Sutton, & Douglas, 2005; Hornsey & Imani, 2004; Hornsey, Oppes, & Svensson, 2002; Hornsey, Trembath, & Gunthorpe, 2004; for a review see Hornsey, in press). This tendency to respond more favorably to internal than to external criticism of groups is known as the "intergroup sensitivity effect" (ISE).

In this chapter, we attempt to integrate insights from research on the ISE, which is located largely in the tradition of research inspired by Social Identity Theory (Tajfel & Turner, 1986), with those from research on the norms that proscribe the open expression of stereotypes and prejudice. Our aim in this is to contribute to current knowledge of the factors that encourage and discourage speakers from voicing negative stereotypes, and those that lead audiences to resist or be influenced by those criticisms. Along the way, we aim to turn up some answers to questions such as "Who is conventionally entitled to criticize groups?" "Why are they so entitled?" "What are the conventions that restrict the open expression of negative ideas about groups?" and "To what extent are these conventions likely to restrict other modes of stereotype communication?" Throughout this chapter we use terms such as norms and conventions interchangeably, intending them to refer to (tacit or explicit) cultural injunctions that determine whether criticisms are perceived as appropriate (Cialdini & Trost, 1998).

We will argue that belonging to the group being discussed tends to exempt critics from the norms that regulate the expression of stereotypes and prejudiced attitudes. Insiders' criticisms tend to be seen as stemming from noble intentions rather than from prejudice. In contrast, criticisms voiced by outsiders tend to be seen by observers—whether or not those observers belong to the group in question—as more malevolent than benevolent (Hornsey, this volume; Sutton, Elder, & Douglas, 2006). In a nutshell, outsiders' but not insiders' criticisms are likely to be viewed as expressions of prejudice, and thereby are likely to attract the consequences of violating prohibitive norms.

Nonetheless, our results suggest that social norms do not grant insiders an automatic license to say what they want about groups and do not require that outsiders forever hold their peace. Rather, social norms directly govern critics' psychological states and perhaps especially their intentions. Observers use speakers' social identities as a heuristic, probabilistic cue to those intentions, rather than an absolute determinant of their entitlement to speak. By and large, these conclusions converge with research on the ISE (Hornsey, this volume) but differ principally in that they attribute observers' responses to social conventions rather than defensiveness springing from social identity attachment.

In the following pages, we begin by providing a brief overview on the research on social conventions and the ISE, respectively. We then discuss the relation between these strands of research, and review and report the results of our recent research which is drawn from both strands. We then consider broader implications for the communication of stereotypes and intergroup relations.

RESEARCH ON THE NORMATIVE CONSTRAINTS ON THE EXPRESSION OF PREJUDICE

Research has shown that there are normative restrictions on what people may say about particular groups. In a given cultural context, some groups may be viewed as legitimate targets of prejudice, whereas other groups are relatively protected from it. In pilot research by Franco and Maass (1999), Italian participants indicated that it was socially unacceptable to express prejudice towards Jews, whereas Islamic fundamentalists were seen as fair game. In the experimental phase, language abstraction, which is an implicit and difficult-to-inhibit index of prejudice (see also Douglas, Sutton, & Wilkin, under review), was correlated with overt prejudice for the unprotected Islamic fundamentalist targets but not the protected Jewish targets. Also demonstrating that some groups are more protected than others, Crandall et al. (2002) sampled North American undergraduates' perceptions of the normative acceptability of prejudice toward 105 different groups. On a scale from 0 ("Definitely not OK to have negative feelings towards this group") to 2 ("Definitely OK to have negative feelings about this group"), the acceptability of prejudice toward some groups, including blind people, family men, Black Americans, and Canadians, neared floor (<0.20), and that toward other groups, including rapists, terrorists, members of the Ku Klux Klan (KKK), and drunk drivers, approached ceiling (>1.80).

Beyond norms that specify how particular groups ought to be treated, Crandall and Eshleman (2003) argued that norms constrain overt prejudice generally. For example, values such as "liberalism, egalitarianism, sympathy for the underdog . . . and humanitarian values" (p. 415) may suppress the expression of prejudice. The extent to which people express prejudice towards any given group is determined not simply by the extent to which they are prejudiced. It is also determined inversely by the extent that the expression of prejudice is seen as socially unacceptable, and directly to the extent that people may be able to justify their prejudice to themselves and others.

Crandall et al. (2002) obtained evidence in support of this view of how norms may constrain prejudice against groups in general. Across the 105 groups included in their study as potential targets of prejudice, there was a very high correlation between participants' perceptions that prejudice toward that group was permitted according to prevailing social norms, and the prejudice they personally expressed toward that group. Indeed this was as high as $r = .96$ in their first study. While there was much variation in how much different groups were seen to be normatively protected from prejudice, the key point is that across all groups (from rapists to blind people), prejudice was expressed to the extent that to do so was seen as permissible.

Mae and Carlston (2005) contributed to this tradition of research by examining how observers respond to verbal expressions of intergroup prejudice. They found that speakers who made prejudiced remarks about ascribed groups (e.g., Blacks, elderly, and gay men) or assumed groups (e.g., politicians, lawyers, and artists) were seen as prejudiced and unlikable. Interestingly, speakers were also derogated in this way when their remarks about groups were positively valenced: Making even positive generalizations about groups seems to be normatively dubious. It seems that observers realize that apparently positive or benevolent stereotypes can be seen as ultimately pernicious. Here then seems to be evidence that social norms governing the communication of prejudice are enforced by observers, ensuring that negative social consequences ensue for people who violate those norms.

It makes strong functional sense for societies to enforce restrictions on what people say about groups. The overt, verbal derogation of groups may erode the collective and personal self-esteem of group members, promote discrimination and intergroup conflict (Bourhis, Giles, Leyens, & Tajfel, 1979), and even harm groups' long-term prospects of cohesion and survival (van Vugt & Hart, 2004). However, it also makes strong functional sense for societies not to impose a blanket ban on the criticism of groups. Many benefits may spring from group criticism, such as opportunities for groups to identify and rectify morally dubious or maladaptive practices (Hornsey, Oppes, & Svensson, 2002; Nemeth & Owens, 1996). Criticism may sometimes provide a useful antidote to certain types of group dysfunction such as groupthink (Janis, 1982). Intergroup criticism may also be valuable in allowing minority groups to point out how and why they are being maltreated by majorities. In short, like driving, group criticism is an often beneficial but also a highly risky social activity. The optimal way for societies to deal with such necessary evils is not to forbid them outright but to subject them to normative constraints on how and by whom such actions should be performed.

Yet to be systematically examined are precisely what these normative constraints are. We do not as yet know what leads a particular instance of group criticism to be deemed acceptable or unacceptable. For example, it would be a conceptual mistake to equate verbal criticism of groups with prejudice, given the prosocial motives that may drive individuals to point out failings in a group's behavior, even at the risk of having opprobrium heaped upon themselves. Prejudice is generally defined as an attitudinal and especially an affective orientation toward a group and its members, which may provide a motivational "spur to action" (Crandall & Eshelman, 2003, p. 415). An important social-cognitive task for audiences is to decide whether speakers' prejudices, or a more benevolent state of mind, spurred them on.

More generally, co-operative communication and co-operative living requires that for much of the time, our motives are benign rather than benevolent, and that members of the co-operative are able to reconstruct each others' motives, detecting and sanctioning defectors and malfeasants. For this reason, perceived motives are at the core of many societies' formal and informal justice systems, by which actions are classified as misdeeds and social sanctions assigned (Kaplan, 2001). Reactions to the same outward behaviors may be heavily influenced by the motives to which those behaviors are attributed (Reeder, Kumar, Hesson-McInnis, & Trafimow, 2002). Whatever the special qualities of prejudice, we may see it as an example of malevolent, objectionable motives, and the detection of prejudice as an example of more general social-cognitive tasks.

Thus far, we have argued that the efficacy of social sanctions restricting prejudice is likely to depend on people's abilities to determine whether overt behaviors such as group criticism are really motivated by prejudice. Although some models of prejudice distinguish between dispositional or inner prejudice and overt behavioral expressions of this prejudice, they do not specify the semantic or pragmatic relation between them. That is, they do not provide decoding rules by which social psychologists, and for that matter lay perpetrators, observers, and targets may decide whether overt behaviors signify prejudice. Clearly, given that social norms designed to stem the tide of prejudice depend on these judgments being made in everyday life, an important piece of the puzzle is missing.

RESEARCH ON THE INTERGROUP SENSITIVITY EFFECT

In parallel with the research on the normative constraints on the expression of prejudice, a literature on how people respond to criticisms of their own group has burgeoned (see Hornsey, in press). This research has been informed largely by the tradition of research stemming from Social Identity Theory. Its central insight has been that individuals' responses to criticisms of their group are likely to be informed by the threat to their valued identity that those criticisms represent. In this, it differs from research reviewed in the previous section, which has concerned itself with how observers' reactions to verbal derogation of groups and other significant behaviors are informed by the normative acceptability of prejudice (e.g., Mae & Carlston, 2005).

In the first set of experiments concerned with people's reactions to criticisms of their group, Hornsey et al. (2002) presented criticisms of groups to which their participants belonged (e.g., Australians). These criticisms were attributed either to in-group members (e.g., Australians), or out-group members (e.g., Canadians). Hornsey et al. (2002) found that criticisms elicited greater sensitivity and harsher speaker evaluations when they ostensibly came from an out-group as opposed to an in-group speaker. This ISE, apparent on a range of dependent measures, was not an artifact of simple in-group favoritism; in-group and out-group speakers were rated the same when they made positive statements. Importantly, Hornsey et al.'s (2002) studies on the ISE also included a measure of the extent to which experimental recipients agreed with the comments. Therefore, their studies could directly address the extent to which ideas about groups, once expressed, may be successfully communicated to recipients in the sense that it causes their attitudes to converge with those ideas. Strikingly, they found that the very same criticisms attracted less agreement when attributed to external versus internal speakers. In this sense, internal critics were more able to communicate their critical ideas.

In subsequent studies, the effect of source on agreement has been shown to be mediated by the superior quality of internal critics' intentions, rather than their expertise. For example, Hornsey and Imani (2004) attempted to orthogonally manipulate critics' group identity and level of experience. For example, in one of their conditions the critic of Australians self-identified as Canadian, having been born there, but since infancy had lived in Australia. This critic was therefore external to the group but possessed much experience of it. Results showed that being so experienced did not help the external critic, who aroused just as much sensitivity as highly inexperienced outsiders. The ISE in these studies mediated by the more constructive motives attributed to internal critics, showing that the ISE does not only depend on perceptions of epistemic authority.

In Hornsey and Imani's (2004) theoretical analysis of the ISE, the social identity concerns of audiences whose groups are being criticized are closely linked to the intentions that they ascribe to speakers. Individuals are wont to defend their positive perceptions of their group, and therefore to reject criticisms that threaten those perceptions. Thus they may be prepared to entertain criticism of their group "only if they can find no plausible reason to attribute the criticisms to bias" (Hornsey & Imani, 2004, p. 367). Intergroup bias appears to be naively understood and when group criticisms come from outside the group, motivated individuals are presented with an opportunity to attribute those criticisms to bias (cf. Elder, Douglas, & Sutton, in press; Tajfel, 1970). Once such attributions have been made, "the threat and anger raised by the criticisms might spill over into high levels of negative affect and derogation of the source" (Hornsey & Imani, 2004, p. 367).

Several subsequent pieces of research have supported Hornsey and Imani's (2004) claim that the perceived intentions of critics are crucial (see Hornsey, in press). For example, Tarrant and Campbell (under review) presented university students ($N = 97$) with criticism of students at their university from a fellow in-group member. Participants were told that the in-group critic made the comments at a meeting with a university tutor. The group-normative status of the in-group critic was manipulated via their ostensible performance (good or poor) on a verbal ability test which was framed as a predictor of general academic ability. The results revealed an interaction between participant identification and target status on ratings of sensitivity and speakers' personalities. The effects of target status were apparent for only high identifiers, who were more sensitive to criticisms by antinormative (low status) critics and who also evaluated antinormative critics more harshly. A mediational analysis of high identifiers' responses revealed that the effect of normative status on evaluation of the target was fully mediated by perceptions of comment constructiveness. In short, normative targets who criticized their groups were evaluated more positively than antinormative targets because their comments were believed to be more constructive.

The role played by participants' strength of identification in Tarrant and Campbell's (under review) findings may turn out to be crucial for the ISE literature. Although theoretical accounts of this effect appeal, very plausibly, to audience members' defensiveness in the face of external attack, in fact there has been no other direct evidence that social identity processes play a role in reactions to group criticism. These processes are inferred rather than directly observed. It is important to note that Tarrant and Campell (under review) examined reactions to the normative status of critics, rather than their identity (critics are always internal), and thus far there is no evidence that social identity attachment moderates the preference for internal criticism.

BRINGING TOGETHER IDEAS FROM THE ISE AND THE SOCIAL NORMS LITERATURE

Research on the social norms that regulate expressions of prejudice and research on the ISE have in common a keen relevance to how audiences respond to group criticism. However they have been informed by divergent intellectual traditions, and papers in each literature tend not to cite papers from the other. Research on the ISE and research on prohibitive norms have also diverged in one very important methodological respect. Whereas the ISE research we have reviewed thus far has concerned itself exclusively with the reactions of insiders to criticism of their own groups, research on social norms also examines the attitudes of bystanders to expressions of prejudice towards groups to which they do not themselves belong (Crandall et al., 2002; Mae & Carlston, 2005). This is important because whereas insiders are likely to feel threatened and defensive in response to group criticism, these social identity concerns are likely to be minimal in the case of bystanders. Instead their responses are more likely to be informed by concerns with what is normatively right and wrong. So although it may be tricky to tease apart social identity and social convention concerns when examining the responses of insiders, it may be less so when we also examine the responses of bystanders.

Our central claim in this chapter is that in doing research on insiders' responses to criticisms of their groups, researchers have also been uncovering facts about the acceptability of group criticism according to societal norms. Especially, we claim that insiders tend to be granted a greater normative freedom to criticize their groups compared to outsiders. This freedom stems from the superior intentions that tend to be ascribed to insiders, given that people are intuitively aware of intergroup bias (e.g., Brewer & Kramer, 1985; Elder et al., 2005; Tajfel, 1970). In particular, internal but not external critics are likely to be largely exempt from the charge that their criticisms stem from prejudice.

One of the reasons we make this claim is that, as we have noted, perceived motives are crucial to observers' responses to transgressive and morally ambiguous behavior, even when observers are not the targets of those behaviors (e.g., Kaplan, 2001; Reeder, Kumar, Hesson-McInnis, & Trafimow, 2002). Therefore the central role played by perceived motives in the ISE seems to us to reflect a more general principle in social and moral judgment. Indeed in order for communication to succeed, recipients need to routinely decode what speakers are trying to achieve with their messages, whether those messages are about groups, goatherds, or go-go bars (Brown & Levinson, 1987; Douglas & Sutton, 2006; Grice, 1975).

Another of our theoretical motivations is that we think the importance of source uncovered in ISE literature may help plug one of the important gaps in social psychologists' understandings of how societies restrict the expression of prejudice. Specifically, the tendency to utilize the source of criticism as a cue to the likely motives of the speaker may well be demonstrated by bystanders as well as by insiders. Thus, ISE research points to how observers may decode overt verbal behaviors, using source as a heuristic cue to determine whether an instance of group criticism signifies prejudice. In short, one of our key aims here is to show that the core findings of the ISE may be exported into the literature on proscriptive social norms.

To summarize, our position is that social conventions associated with the appropriate motives for group criticism grant insiders more leeway than outsiders to voice their concerns. In many respects our position entails similar predictions to the social-identity inspired theorizing published elsewhere (e.g., Ariyanto et al., in press; Elder et al., 2005; Hornsey et al., 2002), but differs in some crucial respects. First, our position but not the social-identity position requires that bystanders respond more favorably to internal compared to external criticisms of others' groups. Failure to obtain this finding would falsify our social convention account of the ISE but not the social identity account (it is also important to note that to obtain a positive finding for bystanders would not be sufficient to falsify the social identity account of the ISE, which can be seen to be agnostic with respect to bystanders). Second, the role of perceived intentions is characterized differently. For example, Hornsey and Imani (2004) argued that insiders are motivated to attribute outsiders' criticisms to intergroup bias, or at least that they seize upon the plausibility of this attribution as an excuse to dismiss criticisms and alleviate the threat they represent. In contrast, we argue that both bystanders and insiders attempt to decode the motivations of critics because these motivations speak to the acceptability and even the plausibility of their comments. In so decoding motives, bystanders as well as insiders use critics' social identity as a salient and helpful heuristic cue.

USING ISE CONCEPTS TO UNDERSTAND THE OPERATION OF SOCIAL NORMS

In this section, we review our recent research findings that demonstrate how variables such as source and perceived motives from the ISE literature help explicate the social norms that constrain critical communication about groups.

Bystanders Exhibit the ISE

Sutton et al. (2006) presented Inland Revenue workers in the North of England with very much the same experimental questionnaire as Hornsey et al. (2002) had presented to their Australian student participants. Specifically, criticisms of Australians were attributed to either an Australian or a non-Australian source (a New Zealander, American, or Canadian). The criticism, lifted verbatim from Hornsey et al. (2002) included charges that Australians are racist, intolerant, and uncultured. Dependent measures were also lifted from Hornsey et al. (2002) and included sensitivity to the message, personality evaluations of the speaker, and agreement. The critical variation from the experiments by Hornsey et al. (2002) was that our participants, being British, were not members of the criticized group.

As found by Hornsey et al. (2002), there were no significant effects of the source of positive comments about Australians. Crucially, the British participants responded with lower sensitivity, more generous personality evaluations, and even with greater agreement to criticisms of Australians when made by Australians as opposed to outsiders. In short, bystanders exhibited much the same ISE as had been demonstrated in previous research conducted with audiences of insiders. This finding is important in showing that the ISE is likely to be much more general in scope than demonstrated thus far. Whether or not a given audience contains members of the target group, external critics are likely to have a relatively difficult time making their points heard. As well as establishing the generality of the ISE, the findings help to clarify its causal antecedents. Clearly, being an insider to the group and thus having some desire to defend it from attack is not a necessary condition for the ISE, because bystanders who do not have cause to be defensive exhibit the same preference for internal criticism. Because it is difficult to imagine what other than normative considerations might motivate bystanders to reject external criticisms, the findings suggest that as we had hoped, insights from the ISE literature may be adapted to help understand the normative restrictions on communication about groups.

Perceived Intentions Mediate the ISE, Even for Bystanders

Borrowing ideas from Hornsey's (this volume; Hornsey & Imani, 2004; Hornsey et al., 2002) analysis of the ISE, and from other research on the centrality of attributions of motive for social judgment and action, we have predicted that like insiders, bystanders will exploit source as a cue by which critics' motives may be judged. Going a step further, we may also predict that these perceived motives would mediate bystanders' lower sensitivity, greater agreement and more favorable personality evaluations in response to internal versus external critics. However, bystanders may not be particularly concerned about whether the critic meant to help or harm the group: They have no reason to take the prejudice personally. Therefore, in the eyes of bystanders, internal critics' superior expertise rather than their motives may qualify them to comment (cf. Leyens, Yzerbyt, & Schadron, 1992).

To resolve these questions, Sutton et al. (2006) adapted Hornsey and Imani (2004) who also attempted to disentangle the roles of experience and motives. Critics were either Australian (internal) or Canadian (external), and were either experienced, having lived in Australia since infancy, or inexperienced, having lived in Canada since infancy. To illustrate, critics in the internal, inexperienced cell self-identified as Australian but said that they had lived in Canada since they were babies. Participants' perceptions of speakers' experience and the constructiveness of their motives were also assessed using measures adapted from Hornsey and Imani (2004).

Consistently across all dependent measures (sensitivity, evaluations of the speaker, and agreement), participants reacted more harshly to external than to internal criticism. This replicated Sutton et al.'s (2006) first experiment in which bystanders had been shown to exhibit the ISE. The experience manipulation concerning where the speaker had lived had smaller and less consistent effects, resulting for sensitivity in a modest main effect, for trait evaluation an interaction in which experienced out-group critics were rated more favorably than inexperienced ones, and for agreement, no effects. Crucially, all effects— even those of the experience manipulation—were mediated by perceived intentions and none were mediated by the critics' perceived levels of experience. Relative to external critics, bystanders perceived internal critics to have more constructive motives. By virtue of the superior motives attributed to them, their comments were received more favorably. As we had predicted, bystanders utilized critics' identities as cue by which to judge their motives, which in turn flavored their subsequent evaluative reactions to critics and their criticisms.

In the Abstract, Internal Criticism is Seen as More Appropriate Than External Criticism

The research we have reviewed thus far makes the case that social conventions are likely to underlie the preference for internal criticism, at least in cases where the audience is comprised of bystanders. Thus far however it has not directly demonstrated the existence of relevant social conventions. Nor has it shown whether or not individuals are aware of such conventions.

To address these issues, Sutton et al. (2006) asked participants questions about group criticism without reference to any particular group or intergroup context. Within participants, questions addressed internal and external group criticism. For example, participants were asked, "To what extent is it appropriate for people to criticize groups to which they themselves belong?" and an otherwise identical question that finished "to which they do not belong"

(1 = "not at all"; 7 = "very much"). As predicted, participants indicated that in general, internal criticism ($M = 5.24$, $SD = 1.55$) is more appropriate than external criticism ($M = 3.31$, $SD = 1.67$), $F(1, 89) = 122.91$, $p < .001$, $v^2 = .58$. They also indicated that they would be more reluctant to voice criticisms of out-groups than of their own groups, and predicted that they would react more harshly to external rather than internal group criticism. The extent to which participants anticipated reacting harshly to external (minus internal) criticism, and especially the degree to which they expressed personal reluctance to engage in intergroup criticism, was directly correlated with perceptions that internal criticism was more normatively appropriate.

These results showed that in general, internal criticism is seen as more legitimate than external criticism. Not only do social conventions that are relevant to the ISE exist, but individuals appear to be able to articulate them when explicitly probed. It also provided preliminary evidence that the relevant norms tend to suppress external criticism and may drive audiences to reject external criticism when it is made. However, another of Sutton et al.'s (2006) findings was that the overwhelming majority of participants (80 out of the 90 in total, or 88.9%) could recall voicing a criticism of an out-group, whereas marginally fewer participants (81.1%) could remember criticizing an in-group, $p = .092$. The normative restrictions on intergroup criticism may tend to make people hesitant to speak out against other groups, but do not altogether prevent them from doing so. Indeed the suppressing effect of these societal norms may in many cases be overridden by other factors such as the dimmer view that individuals take of out-groups than of their own. Nonetheless, the results of the study give reason to believe that social norms make intergroup criticism less common than it otherwise would be.

Perceived Intentions are Intrinsic to Communicative Norms

Thus far, we have established that social conventions seem to be crucial in motivating bystanders to reject external criticism of out-groups. However we have not determined what those social conventions are. On one hand, they might be viewed as a charter or set of rules of engagement devoted specifically to the appropriate conduct of group processes and intergroup relations. If groups tacitly sign up to sets of rules about who is allowed to say what about groups, and are prepared to enforce those rules, all groups are ultimately protected from unreasonable external attacks. Such a view is consistent with research on social dilemmas, in which protagonists sometimes protect their own interests and may even maximize collective outcomes by adhering to and enforcing a set of rules (Wedekind & Milinski, 2000).

Alternatively, it is possible that there are no specific rules designed to regulate group criticism, which instead is governed by more general principles of communication (e.g., Brown & Levinson, 1987; Grice, 1975). To illustrate, external criticism may be seen as less appropriate than internal criticism merely by virtue of the fact that it is seen as generally less well intentioned and perhaps less well informed (cf. Baron, 1993; Leung, Su, & Morris, 2001). It may not be necessary to postulate any additional communicative regulations; there may be no hard and fast rule that individuals should not criticize out-groups. Rather, the more general principle that criticism ought to be well intentioned and informed rather than prejudiced may lead participants to perceive that internal criticism tends to be more appropriate. When any given instance of group criticism occurs, speakers may base their judgments of its acceptability on the normative acceptability of speakers' presumed intentions and expertise rather than on their identities. Identity may have no moral significance of its own except as a heuristic indicator of speakers' probable knowledge and motives. This would be consistent with types of moral reasoning that prioritize the psychological states and especially the perceived motives of moral agents, rather than imposing a set of literal prohibitions on particular behaviors (cf. Kohlberg, 1963). It is also suggested by the mediating role played by perceived motives in ISE research (e.g., Hornsey & Imani, 2004; Sutton et al., 2006).

Sutton, Elder, and Douglas (2006) have obtained some evidence that group criticism is governed by these general, psychologized injunctions rather than more literal, domain-specific prohibitions. For example, in Study 2 they ran a randomized, between groups design in which half of the participants were asked questions about types of communication that were pronormative, and the other half of the participants were asked questions about antinormative types of communication. Some of these questions were pitched at the specific level of the appropriateness of intragroup and intergroup criticism. For example, participants in the pronormative group were asked, "How appropriate is it to criticize groups of which you are a member?" whereas the same question for the antinormative participants read, "How appropriate is it to criticize groups of which you are not a member?" Other questions were addressed the more general issues such as perceived intentions and expertise. For example, the pronormative participants were asked about the appropriateness of criticizing groups with the intention to help those groups, and of which one has had much experience. The antinormative participants were asked about the appropriateness of criticizing groups with the intention to cause harm, and of which one has had little experience. Still other questions were concerned with the appropriate motives and expertise of interpersonal criticism.

Elder et al.'s (in preparation) findings mirrored those of Sutton et al. (2006) in that internal group criticism was viewed to be considerably more appropriate than external group criticism. Crucially, however, the between groups design enabled Elder et al. to conduct mediational analyses to determine whether this normative preference for internal criticism is to some extent independent of, or rather boils entirely down to, concerns with underlying motives and expertise. These analyses showed that once the norms that group criticism ought to be well intentioned and well informed were controlled for, there was no difference in the perceived appropriateness of internal and external criticism. Further, controlling for the norms that interpersonal criticism ought to be well intentioned and well informed also eliminated the perception that internal criticism of groups is more appropriate than external criticism.

Apparently, it is not simply that the perceived intentions and expertise of group critics are important to observers in shaping their responses to criticism that may have violated social norms. Instead, their intentions and knowledge seem to be intrinsic to the social norms themselves. Put differently, there seems to be no rigid prohibition on intergroup criticism, which instead appears to be controlled by an ethical system that is concerned directly with critics' motives and epistemic authority.

Further, it appears that the normative restrictions that affect intergroup criticism are not even specified at the group level. The same psychological restrictions are also applied to interpersonal criticism. When we control for beliefs about the normative acceptability of intentions and expertise at the interpersonal level, we eliminate the normative preference for internal group criticism. Despite its many unique feature and repercussions, we can see prejudice as belonging to the class of antisocial attitudes and behaviors that require regulation if co-operative life is to succeed. In accordance with this general perspective, the present findings suggest that still more general than norms proscribing prejudice, those proscribing malice and ignorance are responsible for the greater license afforded internal critics.

Using Normative Concepts to Understand
Why Insiders Might Exhibit the ISE

In sum, the evidence presented thus far seems to establish that it is possible to translate Hornsey's insights (e.g., Hornsey et al., 2002; Hornsey & Imani, 2004) regarding how insiders respond to criticisms of their group to how bystanders, motivated by normative considerations, respond to criticisms of others' groups. Research on the norms constraining prejudice may, in turn, have something to offer research on the ISE. Most importantly, it offers a different way of conceptualizing insiders' responses to criticisms of their group. Although the threat to their valued identity seems bound to be important in shaping how they react to criticism overall, their differential preferences for internal criticism may rest on normative rather than social identity concerns. The similarity of bystanders' responses to group criticism to those of insiders raises questions about whether the processes underlying their responses really are different. The experiments by Sutton et al. (in press) do not address the responses of insiders and therefore do not speak directly to why they display the ISE. Here we report a new experiment that addresses whether social identity attachment moderates reactions to internal and external criticisms of groups.

In this experiment, as in Sutton et al. (in press) we manipulate the source of the criticism and speakers' levels of experience. However we use stimulus groups that are more psychologically remote from the English (specifically the Chinese and the Spanish) than Australians who were the focus of our previous experiments. As before, we predict that the ISE will occur for both insiders and bystanders and that these effects would be mediated by the perceived intentions of the speaker. We also manipulate whether or not the criticism is targeted at participants' own group, and we measure the extent to which they identify with the criticized group (whether or not it is their own).

Summary of Method

Participants were 233 English undergraduate psychology students at Keele University (177 female, 56 male, $M = 19.65$ years, $SD = 3.05$). They were randomly assigned to the cells of a 2 (criticized group: in-group or out-group) $\times$ 2 (source: internal or external) $\times$ 2 (experience: high or low) between groups design.

The materials and procedure of the present experiment were highly similar to those of Sutton et al. (in press), using for example the same measures of sensitivity ($\alpha = .92$), speaker evaluations prior to ($\alpha = .82$) and after ($\alpha = .91$) the criticism, perceived constructiveness ($\alpha = .72$), agreement and perceived experience. We measured the extent of participants' identifications with the target group using a three-item scale, $\alpha = .91$. The item stem read "To what extent do you" and participants responded on a seven-point scale (1 = not at all; 7 = very much). We adapted an item from Hutchison and Abrams (2003), which read "Identify with [e.g.] Chinese people as a group". Another item was adapted from Doosje, Ellemers, and Spears (1995), and it read, "Feel strong ties with Chinese people." The third item read, "Feel yourself to be similar to many Chinese people."

We then presented biographies of the speaker and obtained initial impressions of them using the personality evaluation scale. The criticisms were presented and the dependent measures obtained. We selected the Spanish and the Chinese as target out-groups because they had been rated by pilot participants as less similar to the English than were Australians, who had been the target group in Sutton et al. (in press). The Chinese were also rated significantly less similar to the English than were the Spanish. We constructed criticisms of the group based on descriptors of each group that were commonly generated by pilot participants and which also, in total, were rated as being equally negative. The comments by the internal English critic were as follows:

> When I think of the English I think of them as being fairly arrogant about themselves. I also think that they're a nation of binge-drinkers. Culturally I think that they're stressed and don't know how to relax properly.

These comments were attributed to an English speaker in the internal source condition and to either a Spanish or a Chinese speaker in the external source condition. The paragraph criticizing Chinese people alleged that they are unsociable, gamble too much, and are noisy in public places. The paragraph criticizing Spanish people charged them of being lazy, being loud, and having a bad attitude about life. These criticisms were again attributed to either Spanish or Chinese speakers as appropriate to the experimental condition. There were no differences in responses to criticisms of the Spanish or Chinese, so we collapsed across these to form the out-group condition of the target group factor. As in Hornsey and Imani (2004) and Sutton et al. (in press), the inexperienced critic had resided since infancy in a country other than that whose citizens they were criticizing. The experienced critic had resided since infancy in the target country.

Results

Descriptive statistics are presented in Table 15–1. For each dependent variable, we applied a planned 2 (criticized group: in-group or out-group) × 2 (source: external or internal) × 2 (experience: experienced or inexperienced) between groups ANOVAs. Results were very similar across dependent measures. To save space we therefore report the test statistics only for sensitivity.

For sensitivity, there was a main effect for source such that internal critics ($M = 3.33$, $SD = 1.22$) aroused less sensitivity than external critics ($M = 4.56$,

TABLE 15–1.
Effects of the Group Membership and Experience of the Critic
on Bystanders' and Insiders' Evaluative Judgments

Judgments	Insiders' Responses (e.g., when English are criticized)				Bystanders' Responses (e.g., when the Spanish or Chinese are criticized)			
	Internal Critic		External Critic		Internal Critic		External Critic	
	Critic's Level of Experience							
	Low	High	Low	High	Low	High	Low	High
Sensitivity	3.33	3.51	4.93	4.46	3.37	3.13	4.78	4.08
	(1.12)	(1.23)	(1.01)	(1.09)	(1.22)	(1.35)	(1.11)	(1.28)
Personality	4.44	4.27	3.56	4.14	3.99	4.36	3.29	3.91
	(0.87)	(1.00)	(1.13)	(0.98)	(1.00)	(0.99)	(0.86)	(1.03)
Constructiveness	3.46	3.54	2.25	2.54	3.50	3.78	2.48	1.66
	(1.41)	(1.37)	(1.10)	(1.00)	(1.20)	(1.31)	(1.20)	(0.70)
Agreement	4.29	4.19	2.85	3.64	2.84	2.96	1.76	2.25
	(1.24)	(1.45)	(1.15)	(1.68)	(1.41)	(1.45)	(1.09)	(1.14)

$SD = 1.17$), $F(1, 224) = 61.73$, $p < .001$, $v^2 = .21$. Thus the ISE was powerfully exhibited in this experiment. As in Sutton et al. (in press), constructiveness was shown to partially mediate the effects of source on sensitivity, Sobel's $z = 4.94$, $p < .001$ and all other DVs, including agreement, Sobel's $z = 5.08$, $p < .001$. Also as in Sutton et al., effects were not mediated by the measure of perceived experience.

Participants were only marginally affected by speakers' experiences, being somewhat less sensitive to the comments of experienced speakers ($M = 3.75$, $SD = 1.32$), than inexperienced speakers ($M = 4.14$, $SD = 1.34$), $F(1, 224) = 3.86$, $p = .051$, $v^2 = .02$. Neither was the interaction between experience and source significant, $F(1, 224) = 3.13$, $p = .078$, $v^2 = .01$. Crucially, the identity of the group being criticized, and therefore participants' status as insiders or bystanders, did not interact with the source of the criticism, $F < 1$, nor the speakers' experience, $F(1, 224) = 1.05$, $p = .307$; nor was there any three-way interaction between criticized group, source, and experience, $F < 1$.

Quite to our surprise, the main effect of the criticized group did not attain significance, $F(1, 224) = 2.00$, $p = .158$. That is, participants were not significantly more sensitive to criticism of their own group than to criticism of out-groups. From social-judgability theory, we developed an explanation for this finding and examined whether the data set supported it. This turned up a very interesting set of findings which we think may illuminate some of the complexities of social identity processes in responses to criticisms of groups. However it should be borne in mind that these analyses were conducted posthoc.

In part, the explanation was suggested by another finding that was at first surprising. Specifically, people tended to agree more with criticisms of their own group ($M = 3.76$, $SD = 1.49$) than of out-groups ($M = 2.42$, $SD = 1.35$), $F(1, 225) = 53.86$, $p < .001$, $v^2 = .19$. We did not predict this result, but it is consistent with the idea that participants felt entitled to make judgments of their own group, and to agree with criticisms of it, by virtue of their expertise as insiders (Yzerbyt et al., 1994). It then occurred to us that insiders' tendencies to agree more with group criticism may suppress their otherwise higher level of sensitivity to it. Agreeing more, insiders were somewhat less sensitive than they might otherwise have been, and in this case, not significantly more sensitive than bystanders.

In Step 1 of a series of regressions, we confirmed that target group predicted agreement, $\beta = .427$, $t(231) = 7.15$, $p = .001$. In Step 2, we confirmed that target group did *not* directly predict sensitivity, $\beta = .065$, $t(231) = 0.99$, $p = .324$. In Step 3, target group emerged as a significant predictor of sensitivity when agreement was controlled for, $\beta = .286$, $t(230) = 4.46$, $p < .001$. This satisfies the conventional criterion for a suppressor effect, whereby an effect is augmented when the suppressor is controlled for (Baron & Kenny, 1986). The candidate suppressor, agreement, was also a significant predictor of sensitivity in Step 3, $\beta = -.585$, $t(230) = -8.34$, $p < .001$. A Sobel test showed that the inverse mediated effect was significant, $z = 5.42$, $p < .001$. These analyses support the conclusion that insiders' greater sensitivity to criticism is suppressed by their tendency to agree more with that criticism.

These findings are of theoretical interest in their own right, because they highlight an opposition between different social identity processes. On one hand, people are apt to defend from attack the esteem in which they hold their groups, as suggested by Social Identity Theory (Hornsey & Imani, 2004; Tajfel & Turner, 1986). But on the other, they may feel more entitled to agree with judgments of their own group and its members, as suggested by social-judgability theory (Leyens et al., 1992). The present results suggest that one process (defensiveness) leads to greater sensitivity by insiders, and the other (entitlement to agree) counteracts this sensitivity.

Of course, we must reiterate that these analyses were conducted posthoc. We also acknowledge that in the present study, the group being criticized (and therefore participants' status as insiders versus bystanders) is confounded with the content of the criticism. Although the structure and intensity of the criticism appears to be matched, the specific charges being leveled at participants' own (English) nationality and others' were different. We should therefore approach the suppressor effect with caution until it is replicated in the absence of this confound.

We finally turned to the possible moderating role of participants' measured identifications with the criticized group. As might be expected, participants identified much more with their own national group ($M = 5.12$, $SD = 1.14$) than the other national groups ($M = 2.81$, $SD = 1.26$), $F(1, 231) = 216.53$, $p < .001$, $v^2 = .48$. We first examined the role played by strength of identification in insiders' responses to group criticism. As might be expected, strongly identifying insiders were more sensitive to criticism of their group overall, collapsing across internal and external sources, $r(130) = .21$, $p = .016$. However in hierarchical regression modeling, strength of identification did not predict insiders' preference for internal (versus external) criticism, $t < 1$. Taken together, these results showed that strength of identification predicted overall sensitivity, but not the ISE. This result tends to disconfirm the notion that a sense of attachment to one's group motivates one to reject external criticism while being relatively accepting of internal criticism.

The meaning of bystanders' responses on identification scales may be different to those of insiders. Here some kind of empathic or sympathetic identification may be at play rather than a self-referent sense of identity. Nonetheless we thought that even this different form of social identity may be relevant to responses to group criticism. Individuals may feel offended or threatened on behalf of other groups, and this may be especially true of target groups that are subjectively similar to the in-group. Thus it might be possible that some kind of secondary or vicarious social identification, and therefore a modified version of the social identity account, may be able to account for the results of our bystander experiments. Correlational analyses however showed that the strength of identification with criticized out-groups had no relation with sensitivity overall, $r(113) = -.14$, $p = .129$, nor with the extent to which internal criticism was preferred relative to internal criticism, $t < 1$.

Discussion

Care is required when interpreting null effects, but it is clear that the present findings do not offer any support for the claim that the ISE stems from insiders' attachment to their social identity. As in the experiments by Sutton et al. (in press), bystanders demonstrated the ISE, preferring criticisms of the Spanish and Chinese out-groups to emerge from within those groups. The present results went further by showing that bystanders exhibit the ISE just as strongly as do insiders. Similarly, highly identifying insiders did not exhibit the ISE any more strongly than low identifiers, even though they were more sensitive to criticism overall.

The results tend to disconfirm certain interpretations of the role played by social identity processes in the ISE. One such interpretation is that insiders and bystanders' responses are informed by the same social conventions, but that insiders exploit those conventions as an excuse to reject external criticism (cf. Hornsey & Imani, 2004). Here we would surely expect insiders to exhibit the ISE more strongly than bystanders. Also, if people really do seize upon the dubious motives of external critics as a means to dismiss criticisms and protect their group, it seems odd that high identifiers, who presumably experience such threats more acutely and are more determined to defend their group, do not show the ISE more strongly than low identifiers. We think it more plausible that social norms drive the ISE for both bystanders and insiders.

However we must acknowledge that the present study represents only a preliminary investigation of the role of social identity processes, as distinct from wider social conventions, in people's preference for internal criticism of their own groups. Thus, it would be premature for us to claim that we should reject the social identity perspective on the ISE. Importantly, we would note that although bystanders and insiders may be no different on the pen-and-paper measures used here (also Hornsey et al., 2002; Hornsey & Imani, 2004; Sutton et al., in press), differences in their reactions to external and internal criticism may emerge on other measures. For example, behavioral measures such as willingness to engage in conflict with the critic may reveal that compared to bystanders, insiders show more differential harshness to external critics (Elder, 2005). It might also be that differences emerge over time; bystanders may rapidly forget about the criticisms they have read and especially their source, whereas each may burn in the memory of insiders whose group has been slighted.

Another caveat is that although some of the null effects observed in the present study are not encouraging for the social identity perspective on the ISE, we do not glean any direct evidence that concerns with the normative appropriateness of criticism drives the ISE. To be fair, it is not clear what other than social conventions might motivate bystanders to exhibit the ISE. However we do not directly measure or manipulate normative concerns (cf. Crandall et al., 2002) and establish that they moderate the ISE. The operation of social conventions is thus far inferred rather than directly observed.

CONCLUSIONS AND BROADER IMPLICATIONS

In researching insiders' responses to criticism from a social identity perspective, it is clear that researchers have also been uncovering general facts about the normative constraints on communication about groups. One such fact is that insiders are more normatively entitled to voice their criticisms than are outsiders (Hornsey et al., 2002). This is not an automatic entitlement but rather one that is contingent upon the tendency for internal critics to be seen as having their groups' interests at heart, compared to external critics who are seen to be motivated by less benign attitudes (Hornsey & Imani, 2004; Sutton et al., in press). Put differently, intergroup criticism appears to be viewed by insiders and bystanders alike as an expression of prejudice, whereas intragroup criticism is not—no matter how ill-advised or unfortunate it might be.

A number of interesting hypotheses about intergroup relations and stereotype communication follow from these conclusions. For example, the normative difficulties that people encounter when criticizing others' groups call attention to something of a paradox. Relative to out-group members, in-group members are motivated to see their own group in positive terms, and may at times be rather blind to its faults (Janis, 1982; Tajfel & Turner, 1986). Even when in-group members attain a balanced perception of their groups' weaknesses and strengths, they appear to suppress the former and emphasize the latter when communicating publicly about their groups, especially when their comments are available to out-group members (Klein & Azzi, 2001). In short, those who are most likely to perceive the limitations of a group (i.e., out-group members) are least permitted to communicate them. Arguably therefore, societal restrictions on group criticisms place greater weight, in practice, on the prevention of harm than on the facilitation of positive changes that might stem from criticism.

Another implication of the findings we have reviewed and reported in this chapter is that we might expect the greater normative pressures on external critics to cause their criticisms to differ from insiders' in substance and style. The ISE research we have reviewed thus far has not given participants an opportunity to formulate their own criticisms, but instead has elicited their responses to criticisms constructed by experimenters. Nonetheless, to criticize a group is to create and transmit a symbolic product, the details of which will affect evaluations of that product and its maker. In this regard, we might expect that compared to insiders, outsiders will do more to mitigate their criticisms, perhaps by using qualifiers, hedges, and especially by attempting to justify the epistemic basis of their comments and the quality of their intentions (for example, "A lot of my best friends are Australians but . . .").

In contrast, insiders ought to be able to assume that their expertise, intentions and entitlement may be taken for granted. When the group membership of the speaker is not known to the audience, we would expect internal more than external critics to point out their identities, and by implication, their entitlements. The more salient are the social conventions, the more we would expect these effects to occur. In short, the social conventions reviewed in this chapter may affect not just when criticism is voiced, but also how people voice it. We might also expect that these sorts of mitigating strategies will be more effective in defusing sensitivity for external than for internal critics. Indeed Hornsey, Robson, Smith, Esposo, and Sutton (in preparation) found that the ISE is diminished when speakers accompany their criticisms with praise of the group, which suggests to members of the group that the speakers' intentions are not malicious.

It remains to be seen whether these findings, obtained with samples of insiders, will generalize to bystanders. However we think there is a case that they will not: Bystanders may not experience sufficient levels of threat and engagement for them to notice these rhetorical variations or to use them to reconstruct critics' motives. This line of reasoning entails that insiders and bystanders will not always respond to criticism in the same way. Indeed, as observed in this suppressor effects reported in this chapter, psychological corollaries of belonging to groups, such as social judgability and identity attachment, do appear to affect responses to group criticism causing them to respond differently, even if these differences are not immediately apparent.

Our theoretical account of the ISE holds that critics' perceived motives are crucial to insiders' and bystanders' responses to their criticisms. Critics' social identities are likely to be a blatant, powerful cue to their probable intentions, being salient and meaningful to insiders and bystanders alike. However other more subtle contextual (Elder et al., 2005), rhetorical (Hornsey et al., in preparation), and linguistic (Hornsey et al., 2004) factors may be used only by highly motivated insiders to evaluate the likely motives of the speaker and the consequences of their comments for the group. Bystanders, having little personal stake in the criticized group, may either fail to notice these subtle cues or may not devote sufficient cognitive resources to decoding their pragmatic implications. Which cues are exploited by different audiences is an empirical question, but as a provisional organizing principle, we would suggest that cues requiring greater attention and cognitive resources will tend to affect insiders more strongly than bystanders.

Some of our recent results provide support for this notion. Elder, Sutton and Douglas (2006) presented participants with criticisms of groups, where internal speakers opted for the first-person plural pronoun (e.g., "we are a nation of binge-drinkers"), the third-person plural pronoun (e.g., "they. . ."), or no pronoun (e.g., "the English. . ."). Participants in Experiment 1 were members of the group being criticized, and showed a clear preference for criticisms expressed in the first person, being less sensitive and showing greater liking for the speaker, relative to criticisms expressed with third-person pronouns or no pronouns. These effects were mediated by the superior motives attributed to internal critics who opted for the first-person pronoun. In contrast, Experiment 2 examined the responses of bystanders to internal criticism of another group (e.g., English participants' reactions to criticisms of Australians by an Australian). Here, the linguistic choices of the internal critic made no difference to sensitivity or liking. Neither did these variations in pronouns influence attributions of motive. As predicted by our normative account, reactions to criticisms were still strongly predicted by critics' perceived motives. However, only insiders' perceptions of motive were affected by critics' linguistic choices.

Another factor that might be of interest uniquely to insiders is that of internal critics' normative status. As we have noted, Tarrant and Campbell (under review) found that insiders' preference for group normative as opposed to antinormative internal critics was moderated by their own level of identification with the group. High identifiers responded more favorably to the criticisms of normative group members rather than deviants, whereas low identifiers were not much affected by the manipulation. The moderating role played by identification here provides positive evidence that recipients' social identity attachments affect their sensitivity to the cue provided by critics' status.

MIGHT THE ISE GENERALIZE TO OTHER FORMS OF STEREOTYPE COMMUNICATION?

ISE research has been concerned with explicit criticisms of groups. However, as much of this volume demonstrates, there are other, less direct but very important means by which people maintain stereotypes in communication. For example, people may choose to talk about the actions and traits of group members that are consistent with group stereotypes, remaining relatively silent about stereotype-inconsistent individuals (e.g., Lyons & Kashima, 2003). For example, if we accept that *hostile* is an attribute stereotypically associated with African Americans, individuals may perpetuate this stereotype by talking more about the behaviors and traits of Mike Tyson than of the relatively agreeable entertainer Will Smith. Another way in which communicative acts may contribute to stereotypes is by speakers' choices of language. Research on the linguistic intergroup bias (LIB; Maass, 1999) shows that people use abstract, dispositional language to describe stereotype-consistent behaviors (e.g., Mike Tyson was violent), but more concrete language for stereotype-inconsistent behaviors (e.g., Mike Tyson walked away from the guy who called him a jerk).

These indirect forms of stereotype communication are likely to be somewhat less subject to normative restrictions governing what may be said about groups, including those resulting in the preference for internal critics. One reason for this is that whereas it may be relatively easy to refrain from explicit derogation of groups, it may be much more difficult for speakers to suppress less direct forms of stereotype communication such as the LIB (Douglas et al., under review; Franco & Maass, 1999)

Another reason is that what we say about given individuals is less obviously diagnostic of our group-level prejudices than is what we say directly about groups. Of course, our talk about individuals may often be somewhat diagnostic of our group prejudices. Imagine for example a dinner party at which a guest asserts "Will Smith is hostile." This statement is not obviously supported by public knowledge of the individual (cf. "Mike Tyson is hostile"). When statements about individuals are discrepant from audiences' own understanding of that individual, they are likely to bring the speaker into focus as the target of impression formation processes (Wyer, Budesheim, & Lambert, 1990). In this example, the possibility that the speaker has been influenced by a prevailing stereotype may well be salient.

Nonetheless, even baiters of Will Smith will be able to deny that they endorse the relevant stereotype, so long as they have not explicitly voiced it. There would be no need, necessarily, for them to fetch their coats and beat a hurried retreat from the party. In contrast, when guests at any civilized dinner party blurt out stereotypes and make the same derogatory claims about an entire racial group, it is really time for them to go home. Clearly, due to its greater ability to be diagnosed, direct stereotype communication (as studied in the ISE literature) is likely to be more subject to social sanction than is indirect stereotype communication.

This differential restriction (in practice) on direct versus indirect forms of stereotype communication appears, at least at first sight, to protect groups from some of the worst possible consequences of prejudiced communication. Group criticism has the potential to be a highly efficient means by which stereotypes may be inculcated in recipients who are prepared to accept speakers' statements at face value. We can imagine for example that prejudiced parents may employ this form of stereotype communication to indoctrinate their children, and that hate groups may use it to reinforce the prejudices of new recruits (Douglas, McGarty, Lala, & Bluic, 2005). There is no need for a large, skewed sample of statements in order for a stereotype to be conveyed, when a single statement from an authoritative speaker might do the job.

However this restriction on explicit intergroup criticism may have the perverse consequence of making existing stereotypes harder to change. To explain, the indirect forms of stereotype communication seem largely to depend upon, and to perpetuate, a previously existing stereotype. For example, speakers communicate stereotype-consistent data in more dispositional terms because the stereotype has affected how they encode those data (e.g., Wigboldus et al., 2000). Speakers may selectively communicate stereotype-consistent behaviors because they understand the stereotype to be endorsed by their recipients (e.g., Lyons & Kashima, 2003). Although these indirect modes of stereotype communication may not be entirely confined to the transmission and maintenance of stereotypes (e.g., Douglas & Sutton, 2003), they are more relevant to these functions than to stereotype formation and change (cf., Maass, 1999). In contrast, even a single, explicit instance of group criticism (or praise, as in Mae & Carlston, 2005) may do much to establish a perception of a group or challenge accepted wisdom about it.

So, it is possible to argue that direct modes of stereotype communication, which are potentially the most capable of instituting stereotype change, are also the most normatively restricted. In contrast, less direct modes that are more or less bound to transmit and maintain stereotypes are less restricted. Ironically, these differential restrictions may contribute to the tendency for stereotypes to reproduce themselves through communication. They may also make it difficult for individuals to articulate and debate stereotypes, and even to identify which stereotypes are endorsed by whom.

By their nature, social conventions are conservative. In this case, they may not only conserve groups from the severe indignities and harms that may arise from overt criticism: They may also conserve prevailing and in many cases deleterious stereotypes of those same groups from public scrutiny and negotiation. Of great interest to social psychologists would be a systematic, empirical assessment of the upsides and downsides of the current normative restrictions on communication about groups. Perhaps of still greater interest might be research into how normative restrictions might be adjusted so that they optimally serve the egalitarian purposes for which they are presumably designed.

ACKNOWLEDGMENTS

We acknowledge the support of the Economic and Social Research Council, Grant Res-000-22-1150 awarded to Robbie M. Sutton and Karen M. Douglas for some of the research reported in this chapter.

REFERENCES

Ariyanto, A., Hornsey, M. J., & Gallois, C. (in press). Group-directed criticism in Indonesia: The role of message source and audience. *Asian Journal of Social Psychology*.

Baron, R. A. (1993). Criticism (informal negative feedback) as a source of perceived unfairness in organizations: Effects, mechanisms, and countermeasures. In R. Cropanzano (Ed.), *Justice in the workplace: Approaching fairness in human resource management* (pp. 155–170). Hillsdale, NJ: Erlbaum.

Baron, R. M., & Kenny, D. A. (1986). The moderator-mediator variable distinction in social psychological research: Conceptual, strategic, and statistical considerations. *Journal of Personality and Social Psychology, 51*, 1173–1182.

Bourhis, R., Giles, H., Leyens, J. P., & Tajfel, H. (1979). Psycholinguistic distinctiveness: Language divergence in Belgium. In H. Giles & R. St Clair (Eds.), *Language and social psychology* (pp. 158–185). Oxford: Blackwell

Brewer, M. B., & Kramer, R. M. (1985). The psychology of intergroup attitudes and behaviours. *Annual Review of Psychology, 11,* 219–243.

Brown, P., & Levinson, S. C. (1987). *Politeness: Some universals in language usage.* Cambridge, UK: Cambridge University Press.

Cialdini, R. B., & Trost, M. R. (1998). Social influence: Social norms, conformity and compliance. In D. T. Gilbert, S. T. Fiske, & Lindzey, G. (Eds.), *The handbook of social psychology Vol. 2* (4th ed., pp. 151–192). New York: McGraw-Hill.

Crandall, C. S., & Eshleman, A. (2003). A justification-suppression model of the expression and experience of prejudice. *Psychological Bulletin, 129,* 414–446.

Crandall, C. S., Eshleman, A., & O'Brien, L. (2002). Social norms and the expression and suppression of prejudice: The struggle for internalization. *Journal of Personality and Social Psychology, 82,* 359–378.

Devine, P. G. (1989). Stereotypes and prejudice: Their automatic and controlled components. *Journal of Personality and Social Psychology, 56,* 5–18.

Doosje, B. J., Ellemers, N., & Spears, R. (1995). Perceived intragroup variability as a function of group status and identification. *Journal of Experimental Social Psychology, 31,* 410–436.

Douglas, K. M., McGarty, C., Bliuc, A. M., & Lala, G. (2005). Understanding cyberhate: Social competition and social creativity in on-line White-supremacist groups. *Social Science Computer Review, 23,* 68–76.

Douglas, K. M., & Sutton, R. M. (2003). Effects of communication goals and expectancies on language abstraction. *Journal of Personality and Social Psychology, 84,* 684–696.

Douglas, K. M., & Sutton, R. M. (in press). When what you say about others says something about you: Language abstraction and inferences about describers' attitudes and goals. *Journal of Experimental Social Psychology.*

Douglas, K. M., Sutton, R. M., & Wilkin, K. (2005). *Could you mind your language? On the (in)ability to inhibit linguistic bias.* Manuscript submitted for publication.

Elder, T. J. (2005). Reactions to criticisms of groups: Where social identity and communication processes meet. Unpublished doctoral dissertation, Keele University, U.K..

Douglas, K. M., & Sutton, R. M. (2006). When what you say about others says something about you: Language abstraction and inferences about describers' attitudes and goals. *Journal of Experimental Social Psychology, 42,* 500–508.

Elder, T. J., Douglas, K. M., & Sutton, R. M. (in press). Perceptions of social influence when messages favour "us" versus "them": A closer look at the social distance effect. *European Journal of Social Psychology.*

Elder, T. J., Sutton, R. M., & Douglas, K. M. (2005). Keeping it to ourselves: Effects of audience size and composition on reactions to criticisms of the in-group. *Group Processes and Intergroup Relations, 8,* 231–244.

Elder, T. J., Sutton, R. M., & Douglas, K. M. *A hierarchy of communicative norms.* Manuscript submitted for publication

Elder, T. J., Sutton, R. M., & Douglas, K. M. (2006). *"Us" versus "them": Reactions to speakers' use of language regarding groups.* Poster presented at the Meeting of the Society for Personality and Social Psychology, Palm Springs, CA.

Grice, H. P. (1975). Logic and conversation. In J. H. Greenberg (Ed.), *Universals of language* (pp. 58–90). Cambridge, MA: MIT Press.

Franco, F. M., & Maass, A. (1999). Intentional control over prejudice: When the choice of the measure matters. *European Journal of Social Psychology, 29,* 469–477.

Hornsey, M. J., & Imani, A. (2004). Criticizing groups from the inside and the outside: A social identity perspective on the intergroup sensitivity effect. *Personality and Social Psychology Bulletin, 30,* 365–383.

Hornsey, M. J., Oppes, T., & Svensson, A. (2002). "It's OK if we say it, but you can't": Responses to intergroup and intragroup criticism. *European Journal of Social Psychology, 32,* 293–307.

Hornsey, M. J., Robson, E., Smith, J., Esposo, S., & Sutton, R. M. Testing the effectiveness of rhetorical strategies designed to overcome defensiveness in the face of group criticism. Manuscript submitted for publication

Hornsey, M. J., Trembath, M., & Gunthorpe (2004). 'You can criticize because you care': Identity attachment, constructiveness, and the intergroup sensitivity effect. *European Journal of Social Psychology, 34*, 499–518.

Hornsey, M. J. (in press). Kernel of truth or motivated stereotype? Interpreting and responding to negative generalizations about your group. In Y. Kashima, K., Fiedler, & P. Freytag (Eds.). *Stereotype dynamics: Language-based approaches to the formation, maintenance, and transformation of stereotypes,* (pp. 323–343). Mahwah, NJ: Erlbaum.

Hutchison, P., & Abrams, D. (2003). In-group identification moderates stereotype change in reaction to in-group deviance. *European Journal of Social Psychology, 33,* 497–506.

Janis, I. L. (1982). *Groupthink: Psychological studies of policy decisions and fiascos.* Boston, MA: Houghton Mifflin.

Kaplan, L. V. (2001). Intentional agency, responsibility, and justice. In B. F. Malle, L. J. Moses, & D. A. Baldwin (Eds.). Intentions and intentionality: Foundations of social cognition, (pp. 367–379). Cambridge, MA: MIT Press.

Klein, O., & Azzi, A. (2001). The strategic confirmation of metastereotypes: How group members attempt to tailor an out-group's representation of themselves. *British Journal of Social Psychology, 40,* 279–293.

Kohlberg, L. (1963). The development of children's orientations toward a moral order: I. Sequence in the development of moral thought. *Human Development, 6,* 11–33.

Leung, K., Su, S., & Morris, M. W. (2001) When is criticism not constructive? The roles of fairness perceptions and dispositional attributions in employee acceptance of critical supervisory feedback. *Human Relations, 54,* 1155–1187.

Leyens, J. P., Yzerbyt, V. Y., & Schadron, G. (1992). Stereotypes and social judgeability. In W. Stroebe & M. Hewstone (Eds.), *European review of social psychology* (Vol. 3, pp. 91–120). Chichester, England: Wiley.

Lyons, A., & Kashima, Y. (2003). How are stereotypes maintained through communication? The influence of stereotype sharedness. *Journal of Personality and Social Psychology, 85,* 989–1005.

Mae, L., & Carlston, D. E. (2005). Hoist on your own petard: When prejudiced remarks are recognized and backfire on speakers. *Journal of Experimental Social Psychology, 41,* 240–255.

Maass. A. (1999). Linguistic intergroup bias: Stereotype perpetuation through language. *Advances in Experimental Social Psychology, 31,* 79–121.

McConahay, J., Hardee, B., & Batts, V. (1981). Has racism declined in America? It depends on who is asking and what is asked. *Journal of Conflict Resolution, 25,* 563–579.

Monteith, M. J. (1993). Self-regulation of prejudiced responses: Implications for progress in prejudice-reducing efforts. *Journal of Personality and Social Psychology, 65,* 469–485.

Nemeth, C., & Owens, P. (1996). Making workgroups more effective: The value of minority dissent. In M. A. West (Ed.), *The handbook of workgroup psychology* (pp. 125–121). Chichester, UK: Wiley.

Reeder, G. D., Kumar, S., Hesson-McInnis, M., & Trafimow, D. (2002). Inferences about the morality of an aggressor: The role of perceived motive. *Journal of Personality and Social Psychology, 83,* 789–803.

Rutland, A., Cameron, L., Milne, A., & McGeorge (2005). Social norms and self-presentation: Children's implicit and explicit intergroup attitudes. *Child Development, 76,* 451–466.

Sutton, R. M., Elder, T. J., & Douglas, K. M. (2006). Reactions to internal and external criticisms of outgroups: Social convention in the Intergroup Sensitivity Effect. *Personality and Social Psychology Bulletin, 32,* 363–575.

Tajfel, H. (1970). Experiments in intergroup discrimination. *Scientific American, 223,* 96–102.

Tajfel, H., & Turner, J. C. (1986). The Social Identity Theory of intergroup behaviour. In S. Worchel & W. G. Austin (Eds.), *Psychology of Intergroup Relations* (2nd ed., pp. 7–24). Chicago: Nelson-Hall.

Tarrant, M., & Campbell, S. (2006). *Effects of normative status on sensitivity to intragroup criticism.* Manuscript submitted for publication.

van Vugt, M., & Hart, C. M. (2004). Social identity as social glue: The origins of group loyalty. *Journal of Personality and Social Psychology, 86,* 585–598.

Wedekind, C., & Milinski, M. (2000). Co-operation through image scoring in humans. *Science, 288,* 850–852.

Wyer, R. S., Budesheim, T. L., & Lambert, A. J. (1990). Cognitive representation of conversations about persons. *Journal of Personality and Social Psychology, 58,* 218–238.

Chapter 16

The Interplay of Stereotype Threat and Regulatory Focus

Johannes Keller and Herbert Bless
University of Mannheim, Germany

As Swim and Stangor (1998) pointed out not too long ago, mainstream research on stereotyping and prejudice carried out by social psychologist during the last decades largely focused on the perceiver's perspective; that is, researchers in the field were particularly interested in the analysis of the emergence, structure, and maintenance of the mental representations that people hold of groups and social categories. They were eager to understand how such mental representations affect cognitive and behavioral processes in persons who hold a specific mental representation of a given target group (e.g., processes in the perceiver; cf. Fiske, 1998; Smith, 1998). If we move beyond this rather intrapersonal focus, other, more interpersonal aspects emerge. How are stereotypes communicated? Does the form of the communication influence later consequences in the recipient? How are these consequences mediated? These kinds of questions can be applied to two different types of communication recipients: (a) those who are not associated with the stereotype and (b) those who may be. With respect to the latter, the research agenda in the field experienced a significant modification when researchers began to systematically address the target's perspective. Accordingly, the focus of research on stereotyping and prejudice was broadened in an attempt to understand the role that stereotypes and prejudice play in affective, cognitive, and behavioral processes in persons who are members of groups or social categories targeted by stereotypic beliefs and prejudice (for an overview of research programs taking this perspective, see the volume edited by Swim and Stangor, 1998). Not surprisingly, being exposed to communication that transports a stereotype that can be applied to oneself may have dramatic consequences. Communicating the stereotype to the target itself affects a wide spectrum of aspects.

In this chapter, we focus on the consequences of communication that explicitly or implicitly comprises stereotypic expectancies about cognitive performance. Research in this regard has received considerable attention ever since the introduction of the stereotype threat concept (Steele, 1997; Steele & Aronson, 1995). The phenomenon termed stereotype threat was first demonstrated in the seminal work by Steele and Aronson (1995). Their research showed that exposure to communication concerning negative stereotypic expectancies (e.g., negative expectancies concerning the intellectual abilities of African Americans) undermined participants' test performances. In this chapter, we will discuss this highly influential research and propose a new theoretical perspective focusing on motivational mechanisms as central determinants of how the communication of positive and negative stereotypic expectancies influences test performance.

CHAPTER OVERVIEW

Our main goal in this chapter is to draw the readers' attention to several distinct methodological, as well as conceptual, aspects of previous research on stereotype threat and to present the specific theoretical perspective we are pursuing in our own examination of the effects that the communication of positive and negative group-based expectancies can have on test takers' performance outcomes. We start with a discussion of methodological and conceptual trends pointing out that previous research on the impact of group-based performance expectancies narrowly focused on the effects of *negative* performance expectancies and the analysis of *mediating* mechanisms that may explain the detrimental effects triggered by the communication of negative group-based expectancies; that is, only little research applied an experimental approach testing factors that may moderate the effect of group-based expectancies on performance. The fact that *positive* stereotypic expectancies may also build a basis of threat and performance decrements has been largely neglected. In addition, we argue that the potential impact of *motivational* mechanisms (e.g., self-regulatory orientations) has been insufficiently addressed in the search for mediators and moderators in previous stereotype threat research.

Following this critical reflection on previous research, we propose a conceptual refinement arguing that two forms of stereotype threat can be differentiated: (a) positive expectancy threat and (b) negative expectancy threat. We then present our theoretical framework that focuses on the analysis of boundary conditions of expectancy threat effects, emphasizing the critical role of "hot" motivational mechanisms of self-regulation. The crucial assumption characterizing our framework holds that detrimental effects of *negative* group-based expectancies are most likely to emerge under conditions where self-regulatory mechanisms are guided by a focus on duties and security emphasizing the importance of avoiding negative outcomes (*prevention focus*; Higgins, 1998). In contrast, we argue that it is most likely to observe detrimental effects of *positive* group-based expectancies under conditions where self-regulatory mechanisms are guided by a focus on ideals and aspirations, emphasizing the importance of achieving positive outcomes (*promotion focus*; Higgins, 1998). In the concluding sections of the chapter, we review results of our research program that support these basic assumptions.

STEREOTYPE THREAT THEORY AND RESEARCH: AN OVERVIEW

Stereotype Threat Theory (Steele, 1997; Steele & Aronson, 1995) holds that members of groups or social categories that are associated with negative stereotypical beliefs may be susceptible to a distinct experience termed "stereotype threat." This phenomenon has been defined as the fear that arises in situations where one is afraid of being judged or treated on the basis of a negative stereotype, or in settings where one runs the risk of inadvertently confirming a negative stereotypic expectancy about one's group (Steele, Spencer, & Aronson, 2002). According to stereotype threat theorists, this unsettling experience may be associated with a diverse set of problematic consequences for the person facing stereotype threat (cf. Steele et al., 2002).

Most of the research on this phenomenon has focused on the potential consequences of stereotype threat in a specific context—test-performance settings—and it has been suggested that in testing situations, negative stereotypic expectations undermine the performance of persons targeted by them. Hence, it is assumed that members of social groups who are confronted with negative stereotypes about their ability in a specific field are negatively affected by these stereotypic expectancies. For example, women are seen as negatively affected by the stereotype "women can't do math." Some minority group members are seen as negatively affected by the negative expectancies concerning their cognitive abilities in general, one example being African Americans who are confronted with the stereotype "African Americans are not intelligent."

In their pioneering work, Steele and Aronson proposed Stereotype Threat Theory (Steele & Aronson, 1995) to account for detrimental effects of negative stereotypic expectations on performance. They suggested that the applicability of negative stereotypic expectations impairs test performance through an interfering pressure—the pressure of one's performance being judged by or seen as confirming the negative group-based expectancy. In line with this

assumption, there is now a consistent and impressive body of research showing that stereotype threat results in decreased performance by the targets of
negative stereotypic performance expectations. Numerous studies found that
rendering stereotypic expectations irrelevant to the testing situation eliminated
performance pressure and, in turn, underperformance; these effects obviously
are not restricted to the highly controlled laboratory setting. For example, in a
study we conducted in the everyday setting of high-school classrooms, we found
that the elimination of negative stereotypic expectancies concerning the math
ability of females (by describing a math test as gender-fair, cf. Spencer, Steele
& Quinn, 1999) resulted in a significant performance boost in our female participants working on a difficult math test (see Fig. 16–1). As a consequence,
the gender gap that emerged under conditions where negative stereotypic expectancies were salient and applicable (e.g., under stereotype threat conditions) disappeared when the math test was introduced as gender-fair.

A large number of studies (for an overview, see Steele et al., 2002) examining the impact of the communication of negative group-based expectations
on cognitive performance found similar results. For example, the effect has
been replicated in elderly persons performing memory tasks (Levy, 1996;
Rahhal, Hasher, & Colombe, 2001), in students from low socioeconomic backgrounds working on IQ test items (Croizet & Claire, 1998), in African American and Hispanic students working on different kinds of cognitive tests (Blascovich, Spencer, Quinn, & Steele, 2001; Gonzales, Blanton, & Williams, 2002),

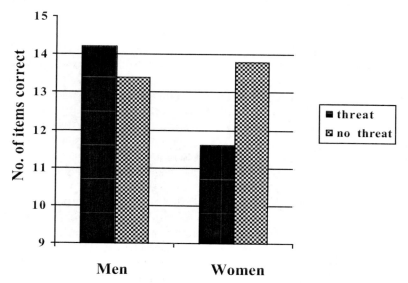

FIGURE 16–1.   Math performance levels as a function of gender and test description
(findings reported by Keller & Dauenheimer, 2003).

in women performing math and spatial tests (Keller, 2002, Spencer et al., 1999; Sharps, Welton, & Price, 1993) or a negotiation task (Kray, Thompson, & Galinsky, 2001), and in men working on an affective sensitivity task (Leyens, Désert, Croizet, & Darcis, 2000).

The Second Generation of Research on Stereotype Threat

Soon after the introduction of the stereotype threat phenomenon, a second generation of research began to analyze possible underlying mechanism that drive the effect. In fact, a large number of potential mediators has been proposed and tested in stereotype threat research. In their seminal paper introducing the concept of stereotype threat, Steele and Aronson (1995) already addressed the "How" question ("How does stereotype threat lead to reduced performance outcomes?") and discussed several potential mediating mechanisms. They suggested (a) arousal, (b) effort withdrawal, (c) attention diversion, (d) self-consciousness, and (e) performance expectations as mechanisms that could be involved. Yet the authors did not provide a clear theoretical framework, including a more detailed elaboration on how and why these variables should function as mediators.

In the empirical studies reported in the article, the authors found first evidence that stereotype threat activates knowledge related to the negative stereotype and elicits self-handicapping strategies, as well as self-doubt in participants targeted by negative stereotypic expectancies. In addition, Steele and Aronson (1995) tested whether stereotype threat was related to affective mechanisms such as anxiety and frustration, but failed to find any effects of the stereotype threat manipulation on these affective variables.

It is noteworthy that Steele and Aronson discussed and tested potential mediators that reflected affective, cognitive, and motivational mechanisms. As is evident when reading across the relevant studies, researchers in the field have tested a host of variables related to a variety of affective, cognitive, and motivational mechanisms. But the interested reader searching for a broad theoretical framework guiding this research will soon realize that no such framework exists. Nonetheless, some studies did find mediational evidence, and the respective mediator variables represent a diverse set of affective mechanisms: (a) anxiety (see Spencer et al., 1999), (b) dejection (see Keller & Dauenheimer, 2003), (c) cognitive mechanisms (mental load; see Schmader & Johns, 2003; Croizet et al., 2004), (d) stereotype activation (see Davies, Spencer, Quinn, & Gerhardstein, 2002), (e) negative thinking (see Cadinu, Maass, Rosabianca, & Kiesner, 2005), (f) motivational mechanisms (goal setting; see Kray, Galinsky, & Thompson, 2002), (g) performance expectancies (see Cadinu, Maass, Frigerio, Impagliazzo, & Latinotti, 2003), and (h) self-handicapping (see Keller, 2002).

Taken together, these findings reveal that some progress has been made in the search for mechanisms underlying the stereotype threat-performance link;

however, given the heterogeneity and inconsistency of findings (the supportive evidence found in some studies appears alongside contradictory evidence
in most cases), stereotype threat theorists tend to adopt a fairly vague position on this issue. For example, Steele and colleagues (2002, p. 406) close their
discussion of mediating mechanisms in their recent review chapter by referring to the multifaceted nature of stereotype threat, which leads them to the
conclusion that it is "almost unimaginable" that the phenomenon is "mediated
consistently through a single psychological process." This reflects the openness
(or inconclusiveness) of stereotype threat theorists' perspective on this important issue, and it would appear that there is still quite a lot work to be done
(both on theoretical and empirical grounds) in the attempt to come to a closer
understanding of the stereotype threat-performance link.

     Another line of research in the second generation of research on stereo-
type threat has focused on the analysis of interindividual differences in the susceptibility to stereotype threat. Parallel to the efforts to elaborate the mediating processes, the results obtained in this field have revealed a diverse set of
moderating personality factors and interindividual difference variables, such
as (a) a coping sense of humor (Ford, Ferguson, Brooks, & Hagadone, 2004),
(b) endorsement of the respective stereotype (Schmader, Johns, & Barquissau,
2004), (c) identification with the domain of ability (Aronson et al., 1999; Keller,
in press; Leyens et al., 2000; Stone, 2002), (d) identification with the target
group (Schmader, 2002), (e) self-monitoring tendencies (Inzlicht, Aronson,
Good, & McKay, in press), (f) stigma consciousness (Brown & Pinel, 2003),
and (g) testosterone level (Josephs, Newman, Brown, & Beer, 2003). These
findings reveal that there are quite a number of relevant personality dimensions that tend to increase the susceptibility to the detrimental effects of stereotype threat, and the respective studies represent important contributions to
the field; however, the conclusions that can be drawn from these studies are
somewhat limited because the evidence is correlational in nature, which implies that causal conclusions are not warranted based on these results. Although many of the established moderator variables (or at least the relevant
theoretical constructs behind them) could be experimentally varied (for example, Keller & Bless, 2005, applied an ease of retrieval manipulation in order to vary the subjective validity that participants attribute to the stereotypic
association between gender and emotional intelligence), the relevant experimental approach has not been pursued systematically. Thus, the actual causal
impact of the moderating factors established in these correlational studies
can hardly be evaluated.

     More recently, some researchers have started to explore the moderation is-
sue by applying an *experimental* approach. For example, O'Brien and Crandall
(2003) demonstrated the crucial role of task difficulty by varying the difficulty
level of the tasks participants had to work on. Aronson and his colleagues
(Aronson, Fried, & Good, 2002) documented that lay theoretical beliefs concerning the stability or malleability of intelligence function as a moderator of

stereotype threat effects on the performance of African American college students. Ambady, Paik, Steele, Owen-Smith, and Mitchell (2004) reported that individuation (the disclosure of personal information) eliminated detrimental effects of previously activated negative stereotypes. Moreover, Marx, Stapel, and Muller's (2005) work demonstrates that rendering positive social comparison information accessible can eliminate the disrupting stereotype threat effect on women's math performance (see also Marx & Roman, 2002). The work reported by Ben-Zeev, Fein, and Inzlicht (2005) reveals that stereotype threat effects on women's math performance can be attenuated when women have the opportunity to misattribute their arousal to an external source. In line with these latter results, Johns, Schmader, and Martens (2005) found that women who learned that the anxiety they might experience while working on a math test could be attributed to the negative stereotypes that are widely known in society did not show stereotype threat effects that were obtained in a control condition.

Given the multitude of factors that have been explored and the range of findings that have been obtained in the research on stereotype threat, a conclusive summary of where the field finds itself at this time is hardly possible. We think, however, that it is appropriate to emphasize three aspects in concluding this overview on stereotype threat research. First, the second generation of research on stereotype threat appears to be methodologically biased in the sense that most researchers have addressed either the mediation question by conducting mediational analyses, or they have tested interindividual difference factors that may moderate the stereotype threat effect on performance. Because both approaches are correlational in nature, the conclusions that can be drawn from the obtained findings are to some extent limited. Moreover, the findings obtained in the search for mediators are somewhat inconsistent and far from conclusive. Given these interpretative restrictions, surprisingly little research on stereotype threat has applied an experimental approach to the study of moderating factors.

Second, research on the impact of stereotypic group-based expectancies on test performance has almost exclusively addressed *negative* group-based expectancies (e.g., women can't do math; African Americans are not intelligent; elderly people are forgetful), although there is good reason to assume that—at least under certain circumstances—positive expectancies (e.g., men are naturally talented in math, Asians are gifted in mathematical reasoning) can elicit threat experiences in target persons as well. Thus, there also seems to be a bias at the conceptual level (and as a consequence in the research agenda): stereotype threat has been defined fairly narrowly with a focus on negative stereotypic expectancies. As a consequence, the fact that positive group-based expectancies may also form the basis of threat experiences and performance decrements has been neglected

Third, since stereotype threat theory is more or less neutral concerning the mechanisms that drive the effect of stereotypic expectancies on performance, the search for the underlying mechanisms has not been guided by a systematic theoretical perspective, but can be described as a piecemeal analysis of a diverse set of potential mediating variables. Moreover, we believe that motivational mechanisms of self-regulation have been insufficiently addressed in the second generation of research (researchers seem to focus on affect- and arousal-based processes on the one hand, and on cognitive processes on the other, thus largely neglecting "hot" motivational mechanisms of self-regulation; but see Seibt & Förster, 2004).

We elaborate on these issues in the remainder of this chapter. In the section that follows, we outline our suggested refinements to the concept of stereotype threat. This conceptual aspect leads us to the core issue that we address in our research program: the boundary conditions of stereotype threat experiences in test-performance settings.

A CONCEPTUAL REFINEMENT:
POSITIVE AND NEGATIVE EXPECTANCY THREAT

As previously mentioned, research on stereotype threat thus far has focused exclusively on how the communication of negative stereotypic expectancies influences test performance; however, one may argue that positive expectancies can be associated with threat experiences and reduced performance as well. For example, Baumeister, Hamilton, and Tice (1985; see also Baumeister, Hutton, & Cairns, 1990) found that positive expectancies held and communicated by an audience can constitute a performance pressure (e.g., a threat) and harm performance. In a similar vein, Seta and Seta (1995) were able to show that participants' performance levels decreased in the presence of an audience holding a positive expectancy based on the target's prior success at the task. Most important in the present context are the findings reported by Cheryan and Bodenhausen (2000). Addressing specifically the impact of *stereotypic* expectancies, these authors found that the performance of Asian American participants on a math test decreased under conditions where the Asian identity and stereotype had been activated. In this case, the positive performance expectancy derived from the Asian stereotype resulted in decreased test performance (similar findings are reported by Shih, Ambady, Richeson, Fujita, & Gray, 2002). In these studies, the participants confronted with a *positive* self-relevant expectancy probably experienced an added performance pressure (a threat) based on the fear of not being able to live up to (or conform to) the respective positive expectancy.

These findings suggest that detrimental effects of stereotypic performance expectancies are *not* restricted to negative group-based expectations. Accordingly, we propose that two forms of expectancy threat effects on performance should be differentiated: (a) positive expectancy threat and (b) negative expectancy threat. We argue that negative expectancy threat can be understood as the fear of confirming a negative stereotypic expectancy (which is in line with the "classic" definition of stereotype threat as a negative expectancy phenomenon). Going beyond this "classic" definition, we argue that threat experiences can also emerge in situations where people experience the fear of not being able to conform to a communicator's positive stereotypic expectancy. We assume that in both cases, the targets of group-based expectancies experience a fear of failure (note, however, that different types of failure are relevant in each case) and a state of defensiveness (based on the desire to avoid failure). Also, we assume that *defensiveness* represents a basic mechanism underlying stereotype threat effects on performance. Such states of defensiveness can be triggered not only in situations where a negative standard serves as reference point (defensiveness based on the fear of failing to reject or refute a negative stereotypic expectation), but also in situations where a positive standard serves as reference point (defensiveness based on the fear of failing to meet a positive stereotypic expectation).

This conceptual refinement leads us directly to a question that we believe has been only marginally addressed in the research on stereotype threat: what are the crucial boundary conditions that determine when we may expect positive and negative stereotypic expectancy threat effects on performance? To address this fundamental question, we started from the assumption that the experience of threat and defensiveness is a state that emerges in situations when people are involved in the process of self-regulation in an attempt to bring the self into alignment with preferred standards (Baumeister & Vohs, 2004) and perceive a possibility that they might fail to reach the respective standard. Accordingly, we propose that self-regulatory mechanisms are involved in the stereotype threat-performance link. As a consequence, we hypothesize that the mode of self-regulation (e.g., the orientation that is guiding the self-regulatory mechanisms in the person) represents a basic boundary condition that has a crucial impact on the sensitivity to positive and negative standards, and hence on the likelihood of positive and negative expectancy threat effects.

It is noteworthy that up to now, "hot" motivational mechanisms of self-regulation[1] have not received much attention in stereotype threat research,

---

[1] A clarification regarding what the term "hot" motivational mechanism reflects in our framework seems necessary because some authors in the field of social cognition refer to "hot" mechanisms when they discuss the impact of affective/emotional states on human information processing, whereas others have used the term to refer to the impact of goals on information processing. In our view, "hot" motivational mechanisms are characterized by the following aspects: (a) the self-concept is actively involved in the process; (b) motives (or goals) energize the psychological system (the desire to reach a distinct end-state is activated); (c) the process involves sensations of energetic arousal (an *experiential state* of alertness and activation); and (d) distinct patterns of physiological arousal (e.g., heart rate, change in cortisol levels) are likely to be involved. From our perspective, "hot" motivational mechanisms should be differentiated from "cold" associative processes. Accordingly, we propose that "hot" motivational mechanisms reflect

even though the definition of stereotype threat refers to concepts that clearly reflect the "hot" motivational and self-regulatory nature of the phenomenon (stereotype threat as the fear of confirming a self-relevant negative stereotype). Thus, our theoretical perspective can be seen as an attempt to bring the hot motivational component of stereotype threat front and center in the field of stereotype threat research.

THREAT EFFECTS AND REGULATORY FOCUS THEORY

In pursuing what appears to be a neglected question, we emphasize the role of motivational and self-regulatory determinants (while readily acknowledging the potential relevance of affective and cognitive influences in the stereotype threat-performance link). We are proposing a theoretical idea that integrates expectancy threat effects into one of the most prominent general motivational frameworks in the social psychological literature to date: regulatory focus theory (Higgins, 1997, 1998). The basic characteristics of regulatory focus theory and its link to positive and negative stereotypic expectancies are outlined in the next sections.

Regulatory Focus Theory

Regulatory Focus Theory (Higgins, 1997, 1998) holds that there are two distinct modes of self-regulation: (a) self-regulation with a promotion focus, and (b) self-regulation with a prevention focus. The two foci are related to specific sets of psychological variables. First, input variables are assumed to induce either of the two motivational states. It is postulated that nurturance needs, ideals as relevant standards, and gain/no-gain situations induce self-regulation with a promotion focus, whereas security needs, oughts as relevant standards, and nonloss/loss situations elicit self-regulation with a prevention focus. The mode of self-regulation can be activated situationally (e.g., due to the salience of gains or losses in a situation) as well as chronically (as the consequence of distinct parenting styles).

Second, output variables capture specific psychological consequences that are related to the activation of either mode of self-regulation. Most important for the line of reasoning that we outline below, the activation of a promotion focus is associated with (a) sensitivity to the presence or absence of *positive*

---

more than the simple fact that goals (in the sense of mental representations of end-states) are involved. We argue that the *experiential* aspect of "hot" motivational mechanisms cannot be reduced to and is not reflected in conceptualizations of goal-related processes that focus exclusively on "cold" automatic processes (activation of mental representations of end-states and related behavioral representations).

outcomes and a focus on reaching maximal goals (e.g., goals that differentiate a positive region of outcome-valence from a nonpositive region of outcome-valence, cf. Brendl & Higgins, 1996), (b) eagerness as strategic means (e.g., to insure hits and to protect against errors of omission), and (c) cheerfulness-dejection emotions. In contrast, according to regulatory focus theory, the activation of a prevention focus is associated with (a) a sensitivity to the presence or absence of negative outcomes and a focus on reaching minimal goals (e.g., goals that differentiate a negative region of outcome-valence from a nonnegative region of outcome-valence; cf. Brendl & Higgins, 1996), (b) vigilance as strategic means (e.g., ensuring correct rejections and protecting against errors of commission), (c) risk aversion, and (d) quiescence-agitation emotions. Numerous studies have supported these core assumptions of regulatory focus theory (for reviews, see Higgins, 1998, or Higgins and Spiegel, 2004).

Boundary Conditions of Expectancy Effects: Regulatory Focus as a Crucial Moderator

Using regulatory focus theory as a theoretical background, we hypothesize that expectancy effects on performance are moderated by the mode of self-regulation that is activated in a given situation. Therefore, our basic theoretical assumption is referred to as the Moderation of Expectancy Effects by Regulatory Focus (MERF) hypothesis (Keller & Bless, 2006). The *MERF hypothesis* postulates an interactive relationship between the type of expectancy (positive vs. negative) and the prevailing mode of self-regulation (promotion vs. prevention) in a given performance situation; that is, all else being equal, positive (and negative) expectations should have differential effects on performance, depending on whether a promotion or a prevention focus is activated.

If specific input variables that elicit prevention concerns are present in a situation (e.g., oughts, need for security, potential losses), one should find a special sensitivity to negative expectancies and minimal goal standards (such as the goal of not performing poorly in an attempt not to confirm a negative expectancy). We predict that negative expectancies are most likely to be perceived as threatening when the prevention mode of self-regulation prevails, because people are most likely to experience apprehension about meeting minimal goal standards (such as avoiding the confirmation of a negative expectancy) when self-regulation is guided by prevention concerns. Accordingly, we expect that negative expectancies lead to reduced performance under prevention focus conditions when compared to positive expectancies. As in research on stereotype threat, we assume that this effect will be especially pronounced if the task at hand is rather difficult.

In contrast, if specific input variables that elicit promotion concerns are present in a situation (e.g., high sensitivity to the implications of personal ideals, need for nurturance, salience of potential gains), we would expect to find a special sensitivity to positive expectations and maximal goal standards (e.g, the goal of reaching a high performance level in an attempt to conform to positive expectancies). Since a positive expectancy per se implies a high standard as the relevant criterion, it is possible that positive expectancies are perceived as threatening. It is most likely that positive (vs. negative) expectancies are perceived as threatening—resulting in negative effects on performance—when the promotion mode of self-regulation is activated, because reaching an ideal or optimal performance level (e.g., reaching a maximal goal) is of critical importance under promotion focus conditions. Hence, we argue that people are most likely to experience apprehension about meeting maximal goal standards (such as conforming to a positive expectancy) when self-regulation is guided by promotion concerns.

The MERF Hypothesis Put to the Test

We set out to put our crucial moderation hypothesis to a test in a series of studies. In these experiments, participants worked on test items under conditions of positive and negative expectancies (which were manipulated using test descriptions that refer to the fair or biased nature of the respective test—a method that has been applied in many previous stereotype threat studies as discussed above), and in which a distinct self-regulatory orientation (e.g., a promotion or prevention focus) was *situationally* induced or assessed as a *chronic* self-regulatory orientation (cf. Keller, 2004; Keller & Bless, 2006).

In one of these studies, we invited female university students into the lab and asked them to work on a test that consisted of items taken from the German driver's license written examination. Participants learned that the study was part of a research project on differences in general knowledge between social groups, and that this particular study addressed differences with regard to knowledge of traffic rules. The test was given with different sets of instructions designed to manipulate the valence of the performance expectancy, as well as situational regulatory focus. Performance expectancy was manipulated using a method that is commonly applied in stereotype threat research (cf., Spencer et al., 1999): half of the participants read that the test had been shown to produce gender differences in favor of men (negative expectancy), whereas the other half read that the test had been shown to produce gender differences in favor of women (positive expectancy).

The regulatory focus manipulation that we use in most of our studies is an adapted version of a task-framing procedure that has been applied successfully in previous research to induce different modes of self-regulation (e.g., Shah, Higgins, & Friedman, 1998). In order to induce a promotion focus, half of the participants were informed prior to the test that they would receive one point for each item solved correctly, and that no points were deducted for wrong answers. In addition, they learned that a reasonable strategy for achieving a good test result was to try and solve as many test items as possible. In contrast, participants in the prevention focus condition read that they would receive one point for each item solved correctly, but that one point would be deducted from their test score for every wrong or missing test item. Also, they were informed that a reasonable strategy for avoiding a poor test result was to try and avoid errors. Note that participants under prevention focus conditions learned that point deductions would be made not only for wrong but also for missing items. This statement should ensure that participants would not stop working on the test after solving a minimal number of test items; that is, it should prevent a main effect of the focus manipulation on the number of items attempted (and it would appear that we were successful in this endeavor, since a focus main effect on the number of items attempted did not emerge in any of our studies). Following these instructions, participants had five minutes to work on the test items.

As outlined in the introduction to our theoretical framework, the MERF hypothesis predicts an interaction effect involving valence of performance expectancy and regulatory focus. In support of that prediction, we found that test performance was a function of expectancy and mode of self-regulation, reflected in a significant interaction effect (see Fig. 16–2). Specifically, negative expectancies were associated with poorer performance more than positive expectancies when the prevention focus was activated. In contrast, when the promotion focus was activated, positive expectancies were associated with poorer performance more than negative expectancies. This pattern supports our theorizing that the mode of self-regulation activated in a given situation serves a

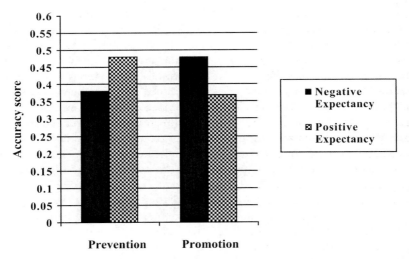

FIGURE 16–2.   Test performance as a function of regulatory focus and valence of performance expectancy.

crucial moderating role regarding the sensitivity that people show toward positive and negative performance expectancies. These results indicate that the communication of both negative and positive expectancies can result in decreased test performance, thus pointing to the need to focus research on stereotype threat not only on negative, but also on positive expectancies as potential sources of threat experiences and underperformance. Moreover, the obtained pattern suggests that—in line with our reasoning—"hot" motivational processes of self-regulation seem to play a prominent role in the stereotype threat-performance link.

Importantly, we successfully replicated this crucial interaction effect involving regulatory focus and valence of performance expectancy in several additional studies. For example, we found that male students reached a lower performance level on verbal tasks when they were confronted with a negative as compared to a positive expectancy under prevention focus conditions, whereas the reverse was true when participants worked on the verbal tasks under promotion focus test-framing conditions (cf. Keller, 2004, Exp. 2). Moreover, we found a significant interaction pattern when we tested female students' spatial ability (cf. Keller, 2004, Exp. 3). Again, the test takers reached lower performance levels under the critical conditions that, according to the MERF hypothesis, are most likely to elicit a threat experience and underperformance (prevention focus coupled with a negative expectancy or promotion focus coupled with a positive expectancy). Given this line of consistent findings supporting the moderation function that we assign to the mode of self-regulation in our theoretical perspective, we argue that there is good reason to assume that self-regulatory mechanisms do play an important role in the stereotype threat/performance link. Moreover, the fact that we applied an experimental approach in studying the moderator function of self-regulatory mechanism allows for comparatively strong conclusions regarding the causal impact that can be attributed to these mechanisms.

In addition, we also conducted a study in which we applied a quasi-experimental research method regarding the regulatory focus factor in an attempt to test whether a parallel pattern of results can be found when assessing chronic regulatory concerns (e.g., interindividual differences in self-regulatory orientations), instead of manipulating regulatory focus experimentally. In this study, we pursued a somewhat more applied strategy in manipulating performance expectancies of female participants who were asked to work on a math test. Rather than manipulating the description of the test (as biased for or against participants' own gender group), shortly before participants started to solve the respective test items, we made use of an intervention paradigm introduced by Aronson, Fried, and Good (2002). In order to induce positive performance expectancies, half of the participants attended two sessions spaced two weeks apart. Participants learned that the study investigated the impact of a mentoring program designed to give younger high-school students encouragement and to foster their academic orientation. In this context, participants were led to believe that they served as mentors and were asked to write two letters (one in each of the two lab sessions) to high-school girls, motivating them to persist in school and to put effort into math classes. As a source of information for their letters, participants received a text that argued that stable and meaningful gender differences in math performance are virtually nonexistent (thus, these participants were confronted with a positive expectancy[2]). In the second session, the procedure was repeated and the participants wrote a second letter, ostensibly to another high-school girl. Participants in the negative expectancy control condition did not participate in the intervention part of the study (e.g., they were expected to enter the math test session holding more negative expectancies concerning women's math ability—which was in fact the case, as a manipulation check indicated—and accordingly felt confronted with the "standard" negative stereotypic expectancies as implied in the "women can't do math" stereotype).

Prior to the math test session, participants in this study also worked on a questionnaire that assessed chronic regulatory concerns in the performance domain (Keller, 2006). This procedure allowed us to test the hypothesis that interindividual differences in self-regulatory orientations qualify the impact of expectancies that participants were chronically confronted with (negative in case of the control group participants) or had been confronted with in the intervention sessions (positive expectancy). All participants were then confronted with the test situation; that is, they worked on a math test. In line with

---

[2]At this point, a critical reader might be tempted to argue that leading participants to believe that there are no gender differences in math constitutes not a positive, but rather a neutral expectancy induction. This seems to be correct from an outsider perspective addressing this issue in what may be termed "an absolute sense." From an insider or target perspective, it seems more appropriate to address this issue in relative terms. For example, it seems questionable to argue that the players of a soccer team that could not manage to win a single match during a season feel confronted with a neutral expectancy when they learn that their team manager expects them to achieve a draw in their next match against the top-ranked team. In absolute terms, this can be construed as a neutral expectancy. However, it is most likely that the players perceive this expectancy as fairly high, and probably even as unrealistically positive in character. Moreover, the term "neutral expectancy" seems questionable in itself. From our perspective, such a term makes sense only under very specific conditions: (a) when someone is performing on a test where none of the existing stereotypic expectancies concerning the ability of social groups or categories apply (for example, on a new type of test designed to assess a completely new type of ability that cannot be related to any of the existing abilities that are already stereotypically categorized), or (b) when someone is performing a task under conditions where he or she is not aware that the task represents a test that allows for an evaluative judgment concerning his or her ability (note that the nondiagnosticity inductions as applied in some of stereotype threat research come closest to an operationalization of a "neutral" expectancy; in these nondiagnostic conditions, participants are led to believe that they are not performing an ability test, but are taking part in a study designed to assess psychological problem solving or some other topic unrelated to intellectual ability).

the MERF hypothesis and the findings obtained using experimental manipulations of regulatory focus, we found that inducing a positive expectancy had
a beneficial effect on those participants who were chronically prevention-
oriented. In contrast, the same positive expectancies impaired the performance of participants who were chronically promotion-oriented, reflecting a
significant interaction effect of chronic regulatory focus and the expectancy
manipulation. Most importantly, the interaction pattern mirrored the results
obtained in the experimental studies mentioned above. These findings bolster
the MERF hypothesis and indicate that the interaction effect that we obtained
in the experimental studies can be replicated even when a fairly different
methodological approach is being pursued.

Taken together, the reported research provides clear and consistent support
for the basic ideas that we put forth concerning the conceptualization of
stereotype threat and the crucial role of self-regulatory mechanisms. Across the
experiments, the interplay of expectancy and regulatory focus consistently affected participants' performance. Specifically, the interaction pattern revealed
that when a prevention focus was activated, negative stereotypic expectancies
impaired performance relative to positive expectancies. In contrast, when a
promotion focus was activated, positive expectancies resulted in poorer performance than negative expectancies. This suggests that our proposed refinement regarding the conceptualization of stereotype threat—a differentiation
between positive and negative expectancy threat—seems well indicated, given
the data we obtained in our studies. Obviously, it is not only negative expectancies that can result in performance decrements. Under certain circumstances—one of which is a promotion-focused orientation of self-regulation—
positive expectancies can disrupt performance outcomes as well. Thus, it
seems to be somewhat misleading to focus attention exclusively on the detrimental effects of negative stereotypic expectancies, as has been the case in
the theorizing and research on stereotype threat so far. Of course, in pointing to this peculiarity of stereotype threat research, we most certainly do not
intent to downplay the prevalence or relevance of negative stereotypic expectancy effects. Rather, we want to direct attention to the fact that there are
critical factors that may contribute to the strength and prevalence of "classic"
stereotype threat effects. It may well be that in everyday environments these
factors are structured in such a way that "classic" stereotype threat effects are
more likely to be observed than positive expectancy threat effects. For example, recent research suggests that rendering group membership salient results in increased prevention concerns in persons who are members of stigmatized social groups (Oyserman, Uskul, Yoder, Nesse, & Williams, 2006).
Hence, there is reason to assume that members of stigmatized social groups
may develop a chronic tendency to react with prevention-focused concerns in
situations where their stigmatized status comes to the fore. If that is true, the
performance of these individuals would most probably suffer in situations in

which negative stereotypic expectations associated with their membership in a stigmatized group are salient. Moreover, it seems plausible to assume that most people show an increased level of agitation, tenseness, worry, and anxiety (e.g., they experience a state which may be characterized as prevention-focused) when they enter a situation in which their intellectual ability is being assessed (of course, people differ in the degree to which they experience such a state of agitation and anxiety in testing situations [cf. Sarason, 1984; Zeidner, 1998]; however, it seems reasonable to assume that the most prevalent reaction to be observed in people entering a testing situation can be described as prevention-focused in character). As a consequence, one may expect negative threat effects to be more prevalent than positive threat effects under standard testing conditions.

From our perspective, the fact that the "classic" stereotype threat effect has been observed rather consistently in experimental research (whereas the reverse pattern that we found under promotion focus conditions did not emerge) may reflect the fact that (a) in general, testing situations as such are likely to trigger a prevention-focused orientation in test takers, and (b) almost all studies testing stereotype threat theory drew on stigmatized participants who are chronically targeted by negative expectancies in the critical domain of ability (e.g., women in the field of math or African American students in academia) and may have adopted a chronic prevention focus orientation associated with the respective field of ability. Note, however, that there are also quite a number of unpublished studies where researchers failed to find the "classic" effect, which, from our perspective, could reflect the fact that prevention concerns were not strong enough in the respective test takers, or not particularly salient in the respective testing situation. On a side note, we want to point out that in testing stereotype threat theory, many researchers (e.g., Croizet & Claire, 1998; Steele & Aronson, 1995) applied a distinct method that is designed to eradicate negative expectancies by eliminating evaluative concerns through a nondiagnosticity manipulation, inducing what may be termed a *neutral* expectancy (see Footnote 2); that is, those studies did not include an appropriate positive expectancy condition that could have triggered a positive expectancy threat of the kind that emerged in our studies when we activated a promotion focus coupled with positive group-based expectancies that were induced using a different manipulation of stereotype threat. Taken together, it comes as no surprise that a negative expectancy threat effect has so far emerged rather consistently in stereotype threat research.

To make this point clear, we do not at all ignore or deny the potentially widespread and very negative consequences of negative stereotypic expectations. What we do want to emphasize is the fact that there are critical boundary conditions—and we specifically refer to "hot" mechanisms of self-regulation—that may help us understand the processes underlying stereotypic expectancy effects on performance.

CONCLUSION

Our aim in this chapter was to draw the readers' attention to several peculiarities that seem to characterize previous research on stereotype threat and—starting off from this introductory overview—to present the specific theoretical perspective we are pursuing in our own examination of the effects that the communication of positive and negative group-based expectancies may have on test takers' performance outcomes. Concerning the peculiarities of stereotype threat research, we referred to methodological and conceptual aspects that stand out. We argued that the research agenda in the field is kind of biased, in two respects. First, in the attempt to explicate the underlying process of stereotype threat effects on performance, most researchers have focused on the assessment of potential mediator variables and have conducted mediational analyses. The alternative strategy that may be applied in order to come to a closer understanding of the mechanisms that are involved in the stereotype threat-performance link—the systematic manipulation of boundary conditions that may qualify the effects of stereotypic expectancies on performance (Spencer, Zanna, & Fong, 2005)—did not receive much attention. Although researchers have tested quite a number of interindividual difference factors that may increase or decrease the susceptibility to stereotype threat effects, the experimental approach to the study of moderating factors that may qualify the stereotype threat-performance link received little attention. Accordingly, a critical analyst referring to the correlational nature of the vast majority of findings obtained in the second generation of research on stereotype threat could argue that this evidence is of only limited explanatory value.

Second, the research agenda is also biased in a conceptual sense. As we explained above, the phenomenon of stereotype threat has been defined fairly narrowly, with the focus on the potential detrimental impact of negative stereotypic expectancies. The fact that threat effects may be elicited by positive group-based expectancies, as well, has been overlooked or neglected thus far in the ongoing research in this field. We argue that this somewhat one-sided perspective should be broadened, given the fact that positive (stereotypic) expectancies have been found to disrupt performance outcomes in several empirical studies. Accordingly, we propose a refinement of the stereotype threat concept by introducing a differentiation of two forms of stereotype threat effects. This differentiation implies that stereotype threat can emerge as the consequence of being the target of (a) negative group-based expectancies ("classic" type of negative expectancy threat), or (b) positive group-based expectancies (positive expectancy threat).

These methodological and conceptual considerations led us to the main theoretical topic that we addressed in the second part of the chapter: the analysis of boundary conditions that determine when each of the two forms of expectancy threat is most likely to emerge. We started from the general idea that stereotype threat can be seen as a phenomenon that is closely related to processes of self-regulation. Based on this assumption, we proposed a moderation hypothesis according to which the mode of self-regulation (promotion vs. prevention) represents a crucial boundary factor that may determine the impact of positive and negative stereotypic expectancies on performance outcomes. More specifically, we hypothesized an interactive relationship between the valence of performance expectancy and the mode of self-regulation activated in the testing situation, such that detrimental effects of negative expectancies are most likely to emerge under prevention focus conditions, whereas positive expectancies are most likely to result in performance decrements under promotion focus conditions.

As described in the final part of our chapter, the results that we obtained in the studies we conducted concur with our hypothesis: negative threat effects consistently emerged under prevention but not under promotion focus conditions, whereas the reverse was true with regard to positive expectancy threat effects. These findings are noteworthy in several respects. First, the evidence reveals that there is good reason to assume that "hot" self-regulatory mechanisms do play an important role in the stereotype threat-performance link. Given the fact that self-regulatory mechanisms have been largely neglected in stereotype threat research so far, our findings documenting the crucial impact of self-regulatory mechanisms are particularly notable.

Second, our research results are clearly less vulnerable to interpretative ambiguities than is the case in studies focusing on interindividual differences in susceptibility to stereotype threat effects, since the experimental (rather than the correlational) approach in studying the boundary conditions of stereotype threat effects took priority in our work.

Third, our findings suggest that being confronted with negative performance expectancies does not necessarily result in detrimental effects on performance. In fact, the pattern of results that we obtained under promotion focus conditions seems to suggest that negative expectancies may even result in a performance boost (although such an interpretation may be premature at this point, since our studies did not include "neutral" expectancy control conditions). The fact that negative performance expectancies do not necessarily result in detrimental effects on performance has also been noted by other authors in the field. For example, Seibt and Förster (2004) found that negative expectancies triggered a careful processing style resulting in enhanced performance on analytic tasks, whereas positive expectancies triggered an eager processing style (focusing on speed rather than accuracy) resulting in decreased performance on analytic tasks. This suggests that the type of task reflects another crucial factor that may determine the performance outcomes of individuals who are confronted with positive or negative expectancies.

Fourth, in documenting the moderating function of self-regulatory mechanisms concerning the effects of positive or negative performance expectancies, we uncovered a factor that may be implemented in educational settings (e.g., in intervention programs) in the attempt to enable students to flourish in achievement settings, even under societal conditions where they may be targeted by widespread negative stereotypic performance expectancies (e.g., women in the field of math), which are obviously very hard to erase. According to our approach, it might be worthwhile to apply an intervention strategy that addresses the motivational orientation that these students bring into performance situations where they are confronted with negative stereotypical expectancies. Our findings suggest that helping such students to approach these performance situations with a promotion rather than a prevention orientation may be a promising strategy in aiding these students in overcoming the added performance pressure associated with the experience of negative expectancy threat. These ideas concerning the potential implementations of our theoretical approach in everyday settings raise our hope that the line of research on the underlying mechanisms of stereotype threat effects on performance we are pursuing may contribute not only to a better understanding of the phenomenon itself, but may also help us to develop feasible strategies for overcoming the negative consequences of stereotype threat in those who are targeted by stereotypic expectancies concerning their ability.

REFERENCES

Ambady, N., Paik, S. K., Steele, J., Owen-Smith, A., & Mitchell, J. P. (2004). Deflecting negative self-relevant stereotype activation: The effects of individuation. *Journal of Experimental Social Psychology, 40*, 401–408.

Aronson, J., Fried, C. B., & Good, C. (2002). Reducing the effects of stereotype threat on African American college students by shaping theories of intelligence. *Journal of Experimental Social Psychology, 38*, 113–125.

Aronson, J., Lustina, M. J., Good, C., Keough, K. Steele, C. M., & Brown, J. (1999). When white men can't do math: Necessary and sufficient factors in stereotype threat. *Journal of Experimental Social Psychology, 35*, 29–46.

Baumeister, R. F., Hamilton, J. C., & Tice, D. M. (1985). Public versus private expectancy of success: Confidence booster or performance pressure? *Journal of Personality and Social Psychology, 48*, 1447–1457.

Baumeister, R. F., Hutton, D. G., & Cairns, K. J. (1990). Negative effects of praise on skilled performance. *Basic and Applied Social Psychology, 11*, 131–148.

Baumeister, R. F., & Vohs, K. D. (Eds.). (2004). *Handbook of self-regulation: Research, theory, and applications.* New York, NY: Guilford Press.

Ben-Zeev, T., Fein, S., & Inzlicht, M. (2005). Arousal and stereotype threat. *Journal of Experimental Social Psychology, 41*, 174–181.

Blascovich, J., Spencer, S. J., Quinn, D. M., & Steele, C. M. (2001). Stereotype threat and the cardiovascular reactivity of African-Americans. *Psychological Science, 12*, 225–229.

Brendl, C. M., & Higgins, E. T. (1996). Principles of judging valence: What makes events positive or negative? In M. P. Zanna (Ed.), *Advances in experimental social psychology* (Vol. 28, pp. 95–160). San Diego, CA: Academic Press.

Brown, R. P., & Pinel, E. C. (2003). Stigma on my mind: Individual differences in the experience of stereotype threat. *Journal of Experimental Social Psychology, 39*, 626–633.

Cadinu, M., Maass, A., Frigerio, S., Impagliazzo, L., & Latinotti, S. (2003). Stereotype threat: The effects of expectancy on performance. *European Journal of Social Psychology, 33*, 267–285.

Cadinu, M., Maass, A., Rosabianca, A., & Kiesner, J. (2005). Why do women underperform under stereotype threat? Evidence for the role of negative thinking. *Psychological Science, 16*, 572–578.

Cheryan, S., & Bodenhausen, G. V. (2000). When positive stereotypes threaten intellectual performance: The psychological hazards of "model minority" status. *Psychological Science, 11*, 399–402.

Croizet, J. C., & Claire, T. (1998). Extending the concept of stereotype threat to social class: The intellectual underperformance of students from low socioeconomic backgrounds. *Personality and Social Psychology Bulletin, 24*, 588–594.

Croizet, J. C., Després, G., Gauzins, M.-E., Huguet, P., Leyens, J.-P., & Méot, A. (2004). Stereotype threat undermines intellectual performance by triggering a disruptive mental load. *Personality and Social Psychology Bulletin, 30*, 721–731.

Davies, P. G., Spencer, S. J., Quinn, D. M., & Gerhardstein, R. (2002). Consuming images: How television commercials that elicit stereotype threat can restrain women academically and professionally. *Personality and Social Psychology Bulletin, 28*, 1615–1628.

Fiske, S. T. (1998). Stereotyping, prejudice, and discrimination. In D. T. Gilbert, S. T. Fiske, & G. Lindzey (Eds.), *Handbook of social psychology Vol. 2* (4th ed., pp. 357–411). New York, NY: McGraw Hill.

Ford, T. E., Ferguson, M. A., Brooks, J. L., & Hagadone, K. M. (2004). Coping sense of humor reduces effects of stereotype threat on women's math performance. *Personality and Social Psychology Bulletin, 30*, 643–653.

Gonzales, P. M., Blanton, H., & Williams, K. J. (2002). The effects of stereotype threat and double-minority status on the test performance of Latino women. *Personality and Social Psychology Bulletin, 28*, 659–670.

Higgins, E. T. (1997). Beyond pleasure and pain. *American Psychologist, 52*, 1280–1300.

Higgins, E. T. (1998). Promotion and prevention: Regulatory focus as a motivational principle. In M. P. Zanna (Ed.), *Advances in experimental social psychology* (Vol. 30, pp. 1–46). San Diego, CA: Academic Press.

Higgins, E. T., & Spiegel, S. (2004). Promotion and prevention strategies for self-regulation: A motivated cognition perspective. In R. F. Baumeister & C. Vohs (Eds.), *Handbook of self-regulation* (pp. 171–187). New York: Guilford.

Inzlicht, M., Aronson, J., Good, C., & McKay, L. (in press). A particular resilience to stereotype threat. *Journal of Experimental Social Psychology.*

Johns, M., Schmader, T., & Martens, A. (2005). Knowing is half the battle. *Psychological Science, 16*, 175–179.

Josephs, R. A., Newman, M. G., Brown, R. P., & Beer, J. M. (2003). Status, testosterone, and human intellectual performance: Stereotype threat as status concerns. *Psychological Science, 14*, 158-163.

Keller, J. (2002). Blatant stereotype threat and women's math performance: Self-handicapping as a strategic means to cope with obtrusive negative performance expectations. *Sex Roles, 47*, 193–198.

Keller, J. (2004). *Expectancy effects in performance situations.* Lengerich, Germany: Pabst Science Publishers.

Keller, J. (in press). Stereotype threat in classroom settings: The interactive effect of domain identification, task difficulty, and stereotype threat on female students' math performance. *British Journal of Educational Psychology.*

Keller, J. (2006). *Development and validation of a self-report scale assessing performance-related chronic self-regulatory concerns: The regulatory concerns questionnaire.* Manuscript in preparation .

Keller, J., & Bless, H. (2005). When negative expectancies turn into negative performance: The role of ease of retrieval. *Journal of Experimental Social Psychology, 41*, 535–541.

Keller, J., & Bless, H. (2006). *Expectancy effects on cognitive test performance: Regulatory focus as a catalyst.* Manuscript submitted for publication.

Keller, J., & Dauenheimer, D. (2003). Stereotype threat in the classroom: Dejection mediates the disrupting threat effect on women's math performance. *Personality and Social Psychology Bulletin, 29,* 371–381.

Kray, L. J., Thompson, L., & Galinsky, A. (2001). Battle of the sexes: Gender confirmation and reactance in negotiations. *Journal of Personality and Social Psychology, 80,* 942–958.

Kray, L. J., Galinsky, A., & Thompson, L. (2002). Reversing the gender gap in negotiations: An exploration of stereotype regeneration. *Organizational Behavior and Human Decision Processes, 87,* 386–409.

Levy, B. (1996). Improving memory in old age through implicit self-stereotyping. *Journal of Personality and Social Psychology, 71,* 1092–1107.

Leyens, J.-P., Désert, M., Croizet, J.-C., & Darcis, C. (2000). Stereotype threat: Are lower status and history of stigmatization preconditions of stereotype threat? *Personality and Social Psychology Bulletin, 26,* 1189–1199.

Marx, D. M., & Roman, J. S. (2002). Female role models: Protecting women's math test performance. *Personality and Social Psychology Bulletin, 28,* 1183–1193.

Marx, D. M., Stapel, D. A., & Muller, D. (2005). We can do it: The interplay of construal orientation and social comparison under threat. *Journal of Personality and Social Psychology, 88,* 432–446

O'Brien, L., & Crandall, C. S. (2003). Stereotype threat and arousal: Effects on women's math performance. *Personality and Social Psychology Bulletin, 29,* 782–789.

Oyserman, D., Uskul, A., Yoder, N., Nesse, R., & Williams, D. (2006). *Unfair treatment and self-regulatory focus.* Manuscript submitted for publication.

Rahhal, T. A., Hasher, L., & Colombe, S. J. (2001). Instructional implications and age differences in memory: Now you see them, now you don't. *Psychology and Aging, 16,* 697–706.

Sarason, I. G. (1984). Stress, anxiety, and cognitive interference: Reactions to tests. *Journal of Personality and Social Psychology, 46,* 929–938.

Schmader, T. (2002). Gender identification moderates stereotype threat effects on women's math performance. *Journal of Experimental Social Psychology, 38,* 194–201.

Schmader, T., & Johns, M. (2003). Converging evidence that stereotype threat reduces working memory capacity. *Journal of Personality and Social Psychology, 85,* 440–452.

Schmader, T., Johns, M., & Barquissau, M. (2004). The costs of accepting gender differences: The role of stereotype endorsement in women's experience in the math domain. *Sex Roles, 50,* 835–850.

Seibt, B., & Förster, J. (2004). Stereotype threat and performance: How self-stereotypes influence processing by inducing regulatory foci. *Journal of Personality and Social Psychology, 87,* 38–56.

Seta, C. E., & Seta, J. J. (1995). When audience presence is enjoyable: The influences of audience awareness of prior success on performance and task interest. *Basic and Applied Social Psychology, 16,* 95–108.

Shah, J., Higgins, E. T., & Friedman, R. S. (1998). Performance incentives and means: How regulatory focus influences goal attainment. *Journal of Personality and Social Psychology, 74,* 285–293.

Sharps, M. J., Welton, A. L., & Price, J. L. (1993). Gender and task in the determination of spatial cognitive performance. *Psychology of Women Quarterly, 17,* 71–83.

Shih, M., Ambady, N., Richeson, J. A., Fujita, K., & Gray, H. M. (2002). Stereotype performance boosts: The impact of self-relevance and the manner of stereotype activation. *Journal of Personality and Social Psychology, 83,* 638–647.

Smith, E. R. (1998). *Mental representation and memory*. In D. T. Gilbert, S. T. Fiske, & G. Lindzey, (Eds.), *Handbook of social psychology Vol. 1* (4th ed., pp. 391–445). New York, NY: McGraw Hill.

Spencer, S. J., Steele, C. M., & Quinn, D. M. (1999). Stereotype threat and women's math performance. *Journal of Experimental Social Psychology, 35*, 4–28.

Spencer, S. J., Zanna, & M. P., Fong, G. T. (2005). Establishing a causal chain: Why experiments are often more effective than mediational analyses in examining psychological processes. *Journal of Personality and Social Psychology, 89*, 845–851.

Steele, C. M. (1997). A threat in the air. How stereotypes shape intellectual identity and performance. *American Psychologist, 52*, 613–629.

Steele, C. M., & Aronson, J. (1995). Stereotype threat and the intellectual test performance of African Americans. *Journal of Personality and Social Psychology, 69*, 797–811.

Steele, C. M., Spencer, S. J., & Aronson, J. (2002). Contending with group image: The psychology of stereotype and social identity threat. In M. P. Zanna (Ed.), *Advances in experimental social psychology* (Vol. 34, pp. 379–440). San Diego, CA: Academic Press.

Stone, J. (2002). Battling doubt by avoiding practice: The effects of stereotype threat on self-handicapping in White athletes. *Personality and Social Psychology Bulletin, 28*, 1667–1678.

Swim, J. K., & Stangor, C., & (Eds.). (1998). *Prejudice: The target's perspective*. San Diego, CA: Academic Press.

Zeidner, M. (1998). *Test anxiety: The state of the art*. New York, NY: Plenum Press.

Author Index

Subject Index

A

Accountability, 35–36, 50, 196, 201
Anonymity, 330
Assertiveness, 85, 146–148, 151
Attribution, 148, 169, 216, 321, 323, 325–329, 331, 333, 345, 347–348, 360
Audience design, 247–248, 250, 255

B

Back-translation paradigm, 99, 113
Bonding, 80–81
Bridging, 79–82

C

Cognitive bias, 98, 191, 198
Cognitive resources, 33–34, 38, 49, 179, 206, 359
Collective mobilization, 263
Common ground, 44, 64–66, 68–69, 72, 76, 80, 84, 213, 219, 228, 243–244, 248, 255, 259, 274–275, 277–279, 281–282, 285, 296, 307–309
Common knowledge effect, 272, 274
Computer-mediated communication, 193, 195
Consensualization, 263, 265–268, 275–277, 287
Construal, 34–35, 268
Cue system, 98, 103–104, 106, 108, 110–111, 113–114
Culture, 59–60, 151, 244, 297–298, 318–319, 321–322, 324–325, 329–331, 348

E

Encoding, 100, 102–103, 105, 107, 110, 170–177, 179–184, 206, 243
Expectancies
  Performance expectancies, 368, 371, 374, 380, 385–386
Grice's maxims, 280, 285

G

Grice's maxims, 280, 285
Grounding, 11, 63–65, 81, 275–278, 285, 287

I

Identifiability, 193–197, 201–202
Information sampling, 271, 273
Information sharedness, 266, 272, 275
Inhibition, 198, 205
Intergroup sensitivity effect, 5, 321–326, 328–330, 332–333, 340, 344

L

Language abstraction, 165, 168, 170, 177–184, 191, 192–208, 342
Leadership, 97, 139–140, 143, 148–151, 153–155, 271, 278, 320, 331
Linguistic category model, 15, 100, 166, 190, 199, 201, 216, 218, 245
Linguistic expectancy bias, 4, 168, 191, 199, 205, 217–218, 245–247, 250, 259